Scott

W9-BWD-519

Miss Tallulah Bankhead

RELEASE

Miss
Tallulah Bankhead

PM
2287
,B17
I8

LEE ISRAEL

G. P. Putnam's Sons, New York

ST. JOSEPH'S UNIVERSITY

3 9353 00235 4163

Acknowledgments

I AM enormously grateful to Eugenia Bankhead for sharing her memories of childhood with me.

I wish to thank the staff of the Manuscript Division of the State of Alabama's Department of Archives and History for making available the Bankhead family correspondence.

Additionally, I am indebted to the entire staff of the Theater Collection at the Library of the Performing Arts, Lincoln Center.

For their time, insights, and interest, I owe special thanks to: Stephan Cole, Ted Hook, Cal Schumann, Robert Williams, Estelle Winwood, Glenn Anders, Kenneth Carten, Tom Ellis, Morton Da Costa, Ed Meyers, James Kirkwood, Herbert Machiz, "Johnny," Laura Mitchell, Cathleen Nesbitt, Otto Preminger, Irving Rapper, Liz Smith, Marian Seldes, the Honorable Harold A. Stevens, Robert Whitehead, Mary Louise Baker, Tamara Geva, Mrs. Claude McGowin, Jr., Barbara Baxley, Buff Cobb, Sidney Blackmer, Joan Blondell, Al Morgan, Joe Rosenfield, Jr., Edith Van Cleve.

Also my thanks to: Goodman Ace, Walter Will Bankhead, Ed Baylies, C. Lawton Campbell, Louisa Carpenter, Harold Carthage, Marc Connelly, Marian B. Crow, George Cukor, Jean Dalrymple, Jimmy Daniels, W. A. Darlington, Selma Diamond, Dorothy Dickson, Mildred Dunnock, Entovan Collection, Victoria & Albert Museum, London, England, Morris Ernst, Julia

8   Miss Tallulah Bankhead

Garland, Margalo Gillmore, Douglas Grant, Merv Griffin, Betty Harmon, Gladys Henson, Katharine Hepburn, Hoblitzelle Theatre Arts Library, University of Texas, George Hyland, Dr. Brannon Hubbard, Elia Kazan, Patsy Kelly, Max Leavitt, Harriet Lyons, Charles Martin, Frank Milton, Julie Mitchell, Ruth Mitchell, the Honorable Fred G. Morritt, Michael Myerberg, Dr. Milton Reder, Sophie Rosen, Robert Ryan, Jim Sheridan, Steve Sheppard, Jean Soames, Vivian Vance, Alan Vincent, Phil Weltman, Betty Wharton, Leigh Whipper, Dorothy Wilding, Maurice Zolotow.

LEE ISRAEL

Contents

Illustrations follow page 256.

1

The Contest

APPLICATION BLANK

I am desirous of becoming a motion-picture player. I have never had any professional experience on either the stage or screen.

Name.............................
Address.............................

Age......   Color of eyes......
Height......   Complexion......
Weight......   Color of hair......

My preference of character roles is ....
....

PICTURE-PLAY MAGAZINE . . . JUNE 1917
SCREEN OPPORTUNITY CONTEST

Your last chance to enter.
Marjorie Rambeau now a judge.

The end of Picture-Play's screen opportunity contest, and the bright beginning of twelve motion-picture careers, which will automatically follow, are both close at hand. The last chance you will have to make your future one of those twelve has arrived. If you have not already become a contestant, now is the time.

No doubt you know just what the result of this contest means to the winners. Twelve people, regardless of age and sex, are

to be chosen from entries by the judges, and these twelve people will have their expenses paid to New York and be paid a
salary of at least twenty-five dollars a week while they act in a
feature picture. Each of the winners will be given a real part,
not that of an extra, in a five-reel production made by Frank
Powell Producing Corporation, and personally directed by
Frank Powell, the man who discovered Theda Bara and
Blanche Sweet.

It was a late Indian summer afternoon in Washington, D.C.,
as the Bankhead sisters, Tallulah, fifteen, and Eugenia, sixteen,
left their apartment house at 1868 Columbia Road on their daily
foray to the neighborhood candy store. *Picture-Play* had failed
cleverly to specify the issue in which the winners of the Screen
Opportunity Contest would appear. So, for the last several
months, Tallulah Brockman Bankhead had ripped anxiously
through the pages of several *Picture-Plays* to see if the winners
were announced and whether she was among them.

She spotted the brand-new September, 1917, issue, featuring
a becurled Mary Pickford on the cover, and grabbed the magazine
off the counter. "It's in this one, Sister," she said to Eugenia.

ANNOUNCEMENT OF CONTEST WINNERS

Judges complete decision of
Screen Opportunity Contest Winners.

At last the anxiously awaited announcement of contest winners can be made. On the first twelve pages of this issue of
PICTURE-PLAY MAGAZINE the photographs of the winners
appear. These pages, as readers of this magazine know, are usually reserved for the photographs of screen stars, and in devoting
this space to our winners we wish to imply the hope that they
will some day be shining luminaries in the film firmament.

Tallulah flipped past eleven of the winners, including potential luminaries Henrietta L. Gant; Lela Sue Campbell; and Myrtle
Owen Anderson of Tulsa, Oklahoma, mother of two. She closed
her eyes and froze with yearning.

"Go on, Sister, turn the page," Eugenia implored. "It may be you."

There was so much that was new and exciting in Tallulah's world since she had suddenly, almost visibly with the onset of menstruation, shed layers of hard-earned fat and become quite beautiful. And it was Tallulah, no longer Eugenia, whom relatives now compared to their dear, departed, and extraordinarily lovely mother.

Eugenia was certain, however, that the twelfth winner would *not* be her sister. This was not the first contest of its kind that Tallulah had entered, and they both had been through this state of highly charged expectancy before. Tallulah, of late, was always scraping together pennies to have her picture taken; to submit new moods, another angle to the camera as if to verify the glad tidings of her mirror, and to verify doubly by sending out the picture to have it compared, in some official way, with other pictures.

"It can't be me," Tallulah said to Eugenia in her scalloped, foggy voice. "Turn the page for me, Sister, I can't bear it."

Eugenia turned the page.

"I'll be damned, Sister," she said. "It *is* you."

Tallulah's picture appeared: an artistic, darkling left profile, dominated by a flamboyant wide-brimmed hat, atop a fashionable borrowed fur.

"Sister," Tallulah shouted, "I've won! I've won! I've won! I've won!"

She galloped up the block, back to the apartment house, waving *Picture-Play* in the air. Eugenia caught up with her, having lingered a moment to pay for the magazine.

In their excitement, neither of the Bankhead girls noticed the headline under Tallulah's picture: WHO IS SHE? or the *Picture-Play* text which amended it. Tallulah had neglected to identify herself when she sent the original picture to the magazine, and the editors now were beefing up the contest with a Cinderella theme. To wit:

ONE OF THE TWELVE UNKNOWN

It is interesting to note that after the winners were selected it was found that one fair beauty among them was unidentified. It was discovered that her name and address did not appear on the photograph and—pity of pities—her letter and application blank had been lost. At first the predicament seemed hopeless. In fairness to the winner the judges did not wish to be forced to substitute someone in her place. It seemed to them that it was a sort of Cinderella problem reversed. Her name, which corresponded to the slipper, was missing and had to be found. The search for it was still going on. It was decided to publish her picture along with all the other winners in the hope that she would see it and then come forward and make herself known.

They ran first to the sixth floor of the apartment house. There Tallulah was residing with her grandparents: the first Tallulah Brockman Bankhead, a warm, handsome woman, like most of the Bankhead females square and squat with fat. Though Tallulah had lived through her childhood alternately with several relatives, she ended all her letters to the old woman, "You are my one and only Mamma and I love you with all my heart." Mamma hugged Tallulah when she heard the news, but she tabled her real feelings about the contest for the present.

Her husband, Tallulah's grandfather, was Senator John Hollis Bankhead of Alabama. A dour, towering figure with a face like a Boston bulldog, he was at his office when Tallulah came galloping home. They called him Captain John; he had begun his political career as a thrice-wounded Confederate hero. The year before the *Picture-Play* contest he had shamed the Senate into appropriating monies for a proposed bust of Robert E. Lee by donning his Confederate uniform and sitting through the session proud and accusing. His colleagues respected him. His family feared him. *Both* Tallulahs managed him adroitly.

From their grandparents' apartment on the sixth floor, they ran to their father's on the seventh. Only months before the

Screen Opportunity Contest, William Brockman Bankhead had been elected to Congress from the harsh and poor Tenth District of Alabama in a bitter campaign that embraced prohibition, women's suffrage, foreign entanglements, and the more explosive issue of whether his Senator father and Congressman brother had redistricted the Tenth as a kind of present to Will. He had recently sat in the Lower House while President Wilson solemnly asked for consent to declare war on Germany.

Three years before the declaration of war, Will had married flighty Florence McGuire, who was then twenty-five years old. Eugenia now lived with the couple while Tallulah stayed with Grandmother and Grandfather. The arrangement was a wise one. Tallulah harbored fierce resentment against Florence, the interloper, and Florence had neither the patience nor the maturity to quell the girl's adolescent fury.

Will's wife was out shopping when the Bankhead girls broke in. Tallulah telephoned her father at the Capitol to tell him the good news. He had serious reservations, but for the time being he kept them to himself. Certainly, during that telephone call, he had little choice since his garrulous daughter seldom paused for breath.

Though many girls claimed to be the mystery woman of the photograph, proving Tallulah was in fact the lovely in the borrowed fur and the stylish hat was simple. A duplicate photo, accompanied by a letter written by Grandfather on his Senatorial stationery more than convinced the editors of *Picture-Play* that Tallulah Brockman Bankhead was indeed the Cinderella of this particular story. The real problem was whether or not the fifteen-year-old ought to be allowed to go to New York and pursue a theatrical career. Tallulah had always had dramatic ambitions; the contest merely moved the decision up a year or two. To deal with this question, the Bankhead family caucused that evening and for many evenings thereafter.

Grandmother Bankhead, a formidable matriarch, was violently opposed. Tallulah was obviously not destined to take the most natural and desirable Cotillion-Goucher route. But that was no reason to throw her to the devil. Florence was as bubbly and excited as Tallulah, less at the victory than at the idea of unloading at least one of Will Bankhead's indulged daughters. Will Bankhead himself wasn't sure. Tallulah was young, totally inexperienced, and certainly not equipped to live by herself in New York City. Who would guide the child? Who would pay the bills until she became, if ever, self-sufficient?

While her elders debated the vectors and salients of the issues, Tallulah made her position clear. She could not, indeed would not, agree to go on living if this opportunity were taken from her. She commenced a hunger strike. In truth, the strike served a two-fold purpose since she would need to be as thin as possible in that two-reel production personally directed by Frank Powell. Knowing her family and feeling her fate—usually in the pit of the stomach, even when it was empty—she could not conceive that they would not ultimately, after a respectable period of torturous debate, allow her to go to New York.

It was finally Captain John who turned the tide. He convinced his wife that to deny Tallulah this opportunity was to court disaster. The child was, after all, her father's daughter. And Will's life, prior to the time he met Florence, was strong testimony to the effect that demons breed best in the Stygian dank of frustration and personal unhappiness.

The child had to do what she had to do, and Captain John offered to pick up all the bills while she did it; he would pay the way, too, for his daughter, Tallulah's Aunt Louise, if she agreed to act as chaperone. Louise consented happily.

Will Bankhead, dazzled and relieved by his father's generosity, nodded his approval, drawing down the side of his mouth in the style of Edwin Booth to say: "Anything for peace."

2

Ada and Will

HER MOTHER, Adelaide Eugenia Sledge, "Ada," died of blood poisoning following Tallulah's birth in Huntsville, Alabama.

She had married William Brockman Bankhead on January 31, 1900. Their first daughter, Ada Eugenia, arrived almost a year later, on January 24, 1901.

Most reports indicate that Tallulah Brockman Bankhead was born on her parents' wedding anniversary, January 31, 1902. A preacher's letter, however, written about Ada's death, a day after the tragic event, would place Tallulah's birth closer to February 12. The preacher in this letter of February 24 refers to Tallulah as "an infant about 12 days old."

The witnesses around Ada at the time of Tallulah's birth include Will, who went crazy with grief after his young wife's death, the preacher, and Marie Owen, Will's sister. Marie would become the official historian of the state of Alabama, but she was also an unabashed sentimentalist. The possibility exists that Marie chose or acceded to the choice of January 31 to mark Tallulah's birth, hoping thereby simultaneously to memorialize the tragically short-lived union of Ada and Will.

There were no birth certificates at the time, and the reports that do exist issue from Marie Owen's testimony.

The witness-preacher attended Ada through her illness to her death. "She lately came here to live as a bride only 21 years of age," he wrote. "She was a beautiful little woman and from the first became devoted to me as her pastor. I was with her during her painful illness and administered Holy Communion. She was perfectly conscious almost to the last and said to me: 'Mr. Banister, do you think God will take me to Heaven?' On reporting to her the assurance of our Lord to all who freely turn to Him, a sweet smile brightened her beautiful countenance and then expressing sorrow at leaving her little babe, she seemed to trustfully submit to the will of God."

Ada's submission to the will of another was a rarity. Like her own Tallulah, she was a second daughter who had lost her mother soon after her birth. She was doted upon by a gyneolatrous Southern father, the son of a wealthy planter who served for a time as president of the Tennessee Cotton Exchange. The family bred and fought the fiercest, finest cocks of the day, the famous Sledge Hammers. Governesses and mammies waited dutifully upon the motherless Ada Sledge. Captain John would say that Will had spent the entire two years of his marriage trying to keep Ada "from gettin' too ruffled." The Sledge temper was apparently not confined to their fighting cocks. She was spoiled, headstrong, imperious, willful, indulged, and extraordinarily lovely. Her dark-eyed, cherubic beauty was legendary in the South.

When she married William Brockman Bankhead, impetuously and in spite of an engagement to another, Ada's father presented the young couple with a splendid carriage and a pair of matched chestnut horses. Dressed in a striped, green-taffeta riding costume comprising yards of billowing skirt and a brown ostrich-plume hat, Ada won the prize in the county flower parade proudly pulled by her fine chestnut mares. When Will Bankhead, years after his wife's death, could finally talk about her without sobbing, he told his daughter Eugenia, "I couldn't afford to buy food for your *mother*, let alone the chestnuts."

As she lay dying, Ada Sledge reportedly told Marie Owen, "Take care of my baby Eugenia. Tallulah will always be able to take care of herself."

The girls were told of their saintly mother's last words. As reminiscing adults they would often refer to them.

"You know what Mother said on her deathbed, Sister," Eugenia chided once.

To which Tallulah replied exegetically, "I know what Mother said on her deathbed, Sister. But she didn't say *I* had to take care of you!"

Ada had, no doubt, been mindful of Eugenia's frail health when she uttered those final instructions to Marie. During the first year of her life, Eugenia was a fragile, sickly child, carried about on a satin pillow, tottering between life and death. It would be said in the Bankhead family that Ada had not known she was pregnant again when she nursed Eugenia and that, because of the new conception, her milk had deteriorated. Eugenia contracted, in early infancy, an infection which would plague her for years. With the demise of the source, both Eugenia and Tallulah were raised on goat's milk.

Tallulah was christened beside her mother's coffin and named after Will's mother, who was purportedly conceived during the migration of her parents from South Carolina to Alabama, at a stopover in Tallulah Falls, Georgia. There are divergent stories about the eponymous Tallulah: the original Tallulah after whom the waterfall was named. Some claim she was an Indian princess. "Tallulah" means "delightful sound" in Choctaw and "terrible waters" in another dialect. Though it was a unique choice, "Tallulah," for Southerners, was not an unusual *sound*. Women were often called after geographical places, many of which have similarly soft, mellifluous Indian names.

Right after the christening, the babies were bundled up and taken to their grandparents in Fayette, Alabama. Will remained alone in Huntsville for five years, eking out a living at the law and drinking staggering quantities of white lightning. The last thing he wanted to see was the responsible infant.

As an adult, Tallulah frequently denied having experienced any guilt as a result of her mother's pregnancy-related death. She would admit, however, that as a child she had felt Daddy had blamed her for Ada's death. But then Ada she had never known; Daddy was the love of Tallulah's life.

Tallulah's father, William Brockman Bankhead, was a man of Southern sensibilities, large and well liked, with vivid, celestially blue eyes and bushy, demagogic brows. He had a handsome face, puttied in the service of his oratorical muse. He was twenty-eight when he lost Ada, and behind him were years spent studying Dixie spellbinders, atop the pulpit; on the electoral stump; most excitingly, on the stage at a time when passions were not only torn to shreds but pulverized. Will's greatest love was heroic theater, but he had settled for the law.

At Will's birth, in Moscow, Alabama, nine years after the Civil War, his father, John Hollis Bankhead, was running a cotton mill, one of the many erstwhile captains of the Confederacy who sought to rebuild the ravaged South through the creation of local and self-sufficient industry. Will was one of five children: Marie, Louise, and John came before him; only Henry was younger.

Will's earliest memories were of a baptism in which he sputtered helplessly and almost drowned; a tug of war where his pants split wide open; swimming in Coon Creek; a trek by mule train to Wetumpka, Alabama, when his father was appointed warden of the state penitentiary. He wrote, in one of the many diaries he kept fitfully throughout his life, that the five years spent at the prison were "happy years with my brothers for playmates and nothing save an occasional licking to hinder our mischievous machinations."

In 1887, when Will was thirteen, his father was elected to Congress, where he served for eighteen continuous years in the Lower House. Captain John was defeated only once in his political career, by a more colorful veteran of the more recent Spanish-American War, but he was nominated almost immediately to the United States Senate, where he remained until his death in 1920, the oldest Confederate veteran in the Senate.

When he himself was elected to Congress, Will told an interviewer, "I have eaten of political pabulum. I have breathed the air of the conference, the hustings, the forum. I guess it might be said it is the breath of my nostrils." His lessons in loyalty to the Democratic Party were catechismal. It was the party of the South, of survival, of everything that was grand and glorious and nice; Republicanism was the apostasy of the Yankee, the harbinger of doom, miscegenation, philistinism.

But to the growing Will Bankhead, politics was the family business, the breath of his nostrils perhaps, not the stuff of his loins. His obsession with drama, rhetoric, gesture—the art of enthrallment—began very early. He remembered the first time he was called upon to recite in grade school. "When Professor DuBose called out 'Willie Bankhead,'" he wrote, "I thought I would faint. My courage, which I had thought was with me, stampeded in all directions, and although I managed to get up on the stage, that was all. I sought asylum in tears and began to boo hoo. I was commanded to make a bow and come down. With my fist in my eye, I did so and sat down. My first forensic effort, an ignominious failure."

That would never happen again. He began to read Shakespeare and the Bible, to marginalize new words, to scrutinize the performances of ministers, politicians, and actors. "He is the most impressive minister I ever saw," he commented after watching a visiting cleric from Atlanta in action. "His every movement is grace, his language chaste and forceful, his logic profound." On the performance of an actor in a play called *The Sign of the Cross*, Will wrote: "He is a little handicapped for a heroic role on account of the lack of voice to suit. He has a strong, soft voice, but he cannot become thunderous and awesome as I have seen players attain in certain climaxes for heroics."

The teeter-totter between theater and politics began. When he was fourteen, unknown to anyone in the family, he rode from Alabama to Washington in overalls and a straw hat for the inauguration of President Benjamin Harrison. During that sojourn, he sneaked into a theater to see *The Count of Monte Cristo*. While the pageantry of the inauguration impressed Will, the thundering performances in the heroic play fired his blood. He made a solemn vow to himself that he would never allow his family to deter him from making his mark upon the stage.

That particular pledge was soon broken, and he permitted his mother and father to supply to him the more traditional outlet for his public speaking flair: politics via the law. He enrolled at the University of Alabama. There he won a gold medal for public speaking and a Phi Beta Kappa key. He was fullback and captain of the football team and president of his junior class. After graduation, he took his law degree at Georgetown and, once again, distinguished himself as speaker, scholar, holder of elective office, and bon vivant.

Will Bankhead was grand, expectant, convivial, fun-loving, weak, sensitive, possibly alcoholic, and just a bit of a fool. While at Georgetown, he went out on the town one night. "We first concluded to take one drink of claret at Drivers saloon," he wrote. "One drink led to another until we concluded that we didn't want to go home just yet. We met a gang of boys and girls out for a time, all adjourned to Bill's Inn, a place of very meagre proportions. The 'professor' played tunes and sang songs, the girls did the split and high kick." The next morning he experienced what he termed "a subdued, *je ne sais pas* feeling among my anatomy. . . . Iced-water tastes remarkably well for some reason today."

He knew apparently less about business than he did about hangovers. He had a buddy named Campbell at Georgetown who convinced him to invest several hundred dollars in "a certain venture which lay in New York." Campbell took Will's money to the big city and wrote presently that it had been burned in a fire. The money was in Campbell's pants, close to the stove, when Campbell retired for the night. A high wind caused a gas jet to burn the kitchen curtain, which alighted the propinquous pants, "destroying them and their contents." Campbell assured Will, though, that his investment had been "doubled in three days." Unfortunately, the healthy return on Will's money was also in Campbell's pants. Throughout his life, Will would less literally continue to burn up money in unfelicitous and highly speculative investments.

Will Bankhead never lacked for company. He had a talent to amuse and a sort of grandiloquent Southern jock mentality. He loved to goose his roommate, John Nored, who boasted of having killed two people in a lumber camp. "One of them," Will wrote, "was a Yankee making offensive remarks in John's presence about negro rights and social equality. John promptly shot him twice in the stomach. The Yankee afterwards died of heart failure. I love him."

He would become, in his political ascent, associated with the egalitarian *Realpolitik* of Franklin Delano Roosevelt. But certainly in his younger days he was a product of his time and of his region, no better and no worse than most. In his "Impressions of Washington," a diary he kept in 1893, Will reminisced about an old black man he had met once who had had both legs shot off above the knee while fighting for the South in the Civil War. "I let him black my shoes as much as possible and considered that I was, in a small degree, pensioning him," Will boasted.

Up from Alabama, Washington was a shocking abomination to Will Bankhead:

> I was amazed the first time I went to the theatre to see big buck negroes and their dusky damsels march in and complacently seat themselves in the front row of the dress circle. They are always boisterous in their laughter and applause. On the streetcars and in public parks they monopolize the seats, the presence of a white lady *standing* making not the least difference to these courtly gentlemen. One thing that tested my patience on the cars was the sight of white young men giving up their seats to the aromatic colored ladies: "Judgment thou art fled to brutish beasts."
>
> On occasions of public display or exhibition negroes hold forth in their supremest exuberance. They get up early in the morning and by nine o'clock the public thoroughfares are jammed with a heterogeneous conglomeration of coons. Big niggers, little niggers, fat and attenuated dudes and raggy muffins, belles and despised ones, aristocratic 16th Street niggers, and the more unpretentious, but nevertheless loud smelling South Washington coon, the barber and shoe black, the washed and the unwashed, the latter prodominantly. There they are! Behold them in their pride and conceit! Harriet B. Stowe, how do you like your incubated proselytes of freedom!

After graduating from Georgetown and failing, despite his father's influence, to obtain a position in Indian Territory, Will settled in Huntsville, Alabama. There he began to practice law and prepared, by modest increments of self-advertising, for a political career. He church-hopped, sang in a choir, made an occasional and fiery speech, lost more cases than he won, rode a bicycle, cultivated friendships, called on a Miss Borden and a Miss Halsey, suffered agonizing bouts of rheumatism that only morphine would appease, and wept copiously over the stirring, sensitive fiction he read alone in his room.

His effusive, optimistic diaries soon deteriorated into listless, stringy jottings:

> May 9, 1896: Work. Went to Nora Robinson's in evening to learn a solo for Sunday.
> May 14, 1896: Worked at office. Bicycle riding in evening. Club meeting.
> May 16, 1896: Argued the case and went to jury.
> May 17, 1896: Verdict returned against us.
> May 19, 1896: Doing same. It's always the same.

Disenchanted with life and law, yearning for something more exciting, he yawed off course, leaving Huntsville to travel East. He stopped over in Boston on his way to New York and picked up a theatrical newspaper. There he saw a call for a young actor with a Southern accent to join a stock company. Will auditioned for the company manager on Friday and was asked to report for work the following Monday. Somehow his family got word of Will's temptation. On Sunday, a special delivery letter arrived from his mother, imploring him to eschew the stage and continue with his political career.

Will spent the day ruminating, brooding, and, no doubt, posturing in the Boston Commons. He did not report to his acting job on Monday, continuing instead his journey to New York, where he began a short, penurious, but exciting time campaigning for the mayoral candidate, Robert Van Wyck. He stumped up and down the Bowery, orating on street corners and off the backs of trucks.

Either homesickness or poverty or a combination of both impelled him to return to Alabama. Soon after, he met and married the beautiful Ada Sledge. For two years, life matched his expectations.

In 1904, when he was able once again to resume his diaries,

Will composed a moving entry in which he referred to the love letters he and Ada had exchanged, expressing the hope that his daughters would someday read them and understand thereby the loveliness and the intensity of what he and his late wife had felt for each other: "Those letters tell the story of our courtship with a tenderer diction than I now can write—for then joy and beautiful anticipations ran my pen, while now I write in the shadow of the loss while choked with the anguish of absence."

He referred, in that same entry, to their wedding day and the "matchless beauty of my bride. I have her wedding gown. She wore it only once. I have never had the courage to look upon its silken folds since she went away to God."

3

Daddy

THROUGHOUT HER CHILDHOOD, Tallulah Bankhead dreamed the same dream. She was alone in a jungle, walking soundlessly along a path lined with pawing, snarling animals. She awoke screaming in a series of beds.

First there was the huge, soft canopied bed in Grandfather Bankhead's house—in Fayette for a short time and then in Jasper, Alabama. Jasper is a small mining town in northern Alabama, about seventy miles out of Birmingham. Tallulah slept with Eugenia at her side and the servant's girl, Rila Mae, on a pallet by their feet.

Will remained in Huntsville, a day's ride away from Jasper,

building himself a reputation as a pugnacious and weepy town drunk. Though he could not yet contribute to his daughters' support, he visited them once a month, on holidays, and for Eugenia's birthday. Since their birthdays were only a week apart, Tallulah's—the preacher's letter notwithstanding—on January 31 and Eugenia's on the twenty-fourth, they celebrated on the earlier date with a joint cake. Daddy's arrival was in and of itself a holiday for both Bankhead girls. One birthday, he bought them a sack of oranges. And when the fruit was gone, they played for weeks with the paper wrappers.

When Tallulah was two, Eugenia was separated from her for a time. Marie Bankhead Owen was visiting her parents when she noticed that the elder girl, just over a siege of measles and chicken pox, was strangely unresponsive.

"I think the child's blind," she said.

Grandmother Bankhead, Mamma, had noticed the condition and was intending to take Eugenia into Birmingham for treatment.

"Wrap her up," Marie exhorted in the Bankhead manner. "I'm taking her to Dr. Thigpen in Montgomery today."

Thigpen and a consultant in Washington advised cool ablutions and the avoidance of all sunlight. Eugenia slept in the sultry, sun-flooded Montgomery afternoons and played at night. When she could not sleep, Aunt Marie, a massive woman in a loose-hanging white shift, fanned her with a palmetto to keep her cool and comfortable. When Eugenia was six, her eyesight became somewhat restored, and Tallulah had her back as her constant companion.

The sisters peregrinated between Jasper and Montgomery. Tallulah ate ravenously and grew fatter, stronger, and more imposing than frail Eugenia, whose sun-sensitive eyes required that she sit low, low at the dining-room table on a footstool, facing a leggy netherworld and feeling, a good deal of the time, like the family pet. But she got the best pieces of chicken, most of the attention, and, when they were under the same roof, the seat next to Will.

In Montgomery, Tallulah foraged after dinner. She barged in

on one particular neighbor of Aunt Marie's, who she knew customarily ate later than the Owen family did. They had just finished the traditional cold salad supper of the South and several plates remained full of the tomato drippings and dressing. Tallulah drained each plate individually and advised the diners that they had left the best part. The neighbors concluded that perhaps Miss Marie was not feeding the motherless child well enough.

This, of course, was not true. Tallulah loved Aunt Marie, who was married to Dr. Thomas Owen, historian and chief archivist for the state of Alabama. She and Dr. Owen had a boy named Tom with whom the Bankhead girls played and at whom Tallulah, to the stunned and admiring amusement of the neighborhood children, directed her first cuss words: "wall-eyed" and "yellar-bellied." He was both.

Marie lived in a pebble-dash corner house on Adams Street, within walking distance of the Montgomery Capitol Building. The lawn was manicured, the house dark with vellum curtains and black Chinese teak armchairs. Her good friends, the Saffolds, who occupied the Amen Corner at the Presbyterian church and reared several daughters to show sufficient cleavage to advance themselves in life, kidded her about her teak tendency. "Miss MAH-reeee," they would tease, "had gone Chinese crazy."

Marie Owen wrote a very popular social column for the Montgomery *Advertiser*. And, like her brother Will, she had a secret place. Her romantic novels, poems, and screen treatments remain to this day in typescript at the Montgomery Archives. A typical passage from Marie Owen's novel *Executor with Bond* reads: "Jude's heart skipped two beats. They stood looking down at the city for a long, silent moment, hand clasped with hand, shoulder touching shoulder. Then Jude caught her up in his arms and ran with her into the desert."

She wrote often, too, of perfectly lovely but star-crossed octoroons who become cumbersomely involved with purebred white Southerners. One such hybrid was the heroine of her motion-picture scenario *Children of the Night*, which begins with the direction: "Lillymay Jenkies, a half-educated school teacher who is secretly a life insurance agent, enters the scene through the wood's path." To research her sympathetic literary involvement with the plight of the octoroon, she traveled with a female friend to Tuskegee University and lunched with the colored students.

Will was summoned home from Huntsville by Captain John, ordered to shape up and look to his responsibilities. He entered law practice in Jasper with his level-headed older brother, John. His daughters rejoined him there in time to begin kindergarten together. They all lived in Captain John's house.

The big white house in Jasper was full of distant relatives, sleeping porches, and the sweet smell of Grandmother Tallulah Bankhead's jelly kitchen. At one particularly populous time, eighteen persons were staying in the house. Besides Will, his parents, and the Bankhead girls, there were: Great-grandmother McAuley; Louise and her two children; young John Bankhead, Henry's son (Henry was off doing government work in the Philippines); and two children called Virginia and John Robinson, the exact nature of whose kinship eluded Eugenia and Tallulah.

In the morning, the sisters played tag, or picked berries in the woods, or seesawed on a rigged-up plank that Will had balanced through the barn windows. Tallulah outweighed Eugenia by many pounds, and she fumed when her lithe sister enjoyed the buoyant benefits of the airborne end of the plank while she straddled the grounded side. One day, when the dinner bell rang, Tallulah, whom Will called Dutch for her dour and hefty Dutch-boy mien, simply got up off the seesaw, and Eugenia, whom he called Nothin' Much for her petiteness, tumbled into the compost heap.

Before their afternoon naps—in the years before the old woman's death—Tallulah and Eugenia took great delight in visiting Great-grandmother McAuley's room. She was the elder Tallulah Bankhead's mother, properly Mary Elizabeth James (of Jamestown) Brockman McAuley.

For the first ninety-six years of her life, Great-grandmother McAuley was erect, ambulatory, and lucid. Toward the end, in the berry-smelling house in Jasper, she passed through a short moribund dotage with her great-grandchildren standing by. Tallulah was delighted when the old woman inquired about Beau, Beau being the famous General P. G. T. Beauregard, who began the fighting at Fort Sumter.

"Where's Beau? Where's Beau?" the old woman asked.

Tallulah and Eugenia would giggle then, and one of them replied invariably that he was in the parlor, waiting to call.

"Send him up, Tally," the old woman commanded, raising her gnarled hand languorously to indicate an imaginary wrap. Eugenia threw a mock scarf around her shoulders, while Tallulah slipped off to find Daddy's overcoat. She reentered the room as General Beauregard, wrinkling her brow to indicate age through solemnity.

"I wonder what my life would have been like if I'd married you, Beau?" Great-grandmother McAuley speculated coquettishly. And then it began. If Beauregard were not interrupted by the demands of her nap, they could talk on for hours about Sumter, the Civil War, Alabama, and the colored race. Tallulah eventually believed the coat; Eugenia was drawn into the conversation. Thus the three wacky fantasists, Mary Elizabeth McAuley, ninety-seven; Ada Eugenia Bankhead, seven; and Tallulah Brockman Bankhead, six, passed many pleasant *matins*.

Before their afternoon naps, in the big canopied four-poster, the girls played Marion and Elizabeth. Tallulah was called Marion, for their older cousin, Marion Bankhead; Eugenia was Elizabeth, because she liked the name.

The fantasies in which they indulged were modest and regional and predominantly Tallulah's, having to do with mature conceptions, a certain area of exclusivity, and the wish for just a jot of self-control:

"And what did you do today, Marion?"

"Oh, nothing much. I had an appointment with the doctor."

"You had an appointment!"

"Yes, I phoned for an appointment."

"Did you see any of your friends, Marion?"

"Oh, yes, I saw some of my friends."

"Who were they?"

"You don't know them, Elizabeth."

"I thought I knew *all* your friends, Marion."

"Well, these are some you don't know."

"What did you do?"

"Ate milk and cookies."

"I bet that you ate too many chocolate cookies, Marion."

"You know I'm not eatin' too many chocolate cookies anymore, Elizabeth. I promised Mamma that I wouldn't."

"Did you clean your room?"

"Of course, I cleaned my room, Elizabeth. How im-*poi*-tenant of you to ask."

In late afternoon, the children would gather in a big rumpus room with their mammies. Virginia Robinson played "Two Little Girls in Blue" on the piano, a song about two sisters, one of whom dies tragically young. The beribboned Bankhead girls sang along gamily, dissolving regularly and simultaneously into tears, each identifying with the surviving sister.

At the Jasper public school, Will one evening moderated a local talent recital. When one of the acts failed to show up, he was ready to go on to the next when Tallulah bellowed from the audience, "We'll recite a poem, Daddy!" She grabbed Eugenia's reluctant hand, pulled her up to the stage, and they went into their standard "Old Ironsides" with appropriate gestures.

Tallulah confided to her kindergarten teacher, Miss Bessie Hawes, her desire to be a great actress someday, and she performed passionately at every opportunity. Only in one kindergarten play did Eugenia outshine Tallulah theatrically. The elder Bankhead girl played a colorful, talky rainbow in a production about the elements. Tallulah, in her autobiography, *Tallulah*, admits to having played a subsidiary role to Eugenia in that play, but she remembered playing the moon, a cameo part rather than a minor one and one for which her wide, resolute face would have eminently qualified her. Eugenia insists that Tallulah was not even the moon, but one of several, undistinguished raindrops, dressed in dull brown crepe paper.

Through her performances, formal and informal, Tallulah learned how to please her desultory Daddy. For the first ten years of her life, Will lived a great deal behind closed doors, emerging wobbly and sobbing. He frequently grabbed Eugenia up in his arms, rocked her back and forth, and called Ada's name. At such times, Tallulah would somersault on the living-room floor or endeavor to perfect her cartwheel, all the time bidding Will, "Look at me, Daddy! Look at me!"

"Tallulah, stand up straight," Will would reply, his use of her full name designating his displeasure.

But he was not always so flinty in his appreciation of her talents, and those were the times she cherished. On two occasions, he returned home after a night of choir practice, accompanied by a group of his chums. They promptly got high and rowdy and awakened the girls, who stood at the head of the steps in their flannel nightgowns.

"Come down," Will called conspiratorially one night. "Come down."

Eugenia seemed somewhat wary. Tallulah bounded down the steps, leaped into Will's arms, and was hoisted atop the dining-room table. There she recited poetry and sang off-color songs while the gang roared their approving laughter. A feisty time was had by all, and Tallulah talked about that night for years. When it happened again, however, Grandmother Bankhead trooped down the steps, glared at her son, directed the girls to bed, and hissed Will's friends home where they belonged.

Aside from frequent bouts with a racking croup for which scalding mustard plasters were applied to her chest and in reaction to which she suggested, "Burn Sister! Burn Sister, too!," Tallulah was a healthy child with a wide, earnest face and a chunky, going-on-fat physique. Her hair was short, naturally wavy, and storybook blond, full of sun and pigmentation. Long, home-cut bangs awned her deep-set, wide-apart blue eyes. Her voice, like Eugenia's, was strong and bronchial, its natural deepness exacerbated as a result of a tonsillectomy in which a surgeon inadvertently cut into her uvula.

She chattered a great deal and loudly. She scampered up trees. She hugged often and very tight. She expressed love easily. She was a bit of a bully. Had she been born sixty years later, her enormous energies would have been designated hyperkinetic.

She had frequent tantrums, but only in Will's absence. They

were frightening displays, near seizures, in which she slapped herself down on the floor, beat her arms, and bobbed her head and turned purple in the face. Rainy days made a hyena out of her, and Eugenia, to escape her frightening pace, often hid in the closet. When Will returned from the office on such days, he would call out "All right, Nothin' Much, you can come out now. I'm home."

Tallulah's tantrums did not, as it was hoped, abate. They were often staged alongside Grandmother Bankhead's rocker. Glancing down at the mad Tallulah, the old woman warned, "I'm gonna get the bucket if you don't stop kickin'. Okay, Tallulah, I'm gettin' the bucket." She sloshed bucketfuls of cold water on the child. To no avail. Long before Tallulah ran out of steam, Grandmother ran out of cold water.

Grandmother Bankhead tried to raise the girls to be proper Southern ladies. She taught them to pick up after themselves, to accumulate good deeds in this life in preparation for the life hereafter, to stand when elders entered or left the room, to cultivate *nice* friends because people were, after all, judged by the company they kept. When angered, she threatened, "I'll make young ladies out of you or see you lyin' in your graves."

They rode with Grandmother every Thursday into the Negro section of Jasper. Many of the residents there were descendants of the slaves whom the elder Tallulah's mother, Grandmother McAuley, had brought with her from South Carolina. The Senator's wife brought baskets of food, her dirty laundry, and a well-developed sense of responsibility. On her own land, she maintained a sort of commissary to which Negroes came on Saturday for their cornmeal. She kept a little black book in which she recorded their births and deaths and thereby knew how much cornmeal was actually required by each family and whether or not any of it was being fed to the chickens. That she would not tolerate.

During election years, the girls stumped through northern Alabama with their imposing Grandfather, Captain John. They started out early in the morning in a horse-drawn surrey. Tallulah looked forward to the whole barbecued steers, the tons of potato salad, and the hot biscuits along the campaign trail. To the question "And who might you be little girl?" Tallulah was primed to respond, "I'm Tallulah Bankhead. My Granddaddy's running for Congress. I hope you'll vote for my Granddaddy."

Eugenia was petrified of him; Tallulah knew better. If he scowled or looked cross, his youngest granddaughter approached him very directly and stared straight into his blue eyes. She smiled. "You're not gonna be cross with me, are you, Granddaddy?" She came still closer and whispered into his ear, "You know I'm your favorite."

"Don't say that, Tallulah. You know we don't have favorites in this family."

"Give me a nickel, Granddaddy."

The old gentleman reached into his pocket. "Shouldn't we give Sister a nickel, too?"

"All right, Granddaddy. You can give Sister a nickel. Sister, come and take Granddaddy's nickel."

Tallulah and Eugenia talked about those favorites that the Bankhead family *didn't* have when they rode together on their ponies into the woods adjacent to the house. They went there to fetch blackberries regularly for Grandmother's jelly kitchen.

"I'm Grandmother and Granddaddy's pet," Tallulah would say matter-of-factly. "But Daddy loves you the best." She almost always picked more berries than Eugenia, whose eyesight was yet far from normal, and when she didn't, she ate from Eugenia's basket to equalize the yield.

Will Bankhead had good days and bad. On his worst days, after drinking excessively with his friends, he frequently got into brawls and returned to the house swathed in bandages. While Tallulah dreamed her jungle dream, Eugenia dreamed recurringly of a coffin being carried up the driveway toward their house. It was set down. She approached it. Gazed in and saw her father: a corpse with a swath of bandages around his head. She ceased having that dream only way into her adulthood, after Will's death.

After he'd been drinking, he brandished a pistol sometimes and threatened to end his lugubrious yearning for Ada. When she was eight, Eugenia passed him one day on the stairs and noticed he was hiding something behind his back. Fearing the worst, she followed him up to Grandmother's room. Will entered, leaving the door slightly ajar. Eugenia watched as he kneeled chivalricly at his mother's feet, hoisting an unopened liquor bottle in the air. He swore in behalf of Ada and for the sake of his daughters that he would forsake the bottle and never again expose the girls to his Stygian depressions. With one hand, Grandmother Bankhead comforted her sobbing son, and with the other she motioned Eugenia away.

What seven-year-old Tallulah felt about Will's suicide threats can only be surmised. Neither she nor Eugenia ever spoke about them. Her jungle dream undoubtedly had something to do with a fear of abandonment, of being left alone and unprotected in a hostile world. Tallulah had been abandoned by Will, first by his separation from her physically and then by his drunken, melancholic lack of approachability.

If Tallulah now feared permanent abandonment—Daddy's death through suicide—she reacted with a fierce curiosity about the phenomenon in general. One afternoon, in Jasper, when she was seven, the family was sitting down to their long midday meal. Will customarily walked home from the office to eat with the girls.

"Where's Tallulah?" he asked Eugenia.

"I don't know, Daddy," Eugenia said. "We went into town on our ponies, and she said she was going to see the bodies."

"What!"

"You know, Daddy. The people that died."

The day before, in Jasper, there had been two deaths, an extraordinary number for a town that size. An old man was drowned, and a teen-age boy had stabbed himself to death. Just as Will was about to ride into town to fetch Tallulah, the telephone rang. It was the town mortician, hideously named Mr. Legg, who wanted to know what to do about Tallulah.

"What's happened to her?" Will replied.

"Oh, nothing's happened to her, Mr. Will. But she's been sitting here on a box between the two corpses for hours. She looks at one, and then she looks at the other. I told her it was time to go home for lunch, but she hasn't moved."

Will ordered Tallulah home at once. She came in, sat down at the dining-room table, and grabbed a biscuit. Will cleared his throat and asked gently what she had been doing at Mr. Legg's.

"I was lookin' at 'em," Tallulah said.

With intense concern, Will Bankhead asked why she was so interested in viewing the bodies of two men whom to his knowledge she did not even know.

"They were alive yesterday. And they're dead today. And I was just tryin' to understand why," she said.

"To me," Tallulah wrote about Will, "he was a fusion of Santa Claus, Galahad, D'Artagnon, and Demosthenes. He was the gallant, the romantic, the poet, above all, the actor."

He was, in fact, all those things, however fitfully. There is no question but that, when Will Bankhead was good, he was very, very good—or, at least, bountiful. He took his daughters on all-night camping trips, though he confided to Tallulah during one that he had wanted a son. He read them Shakespeare and the Bible resoundingly. He extricated them quixotically from trouble and woe.

In 1910, Will promised to take the girls to the circus. Instead of napping as they should have to prepare for the event, Tallulah and Eugenia, accompanied by their cousin John, roamed around in back of Grandmother's greenhouse and found there an unsmoked, long cigar. Tallulah suggested that they try it. They did and were caught, sent to bed by Grandmother Bankhead with only bread and milk, and informed that the circus was out. Eugenia accepted her fate. Tallulah fumed and hurled pellets of bread at everything in sight.

Just before dark, they heard a rap on the window. Will, in a new black suit and probably several under his belt, had climbed up a ladder to rescue them.

"Get dressed," he whispered. "We're going to the circus."

Following a subsequent breach of conduct, Grandmother Bankhead insisted that he spank both girls soundly. Will feigned a sober, fatherly glare, sighed mightily, and took them each separately into an adjoining room. "I'm sure you haven't been as bad as Tallulah," he told Eugenia. "But if I spank her, I've got to spank you. I'm gonna slap my knee and I want you to howl as if I were spanking you." Years later, the sisters compared notes and Eugenia discovered that he had said exactly the same thing to Tallulah.

Tallulah came to cosset and glorify the memory of her sundry childhood illnesses. In her autobiography she listed all of them proudly: whooping cough, measles, pneumonia, the mumps, erysipelas, croup, tonsillitis, even smallpox. "I was sickly too," she boasted, "but I got little sympathy because I was so plump." Illness meant, of course, special attention, the special and exclusive attention of Will.

She remembered clearly coming perilously close to death when she was five or six after being bitten by a snake while on a picnic alone with Daddy. She wrote, "Quick as a flash, Daddy snatched off my panties and sucked the blood from the wound. Subsequently, he was quite ill. He had an abrasion in his gums and the poison infected him."

When Tallulah recalled the incident to her sister in 1943, Eugenia had no memory of a snakebite at all. Tallulah became incensed and showed her a scar on her upper thigh as proof. The elder Bankhead sister remembered the cause of that scar: a nasty, multiheaded carbuncle, the lancing of which had been particularly gleeful to Eugenia because she had been asked to sit on Tallulah's head.

Just about the time Tallulah suffered with her carbuncle, Uncle John was bitten by a snake and Will did assist in his treatment. Tallulah could have introjected the events. The possibility exists that her snakebite was a screen memory, primal, emblematic, and complete even to Will's punishment.

4

Convent Cavalcade

THOUGH WILL BANKHEAD TRIED, he was unable to cope with his motherless children and his own demons while the patriarchal Senator Bankhead and his wife were in Washington for the Congressional sessions. Tallulah and Eugenia spent a good part of 1910 and 1911 in Montgomery with their bustling and literary Aunt Marie.

The girls played among the heroic Capitol statuary, a chalky Arcadia of dead heroes, working cannons, and granite poesy, which Tallulah recited in Daddy's tremulous tones:

> When this Historic Shaft Shall Crumbling Lie
> In Ages Hence, In Women's Hearts Will Be
> A Folded Flag, A Thrilling Page Unrolled,
> A Deathless Song of Southern Chivalry.

Tallulah did her usual quota of showing off. Aunt Marie had a watermelon party in her honor, and she monopolized center stage with a devastating impression of Miss Gussie Woodruff, her teacher, whom Sara Mayfield described in *The Constant Circle* as "a white-haired maiden lady who always dressed in high net collars and long black silk dresses with a pince-nez pinned to them by a gold fleur-de-lis." Tallulah's impression was right on target.

At Miss Gussie's grammar school, the girls scored effortlessly and virtually identically in the mid-90's. The most significant difference was in their deportment marks, where Tallulah, with a 93, scored two points behind Eugenia. Miss Gussie had apparently not caught Tallulah's act. Withal, Tallulah was obviously not a behavior problem in school. She and Eugenia were always in the same grade since the latter's early illness had delayed her schooling for a year.

They spent the following summer back in Jasper. One rainy day they were rummaging through some old trunks of Will's in the attic and came across Ada's taffeta riding costume, feather plume and all. Eugenia, who was thin, darker than Tallulah, and often compared to her late mother, pushed her hair up into the hat, squeezed on the dress, and stood within Will's line of vision as he walked wearily home from work.

"Wh-eeeeel! Wh-eeeeel!" she called to him, waving airily.

He had turned ashen before Eugenia, realizing what she had done, assured him, "It's only me, Daddy."

La gauche femme fatale and the exhibitionist were sent away to school that fall.

Will accompanied them to the Convent of the Sacred Heart, in Manhattanville, New York. A Catholic school was chosen, over the anxious demurrals of their anti-Catholic grandmother, simply because there was no existing choice. Only they took boarding students as young as ten and eleven. The consensus, moreover, among the family and the townfolk was that a strict Catholic education would probably do the Bankhead girls—especially that Tallulah—some good.

"Started the incubator this morning," Will wrote to his father in Washington. "If you go to New York, please do not fail to see the children. They are awful homesick and would be so happy to see you."

The convent was an enwalled, bucolic spot where the girls wore navy blue uniforms with grosgrain ribbons, bathed with their chemises on, and held their hands stoically still for a smart ruler's rap. Here Tallulah experienced a trinity of firsts: snow, nuns, and jokes about her name. There had been no jokes in Alabama. Montgomery alone boasted a family which called its daughters after the states of the Confederacy: Alabama, Florida, and Georgia. The derision started when one of the nuns suggested that "Tallulah" was a "pagan sound."

The girls had been reared theoretically as Episcopalians, Will having elected that they follow the faith of their mother. Exigency and alternating relatives had ecumenicized them, however, and they had attended a variety of Protestant services, some of which featured curdling descriptions of unsaved souls roasting and wriggling throughout eternity. And though Tallulah abhorred being away from home, she rather liked what she now saw of the Catholic church. It was a cool medium with a certain cachet. She viewed the kneeling nuns, the incense smell, and the strange chanting with a mixture of terror and fascination.

She incorporated some of the devout attitudes and a couple of the splashier rituals into her dramatic repertory, which, at the time, ranged from "Old Ironsides" to Lady Macbeth's mad scene. Eugenia walked into their room one day to find her rotund ten-year-old sister staring autohypnotically into a mirror, at the same time making strange, wide balletic movements with her arms.

"What's wrong, Sister?" she asked.

"Nothin's wrong. Don't you recognize an actress when you see one?"

Her actress daydreams were among a complicity of factors which prevented Tallulah from attending to her work at school. She was restless and high-strung. She woke up many nights still screaming in that jungle. She was angry at Will for sending her away, and the stern rules of behavior at the convent were simply unacceptable to her.

The nuns got the first real taste of Tallulah's temper during the first round of awards for the semester. Those students who were awarded three laudatory *très biens* for excellence in classwork were permitted to wear a special and very dapper satin sash for a month. Tallulah never expected to get the sash herself, but she was counting on Eugenia's superior scholarship. Sister copped two *très biens*, but on her third attempt was given a mere *bien*. Convinced that her sister had been unjustly graded, Tallulah flung an inkpot against the classroom wall. The mother superior confined her to quarters. She was forbidden to attend the upcoming school bazaar which both she and Eugenia had been looking forward to for weeks.

On the big day, Eugenia dressed for the bazaar while Tallulah paced their room. The pacing finally yielded a solution. At the fair, for a penny, the students were to be given the opportunity to fish chances out of a giant bowl. The prizes included chocolate cake slices, dolls, books, and special dispensations. Would it not be reasonable to assume, that given twenty-seven opportunities—Eugenia had fourteen pennies and Tallulah thirteen—Sister could buy *one* dispensation to be used to free Tallulah so she could enjoy at least *part* of the bazaar? Eugenia was dispatched.

Tallulah stood at their window and watched the fairgrounds: saw Eugenia stroll up to the fishbowl, win and eat several pieces of chocolate cake, choose a doll and a little book of poetry. The afternoon cranked on and on with no dispensation in sight. The fairgrounds had almost emptied when Eugenia looked up to Tallulah in the room to indicate that she had spent the last penny.

Tallulah jumped up and down with rage. She yanked out several hanks of the hair that Aunt Marie had compared to spun gold, flung open the window, and hurled them out willy-nilly. She was never entirely sure that Eugenia had not bought a dispensation and simply pocketed it.

The girls went home to Jasper that summer. Grandmother commented on their growth and a considerable improvement in Tallulah's behavior. Tallulah begged not to be sent away again, but there was little choice. All the Bankheads were too busy. Marie was ministering to Dr. Owen, who was ailing. Grandfather was working particularly hard to pass a bill which would appropriate millions of federal dollars to Alabama roads. Will was knocking on doors collecting signatures for his first Congressional campaign. He was resolute, hardworking, sober, and, as it turned out, enormously savvy in the ways of local politicking.

He wrote to his father that year: "There is a man in the Penitentiary at Wetumpka by the name of Can A. Pate who was sent up from Pickens County for murder in 1906. He has a large number of relatives and friends in Pickens and Tuscaloosa County who are very anxious to secure a permanent parole for him. He does not want a pardon as there is another indictment still hanging over him in Pickens County. . . . I want you to write Governor O'Neal a very strong personal request asking him to permanently parole this prisoner . . . at once if possible so that he can do some work before the Primary."

While Can A. Pate got his parole, Tallulah and Eugenia were sent up once again: They were entered, in the fall of 1913, at Mary Baldwin Seminary in Staunton, Virginia. It was near enough to Washington so that they could see their grandparents regularly. Their older cousin Marion Bankhead was enrolled there. Surely, Tallulah would be less homesick and obstreperous there than she had been at Sacred Heart.

But it didn't work that way. Tallulah, at eleven, was the youngest student in the school and possibly the fattest. There was no doubt in anyone's mind that she had inherited the traditional Bankhead frame. The tendency was aided and abetted by the regular after-hours feasts she and Eugenia enjoyed in their darkened room. To make matters much worse for a budding Thespian, her face was beginning to break out.

The girls at Mary Baldwin, however, would not soon forget Tallulah Bankhead, pimples or no. After she was turned down for the school play, she attended the production with Eugenia and made it a point to talk loudly throughout. At a Halloween party she somehow got hold of a jug of hard cider, drank some, rather liked the effect it had on her, and turned a couple of dexterous cartwheels. Her classmates gathered around as she drank more cider, turned some rather more daring cartwheels. Tiring of the trick, she rigged up an ersatz trapeze and swung by her feet, laughing boisterously the whole time. Tallulah had figured out that she did not need the appurtenances of the theater to reap its most satisfying reward: an audience.

Her performance was rudely interrupted by one of her least favorite teachers, a Miss Wyman, who first ordered Tallulah down and then attempted forcibly to disengage her from the trapeze. She bit Miss Wyman on the hand. The girls were sent home before Thanksgiving.

Though Tallulah rejoiced, Eugenia this time was annoyed at

the consequences of her sister's exhibitionism. *She* was enjoying Mary Baldwin. The older students had just begun to accept her and were using her to run messages to the cadets at nearby Staunton Military Academy. The intrigue was fun, and the cadets, in their snappy little uniforms, were extraordinarily attractive.

Tallulah was bitterly disappointed that same fall when her father lost the Congressional election. His opponent had charged that "Little Willy" was not only a drunk but an apostatic drunk who had chosen to educate his daughters outside the glorious state of Alabama. By the time of his defeat the motile Bankhead sisters were enrolled in their third school, the Convent of the Visitation, which was also in the Washington area.

Tallulah fell in love that year, wildly, totally, obsessively in love —with a rangy schoolyard nun. She could not eat or sleep or study without thinking of the nun, and when she did think about her, she experienced something close to nausea but much nicer.

"I've got a crush on Sister Ignatius," she told Eugenia. But Eugenia was much too busy with thoughts of Staunton Military to pay her much heed.

Tallulah's feelings had begun to churn up when Sister Ignatius had taken her part in a schoolyard brawl. Since then, Tallulah had hung around her, run errands, talked continuously to anyone who would listen about the kindly nun. She was the first of a series of teachers on whom Tallulah developed schoolgirl crushes.

For the unlovable but certainly not unloving Tallulah, it was usually a matter of being defended. If a particular nun took her part, or spoke up on her behalf, or complimented her, or showed her just a little preferential warmth, Tallulah was smitten for weeks. Her separation from Will became less intolerable.

But these crushes had more to do with Ada than with Will. Tallulah and Eugenia had never discussed their feelings about not having a mother. They had been told that Ada was a beautiful angel whose hair was filled with white gardenias—and that was that. They would comment occasionally on the mothers of the other girls who came to the convent to visit. If a particular mother was ugly or shrewish, the Bankhead sisters would get beamy and self-congratulatory.

After watching one of them carp at and criticize her daughter, Tallulah whispered to Eugenia, "Maybe we're better off, Sister." And when Eugenia pointed out the mother of one of their friends, who seemed nice enough and very pretty, Tallulah said, "You can't always tell by looks."

In spite of the young Tallulah's cynical defenses, she seemed to be keening now over a terrible absence in her life and choosing approving teachers as surrogate mothers. In later years, she would jest bawdily about herself and the convent nuns. As with most of her mature humor, her nun stories contained a kernel of emotional truth protected and distorted by layers of sexual travesty.

During their stay at Visitation, Will Bankhead remarried. The woman was Florence McGuire, the daughter of a Jasper attorney. She was an attractive, dark-eyed, auburn-haired child-woman in her mid-twenties who had done some secretarial work for Will and had been dating him for several years before the nuptials. Tallulah and Eugenia were told of his marriage by Grandmother Bankhead, who was less than overjoyed at the prospect. She never liked Florence and referred to her as "that woman." Eugenia and Tallulah decided between themselves that they would try at least to be civil to Florence McGuire.

Soon after the marriage, Will took the girls on a vacation trip to Myrtle Beach, South Carolina. He had his first car that year, a Hudson with isinglass windows. Eugenia was sitting up front next to Will, Tallulah was in back, between Florence and Miss Douglas Lacy Long, Will's current secretary and a good friend to the Bankhead girls. It was the kind of venture—new car, rustic country—which ordinarily would have excited Tallulah. But she was unusually quiet that trip, until she screamed suddenly, "Stop the car, Daddy, I'm dying!" Her first menstrual blood had trickled onto the back seat.

In fact, Tallulah had not been unprepared. She had questioned her older cousin Marion doggedly about "the curse," with the ruthless curiosity that she evinced in many matters of life, death, and sexuality. Just months before, Eugenia had walked into the room at the convent and discovered Tallulah sort of poking herself.

"What in heaven's name are you doin', Sister?" Eugenia asked.

"I'm lookin' for the blood," Tallulah replied, pronouncing it "bloud" as she had heard it said trippingly from the mouth of Will Bankhead during one of his thunderous Shakespearean recitations.

The mood of the Bankhead family in 1915—what with marriage, menarche, Will's continuing political resoluteness in the face of defeat—was one of growth, reform, and amelioration. Appropriate to that mood, Will Bankhead endeavored to do something about his daughter Tallulah's behavior. Since the one constant in Tallulah's life had always been Eugenia, it occurred to him that separation might be the solution.

The Margaret Booth School was chosen for Eugenia. Miss Margaret had opened her portals to the young ladies of Montgomery just the year before. She took only a hundred of the *finest* girls each year, teaching them Latin, English literature, and art history. The term culminated in a pilgrimage to Florence, Italy.

Sara Mayfield wrote of the school: "Mademoiselle Marguerite Dognon drilled French into us by a rigorous system of *précis*, *dictées*, and *cahiers*. A unique cultural feature of the Margaret Booth School was the morning convocation, at which the Lord's Prayer was said, the Marseillaise sung in French, and the roll call answered with quotations of Robert Browning." Zelda Sayre, who became Zelda Sayre Fitzgerald, lived a block away; though she attended the public high school, she chose in later years to educate her daughter, Scottie, at Miss Margaret's.

Tallulah would claim in her autobiography that she had attended Margaret Booth's school, but she did not. Tallulah was enrolled at the Holy Cross Academy at Dunbar, near Washington. With the exception of those years when Eugenia was being treated for her blindness in Montgomery, she and Tallulah had been inseparable throughout their lives. Tallulah was distraught without her and more alone than she had ever felt in her life. Missing Sister desperately, she pleaded to be sent home. When she was not, Tallulah simply went limp. She would not eat or go to chapel or speak in class. She cried by herself in her room. Her misery was relieved only by fantasizing about a time when she would be famous, and beautiful, and loved, and thereby unlonely.

That need was vivified when she sneaked off one day, no doubt emboldened by Will's *Monte Cristo* venture, to see Madame Alla Nazimova, the famous Russian actress, in her celebrated performance of *War Brides*. Tallulah was weak with enchantment but strong enough to sneak back into the Academy undetected.

Back at the school, however, confronted with the brutish facts of her reality, with no Eugenia to tell about Nazimova, she continued her listless behavior. In a matter of weeks, Eugenia was yanked out of Margaret Booth and sent to Holy Cross to keep her younger sister company.

Shortly afterward Tallulah received the sad news that her seventeen-year-old cousin William Perry, the bright and charming son of Aunt Louise and one of the several children with whom she had grown up in Jasper, was dead. He was at the University of Alabama when he contracted walking typhoid. Just before he died, William had shot bolt upright in bed and said to Louise: "Morning, Mother, it's always morning." Louise then locked herself in a closet and buffeted her head against the wall.

Tallulah sent these words to her aunt: "In the middle of the night, I find myself crying to think I will never see dear Billy again and oh I loved him better than I could have loved a brother."

Eugenia began to date. She dreamed not about a stage debut but of Annapolis hops and coming out in Washington society. At fifteen, she was thin, round-faced, risible, with an eager and developing coquettish wit. In spite of her problem eye, she was considered a beauty.

Tallulah, who had reached her full height at 5 feet 3 inches and shocked the scale at 130 pounds, was another matter altogether. Eugenia tried but was unable to get anyone to take her clamorous, stomachy sister out. Tallulah told Eugenia that she didn't care about boys in any case, and perhaps she didn't, but being rejected by them was something else entirely.

From Dunbar they went to Fairmont Seminary in Washington. The small and fashionable finishing school was the last educational institution either Bankhead girl would attend. From the other eight or so schools they had never graduated or stayed more than a year or two before they were either rejected or drifted away. They were enrolled at Fairmont to be made ready for their debuts into Washington Congressional society, for which they would have been eligible solely on the basis of their grandfather's status. Happily, Will redoubled their eligibility in 1916 when he was elected to Congress from the Tenth District of Alabama.

On the day of the election, Tallulah buzzed around Fairmont whispering solicitous Hail Marys. She was taken with a chaperone to watch the election results on a screen in front of a newspaper office on Pennsylvania Avenue. When the good news was flashed on the screen, she ran totally amok.

At school, she studied piano and violin. She was able to play two easy pieces by Chopin on the piano, but she was more ambitious about her fiddle, which Granddaddy had just recently bought for her. While scratching away at it one day, she told Eugenia that if her acting career were for some reason not to fructify, she might consider becoming a concert violinist. Eugenia replied that she would do well to first learn to tune the instrument.

In that fifteenth year, strange and radical changes were happening to Tallulah. Her curls, which had been golden but unextraordinary, took on a marvelous radiance. She shed layers of fat. And her pimples cleared. She discovered interesting and photogenic planes in her face and realized that she was not, after all, going to resemble Aunt Louise. With the encouragement of a burgeoning pulchritude and the example of the successful actresses over whom she swooned, she dieted stoically for the first time in her life. "Suddenly," Eugenia Bankhead recalled, "Tallulah was the beautiful one."

Tallulah was, of course, delighted with the transfiguration. She gazed constantly into mirrors and posed often for a variety of photographers. She pouted, pursed, and pinced her lips like her latest actress idol. In several pictures, she was up on her toes, curls hovering, eyebrows raised, chin shot out in a dancy imitation of life.

On a fishing trip with Daddy and Florence, a photographer was employed to shoot the family standing beside their abundant catch. Tallulah ran up to their room to prepare herself for the arrival of the cameraman; Eugenia, for a lark, locked her in. Before she was able to extricate herself from the room, the man had taken his pictures of Will, Florence, and Eugenia and left. When the developed pictures were sent to the family, Tallulah tore up every single shot in which Eugenia appeared.

5

La Dueña

NINETEEN SEVENTEEN turned out to be a watershed year for the Bankheads, as well as for the world at large.

Captain John succeeded with the most important single piece of legislation in his Methuselahan career. It resulted in the construction of two federally financed transcontinental road systems, both originating in Washington, D.C.: the Lincoln Highway, stretching northward, and the Bankhead Highway, heading south from the Capitol and then west to the Golden Gate Bridge. In Washington, at the junction of the two roads, an ecumenical marker contains the granite likeness of each.

Will Bankhead went into his first year as United States Congressman, determined to follow the sage advice of his father vis-à-vis advancement within the ranks: "Learn the rules." A well-liked parliamentarian was bound to go far.

Eugenia Bankhead, sixteen, met Morton Hoyt, the charming scion of a prominent Washington family. Hoyt introduced himself at four in the afternoon. They were married by nine that same night. It was her first, his first, and *their* first marriage. Though this particular ceremony was annulled forthwith, she and Hoyt would marry each other on several subsequent occasions.

Tallulah, fifteen, arrived in New York City with Aunt Louise and Ola Davis, her dead son William's erstwhile fiancée, who sang as sweet as she looked.

The motion-picture promoter who contracted with *Picture-Play* magazine to bring Tallulah and the rest of the contest winners to New York and photograph them in a five-reel production personally directed by Frank Powell originally had no intention of living up to his promises. The buck passed from hand to hand, but Senator Bankhead and some influential allies in New York pressured the magazine into exacting from the promoter at least minimal compliance.

Tallulah, Aunt Louise, and Ola were summoned to New York. The smoldering fifteen-year-old was employed for a period of three weeks at a motion-picture studio in Brooklyn. The ladies were instructed to proceed with caution through the unsettled Brooklyn streets. Tallulah was paid $25 a week for her work, the first money she ever earned. There is no evidence that the resultant footage was ever released or indeed that someone cared enough to load the camera. The magazine, however, was off the hook.

Senator Bankhead was not. He had promised not only to allow his favorite grandchild to avail herself of the opportunities presented by *Picture-Play*—that would have been a legalistic sleight of hand which would have solved or proved nothing—but to stake her over a sensible period of time until she gave up, got it out of her system, or succeeded. No time limit was set, but it was understood that recall was always a possibility.

He did all he could to help her and protect her, establishing on Tallulah's behalf a network of interest, influence, and surveillance. After thirty years in national politics, the Senator naturally had a legion of friends in high places. Through his man in New

York, a lobbyist for the American Chicle Company named Knox "Jimmy" Julian, appointments were arranged for Tallulah with Frederick L. Collins, managing editor of McClure's Publications; Benjamin B. Hampton, vice-president of the American Tobacco Company, who had recently become one of the chief stockholders of Goldwyn and Rex Beach Pictures; Edward Seldon, a play broker; and John Rhinock, a theatrical executive and oil millionaire who had served in Congress with both Senator Bankhead and Louise Perry's first husband.

As late as 1930, the Bankhead family was still making old debts good. Jimmy Julian wrote to Will Bankhead, who was by that time an influential member of Congress, about a man named Leon J. Rubenstein. Rubenstein wanted government support to finance the distribution of some Russian films. "He seems positive [the films] would make wonderful anti-Red propaganda," Jimmy wrote. "He tried to help Tallulah in her struggling days. I do not think he accomplished much but he did try to do anything he could for Tallulah and Mrs. Lund and Ola."

The trio took an apartment on West Forty-fifth Street in a fashionable New York building. Through the winter of 1917 they made rounds, received advice, shopped at Altman's, attended the theater, and reported their progress directly to the Senator. Tallulah resented her aunt in the beginning, but no more than any spoiled, willful adolescent would have resented the presence of a chaperone who had purse power, nay-say, and the responsibility to run interference between the glitter of New York and the ambitions of an innocent right out of the convent by way of finishing school.

Like her mother and her sister Marie, Louise Bankhead Perry Lund was a square, squat, typically upholstered Bankhead woman. She had married her first husband, Congressman William Perry, when she was very young and lost him the same year that Will's Ada died. William Perry was the son of the famous Governor B. F. Perry of South Carolina, who pronounced to the threatening Reconstructionist elements: "This is a white man's government."

Louise had two children from that first union: William Perry,

Jr., the boy who died at seventeen from walking typhoid, and young Louise, who was back in Jasper rearing her own family. By the time she came to New York with Tallulah, Aunt Louise was remarried to an Arthur Lund, but they were not living together.

The boy William had been the apple of her eye. When she lost him, she became brusque, short-tempered, and a bit resentful of surviving youth. Her life was measured in "good deeds" rather than loving gestures, good deeds for which she expected a just return on the other side. She genuinely loved Ola because William had.

With the two girls in tow, she chased about in New York from spiritualist to spiritualist, trying to communicate with her dead son. Right after his demise, one medium had produced for her the words: "Morning, Mother, it's always morning." Louise was agog, and she expected that New York, with its vast supply of mediumistic talent, could provide her with an encore. The best she got were some spooky shuffling and a couple of table raps.

It was not the spiritualist meetings, which rather entertained Tallulah, but the ubiquity of Ola Davis that eventually turned the budding actress against her *dueña*. Ola wanted a singing career. When Aunt Louise presented both girls, *a duo*, to New York talent agents, Tallulah felt she showed a definite preference for Ola. She ranted and raved and wrote letters home about the situation. Was she to be hobbled even in her sacred ambition by yet another sibling rival!

During this period, they went one day to the office of David Belasco. After they had left the producer and were standing in the hall waiting for an elevator, Louise excused herself and returned to see the producer for a moment. Tallulah had the distinct impression—confirmed, she said later in life, by an eyewitness—that Louise had gone back to bad-mouth her and, for that reason, she was not employed. Tallulah wrote that Aunt Louise had "blackjacked" her.

Certainly it would not have been unlike Louise to take Tallulah's ambitions less seriously than she demanded they be taken. Louise indeed may have chatted amiably with Belasco on her return and, in the course of the conversation, patronized a passion which she could not have apprehended by the very nature of her background and sensibilities. But "blackjack"? Probably not.

In February, 1918, Tallulah, Louise, and Ola moved around the corner to the legendary Algonquin Hotel. They took a modest but airy room with two beds and an armoire. During the first three weeks of their residence there, Tallulah was moody, splenetic, and subject to fitful, thumping headaches. Louise attributed her moodiness to natural bad temper and inactivity. Tallulah typically had not told her aunt or anyone else what the problem was. She fumed and fussed and with childish optimism expected that they would know: January 31 had been her *sixteenth birthday*, and no one, not even Daddy, had remembered.

Finally, on February 23, she received a letter from Will. "I intended to send you a telegram but it slipped my memory," he wrote. "May sweet sixteen be the threshold of your final dreams."

He continued, in his handsome, lucid hand, under the Congressional letterhead:

> I have no son, and maybe never will have. I will depend on you to represent your father and your grandfather by making a real and lasting career as an artist in your chosen profession. It is a fine thing to contemplate how powerful a factor the screen has become on the thought and conduct of the world, and how great the possibilities it offers to you—my daughter. But don't forget, when you get your real chance, don't forget that it takes *steady* sacrifice and inconvenience. There is no royal road to the top anywhere. Let us know your prospects, and keep me advised where and in what picture I may "look upon thine image."

That afternoon, Aunt Louise and Ola went carpet shopping. Tallulah used her headache as an excuse to stay home at the Algonquin, hoping to take the opportunity to prowl the lobby undeterred. She was about to leave the room when the telephone rang. Tallulah was instructed to get over to the Shubert Theater as quickly as possible.

The chain of communications that had unfurled from her sundry appointments had finally yielded fruit. They wanted her to audition for a new play about to depart for a short, pre-Broadway tour. Tallulah grabbed her hat, painted her face in the style of Ethel Barrymore, and rushed over to the theater. She got the walk-on part, rehearsed it, bought her costumes, and returned to the Algonquin, a working actress, in time to hurl herself head-acheless at Aunt Louise and Ola Davis as they walked through the door at six. She was a sputtering, talkative, excited amalgam of terror and jubilation.

The Squab Farm, with Alma Tell and Gladys Sinclair, opened on Broadway in March, 1918. It received hideous notices and ran for less than a month. Jimmy Julian arranged for a full column of publicity about Tallulah to appear in the prestigious "Plays & Players" section of the New York Evening Telegram. The angle of the piece, published beside a big picture of Tallulah, was the distinguished Bankhead family. Several days later, in the same column, the star of The Squab Farm, Alma Tell, was allocated a mere two lines. The untrained and overtouted Tallulah was ostracized by most of the cast.

No matter. She had a beginning. In return for $50 a week her grandparents sent to Aunt Louise for Tallulah's maintenance, she was expected regularly to communicate with them. Grandfather, whose gout was beginning to nettle him, threatened several times to cut off her money when Tallulah became derelict in her letter writing. Now that she had something to tell, however, her affectionate and naïve missives were dispatched with glee. She wrote to her grandmother from the Algonquin:

My Precious Mamma,
Your little name sake is now a full fledge actress. I have made my debut on Broadway and I am so crazy about the stage. I have just returned from the matinee and I can't wait to go back for the evening performance. I expect to have a nice little part soon. In one of the pieces it says I am the star, but of course that is only press stuff. Some girls would pay a great deal of money for the publicity I am getting free.
Your devoted daughter (actress)
Tallulah

Tallulah was not a bit upset even at the short run of the play. Soon after *The Squab Farm* closed, the Russian independent film producer Ivan Abramson, who had been recruited by Granddaddy but was nonetheless enchanted with Tallulah's raw energy and wild beauty, put her in a silent flick, *When Men Betray*. It was an undistinguished effort produced in New York, which had little effect on her progress, but she was emboldened by one of her reviews which described Tallulah as "exquisite of feature, dainty of form, deliciously feminine and with a pair of large eyes that have the power of expressing all their emotions in their glance. Her appearance brings with it the feeling that the very atmosphere is surcharged with energy."

That was more or less how the gang at the Algonquin felt about her. They couldn't help noticing her. She had a little match-girl quality. She was very beautiful, and she was always running in and out of the lobby, generally in a state of physical and emotional disarray. Because it was all so new and exciting and there seemed hardly to be time for anything, she could never settle down properly to comb her hair or dress fastidiously. There was about her an aura of disarray, of spontaneity, and of innocence: all genuine.

To ask her a question was to open a floodgate of untrammeled revelation. With hurried but honeycombed, endless, unpunctuated words she talked about her wish to be a famous actress, about the audition she had just come from and the one to which she was now rushing, about Daddy, who was a handsome Congressman, and Granddaddy, who was a darling Senator, about Ethel Barrymore who had actually spoken to her and almost made her faint.

While she talked, she touched, more than people in New York, even in the theater, were used to being touched. She was demonstrative, loving, totally without ruse and easily moved to tears. Not tears of sadness—that emotion was covered by rage—but tears of feeling. She was also, in those early years and in spite of her tendency to run at the mouth, a studious and deferential listener.

When Tallulah was not working, the excitement of the Algonquin was theater enough for her. Frank Case managed the hotel at the time. He was a good friend to young Tallulah, as he was to everyone in the profession. It was his presence, encouragement, and loyalty which drew to the little Algonquin the cream of the theater world of that day. In his book *Tales of a Wayward Inn*, Case explained the phenomenon with a characteristically modest shrug: "If a man," he wrote, "should stand in Times Square with his heart simply bursting with love for bricklayers, I don't doubt that in time the bricklayers would sense it and gather round."

He proclaimed his love for the people of the theater, and they gathered around. John Drew was among the first, followed in Tallulah's time, by John, Ethel, and Lionel Barrymore; Elsie Janis, the musical comedy star; Frank Crowninshield, who published *Vanity Fair* and hosted, on behalf of Condé Nast, the chicest parties of the day; Douglas Fairbanks, Jr., who lived at the hotel with his mother and father; Constance Collier; Ina Claire; De Wolf Hopper; Raymond Hitchcock; Frank Craven; Jane Cowl; Laurette Taylor; Rex Beach; Anita Loos, a prolific motion-picture scenario writer; Estelle Winwood, who emigrated from England to the United States in the same year that Tallulah came up from Alabama; Jobyna Howland, a statuesque, six-foot actress who had been the model for Charles Dana Gibson's first Gibson Girl and was eternally cast, according to Dorothy Parker, as "Liberty or the Marne or the Spirit of the Ages." When Jobyna roared at Tallulah, who had jettisoned Aunt Louise for a couple of hours and was sitting in the lobby about to light up, "Take that cigarette out of your mouth, you infant," Tallulah took that cigarette out of her mouth.

Joby befriended Tallulah. She was acquainted, too, with Estelle Winwood, Anita Loos, Zoë Akins, the playwright, and an actress she met under the oddest circumstances. Tallulah was in her room one night when she heard a panicky rapping on the door. Aunt Louise was either out or sleeping soundly.

"Have you got a douche bag? I've just been raped," the actress told Tallulah. Being not only virginal but still innocent, Tallulah was mystified. The term had to it a rather ablutionary sound, and Tallulah, taking special pains to be as casual as possible, answered, "No, but I have an enema bag. Will that do?" The actress took the enema bag and left.

Of all the people in and around the Algonquin, the Barrymores were to Tallulah the acme of perfection, glamor, and dizzying distinction. Tallulah would say, in later years, that she had never made up her mind with whom she was more in love: John or Ethel. It was Ethel, in any case, whom she met first, and the distinguished stage actress had even, once or twice, deigned to speak to her.

She was lunching once with Eugenia in the Pergola Room, now the Oak Room, of the Algonquin. At a corner table, underneath the mirrored reflection of a mural of the Bay of Naples, sat Ethel Barrymore. Tallulah saw her and paled over her eggs Benedict.

"My God, Sister," Eugenia said, "you'd think it was the Virgin Mary."

Despite the fact that she was becoming known to an impressive group of Algonquinites, Tallulah's social life was severely limited by the presence of Aunt Louise. Ola had returned discouraged to Montgomery months ago, so she was no longer the problem. The problem was Louise's endeavor to cramp her niece's life-style, indeed to prevent her from having one. Their fiercest altercation resulted from a visit that Tallulah made to the apartment of a young male photographer who took some publicity pictures of her. Louise charged that she had posed half-naked and demanded a full account. Tallulah gave her a full account of her fury.

By the summer of 1919 Tallulah's erratic moods were exacerbated by worry and inactivity. She had not set foot on a New York stage since the closing of *The Squab Farm* in April, 1918. She was less discouraged than fearful that Granddaddy would recall her to Washington. As prospect after prospect failed to fructify she became more and more difficult to live with and to govern.

She told many small lies to Louise and to her family, most of them about her prospects. She firmed up offers that were not firm at all, not to make herself more important to the Bankheads, but to keep them from becoming discouraged on her behalf. Yet, priding herself on her essential veracity, she rankled when distrusted. Her aunt bore the brunt of Tallulah's insecurity and fear.

Louise Bankhead Perry Lund finally could stand no more. "I do not believe there is a human being alive who can control her," she wrote to Senator Bankhead. She thereupon mailed the key to her safe deposit box to her daughter in Alabama, implored the young woman to teach her children the *right things*, and, after encountering a certain amount of difficulty finding a uniform large enough to fit, joined the Red Cross and shipped out to Paris.

6

Morning Glory

AUNT LOUISE'S DEPARTURE was, for a time, only a Pyrrhic victory for Tallulah. Aunt Marie replaced her for a bit. Jim Julian continued to check on her habits and prospects. She was instructed to take Sunday dinner with and telephone regularly a family named Cauble, trusted friends of the Senator's, who lived in New York. Senator Bankhead even asked Frank Case to keep an eye on young Tallulah. Case smiled graciously, but balked subsequently to his family: "I can either run this hotel or look after Tallulah Bankhead. I can't do both."

Jobyna Howland took it upon herself, as well, to instruct her little friend on the subtleties of ladylike behavior. When Tallulah chose starry-eyed to emulate Joby's language, the older actress corrected her: "Watch your mouth, ya little bitch, ya sound like a who-aw."

Tallulah made another silent movie. She hated movie work and refused absolutely to pursue it. Her decision dismayed Daddy, the Senator, Rhinock, Seldon, and Jim Julian, who all agreed that films were the wave of the future. Tallulah argued that her particular destiny was the stage.

There were no offers, however. By mid-1919 she had not worked in the theater for more than a year. Both Tallulah's excuses and the family's patience were running out. They were advised to act. Edward Seldon wrote the Senator: "Don't let Tallulah stay here too long if she does not get an engagement. We don't want her to get shopworn." Jim Julian cautioned, "New York is no place for an idle girl to be."

Without a regular chaperone, recall was imminent. Senator and Congressman Bankhead both agreed that she should not be permitted to remain idle and unguided in a strange and dangerous city too much longer. There was also the fear, unfounded at the time, that Tallulah might have inherited her father's drinking disposition.

Aware of the precariousness of the boat, Tallulah would not rock it by asking her family for anything that was not absolutely essential. There was also the matter of her considerable pride. Of the $50 a week that her grandfather sent her, $25 went for rent, and a good deal of the rest was spent on food and transportation. Her credit at the hotel was close to extinction. Her heels, most of the time, were close to the nails. There remained but a single dress in her wardrobe, a blue coat outfit which Daddy had bought her before she left Washington for New York. When it was being cleaned, Tallulah simply stayed in her room. Her dress and the state of it was a standing joke to some of the more successful Algonquinites; they even considered chipping in to buy her another.

Louise was demobbed soon after she showed up in Paris in a spiffy, tailor-made Red Cross cape. The war was ended. The worst of the wake was over. There was no longer a need for workers. She returned to New York and went immediately to the hotel, making it a point to barge in on Tallulah. She was astonished to find that her niece actually appeared happy to see her. Tallulah *was* happy to see Louise and especially delighted to be taken to *dinner*, where she ate ravenously. It occurred at long last to Louise that the child meant business. She wrote to her father about Tallulah, "I think she would rather starve and go naked than give up the theater."

And Mrs. Cauble, who complained that she eluded, evaded, and mystified her, gave this account of Tallulah's thwarted ambitions: "During one visit, Tallulah complained of a headache. She asked to lie down and went into a bedroom. There issued from the room a cry, almost a howl, which frightened all of us. Tallulah, drawn and frantic, came out of the room and said to me, 'I've got to go on the stage.' I never saw one her age so nervous."

Work finally came. In the early summer of 1919, Tallulah was offered a job with a highly respected stock company in Somerville, Massachusetts. Eager to do something to keep the wolf away from the door and her family off her back, she accepted the offer and worked, for two weeks, as hard as she had in her life: rising at eight, rehearsing a new play from nine until noon, performing the ongoing play twice a day. Learning lines was the easiest part for Tallulah, who engulfed pages by merely hearing the words spoken once or twice. She was an extraordinarily quick study.

But the demands were nonetheless grueling. No, this was not really what she had in mind. At the end of the two weeks, the company manager asked her to stay on for the season. She turned him down. "I can't possibly do it, Granddaddy honey," she wrote in explanation, "because I would be dead."

Tallulah's first words on the New York stage were spoken later in that summer of 1919. The play, written by Rachel Crothers, was called 39 *East*. With stars Henry Hull and Constance Binney, it had opened in April to nice notices and was a big commercial success. 39 *East* was the story of a New York boardinghouse and its inhabitants, "appealing, entertaining and typically feminine," according to one chauvinistic reviewer.

Around the Algonquin, Tallulah had heard that Miss Crothers, whose works were always produced entirely under her own supervision, was looking for an actress to understudy Miss Binney and go on for her in the New York production while the star took long weekends throughout the summer. The replacement would then travel with a second company on a national tour.

Tallulah, whose instincts and training were political, tried to get to Miss Crothers through Mary Kirkpatrick: the co-producer of the show, a Southern girl herself, and a friend of the Bankhead family. She tried for days unsuccessfully to reach Mary, finally waited for her on the street and waylaid her.

Mary told Tallulah that her chances were slim. Miss Crothers was unlikely to hire a feature player as untrained and scantily experienced as Tallulah "even if she were the President's daughter." If Tallulah cared to try, however, auditions were being held at that very moment over at the Broadhurst Theater. Tallulah, of course, hied over to the Broadhurst and waited her turn to read for Miss Crothers. Miss Crothers was impressed. Tallulah looked the part, and she read well. She was hired.

Tallulah wrote to her family immediately: a long, ebullient, unpunctuated account, a part of which began with her reaction to the compliments Rachel Crothers had paid to her:

> I was so happy I just burst out crying! I am going to get a hundred a week and my maids traveling expenses paid my maids salary paid and all my clothes bought so the expenses I will have will be my hotel bill and for fifty weeks in succession I will play which in the long run is much better than making two hundred for several weeks and then laying off for weeks. I can save a lot of money this way and we will play all the big cities and maybe play Chicago for a whole season. Every bodys crazy about the show and my name is going to be on the bill boards "39 East" with Tallulah Bankhead and the season after next I will play leading parts on Broadway. Mary says this part will make me a big stage star. Miss Crothers told her I was a genius and had a great talent and Mary says as long as she has known Miss Crothers she has never known her to give even a small part to a girl without experience much less a big part. . . . I thank you Mamma and dear Grandfather for the check. I will make this last me until I begin getting my understudy money. You all have been wonderful to me and I love you all

to death. Mamma. Grandfather. Sweet Daddy, dear Aunt Louise, dear Florence and the whole family.

TALLULAH

Please send this on to Daddy I could never write another letter My arm is dead.

LOVE

Withal, as visions of billboards, glory, and gratification danced in her head, Tallulah never forgot her manners. She did write to Daddy and, in the letter, asked him to communicate with Mary and thank her directly for being so nice: "She will appreciate it and she will do even more for me because she has a lot of influence with Miss Crothers."

At Miss Crothers' suggestion, Tallulah began to study diction, French, and ballet. She rehearsed the play at the playwright's apartment with Sidney Blackmer. Blackmer was in his early twenties, just back from the front where he had served with the American Expeditionary Forces. He was hired to understudy Henry Hull, fill in for him on the long summer weekends, and eventually tour with Tallulah.

After the rehearsal period, Tallulah began regularly to stand in the wings during performances and watch Constance Binney. She and Blackmer went on together for the first time in midsummer of 1919. Daddy, Florence, and Eugenia came up from Washington to see the performance. Her grandparents were not well enough to travel, but Mamma, who was beginning to enjoy her namesake's success, sent her a note. "I know," she wrote, "you will make my name more famous than ever."

The family was thrilled that Tallulah was the star of a Broadway play and very impressed with her ability. Seeing her up there finally legitimized her aspirations; they would communicate to Senator Bankhead that, chaperoned or not, Tallulah belonged in New York. She was an actress.

What the Bankheads did not perceive, however, was that Tallulah was not really *acting* during that first performance. She was so overcome with nervous tension that her imitative instincts were suppressing her dramaturgical flair. She was copying gesture

for gesture, nuance for nuance, every element of Constance Binney's performance.

As the weeks went on, she overcame her tendency to ape and
tried to act. But her performance in that play never developed or
became really professional. She was unpredictable, neurasthenic,
and aware always of her inadequacies. The latter, most of all,
made Tallulah difficult to work with. Blackmer found her particularly uncooperative.

In 39 *East*, Tallulah played Penelope Penn, resident of the
boardinghouse after which the play was named, a minister's
daughter who had traveled to the big town to find choir work and
send her brother to college. During her search for the proper
choir, she spurns an unsavory character who subsequently abducts
her in Central Park. Blackmer, the hero, enters the park as the
abduction scene has just transpired.

As directed, Tallulah was instructed to enter the park, do a fey
toe dance to some distant calliope, take her brimming sunbon-
net off her head, *place* it on a bench, and disappear. The bonnet
becomes the visual clue for Blackmer. Finding it, he surmises that
Penelope is in trouble.

As Tallulah actually played that scene, there were problems.
She was regularly so taken up with her dance, so undone by adrenaline, that she often failed to place the bonnet where it could conceivably be seen by Blackmer. Instead, she flung it. It landed in
places on the Livingston Platt set that should have been out of
sight or inaccessible to Blackmer: in the distant, misty lake; on
the papier-mâché rock formations; even, one night, around the
head of a mechanical swan.

Blackmer winged it until finally he became annoyed.

"Please, honey," he implored. "Put the hat on the bench. Just
put it on the bench."

Tallulah bristled. "I have too many things on my mind to worry
about where I put the hat."

That she was not cut out for ensemble playing was immediately apparent.

One night backstage, Blackmer noticed that some stagehands
were gathered around staring at Tallulah, who was in the wings

preparing to go on. He followed their collective gazes, gasped, and, being a Southern gentleman, walked discreetly over to Tallulah.

"Tallulah, honey," he whispered into her ear, "you're standing right in front of the lights."

"So!"

"So they're practically undressing you. And all the stagehands are gaping."

"Sidney," she said, "why do you suppose I'm doing it?"

Tallulah's behavior offstage was becoming gradually more colorful and certainly more citable than her undistinguished, though promising, professional accomplishments. Zoë Akins, the playwright, was one of the many luminaries of the day, who was fascinated by the raw, energetic, and still-developing Bankhead personality. She would fashion her central character in *Morning Glory*, Eva Lovelace, after Tallulah.

Morning Glory, which starred Katharine Hepburn in the film version, was about a young actress, half-mad with ambition, who is known around town by the theater community long before she actually does anything *in* the theater community. She is a fetching creature, totally without guile, who talks too much, starves for her art, and performs the balcony scene from *Romeo and Juliet* at parties.

As Eva Lovelace performed Shakespeare, Tallulah, at parties, impersonated some of the most famous actresses of the day. Imitation came easily and naturally to Tallulah. The facility could be a hindrance professionally—*39 East* was not the last time Tallulah would unconsciously ape another's performance rather than create one of her own—and an embarrassment in her personal life. If Tallulah talked to a stutterer, she herself might begin to stutter. If she talked to an Englishman, she might inadvertently begin to pick up the flavor and rhythm of the accent so that, in minutes, she would sound as though she had spent at least a decade in Manchester.

Tallulah *osmosed* the inflections and characteristics of the people around her. Indeed, at eighteen and nineteen, she was *becoming* almost through a process of imprinting. Onto her already bulky, flagrant personality, she superimposed the cool, clipped, trendy insouciance of the Algonquin crowd. She was less an original than an original conglomerate.

Because she adored and studied Ethel Barrymore and because Miss Barrymore had such an eruptive effect on Tallulah, she was able brilliantly and with great subtlety to impersonate her. It was Tallulah's favorite impression and the one most requested at parties. Frank Crowninshield had seen Tallulah's impression and thought it would be fun to have Tallulah do Ethel for Ethel. It was the first Condé Nast party to which Tallulah was invited.

Tallulah did her impression while Miss Barrymore sat directly in front of her. It was well received, though Tallulah never once looked up at her subject. When she was done, she ran up flustered to the formidable actress and begged her forgiveness. Miss Barrymore, who had all her life fought to keep her weight down, said only: "But your impersonation makes me look so *fat*."

Tallulah replied nervously, "It's not my fault. I was imitating you, Miss Barrymore."

Tallulah was slapped smartly across the face.

At least attention had been paid. Anything, for Tallulah, was preferable to being an angel in the wings.

In mid-August, after Tallulah had played only twelve performances of *39 East* on Broadway, she received from Actors' Equity a union card and a letter: "You are hereby instructed to stop playing at once until further notice. By order of the strike committee." The entire company of the Crothers' play struck, as did six other shows in New York. All rehearsals were interrupted. The strike came on the heels of the producers' failure to recognize Equity and its demands for better working conditions, more equitable contracts, and shorter nonpaying rehearsal periods.

The actors gathered in the Old Lenox Opera House to raise money for their strike. The Barrymores were among the illustrious roster of performers who attended and fully supported the movement. Ethel and Lionel enacted a scene from *The Lady of the Camellias*. Lionel spoke impassionedly: "We're proud to be here. We'll be here forever if necessary." Ethel rose for a moment to say, "I don't know how to make a speech really. But I am with you heart and soul and more than that. Don't be discouraged. Stick!"

Tallulah was one of the many ingenues who collected money and showed people to their seats. The goal of the rally was $100,-000. They collected $20,000. Taken up by the religiosity pervading the atmosphere, Tallulah stood up and pledged $100, which she could ill afford especially now that she was out of work. She petitioned Grandfather for the money.

Though the Bankhead family had owned a coal mine in Jasper, where they were reputed to have instituted some rather enlightened unionlike benefits for their workers, Tallulah's own feelings about the strike now were a mixed bag of fear, rectitude, Barrymore-imputed cachet, and a recognition that options did not really exist. She was clearly not yet an ideologue.

She wrote to Granddaddy, when she made her bid for the $100: "I joined Actors Equity because it was the right thing to do . . . all the very biggest stars in the profession belong and it's a wonderful organization. The Barrymores all belong and if you don't you are called a scab and are blacklisted and they called 39 *East* to strike and of course I did. I couldn't play alone anyway and besides it was the right thing to do. We may open any night now."

Her ideological sensibilities were buttressed, too, by Jim Julian's advice that she *not* strike, lest her actions "prejudice her case with her employers." Jim Julian's Henry Jamesian guardianship was becoming a royal pain in the ass.

Before the strike was settled in favor of the actors and their union, Tallulah was striken with an attack of gangrenous appendicitis, the details of which she would talk about all through her life with no small amount of pride. To recuperate, she went home to Washington. She healed there with remarkable celerity and made the social scene for a short time. She was a belle, as she had never been a belle in Montgomery or Jasper, Alabama, and she loved it.

Each settled noncompetitively into her own niche, Tallulah and Eugenia got along famously. Since it was the age in which everything bob-able was bobbed, "Eugenia" was now "Gene." The year before, Gene had made her debut in Washington. President Wilson stood in the receiving line. Meyer Davis supplied the music. She and her fiancé, Morton Hoyt, danced until dawn, spotlighting the evening with their famous, flamboyant, flamingly mod exhibition tango.

Morton was a charming drunk, a friend of Scott Fitzgerald's, and the love of Eugenia's life. It had not been the choice of Hoyt but Eugenia's youth which had precipitated the annulment of two years before. He was the son of the late Solicitor General of the United States and the brother of novelists Nancy Hoyt and Elinor Hoyt Wylie.

During Tallulah's recuperative period, Morton and Eugenia were engaged to be married properly, as they were on August 18, 1920, at Bar Harbor, Maine, with great pomp and ceremony. Tallulah was unable to attend because she was working, but she thoroughly approved of her sister's choice. Morton, in fact, was the only one of Sister's men of whom she would approve.

Tallulah was due back, to tour with 39 *East*, in the fall. The contract, which she had signed with the Shuberts, committed her to a tour running from September 15, 1919, to June 1, 1920. It was the very same deal over which she had rhapsodized in her letter to the family. She decided now, however, that she would not honor that commitment for the same reason that she had not agreed to stay on with the stock company in Somerville, Massachusetts. She produced a note from Dr. Sterling Ruffin of Washington to the effect that Tallulah Bankhead was still too weak to perform and "should not be on the road."

Tallulah would not postpone gratification. With the stock company, taking a different part week after week, she could have begun to pick up the technical ruses of her art. On tour with 39 *East*, the grueling paces of the road could have exposed her to the kind of discipline to which she had never been conditioned. She might have learned in either case the difference between strength and toughness, between slakable, productive vitality and torrid nervous energy.

Tallulah wanted, at the same time, too much and too little, not really theater but exhibition. Indeed, that is all her howling constitution would permit.

In the 1950's, a New York doctor and a young actor named Tom Ellis, whose eyes Tallulah called "silent-movie-star-blue," were driving home from the star's apartment after six in the morning. The doctor had just given Tallulah a hypodermic needle full of sleep elixir of the sort used for patients in extreme, terminal pain. Tom asked the doctor why Tallulah could not sleep.

"Try to imagine," said the doctor, "how you feel when you're about to go onstage before a very important opening night. Think about what your nerves are like with all that adrenaline pumping through your body. Now take that feeling and multiply it ten times. That's how she feels all the time and I suppose it's the way she's always felt."

7

"Precious Mamma....They All Think Your Little Namesake Is Very Clever"

IN 1921 the Belgian dramatist and philosopher Comte Maurice Maeterlinck was the favorite of the New York theater-going cognoscenti. "They stood in line for hours," Dorothy Parker wrote, "to sit through his work in a dreamy-eyed appreciation, each one discovering subtle beauties that no one else had the insight to observe."

To one of these voguish evenings, *Aglavaine and Selysette*, Tallulah, nineteen, was taken by the redoubtable drama critic Alexander Woollcott. She leaned over, during the course of the play, and whispered to him, "There is *less* in this than meets the eye." Nervous next to the 250-pound Woollcott, in his knuckle-thick granny glasses and scarlet-lined opera cape, Tallulah was discombobulated. What she meant to say was a compliant "There is *more* in this than meets the eye."

Woollcott chuckled appreciatively at the time, printed the remark in his column, and repeated Tallulah's serendipitous bon mot to the members of the Round Table at lunch the following day. Tallulah wisely never owned up to the mistake; she simply permitted babble to become bauble. She wrote to her grandmother in Washington exultantly: "Precious Mamma. . . . They all think your little namesake is very clever."

Noting a couple of such attributions, O. O. McIntyre wrote that the young actress, Tallulah Bankhead, was beginning to rival Dorothy Parker's reputation as a wit.

McIntyre, who was never asked to sit down with the Algonquin wits, was overstating the case. It was being said that Mamma Bankhead's little namesake was very clever. Indeed, she was in spite of the fact that her most often-quoted Maeterlinck line was pure accident. Moreover, in regard to "There is *less* in this than meets the eye," it might be contended that Tallulah was more clever to keep her mouth shut about not really meaning it than to have meant it in the first place. All that notwithstanding, Tallulah, certainly at age twenty, had nothing approaching the deadly and literate style, the atomizing whammy of Miss Parker.

What Tallulah did have was a Southern background. She came from a society in which fluid, entertaining talk, a gift of gab, the well-turned phrase were particularly honored and appreciated. With the exception of Captain John and Aunt Louise, all the Bankheads were articulate, mighty entertaining speechifiers. Daddy, as well, had given her not only an almanac of the mind, comprising apt and quotable stuff from Shakespeare, the Bible, and a few of the classics, but also training in the retention of rhythms and styles. She had a flawless ear for dialects and speech nuances.

There was also the matter of style and quantity. Tallulah had a flexible voice range and an instinct for the quintessential emphases of humor. To come down on one word—as in "She's sixteen? That's impossible. Nobody's sixteen"—was to turn a pedestrian phrase into a cynical, quotable, laughter-evoking witticism. Also, Tallulah talked so much that she was bound occasionally to come out with a good one. Finally, she possessed something for which there is no accounting: a sense of humor.

That she was changing in her verbal style was evidenced in the letters she wrote to Mamma from New York in the early twenties. They abounded in the superlative, sometimes Anglophilic style of the day: A party was "divine," "mad." One was "crazy about a new dance." A roommate was "quite the best person I've ever met. Everyone simply adores her."

Tallulah's sophistication was burgeoning. Her celebrity grew somewhat through publicity breaks such as the McIntyre item. She continued to be well known to a small group of theater and literary people. But she was *not*, at any time during her New York tenure, what many writers later said she was. She was not "the most famous woman in New York at twenty"; she was not, by a long shot, "a legend in her time"; she was not even a member of the chichi Round Table. She was known by them, instead, as a sort of "kid flapper"—Margalo Gillmore's designation—on the make for life, a warm, vibrant, penurious, slightly notorious and sometimes rude young beauty who giggled a lot and wanted something which seemed to her to reside in the theater and around its people. She was a joke to the Algonquinites but not a cruel one. They genuinely liked Tallulah, though they had no great regard for her as an actress.

When Tallulah was employed, during the very early twenties, it was most often in the play of Rachel Crothers. Miss Crothers either didn't know or care about Tallulah's malfeasance in 39 East, and in 1921 she cast her in Nice People. Tallulah's efforts were well received, and the play ran for half a season. She played Hallie Livingston and Katharine Cornell was Eileen Baxter Jones. It was Francine Larrimore, as Theodora, creating a small sensation by wearing overalls on stage, who became the real star of the production.

Nice People not only gave Tallulah a chance to work, but offered her a series of heroines from which she partly modeled herself. Rachel Crothers' kid flappers, tense with opportunity and sparring about degrees, embodied the radical chic of 1921. They sipped scotch, smoked cigarettes, wore pearls, stayed out all night with members of the opposite sex, and employed a hot slang in a cool way—the new frankness—to refer to things which had not been discussed before.

> HALLIE: I adore a man who is absolutely mad about me and yet who controls himself in that perfectly marvelous way.
> THEODORA: Oh, I don't know. I'm not so keen about so much self-control.
> HALLIE: Oh I am. I think it's much more subtle.
>
>   *   *   *
>
> EILEEN: Well, I must say I like sort of a frank flash of pash once in a while—so you know where you're at. Elemental stuff, you know.
>
>   *   *   *
>
> THEODORA: Of course no man wants to dance with her if she *will* wear corsets.
> EILEEN: Old Ironsides—they call her.

The plays were not without criticism of the way in which this new generation was leading its life. One of the older, wiser characters in the vehicle, obviously speaking for Miss Crothers, makes a statement about fatuity and waste among the smart set. "The emptiness—the soullessness of it all," she moans. "I've been here three days and I haven't heard her nor any of her friends say a single word or express a thought about anything on earth but their clothes and their motors and themselves. . . . And your house is a bar . . . it pours out at all hours. . . . And the smoking! Those delicate young girls as dependent upon their cigarettes to quiet their nerves as any—Oh, it's too terrible."

She is less shocked at what they are doing than who is doing it: "If they were common little upstarts and parvenus it would be easy to understand. But *nice people!*"

What Miss Crothers called the "general psychology" of most of these "now" characters resonated felicitously with Tallulah's natural rhythms. As she modeled herself after them, so undoubtedly was she modeled after. The kid flappers were slender, vibrating, high-keyed, alert, intense, "finely bred animals of care, health and money . . . dressed with daring emphasis on the prevailing fashion, startling in their delicate nakedness and sensuous charm."

There was a freshness about all this: the plays, the players, and the playing. Though the diction was affectedly English, the energy was strictly American. When the young, impoverished Noel Coward, just over from England with a batch of manuscripts under his arm, dropped in to see *Nice People*, he was astonished.

Coward writes in *Present Indicative:*

> I walked up and down several side streets, looking at the pictures outside the theatres, finally decided upon one, and went into the Klaw Theatre. The play was *Nice People* by Rachel Crothers, starring Francine Larrimore and including, among the smaller parts, Tallulah Bankhead and Katharine Cornell. I thought the production and acting good, and the play poor, but what interested me most was the tempo. Bred in the tradition of gentle English comedy with its inevitable maids, butlers, flower vases, and tea tables, it took me a good ten minutes of the first act to understand what anyone was saying. They all seemed to be talking at once. Presently I began to disentangle the threads and learnt my first lesson in American acting, which was the technique of realising first which lines in the script are superfluous and second knowing when and how to throw them away.

Like Tallulah, these plays were, in our own terms, rather adolescent in their sophisticated innocence. Sexuality underpinned everything, but it was tense and talky: the logical terminus of the frankness, the freedom, and the slight dishabille, but nobody ever got down to business. The heroine's reputation in *Nice People* is almost irreparably sullied because she stays out all night with a man. She is vindicated only when a witness is produced who swears that nothing of an intimate nature happened between the hero and heroine. The kid flappers wanted simply to dance girdle-less and protest their essential innocence.

Tallulah remained a virgin all through these New York years until she was twenty, a virginal virgin up to the age of seventeen, a "technical virgin" up to the time when she left the country. She made that claim in her autobiography, *Tallulah*, and there is no reason to doubt it. "I use the phrase 'technical virgin' advisedly," she wrote. "I had my share of necking. More than once I trembled on the brink of compliance." She dated men, hundreds of them, rich, eligible, and adoring men. But the object was to be seen around town, to be taken to one of Frank Crowninshield's parties, or to hear Galli-Curci sing *Lucia* at the Met.

Taking tea one afternoon with Margalo Gillmore, "The Baby of the Algonquin Roundtable," who had made an enormous hit the season before in *Alias Jimmy Valentine*, Tallulah leaned over and whispered, "I hope you won't think me cheap. But I've allowed John Barrymore to kiss me."

Tallulah had approached Margalo earlier that afternoon, in the lobby of the hotel. Tallulah was in the state of exquisite disarray for which she had come to be known: her hair luxuriant, radiant, but badly and impatiently combed, her latest only dress shiny, going-on-brown, and desperately in need of a good dry cleaning.

She and her best friend, Estelle Winwood—a lisping, dedicated, thirty-eight-year-old English actress, thin as a mobile and unobtrusive as a cat, who seemed always to be staring up at the flighty, wide-brimmed hats she wore all the time—had decided that it would be chic, fun, and educational if each of them hired a French maid, at $25 a week, to teach them their language and impress the natives. This was during one of her many lean periods when Tallulah was forced to live, eat, and pay rent on the $50 a week which her family, in times of need, continued to send her. Though her maid insisted upon speaking only English—the better to pick up the language of her new country—Tallulah did not have the nerve to let the girl go. Consequently, she was often literally penniless.

Tallulah needed five cents in order to get on a streetcar to keep an appointment with John Barrymore, who wanted her to co-star in a movie he was doing. She had four cents. She explained her predicament to Margalo Gillmore, who dipped into her purse and proffered the penny.

"Is that all you need, Tallulah?"

"Yes, just a penny."

"How are you going to get back?"

"I hadn't thought about that."

Miss Gillmore looked at Tallulah's ravaged dress. "Tallulah," she said, "your dress is dirty."

"I know," Tallulah replied earnestly, "but I'm clean underneath."

Tallulah turned down Barrymore's movie and also his sexual overtures. In his dressing room the actor came at her, making fervent little animal noises. She enjoyed the kiss and then ran scared.

Her own sex was less threatening and, in those years, more to her liking. "My family warned me about men," Tallulah would say in later life, "but they never mentioned a word about women."

At a party in 1922 a member of the Round Table walked into the kitchen and found Tallulah sitting on the kitchen table, locked in a mad embrace with another woman. She did not start but merely asked the intruder whether he had a handkerchief. He gave her the handkerchief; she calmly fixed her makeup.

Word filtered down. At a party in Washington, where she was living with Hoyt, Eugenia overheard one of her guests comment, "Everyone knows her sister is a lesbian." Eugenia was chipping ice at the time and, enraged at the allegation, hurtled the ice pick at the offending woman. Fortunately, her aim was bad.

Tallulah and three of her closest friends were called by gossips The Four Horsewomen of the Algonquin. The phrase was catchy and bandied about until it finally appeared as a newspaper item. "I don't care what they say as long as they talk about me," Tallulah said.

Of course, part of her did care passionately about individual people and what they thought, or she would not have gone to such pains to explain the Barrymore episode to Margalo Gillmore. The "they" was an amorphous corpus that somehow had to be made to talk, set in motion, if she were ever going to attain real celebrity status.

The lesbian thing was exaggerated by Tallulah in order to get people to notice. Tallulah's wild, flossy, entirely feminine beauty, however, attracted some of New York's most prominent and interesting homosexual women. At nineteen and twenty, Tallulah was also attracted by them. For several months, she was smitten to the point of obsession with a mannish society girl turned actress. She would refer to her as "the only woman she ever loved." But she was attracted to and involved with several others, many of them considerably older than Tallulah.

Oddly but not untypically, the most telling indication of the importance, place, and authenticity of her early homosexual activities is contained in a letter Tallulah *saved* much later in her life. It was sent to her in 1959, accompanying a scrapbook of clippings. In 1963 she gave the scrapbook and the letter to a friend for safekeeping. The letter, written on a child's floral stationery in an intelligent hand and style, reads in part:

> DEAR MISS BANKHEAD,
> I am the little girl who came to see the great Tallulah Bankhead this past June. This is probably the last time I will bother you. I have only thought of you for a whole year now. I think it's about time to stop that. I am 13 years old. It is not normal for a girl of my age to be like me. I have no intentions of becoming an actress. I have grown up quite a bit in the past six months.
> So the scrapbook will do me no good anymore. I thought you might like to have it. It has taken a year to compose it.
> This letter will be short in comparison to the one I wrote you before. That letter was ten pages long. I received no answer. Good-bye Tallulah Bankhead,
> A ONCE VERY DEVOTED FAN

In 1921, Eugenia and Morton took an apartment on the West side of New York, next door to their closest friends and boon companions, Scott and Zelda Fitzgerald. Tallulah dropped over frequently for lunch. She wrote to Mamma:

> Sister and Morton are so happy. I see them everyday and sister is a very neat and tidy little housewife. You should feel

proud, Mamma dear, because it is all from your good influence and training—and although we were stubborn little kid-
dies and didn't like picking up our nighties, your little
scoldings did not go for nothing, for we are profiting by them
now and are very thankful to our little Mamma.

Indeed, many of Grandmother Bankhead's lessons had not been
wasted, though a neat and tidy little housewife Tallulah never became. "Precious heart," Mamma had written to her favorite
grandchild again and again, "be unselfish and do as many little acts
of kindness as possible, and it will in return bring joy to you."

In accordance with her training and her sensibilities, Tallulah,
even in those lean days, always sent flowers or sweet notes to her
friends who were opening in shows, especially if they were not
important players. She gave away her only winter coat to a girl she
hardly knew; it was cold outside, and the girl was suffering with a
slight cold. She was enormously sensitive to the feelings of old
people, undoubtedly because of her great love for Mamma. Her
gestures were warm, private, and accompanied always by a flush
of empathic tears.

Anita Loos recalled an example of Tallulah's behavior in 1931.
Though this was much later, it was the kind of effusive gesture
which also characterized the younger Tallulah Bankhead. They
both were staying at the old Hollywood Hotel. Hollywood was
just becoming a film community and there remained at the hotel
a contingent of elderly, retired midwesterners:

"They were as truly nice as they were boring," Miss Loos wrote,
"and none of us who worked in films ever bothered to give them
the time of day as they sat rocking their afternoons away on the
front porch. But Tallulah did. And I still carry a picture in my memory of her sitting on the porch of the hotel and allowing an old
lady from Iowa to teach her a crochet stitch. Tallulah, with no intention of crocheting anything, at any time, pretended an interest
out of kindness and as a means of communication."

This kind of touching and tender behavior made Tallulah's
occasional rushes of rudeness even the more shocking. She alienated many people with insults, shortness, and stinging, almost

cruel candor. It was not impossible that these episodes were set off by cocaine.

In 1922, cocaine, or snow, was as *au courant* as marijuana is today. Its illegality embued it with a sort of cachet. Its stimulating, freneticizing "up" qualities were as high as the times. The Beautiful People of 1922 were sending out party invitations which read archly: "Will You Come to My Snow Ball?" *Vanity Fair* reported sardonically on the trendy motif of a glamorous gathering: "The living room was a miniature drug store . . . little packages of cocaine, morphine, and heroin were dispensed. . . . the guests at their departure received exquisite hypodermic needles in vanity boxes."

Once again, her family had fallen short in their advice to Tallulah. They had warned her about alcohol, and she was totally abstemious. But nobody had said a word about cocaine. Tallulah bought it from the urchins who hung around the tea shoppes in the West Forties. It was dispensed in little packages the size of tea bags and sniffed up the nose. The price was $50 a bag, and Tallulah purchased some whenever possible. In the superlative style of the day, one said, inhaling, "Cocaine. It's absolutely divine. Will you sniff some?" When Tallulah did not have $50, she crushed an aspirin tablet and pretended.

There was nothing the curious Tallulah would not try. But of course she needed stimulation as much as Rip Van Winkle required Tuinal. Whenever possible, Estelle Winwood flushed Tallulah's cocaine down Tallulah's toilet. "It made her dirty and rude to people," Estelle Winwood recalled. "I introduced her to two or three friends, and they remarked how rude she was. But that wasn't Tallulah. It wasn't the real Tallulah."

Tallulah sometimes took a bag with her to parties. In the beginning of the evening, she was this piquant little match girl, perhaps showing the picture of her sainted mother, which she carried around with her at all times, to other guests. As the evening wore on, however, when she failed to receive the kind or quality of attention she demanded, Tallulah sniffed some snow and proceeded to do her famous cartwheels. When the cartwheels qua cartwheels ceased to amuse or shock, Tallulah took to doing them without any underwear on.

Toward the end of the run of *Nice People*, she moved into the apartment of Beth "Bijou" Martin on West Fifty-first Street. Miss Martin's mother was traveling abroad. Through the very social Bijou Martin, Tallulah met and began to run around with a young English crowd, including Noel Coward; Jeffrey John Archer Amherst, the fifth Earl of Amherst, who was working on the staff of the New York *Morning World*; and Napier Alington, Napier George Henry Sturt Alington, the third Alington baron. He was called Naps, and his bohemian apartment on Eighth Avenue was called Naps Flat.

Tallulah fell promptly in love with Alington. He was twenty-six, slightly built, a soft-spoken, blond tubercular—well cultivated, bisexual, with sensuous, meaty lips, a distant, antic charm, a history of mysterious disappearances, and a streak of cruelty. Tallulah was fascinated with his unavailability. When he turned around and evinced interest, her fascination waned. They played a neurotic game of teeter-totter.

Naps and Tallulah spent most of the winter of 1922 together. He returned to England. She opened in *Everyday*, a vehicle which Rachel Crothers wrote specially for her. It closed promptly. She played another one of her nervous flappers in *The Exciters*, which opened on September 22, 1922.

Five years in New York! And she was still an actress who occasionally starred in plays, but not a star by a long shot. *Vanity Fair* referred to her again that year as "the world's most subtly amusing imitator of Ethel Barrymore."

One critic commented, reviewing *The Exciters*, that Tallulah was "ripe and gorgeous . . . makes you believe she is going far." Another complained about the behavior of the audience during the first night performance: "She had a lot of silly friends in the theatre who gave her an ovation before she had done a thing. . . . A real case of SAVE ME FROM MY FRIENDS." Burns Mantle was incredibly percipient. He said, "She is a gifted young woman upon whose shoulders we fear success is weighing a little heavily. She looks tired and a bit fed up with her work."

Tallulah was very tired. She wanted something bigger and faster than what was happening to her as an actress-personality in the United States. For an English-speaking performer, the alternative was England. Naps was there; now that he was gone, she thought of him often. Her family, especially Aunt Marie, had spoken to both girls all their lives about the glory of the British Empire, the purity of their English roots. Marie called England their mother country; Mamma's stationery bore an impressive, if not entirely authenticated, royal crest. Estelle Winwood, who had little faith in Tallulah's technical abilities as an actress or in her growth potential, had remarked often to her friend that because of the dearth of beautiful women in London, Tallulah could conceivably become a fabulous star there.

At another of Frank Crowninshield's parties in the late winter of 1922, Tallulah met the illustrious theatrical impresario, visiting from England, Charles Cochran. Cochran had heard about the young actress from Estelle Winwood and Blythe Daly. He'd read about her subtle impersonation of Ethel Barrymore in *Vanity Fair*. He insisted that she perform and was amused with her mimic talents, even more impressed with her beauty and vivacity. He returned to England with a picture of Tallulah in his wallet.

Six weeks later, she received a cable from the Englishman which read: POSSIBLE ENGAGEMENT WITH GERALD DU MAURIER IN ABOUT EIGHT WEEKS. A follow-up letter from Cochran explained that Sir Gerald Du Maurier was the best stage director and manager in London, that Gladys Cooper, among others, owed her high position to his faith and assistance.

Gerald Du Maurier had co-authored and was about to produce a play in which there was a good part for an American girl. "She is somewhat of a siren and in one scene has to dance," Cochran continued in his letter to Tallulah. "This altogether sounds like you. She is, in the play, supposed to be of surpassing beauty. I have told the part authoress and Sir Gerald that I believe you are 'the goods.' They are quite excited about you, and I think there is but little doubt that if you care to take the risk of coming over you will be engaged. In any case, your expenses will be paid."

Tallulah and Estelle frequently journeyed uptown to Riverside Drive to consult the famous seer Evangeline Adams, a dour Scotswoman who predicted the future using a combination horoscope,

cards, and the Bible, which she opened randomly and pricked with
a pin. During such visits, they would invariably giggle nervously,
especially when the mystic dealt the fearsome snake card to
Estelle and Estelle gave it back.

Upon receiving Cochran's letter, however, Tallulah went to see
Miss Adams alone. There would be no giggling this time; the decision was serious business. Evangeline Adams opened the Bible
and selected, at random, a section from 2 Kings which refers to
Jezebel, the notorious wife of Ahab, King of Israel. She remained
mute at the significance of the passage.

Tallulah returned to the Hotel Webster, where she and Estelle
were now living, and told the older actress about what had happened. Estelle said with trepidation, "You realize, don't you, my
dear, that Jezebel was thrown to the dogs?"

Tallulah, who had obviously given the matter some thought, replied, "Yes, I know. But before she was thrown to the dogs, she
rode with kings and queens."

The decision was made.

Tallulah was devastated when, in a matter of days, she received
from Charles Cochran another cable telling her *not* to come. Con-
sorting again with Estelle, she had the solution. She would go anyway, pretending that she had never received the second cable.
They would not have the nerve to send her home after she had
crossed the ocean just to do the part.

Within a week, Tallulah Bankhead had booked passage on the
Majestic. Because she knew her father would not understand her
certainty, her gut feeling in the face of such patent discourage-
ment, she told him the story *up to* the second cable. Since Granddaddy had died two years before and Will believed that her passage
was included in the deal, she was forced to borrow her traveling
expenses—$1,000—from Colonel Coleman DuPont, a rich Con-
gressional friend of Will's.

There were tears and excitement at the boat. A wild delega-
tion of Tallulah's friends came to see her off. At the last minute,
as the *Majestic* signaled its imminent leave-taking in basso tones,
Estelle looked at Tallulah and said, "You don't have a coat."

"Will I need one in England?"

Estelle took off her mink and placed it around Tallulah's shoulders.

Aunt Marie Owen received this letter in Montgomery, from her brother Will, four days hence:

> MY DEAREST MARIE:
>
> You will no doubt be somewhat surprised to hear that Tallulah sailed for London on the Majestic Saturday last. She was guaranteed her passage and expenses and a fair chance of being engaged by the leading English producer Du Maurier (Sir Gerald) for a London engagement. She had gotten somewhat "fed up" in New York, and some of the disappointments she had met—and I thought it only fair to her to give her this extra chance. If her expectations do not materialize, she will at least have had the *sight* of England, etc. She had many wonderful letters of recommendation from the leading dramatic folk in New York.
>
> On top of that, I am sending Eugenia to Reno, Nevada to get a divorce. So, one flies east and one flies west. Oh, this new generation! I feel that very *gradually* both of them are finding themselves. They both have *brains* and sprightliness of mind— for which the Lord be praised.
>
> DEVOTEDLY
> WILL

8

England

PLUMP, EXHILARATED, her long hair down almost to her calves, her mouth an angry jam jar, Tallulah danced her way to London aboard the good ship *Majestic*, repressing with her frenzied activities all thoughts of Charles Cochran's second telegram. By the time she reached Southampton, she had probably all but convinced herself that she had never in fact received the news of Sir Gerald Du Maurier's change of heart.

Her dancing was a supremely appropriate cultural calisthenic. Wealthy, postwar London, in which Tallulah was hoping to make it bigger faster, was obsessed with the subject of the new jazz dances. The newspapers daily ran heated letters on changing rhythms as a social symptom. To the *Daily Mail*, a correspondent wrote: "With the addition of war paints and feathers, the Charleston would rival the antics of a tribe of savages. Let us have dances to conform with our standards of civilization."

At the *ne plus ultra* annual Royal Academy art exhibit, a bitter controversy followed the hanging of John Souter's picture "The Breakdown," which delineated a Negro musician sitting atop a castdown statue of the goddess Minerva, gazing stolidly at a naked white girl who is dancing the Charleston. The fear was not sexual but cultural miscegenation. The picture was removed from the Academy over the protests of the artist, who claimed he was "just illustrating a tendency of modern life."

Daphne Du Maurier, the writing daughter of Sir Gerald, fumed fustily over the changes she saw in the postwar early-1920's: the dance mania that took over once the guns were stilled.

Sir Gerald was himself dealing with the subject in *The Dancers.* This play, in which Tallulah was bound and determined to participate, was a novelettish piece whose two principal female characters are profoundly affected by dance mania. One, a Canadian light-o'-love, uses her dance talents to elevate herself and becomes a world-famous ballerina. The other, an English aristocrat, falls victim to the times and the dance, has what was then called "a moment's lapse" with her dance partner, becomes pregnant, and takes her own life.

The dance was the time: disjunctive, scattered, fitfully energized. And the most visible products of the epoch were the so-called Bright Young Things. They were the jet set of their day, who shocked their more conservative countrymen by devouring cocktails, rollicking all night in cars, accepting and practicing bisexuality, and questioning the existence of God. They *simulated* events at compact, almost hysterical energy levels; thus, the trendiness of the costume ball, the practical joke, and a game called Truth. An anonymous British aristocrat, Lady X, detailed, with incredulity, the cultural shock she experienced when she attended a typical party of the Bright Young Things. In *Victoria Bouquet,* she writes, "The room was dark-blue with smoke, a gramophone blared, and a detachment was playing a game which consisted in ringing up the first name the telephone book opened at and asking it to a party."

Within the London theater, an invasion by American plays, players, and management effected sudden eruptions in the comfortable clubbiness of the prewar era. "A new, rather false atmosphere was apparent," Daphne Du Maurier wrote in the biography of her father, *Gerald.* "It was over-intimate, over-familiar; a gush of insincerity, mingled with too obvious flattery, filled the air in place of the old, easy comradeship and mutual respect. . . . it was the dawn of the superlative age and the vogue of the emphasized adjective: the word 'darling' rose too easily to the lips, and 'marvelous,' 'wonderful,' and 'divine' described the colour of a new lipstick or the texture of a silk stocking. Life was not worth living unless somebody was 'having an affair' with somebody else."

Tallulah was obviously in the right place at the right time.

Unmet, she went directly from the boat to the only hotel she knew, the exclusive, rococo Ritz. Tallulah phoned Cochran immediately and told him that she had come to London in spite of the second communication and that she knew Sir Gerald could be made to change his mind. Cochran was amused by Tallulah's pluck. They met the following day for lunch at the Ivy, London's Algonquin, cozy, elegant and snobbishly casual. They sat at Cochran's regular front room table among many of the aristocracy of the London theater world.

Tallulah told Charles Cochran of her plan. She would simply *pretend* that she had not received the second telegram. Sir Gerald, seeing that she had come all the way to England alone just to be in his play, in a trinity of remorse, pity, and admiration, would simply *have* to award her the part. Cochran agreed to make the first introduction, though it was Sir Gerald's notorious roving eye, not his remorse, that he counted on.

Since the play was scheduled to open in a matter of weeks, there was no time to waste. Tallulah and Cochran dropped backstage at Wyndham's to see Sir Gerald Du Maurier that evening after a performance of *Bulldog Drummond*.

Wyndham's theater was Sir Gerald's principality. As presiding actor-manager, it was his to choose, direct, produce, and act in all the vehicles presented there. *The Dancers* was the first play he had ever written. He and Viola Tree completed the four-act melodrama in a matter of weeks as a kind of stunt under the collective nom de plume Hubert Parsons. Should it have failed, of course poor Hubert would have taken full responsibility.

In 1923, at fifty years old, Sir Gerald was the most popular leading man in England, a romantic figure, considered by some to be the founder of the "natural" school of playing. He was known, on-stage, for his casual, careless, maddeningly insouciant style of lovemaking. After a less than ardent kiss, planted often on the forehead of his leading lady, he characteristically yawned, or lit a cigarette, or rapped the object of his disinterested affection lightly across the face, with a comment something like "You're a little mug, but I love you all the more for it." A kind of aristocratic Bogart, he drove the ladies of the day to distraction. He had a fair, angular face and voice whose stentorian dryness Cecil Beaton once compared to a pumice stone.

In approaching Sir Gerald, Tallulah was going to the top. But the ruse did not come off as expected. Cochran and he talked shop for several minutes. After expressing regret at the confusion, he wished Tallulah good luck and bade her adieu. Tallulah shrugged as though she every day made futile trips across the Atlantic Ocean. She returned to the Ritz and cried a lot.

Cochran rang up the following day and suggested that they try again. He directed Tallulah this time to do herself up to the nines and present herself *hatless* to Sir Gerald. At the first meeting, she had simply thrown together a dress and a hat. She had neither the inner quietude nor the outer amplitude of wardrobe to give dressing up much time. "He absolutely *must* see your hair," Cochran insisted.

At this ensuing meeting, Sir Gerald's attitude was radically altered. He asked Tallulah questions about her exotic name, discussed her professional experience, commented exultantly on her husky voice quality, and stared at her hair, which streamed freely down her back. After Tallulah left, his daughter Daphne said that she was the most beautiful girl she had ever seen, and Sir Gerald apparently agreed. He called Tallulah the next day. She was signed at 30 pounds a week, for the part of Maxine, the Canadian light-o'-love.

In the little time that remained until the play went into rehearsals, Tallulah never once experienced a desire to sight-see in this strange new world capital. Buckingham Palace was a place to pass or to visit. Public transportation was confusing and taxing. She would spend eight years in London without once seeing or thinking to see Westminster Abbey. "She had the egocentricity of a child and all the same sort of lovable qualities," recalled Cathleen Nesbitt, who met Tallulah during those years. Such solo, pedestrian activities were, therefore, beyond her purview, irrelevant. To begin to feel unalien in a place was to be known.

She renewed some old friendships, one with Dorothy Dickson, an American star of musical comedy, who was making a tremendous hit on the English stage. Back in New York, Miss Dickson had tried to interest Florenz Ziegfeld in Tallulah, but he was totally unimpressed. Now, at Miss Dickson's house in Chesterfield in the late morning, sitting on the side of the breakfasting star's bed, Tallulah talked a blue streak about the start of her new career. "There are two girls in the play, dahling," she said. "But Sir Gerald tells me I have the best part by far."

Tallulah had resolved to be cool and distant to Napier Alington when they met in London. It had been more than a year since he left New York to return to his 18,000 acres, his baronetcy, and his famous mother, the redoubtable Edwardian hostess, Lady Alington, who looked like a publican and talked ceaselessly about her children's "wildness." In all that time, Naps had not written once to Tallulah. She was wounded and furious. When he appeared, however, in the lobby of her hotel, dressed in a smart lounge suit with a puppy under his arm, she melted. He smiled and offered the Pekingese snowball to her. "For you, Lulas," he said. They called the dog Napoleon.

Tallulah adored Napier Alington and experienced with him a contentment which she had with few other people in her life. She could be alone with him; he was sufficient environment for her. They quarreled constantly, but they were highly charged lovers' quarrels. She knew about the men in his life. They never appeared to bother her; indeed she was fascinated with the details of these other relationships. Tallulah was, no doubt, attracted by his essential unavailability, his epicene, flattish good looks, and his boyish, careless charm. She was strongly maternal toward him a good deal of the time, and the role pleased both of them. He was probably the man to whom she lost her technical virginity. And it was always in the back of her mind that she would someday marry Naps.

With Naps, Tallulah got around. She met his friend, Lord Ned Latham, theatrical dilettante and designer; Lady Diana Manners, the actress-daughter of the Duke of Rutland; and Olga Lynn, a socially ambitious singer and teacher who concertized her way into the stateliest British homes. Naps' friends were smart, successful Bright Young Things, in attitude, if not in years, and they all were quite taken with Tallulah. They were impressed with her wayward beauty and her loquacious cleverness. Tallulah's bids for attention amused them; her husky Southern drawl delighted them. In New York she had been an oddity; here she was an exotic.

Tallulah went to her first Beautiful Young Thing costume ball with Naps. They dressed as twin brothers from the court of Louis Quatorze, wearing skintight blue satin breeches. Tallulah made everyone laugh at the ball when she said to Naps, "These things are all right for you. But what do I do if I have to pee?"

With Naps, she watched the royal procession of the Duke and Duchess of York and wrote to Will afterward: "The people rode in Golden Coaches more beautiful than in Fairy Tales. Daddy dear, having a King and Queen makes *such* a difference!"

When rehearsals for *The Dancers* began, Tallulah cut out processions, galas, and other frippery. She moved from the Ritz into a small service flat. She stopped smoking so that she would be in top physical condition for her opening dance. The play, for reasons known best to God and Hubert Parsons, opened in a saloon in the "Wild West." The Earl of Chievely, Sir Gerald, in an open shirt and flared riding breeches, is discovered serving drinks with Maxine on his arm. She is dressed in a feather bonnet and a scanty buckskin savage outfit. She goes into a wildly mutant Indian Charleston. Tallulah had problems at first finding the right squawflapper ratio, but Sir Gerald emended that.

Tallulah was punctual, hardworking, and attentive all through the rehearsal period. From Sir Gerald, who reminded her of Daddy, she took direction splendidly. When she lost her temper, he understood that it was just her insecurities. At such times, he took Tallulah to lunch, or bought her little gifts, or told her how brilliant she was bound to be. Sir Gerald was a marvelous woman's director. Most of his stars fell in love with him. Tallulah was no exception. Nor was Audry Carten, the young actress, who was cast as Una, the other woman in Gerald's life. Tallulah and Audry became the closest of friends. They had their adoration for Gerald in common. They revered and emulated him. If Gerald did it, it was chic.

With all his professionalism, Sir Gerald Du Maurier was an almost pathological practical joker. When the moon was right, the stage turned into a virtual minefield of surprises for the actor. Forks and other props bent unexpectedly in the middle. Dinner rolls were stuffed with cotton. Chairs moved just as the sitters were about to sit on them. Sofa cushions made loud and unmistakable noises. After one of his stunts was successfully completed, Sir Gerald retired to his dressing room, where, like the props, he bent helplessly in the middle, collapsed in paroxysms of solitary laughter.

So Tallulah and Audry began doing tricks on people. After rehearsals, Audry frequently went home with Tallulah for a quiet dinner and a game of bridge. After the bridge game, they telephoned complete strangers to tell them that their mates were involved in torrid romances or serious accidents or both. With a group of friends, they awakened Sir Gerald in the middle of the night by serenading him in his garden. Once they called a crematorium and left instructions for the pickup and disposal of several fellow members of *The Dancers*, who were, of course, very much alive.

When they weren't making silly phone calls, Tallulah and Audry sat up late into the night, drinking wine, smoking innumerable cigarettes, and talking about their futures. Tallulah stated baldly that she hoped to make a huge name for herself in England, then return triumphant to her native soil. Audry, who idolized Tallulah for her energy and her apparent self-assurance, was less certain of what she might do. She was not at all sure that her nerves could withstand performing much longer, though Bernard Shaw, among others, had predicted that Audry would be one of the most brilliant actresses of the century.

Audry was a year older than Tallulah, a tall, dark-haired girl with a poignant catch in her voice who had the kind of horsey, long English face which is said to make the French laugh. Audry Carten, originally Bicker-Caarten, had studied for two years at the Royal Academy, where her sensitive, neurasthenic acting had been seen and admired by Shaw, Lady Tree, and finally by the stage manager at Wyndham's, who first called Sir Gerald's attention to her. In a previous production at Wyndham's, one of Audry's first out of school, she had played the part of a maid. A critic wrote of that performance: "The only thing she had to do was scream. But she did it so well and with so much reality that it instantly attracted attention."

At a final dress rehearsal of *The Dancers*, Audry told Sir Gerald that she could not possibly open in the play, that she knew she would faint as soon as she was required to speak her first line. Gerald disappeared. Upon his return, he presented Audry with a beautiful ivory walking stick. She was instructed to take it with her onto the stage, "to lean on, my darling." Though Tallulah was herself petrified of facing the British public for the first time, she was forced to assume a bravado even falser than the one she would otherwise have tried on. One doesn't, after all, complain of a headache in a cancer ward.

The Dancers opened on February 15, 1923. While Prince George, the Marquess of Salisbury, Lady Diana Manners, Miss Aileen Guinness, Miss Gladys Cooper, Lady Wyndham, Lady Du Maurier, and other notables filed into the stalls and boxes at Wyndham's, the women in their tiaras and furs, the men in their white ties and tails with maroon carnations in their buttonholes, Tallulah knelt trembling in her dressing room before a picture of Ada and one of Will. "Please," she petitioned, "don't let me make a fool of myself tonight."

Acts one and four were hers; two and three were Audry's.

She walked onto the stage in her white buckskin outfit, her colorful bonnet, with her incredible hair cascading from beneath. She did her dance, spoke her lines, and walked off. An inquisitorial hubbub went through the audience. Programs rattled. Heads turned. The first-nighters were riveted. Several members of that audience would recall their reactions to the first sight of Tallulah Bankhead: She was simply the most beautiful creature they had ever seen. The radiance of her hair struck them particularly. The huskiness of her voice was an exciting anomaly, its lazy, long Southern tones brand-new to the English ear and very pleasant.

Tallulah was aware of none of this. At the end of the first act, her name was called from several places in the audience. Some especially loud noises emanated from the upper tiers of Wyndham's. Listening to all this from her dressing room, Tallulah assumed she was being booed. Being an American, she could only associate such vociferousness with disapprobation. She was relieved, however, during the second and third acts to discover that Audry was receiving the same treatment. Sir Gerald himself prompted a similar reaction. It was obviously the play then, not the individual performances, which was at fault.

When the final curtain rang down, Tallulah stood in the wings quizzically. She watched what was happening on the stage like a new kid on the block watching a strange game, not understanding it and not knowing whether she would be invited to join in. They called Audry's name. She stood center stage with Sir Gerald, looking about to faint, walking stick or no. Sir Gerald motioned for quiet and spoke about an American girl who had come all the way to England just to appear in his play. Tallulah wondered who that was and marveled at how very much they had in common. Gerald beckoned Tallulah; Tallulah watched him beckon. There was laughter in the house as he walked toward the wings, took Tallulah by the arm, and led her out upon the apron. As she walked into view, the rude noises coalesced into one victorious wall of sound. They liked her.

9

"Climbing"

THINGS BEGAN TO HAPPEN to Tallulah during the ten-month run of *The Dancers* which had never happened before:

She developed a fanatical, burgeoning following of Cockney girls, most of them in their late teens. Many of them wore polo coats and tried to model themselves after Tallulah. They cheered her performances from the gallery with frenetic zeal and waited for her as she entered and left the theater. Tallulah chatted with them, called them by first names, and invited criticism. They numbered no more than twenty.

Tallulah appeared on the covers of several theatrical magazines, among them the popular *Tatler*. In the *Tatler* portrait, which came out only weeks after the opening of *The Dancers*, Tallulah's face was very round, her eyes huge, her lips kewpied, her hair soft, marcelled, and bobbed! Sir Gerald was apoplectic when Tallulah cut her long hair, which had become the talk of the town, between Acts I and IV of his play. But Tallulah knew what she was doing. When she appeared on stage in Act IV with her hair totally restyled in the modern flapper fashion, her Gallery Girls roared their approval. During subsequent performances, several of them cut off their own hair and threw approving hanks at Tallulah on the stage.

Soon after the bobbing incident, Tallulah was asked to move in with Olga Lynn, the ambitious singing teacher to whom Napier had introduced her. Tallulah was delighted. She liked Oggie and her posh house on Catherine Street teeming with servants. Here were ambience, service, and prestige which would have been way beyond Tallulah's still-limited means.

Oggie was an amusing dumpling of a woman, much older than Tallulah, who had begun her musical career singing opera at Covent Garden. There she performed some minor roles successfully, but her high, exquisite voice simply wasn't *big* enough for the kind of success she wanted. She focused on a career in concert halls and drawing rooms, discovering that the social perquisites were as satisfying to her as anything else. Oggie Lynn became a kind of pet of London society.

"To be a friend of Oggie's," wrote Percy Colson, "is a liberal education in *Who's Who* and *What's What*. . . . No small, smart musical party was complete without Oggie, and everywhere she went she made friends, for people found that she was amusing, extremely well-read, a good linguist, and both kind and *serviable*."

Tallulah was attracted to Oggie. From Naps' first introduction, Tallulah actively sought her attention and approval. At a dinner party which playwright Marc Connelly attended, the young actress literally turned cartwheels for Olga Lynn. Success at Wyndham's did not temper her inordinate demands. Tallulah's freneticism stemmed, in part, from her complete inability to hold onto or transmute the love that came to her over the footlights. Though she could not survive without it, it wasn't enough.

Through Oggie Lynn, Tallulah met and cultivated some of the smartest people in London society. She learned about food and wine and the little touches that distinguish the truly well-bred from the crash-coursed. She learned when one went to Venice and what one did once one got there. She began to sojourn to Paris to buy her clothes at Molyneux; it was better to own a few good things than a multitude of dross. She was encouraged to diet off her baby fat. That Tallulah chose to ignore many of the rules Oggie taught her was all right. A lady was a lady who knew which rules she was disobeying. Tallulah was fond of saying "I can say shit, dahling, I'm a lady."

She wrote to Daddy about her new situation. "I live in a divine big house with Olga Lynn who is the most divine woman and has been a great friend to me. She is much older but everyone worships her and she has a lot of influence in every direction." This last phrase, of course, is the very same designation Tallulah used to describe Mary Kirkpatrick's sphere of influence to her father.

Because Tallulah was a passionate, instinctive creature incapable of the coolness and deliberation usually associated with aggressive, self-serving motivations, it was often assumed by the people around her that she was therefore neither ambitious nor career-minded. Because she constantly alienated people who were even more powerful than the ones she did not alienate, it was frequently thought that honesty and spontaneity were the keynotes of her emotions. She alienated people not because she was honest—though she was—but because she had a low, almost nonexistent tolerance threshold. She was, because of that, incapable of cultivating people she disliked. But she was quite capable of cultivating people she liked, indeed of liking the cultivatable. She was fond of Olga Lynn, but fond, no doubt, because of what Olga Lynn could do for her. With Tallulah, as with most truly driven people, ambition and libido were dynamic rather than dichotomous.

Tallulah was a big enough name, after the closing of *The Dancers*, to be billed over the title of her second play, *Conchita*, but only because it was a second-rate vehicle. In *Conchita*, Tallulah played a peppery Latin American serving girl working at a small hotel in Cuba for a powerful politician who treats her in a manner "werry fierce." By the second act on the first night this heavy romantic drama had been transformed into a *succès de rire*, deferring to an audience who simply wouldn't take the play seriously. "Tallulah," one critic wrote, "never gave the impression of being the least bit Spanish."

She played Yvonne, Herbert Marshall's mistress and Cathleen Nesbitt's competitor, in the next but far more respectable failure, *This Marriage*. Miss Nesbitt was the wife who insisted on complete honesty in her marriage; Herbert Marshall was the husband who gave it to her. Told of his affair with Tallulah, the wife suggests a plan whereby he could be shared. Tallulah, as Yvonne, responds, "I think you are behaving like a cross between a god and a lunatic." The gallery cheered at this line, rendered rushed and husky by their idol, as they did at her reading of "Conscience isn't like a liver; you can get on without it."

Tallulah grew especially fond of Cathleen Nesbitt during the run of *This Marriage*. Their relationship began with a dispute over a dressing room. When it came time to assign the only stage-level dressing room in the theater, the stage manager of *This Marriage* could not decide whether to give it to Tallulah Bankhead or to Cathleen Nesbitt. He went to Miss Nesbitt and explained his dilemma. "By all means, give it to Tallulah," she said gallantly. "She's a visitor to our country."

He told Tallulah that the very desirable dressing room was hers. "No, I won't have it," she said. "After all, this is Cathleen's hometown. I'm just a visitor."

This mutual magnanimity put him right back where he started, until Tallulah discovered that Cathleen Nesbitt, the wife of Cecil Ramage, MP, was nursing. Her newly born son was brought to her every afternoon, during the break in rehearsal when the other actors were usually out to lunch. When Tallulah found Cathleen with the child, she demanded that the somewhat older actress take the better dressing room. "I couldn't bear the thought of that divine baby going upstairs for his meals," Tallulah said.

This imperiousness was habit. She styled her hyperbolic lexicon of "divines" and "dahlings" after the smart set with which she associated. But divested of its style, the decent content of Tallulah's behavior went way back to Grandmother Bankhead and the code with which she had raised her grandchild. Tallulah gave Cathleen the better dressing room because it was simply the *right thing* to do.

Tallulah seldom missed a feeding. No matter what else she was doing, she always popped in, laden with gifts from the exclusive White House, to see the infant pull and suck. She was fascinated with everything about the feeding, as fascinated as she had been back at Mr. Legg's funeral parlor. Tallulah had not yet, nor would she ever, lose her sense of awe concerning the quiddities of life. No matter how sophisticated she seemed to become, she was in this respect marvelously childlike.

She was also wickedly interested in other people's love lives. The fact that Cathleen had been engaged to the poet Rupert Brooke at the time of his death in 1915 impressed her. In her personal pantheon, poets were entitled to great reverence. Daddy had taught her that. She pored over a collection of Brooke's published letters, astonishing Cathleen with her insights, not only in regard to what was in the letters but also in regard to what was *left out*.

Many of these letters had originally been love letters written by Brooke to the actress. At the insistence of his mother, however, a good deal of the ardor was extirpated, so much of it that they seemed hardly to be love letters at all. Reading the expurgated versions, Tallulah was not at all fooled. She cried over the denatured letters as though some sixth sense were apprehending the original text.

"These are beautiful love letters," she said to Cathleen.

"How could you tell they were love letters, Tallulah?"

"Any fool would know that," Tallulah responded.

There were other letters in the Brooke collection which were edited differently. They were also love letters to Cathleen Nesbitt. In these, the passion was permitted to remain, but the salutation was changed from "Dear Cathleen" to "Dear X." Tallulah read these and naturally assumed that "X" had been a man.

"I think he was queer," Tallulah said to Cathleen. "These letters were written to another man."

"Don't be ridiculous," Cathleen said. "These letters were written to me."

Tallulah was as perverse in her comments on the latter group of letters as she had been percipient with regard to the former. Throughout her life, Tallulah hit upon hundreds of absurd theories which she maintained pharisaically; no amount of persuasion could disabuse her of any of them. Her suspicions of Rupert Brooke joined the catechism.

After *This Marriage* closed in a jiffy, Tallulah resolved that she would bide her time until a play worthy of her talents was offered to her. She received word, however, that Will would be passing through London on Congressional business in a matter of weeks. She was excited, of course, and eager to impress him. Certainly it would not do to be unemployed. She took the first thing offered to her, a whodunit called *The Creaking Chair*, in which she was to play the mysterious wife of a crippled Egyptologist.

Ironically, because of delays in production and the briefness of Will's London sojourn, he never did get to see Tallulah in *The Creaking Chair*. He was, nonetheless, impressed with the obvious progress of his daughter's career and with the prestigiousness of her acquaintances.

Tallulah was delighted to be able to attend, on Daddy's arm, a sumptuous dinner at the Savoy Hotel. Present also were Lord Birkenhead, Lord Balfour, Lord Beaverbrook, Lady Manners, and Lady Tree—all friends of Tallulah's. Will was called upon to address the dinner. In white tie and tails, he drank to the health of the British Empire and to the pulchritude of its women. "American women are the most beautiful women in the world," he began. "And now I can see why, because they're descended from the English and the Irish."

Tallulah's behavior in Daddy's presence was flawless. At a previous Savoy dinner, she had hailed an uncommunicative earl across a crowded room, "Don't you recognize me with my clothes on?" But there were no such bon mots now, nor were there cartwheels.

Tallulah did everything in her power to keep the colorful side of her life in England from Will. At one point, Aunt Marie, aware of Tallulah's sloppiness in matters like keeping scrapbooks and memorabilia, begged her niece by letter to subscribe to an English clipping service. Tallulah could not bring herself to tell Marie a blatant lie, but she could not possibly have helped supply anyone connected with her family in America with a regular source of English reportage. Though few of Tallulah's escapades and bon mots were printable, one never knew.

By 1925 Tallulah had become the quintessential Bright Young Thing. No chic party was complete without her imitation of Sarah Bernhardt; all gossip of London town had to include at least one tale of Tallulah's most recent outrage against the conventions.

It was said that she received callers stark naked, that she presided over intimate cocktail parties atub. She did. It was good for a laugh. It caused a stir. People talked. That is precisely what she had in mind. Her *modus operandi* was not entirely arbitrary; she had a literal need to exhibit herself.

But in those years that drive was neither sad nor destructive. Considering her enormous demands for attention, her exhibitionism helped her survive. The end result was publicity, people talking about Tallulah Bankhead. That pleased her enormously.

It was said that she enjoyed sex with women as well as with men. But by the time she reached her middle twenties, she had decided that she liked men better than women or at least liked the *idea* of men better than women. For all her notorious individuality, Tallulah continued to care deeply about how other people regarded her. Though she couldn't resist the shocking line, she did not want to be known as a homosexual. Tallulah was, for instance, repelled by the group of close-cropped Sapphists who cavorted around London in tailored suits, collars and cuffs, watch chains, and carnations, whom Cecil Beaton described as looking and talking like "ventriloquists' dummies." She had more lesbian lines than lesbian experiences, and they were widely disseminated along with her other outrageous comments, to wit:

"Dahling, I couldn't possibly go to the marchioness' this weekend. I'm so bloody tired of three in a bed."

"I'm sick to death of all those royal lesbians following me about."

"I don't know what I am, dahling. I've tried several varieties of sex. The conventional position makes me claustrophobic. And the others give me either stiff neck or lockjaw."

Tallulah's wit was devastating and citable, though it was less real, less original than Mrs. Pat Campbell's, for instance, who said

about Tallulah in the late twenties: "Tallulah is always skating on
thin ice. Everyone wants to be there when it breaks." Mrs. Campbell's wit was a genuine mode. It was vicious, angry, hot, and destructive. It issued from the very real hostilities of a frustrated,
frightened old woman. Tallulah's wit issued only from her need to
make people laugh, or shutter, or react. If it was cynical and shocking, it was mostly because cynicism and shock worked for her. If,
for instance, she had ever tried three in a bed, she certainly was not
tired of it.

It was said, too, that Tallulah had abortions the way other
women had permanent waves. She did, in fact, have several performed in private nursing homes in England. Her various "pre-
dicaments" were a natural outgrowth of liberation and promiscuity
combined with ignorance and extreme fertility. But she had no
more, however, and probably fewer than a contemporary of hers,
Meggie Albanesi, who refused to take even the simplest precau-
tions and died, at twenty-four, from repeated curetting.

In areas of sex and sexuality, many contemporaries of Tallulah's
assumed that she wrote the book. In fact, she was abysmally naïve
about contraception, harboring all sorts of myths and misconcep-
tions in that area.

In any case, stories about Tallulah's multiple abortions got
around. They radiated out from the inner circle into the hinterlands. There was undoubtedly some shopgirl in Manchester who
heard that Tallulah had ten abortions in as many months and that
the Prince of Wales was seen donating a mysterious pint of blood
at the Lyric Theatre on the night of her last leave-taking. The
stories were disseminated in their original form by Tallulah, who
had a multitude of favorite abortion throwaway lines, one of them
being: "I'll never go back to that place again. They aborted me
with rusty nails and old razor blades."

There were many aspects of the developing Bankhead super-
image which were based on original truths. People talked, for instance, about her helplessness, her inability to cope with the
normal, the banal, the everyday. That was true to an extent, but
the tendency grew as it was noticed.

Because *The Creaking Chair* turned out to be a potboiler, Tallulah was able, for the first time in her career, to put some money away. She was aided and abetted by her martinet manager and co-star, Aubrey Smith, who had her on a limited allowance for several months. With the couple of hundred pounds she had saved, Tallulah bought herself a little green Talbot. She was taught to drive the automobile and tried to get from her home to the theater in it. She managed, several times, to become irretrievably lost. On one such occasion, worried that she would miss the curtain, she called a taxi and asked the driver to *lead* her to the theater. Subsequently, wanting to drive but fearful of getting lost, she would hail a cab, give the driver the address of the theater, scoot into her Talbot, and follow the somewhat amazed driver to the West End.

When Tallulah told the story to friends, they howled with laughter. It even made the newspapers, and Tallulah never again tried to drive to the theater unassisted. She discarded the Talbot but never jettisoned that particular aspect of her role playing. She was, thereafter: Tallulah Bankhead, maladroit, nondriver. In such a way did her personality form—experimental, jerry-made, subject to approval.

Publicly, her reality diminished. *Cecil Beaton's Diaries* contains this note on Tallulah, who one day dropped in, with a group of friends, to visit the Tower, a famous restaurant in London: "Tallulah arrived late, went to every table and was quickwitted at each. She has developed her personality to such an extent that she always seems natural, but it is only acting."

Though her acquaintances were legion, Tallulah's close friends were few and odd. And they, of course, saw a more real Tallulah. Among the chosen and widely disparate intimates were: Oggie Lynn, with whom she lived for a time and from whom she learned enormously; Gladys Henson, the earthy actress wife of Leslie Henson. Tallulah and Gladys would have seen more of each other except that Leslie Henson was not comfortable with Tallulah. Though she liked him a great deal, Henson, one of the biggest music hall stars of his day, told his wife, Gladys, "I'm just a common man. I can't keep up with Tallulah and her wild crowd."

Audry Carten remained Tallulah's closest girlfriend. Audry had opened in *The Dancers* to some of the most exciting reviews in the history of the English theater, but she was simply unable to cope with the pressure. After *The Dancers* closed, with professional offers pouring in, she retired from the stage, as she told Tallulah she would. She was twenty-three years old.

Audry worshiped Tallulah, and so did her younger brother, Kenneth. Eleven-year-old Kenneth Carten was away at school when Audry began to write to him about a "charming, beautiful American actress." He came home on holiday during the run of the Du Maurier play and was finally introduced by Audry to Tallulah. The shy Etonesque Kenneth, frail and blond in short pants and tennis socks, extended his hand. Tallulah disregarded it and gave him a big, smacking kiss. She then directed her dresser, Mrs. Lock, to run out and buy a copy of *Through the Looking Glass* for him. Kenneth thought she had the reddest lips he'd ever seen and promptly fell in love with her.

Tallulah was quite taken with the shy, motherless boy. She teased him outrageously, listened to his problems, bawled him out from time to time, lavished gifts on him, and began to follow his tennis career with an insane avidity. Kenneth was then the Under Sixteen Junior Schoolboy Tennis Champion of England, a title in which Tallulah came to derive as much pride as he. In long argyle socks and a rakish green tam, she attended every game he played, screaming excitedly at Kenneth's agile scampering: "Hit it! Hit it, you son of a bitch." Tennis was Tallulah's first spectator sport.

When Tallulah wasn't behaving in a somewhat maternal manner toward him, she enjoyed being a child with Kenneth. Every Sunday night, for instance, Audry, Kenneth, and Tallulah, dressed in sportive comfortable clothes, went to a movie in the West End. One Sunday, as they were on their way to the cinema, Kenneth revealed to Tallulah that he expected to cry during the performance. He had learned that the picture, called *The Nurse*, was about an English nanny and predicted that it would probably bring back poignant memories of his own nanny. As soon as the lights were lowered in the cinema, before the title had even appeared on the silent screen, Kenneth began to sob. Tallulah joined him straightaway. Audry watched them incredulously. The picture had not been on for five minutes before the trio was asked graciously to accept a refund and leave the auditorium.

Tallulah spent a great deal of time as well with Sir Guy Francis Laking, whom she was forever extricating from hock and woe. Two years younger than Tallulah, Laking was the first of her freaks: a fat, lisping eunuch who resembled a cretinous Charles Laughton. His grandfather had been physician to the king and had, on more than one occasion, saved the monarch's life. Because of his grandfather's usefulness, Laking inherited a baronetcy, a diamond stickpin, a disastrous arrogance, but hardly any money at all. His eternal complaint was: "What'th the good of a baronethy if one dothent have any money!" Actually, the baronetcy yielded some. He used his title to exact credit from various London jewelers and was at least once compelled by the court to return a precious stone for which he had no means to pay. His background permitted him to know Tallulah Bankhead, who was never unimpressed with title though she feigned disinterest in such matters.

In his way, Laking undoubtedly loved Tallulah. He gave her the diamond stickpin which had been given to his grandfather, though he would have been appalled to discover that she offered it to a reluctant homosexual actor on condition that he sleep with her. Luckily, the actor turned her down, and Laking never found out.

Sir Guy Francis Laking was a kind of court jester to Tallulah. She loved to hear gossip, and he was a veritable fount of it. When he wasn't actually privy to trouble, he started his own and exulted when it began. He was known to speed back and forth from combatant to combatant carrying acidulous messages with utter relish.

Laking's personality amused Tallulah. He was a hoot. She roared at his raffishness, his social idiocy, his outlandish arrogance. Once Tallulah, Laking, and several other notable types were motoring to the races at Brighton. Their car broke down in the middle of the night, in the middle of the countryside. Laking assumed command. He led the party to the side of an old farmhouse where he called up, "Yooo! Hooo! Yooo hooo!"

A man in a nightcap stuck his head out of the window. "What do you want?" he asked charily.

"No cauth for conthern," Laking answered. "We're noble folk from London, and our Bentley ith broken down."

Tallulah doubled over with laughter. She did a good deal of laughing in those early London years. Everything was fun, her career seemed to take care of itself, and her celebrity fattened on every crumb she threw it. One of Aunt Marie's many unanswered letters to her niece in 1925 was addressed to: TALLULAH BANK-HEAD/AMERICAN ACTRESS/LONDON, ENGLAND. Just TALLULAH would have sufficed.

Every Saturday night, Tallulah and an assortment of friends gathered at Tallulah's for what she called her bacchanal. They drank until they got drunk and then they played a trendy game called Truth, in which they were required to answer with candor any question anyone else in the room cared to ask. Tallulah had by this time moved out of Olga Lynn's house into a service flat on Curzon Street.

When Tallulah's turn to respond came, she was sitting curled up on her sofa. Napier Alington sat next to her with one of her tiny feet in his hand.

"I want to ask Lulas a question," he said. "I'd like to know what she would like to have more than anything in the world."

"Careful, Tallulah," Lord Ned Latham suggested. "You might get it."

Tallulah reached over and took one of her Goldflake cigarettes, tapped it hard, and answered, "As long as I can remember, I've been absolutely hagridden with ambition. I think that if I could wish to have anything in the world, it would be to be free of that ambition."

"Failing that, Lulas?" Napier asked.

"Failing that," she said, "I'd like to get my teeth into the tart's part in *Rain*."

The play that she had taken just as a lark in order to show off for Daddy, *The Creaking Chair*, was in its twenty-fifth week when Tallulah received some very exciting news. Producer Basil Dean told her that she was a very serious contender for the role of the prostitute, Sadie, in Somerset Maugham's play *Rain*.

This was a big one. Jeanne Eagels' success in the ongoing American production had been one of the theatrical events of the decade. When Miss Eagels decided against coming to London to re-create her role, there was great speculation about who would do it. Even before Dean approached her, many of the theatrical cognoscenti assumed it would be Tallulah. She seemed so right. She was an American. She was a very popular, albeit inexperienced stage star. She had the husky dynamism, the smoldering anger, the sensuality of Sadie. Even before the deal was set, all London had heard that Tallulah had been signed definitely to do *Rain*. And that had a great deal to do with Tallulah's active mouth. She was obsessed with *Rain* before she had signed anything; this was the part for which she had been waiting.

For the first two years of her London period, Tallulah considered herself "climbing," taking parts willy-nilly with no end in mind except employment and exposure. It was time now to begin to think of a virtuoso part to exhibit the quality of her talent. Tallulah, at twenty-three, assumed that she would someday be a great—which is to say, *serious*—actress, the kind about which Daddy had always talked, the kind on a league with poets. To begin to do that, one had to have one's name identified with a part of substance.

Basil Dean definitely set his mind on Tallulah. He wrote in his recent autobiography, *Seven Ages*, "Although comparatively inexperienced for such a big emotional part, she would be an undoubted box-office attraction." Dean was in desperate financial straits at the time and needed the kind of hype Tallulah and *Rain* could provide. Somerset Maugham, however, had to approve any choice Basil Dean made. And Maugham was a difficult man.

Production was begun with Tallulah. She read the part; started work on her lines; agreed to take 30 pounds a week, a substantial cut in salary should Maugham approve her; and even consented to travel to the United States just to see Jeanne Eagels in the part. She was then to return to England and begin rehearsals. At this point, Maugham was to make his decision.

Tallulah steamed across the Atlantic on the *Berengaria* in March, 1925. Dean left a couple of days before Tallulah in order to begin production talks with the author, who was then in the United States. Ostensibly, Dean's trip and Tallulah's were completely independent. She was going to America to see the play; Dean was going to meet with Maugham. Before Dean left, however, he told Tallulah that he would try to get some kind of reaction from him. Maugham at the time knew nothing about the casting of the English production.

What must have been a tertiary concern of Basil Dean's approached obsession with Tallulah. She was haggard with anxiety all through the crossing and telephoned Basil Dean at the Gotham Hotel as soon as she passed through customs. When she discovered that no decision had been reached, that Maugham had not reacted one way or another to the mention of her name, she fumed with a fury born of impatience. Dean told her that Maugham had gone on to Washington; she decided to follow him there to convince the author somehow that she was the only girl for the part.

She did meet with Maugham but elicited nothing decisive from him. She succeeded only in alienating the author by her aggressiveness. Basil Dean wrote in *Seven Ages:* "This was a mistake in tactics, for Maugham disliked being pestered by women." Dean even persuaded Tallulah not to book passage on the *Aquitania,* the ship on which he and Somerset Maugham planned to return to London, "on the theory that familiarity breeds contempt."

Tallulah stayed with Daddy in Washington for several days, went on to Pittsburgh, where she caught a touring Jeanne Eagels in *Rain,* rhapsodized at the performance, and returned to England —on a ship other than the *Aquitania*—more fired up than ever about the importance of *Rain* to her career.

As per her original agreement with Basil Dean's production company, Tallulah went into rehearsal for *Rain,* her interpretation to be seen and judged by the author. Maugham sat through two run-throughs and then expressed his decision *not* to use Tallulah.

The official explanation for Tallulah's failure to impress Maugham during the *Rain* rehearsal—at least the one told to Tallulah—was that she "lacked personality." And of course, she found that charge positively outlandish. She preferred to believe, at the time, that something other than her acting had alienated Somerset Maugham decisively: either her importunate behavior during that trip to the United States or her tendency to mimic. Of the latter, she wrote: "One of the curses of my gift for mimicry is that unconsciously I will blink if my opponent blinks, lisp if he lisps." Maugham was, of course, a bad stutterer, an affliction pandemic among upper-class Englishmen. "I have a suspicion," Tallulah went on, "that I may have imitated Maugham's stutter."

A more likely explanation is that she just wasn't good enough, that she did, in fact, lack personality. As she would later prove in *The Lady of the Camellias*, Tallulah had a tendency, when she acted in "serious parts," to jettison all her tricks and mannerisms and to underplay. This could have easily been construed as a personality lack. Tallulah's gift for mimicry was not confined to the drawing room, and it is impossible to conceive that her performances for Mr. Maugham were unaffected by the Jeanne Eagels performance she had been sent to the United States especially to see. A mimetic interpretation is always inferior. It was stupid to send Tallulah to the Jeanne Eagels performance in the first place.

In any case, it was Basil Dean's hapless duty to tell Tallulah about Maugham's negative decision. She ran crying out of his office, returned home, and tried to OD with aspirin tablets: her first, last, and not very serious suicide attempt. Her note read, "It ain't gonna rain no mo."

10

Gallery Unreserved

JUST ABOUT THE TIME Tallulah was Maugham chasing in Washington, a new comedy by Noel Coward called *Fallen Angels* had begun production. Scheduled to open in the two-character play were Edna Best and Margaret Bannerman, featured as middle-class housewives getting gradually bombed as they wait for their Godot—the mutual Lothario that neither one of them had married.

Margaret Bannerman unfortunately suffered a nervous collapse five days before the play was scheduled to open, and Noel Coward, in desperation, called Tallulah. Under normal circumstances Tallulah would probably not have consented to undertake learning the enormous part on such cruelly short notice. But, furious at the world in general and Maugham in particular, she accepted the challenge. She worked around the clock and by opening night had the part letter perfect.

In the first public display professionally of her high comedy flair, she was brilliant. On opening night, Coward's curtain speech was delayed for ten minutes while the house, all parts of it, called for Tallulah and Edna Best.

The play was otherwise significant. It more than doubled her income bracket. When Coward called her, she had the good sense to ask for 100 pounds a week. And *Fallen Angels* elevated her position theatrically so that she was considered for plays of far higher quality than those she had been offered previously.

Fallen Angels proved too that Tallulah Bankhead had an absolute Midas touch for publicity. Everything she touched seemed to turn into banner headlines. Though her acting and that of Edna Best's were unanimously lauded, the play itself became a storm center in the battle against filth, smut, and other divertissements on the London stage. A feverish review of the Coward play in the *Daily Express* began: "Drunkenness. Drunken women. Drunken young women. Drunken young married women both confessing to immoral relations with the same man. That is the *bonne bouche* of the new comedy by Mr. Noel Coward. . . ."

It was, in the lexicon of a later day, a money notice.

The campaign against *Fallen Angels* climaxed with the visit of Mrs. Charles Hornibrook to the Globe Theatre. Mrs. Hornibrook, best known for her declamations against the pernicious influence of Eugene O'Neill's work, had recently parted with the London Council for the Promotion of Public Morality, after a disagreement over the militancy of her tactics, and set out on her own. At the end of the second-act drunk scene in *Fallen Angels*, she stood up in her box and proclaimed, "Ladies and gentlemen. I wish to protest. This play should not go unchallenged. . . ." The gallery hooted. A gentleman in the stalls suggested that she shut up. And, while the band struck up "I Want to Be Happy" from *No! No, Nanette!*, which was the hottest ticket in London at the time, Mrs. Hornibrook was gentled out of the theater.

The Hornibrook proclamation hit all of the newspapers and delighted Tallulah, who thrived on *causes célèbres*, as long as they had a certain cachet about them. There was good scandal, and there was bad scandal, both necessary, one infinitely preferable to the other. When the storm centered on a classy Coward play, the attention was particularly divine.

Tallulah pulled a rather astonishing stunt on the opening night of *Fallen Angels*. There was, in the original script of the play, a line, "Oh dear, rain." Somewhere along the way, Tallulah changed that line to "My Gawd, RAIN!" and spat it out with an icy shudder which delighted the audience, all of whom had heard or read of Tallulah's difficulty with Somerset Maugham, all of whom knew how terribly disappointed Tallulah had been not to land that part.

The entire phenomenon was unique. Who else but Tallulah

could have transformed the simple fact that an actress did not get a part into such a big story? The people in the audience knew about Tallulah and Maugham and *Rain* because they had read it in the newspapers. But it was Tallulah's rare ability, a product of her childlike egocentricity, to self-advertise to such an extent that *other* people somehow thought it was important.

This was before the day of the "biographical actor." An actor was considered a personality because he had magnetism, appeal, and a number of mannerisms which came to be identified with him. He was not profiled in depth; an actor's life was separate from his performance. To no one else on the London legitimate stage in 1925 would it have occurred, as it did to Tallulah, to merge life and art this way, to interpolate biography into dramaturgy. To a Gladys Cooper or a Godfrey Tearle or an Edith Evans, such an arrogation would have been unthinkable apostasy. Indeed, they could not have indulged such a whim had they chosen to. Their personal activities were not nearly so well known. Tallulah's position as actress personality was brand-new to the English theater world. There was no one else quite like her.

Nor had there been anyone quite like Iris Fenwick, the heroine of Michael Arlen's *The Green Hat*, which in novel form had been a sensation of prodigious proportions. Iris had somehow encapsulated the energies, the shimmering modernity of the woman of the mid-1920's. She was an essentially noble outcast, a demimondaine who, by her own tragic end—i.e., driving her yellow Hispano-Suiza into an oak tree at 70 miles an hour—exposed the hypocrisy and rottenness of the decent society which had cast her out.

In its first American dramatization in September, 1925, Katharine Cornell turned the play into a kind of personal triumph. The same month, in London, Tallulah tried it. She went method for the part, wearing green ensembles offstage as well as on; taking special delight in the name of the play's hero, Napier; finding similarities in a swim party which she had once attended and the one described in the Arlen text. When her director informed her that Iris had a secret death wish—which is generally true of people who drive their cars into brick walls—Tallulah decided that she had one as well, prognosticating that she would one day meet a violent end.

Not since the opening of *Rain* had such a flurry of excitement attended a production. The first-night audience at the Adelphi Theatre was a microcosm of British society. The Prince of Wales was there with Mrs. Coates of the cotton Coates; Napier Alington came in from his country home in Dorset. Gladys Cooper, who had turned down the part of Iris, looking tan from a holiday in Lido, shared a box with Ned Latham and Mrs. Fred Thompson. Lady Milford Haven, in a lace dress with a Russian headdress, was surrounded by Lord Tweedmouth, Lady Curzon, Mrs. Seymour Hicks, and Lady Du Maurier.

Tallulah fought an uphill battle, uttering lines like: "You've all got Alma Maters instead of minds, and Union Jacks instead of hearts." Among the lines uttered *to* her: "You are a woman with magic eyes and a soft white body that beats at my brain like a whip." It was generally agreed by the critics that the play was preposterous.

Opinion about the performance of Tallulah by the more conventional critics ran violently pro and con. Since the beginning of her London career, she was being taken to task for her inaudibility. As far back as *The Dancers,* someone wrote, "Speak up, Tallulah, and we'll love you." It was a matter not simply of her American accent or her untrained vocal equipment, but more of her rushed, lightning delivery which was becoming a part of her personal style. Several of the daily critics complained that they simply could not understand a lot of what Tallulah was saying. The *Times* dismissed the play and commented: "Miss Bankhead is more than ever inaudible." James Agate wrote, "Miss Tallulah Bankhead brought all her husky charm to the part of Iris, and acted pleasantly and competently without making one feel that the character could have moved in any mentionable circle." Gladys Cooper hated it.

Hannen Swaffer, "the Pope of Fleet Street," the very lively reviewer for the *Express,* was the first of the critics to defer to Tallulah—which is to say that he widened his purview in considering *The Green Hat,* making his critique a consideration of the whole

Bankhead phenomenon. "Tallulah Bankhead," he wrote, "is almost the most modern actress we have. She belongs to the semi-exclusive set of whom Michael Arlen writes. She has beauty and a shimmering sense of theatre. So she made Iris Fenwick a most fascinating study. She has moved starwards in great strides during the last year. Her art saved *Fallen Angels* from dreariness; now she has succeeded in a part about which even Gladys Cooper felt nervous."

By the time Tallulah opened in *Scotch Mist* in January, 1926, she had amassed a gallery following more loyal, fervid, and numerous than any star in London. There were now hundreds of these girls: tailoresses, laundresses, clerks. On an opening night of Tallulah's, they queued for blocks, waiting for their chance to crowd into the overheated gallery section, which comprised backless, hard tiers of pews into which a management man called the shover upper shoved a certain outlandish number of backsides regardless of their girths and dimensions.

Many of the galleryites reserved their place on line as far as forty-eight hours in advance of the opening. They did this not by actually remaining outside the theater for two days—for they were, after all, working people—but by renting or purchasing from the management or Woolworth's little stools which came equipped with chains and name tags. They weren't substantial enough to sit on, but chained to the iron gate which ran outside any London theater, the stool with its marker reserved the spot on line. The marker might say Dora Morris, Kitty Berger, Ted Mortimer, Angie or Sophie Rosen. One had to put in certain hours actually present on line, but the management eased the hardship by serving tea to the galleryites. Sandwiches and cakes were sold on the street.

Tallulah's gallery was notable because of its vociferousness, its size, and its singularly female consistency. But the gallery in general was a respected English theatrical institution. Management deferred to them; the press chronicled them; actors feared them mightily. Their colorful condemnation was loud, rude, and irreversible. Among their tactics was, of course, the rudimentary boo, but unbelievable shades of same were explored, discovered, and taught by a galleryite named Pip, also called "the bad boy of the Lyric Theatre." There was also slow clapping, contagious giggling, the answering of questions posed by an actor to another actor by a member of the gallery, as in:

ACTOR: Where's Ted?
GALLERYITE: Eeee's beyind the curtain, ya bloody fool.

Simple declarative sentences could also issue from an unhappy gallery. Some of them were helpful, as "Speak up, please!" Most of the suggestions were less constructive. "Lights please" was very big in Tallulah's time. So was "Take it off! It's rubbish." This last was the favorite comment of one of Tallulah's most avid Gallery Girls, Fat Sophie. Fat Sophie also had a notorious black umbrella. When she raised it, thunder issued from all parts of the gallery.

Of course, Fat Sophie never raised her umbrella or her voice at a Tallulah play. For her and her sisters, Tallulah Bankhead could do absolutely no wrong. They attended every one of Tallulah's opening and closing nights. In between, they might see that same play four or five times a week. They knew the plays line by line. They cheered, swooned, applauded madly. Linking hands and swaying, they chanted adulatory phrases like "Tallulah you're wonderful!" and "Tallulah! Hallelujah!" When Tallulah looked up at them and blew a kiss, uttering the phrase, heartily felt, with which she was becoming increasingly identified, "Bless you, dahlings," they lost their collective minds.

Tallulah continued to learn most of their first names. She continued as well to elicit and value their judgments although they differed radically from the published critics'. They rhapsodized over *Scotch Mist*, which was about the promiscuous wife of a British Cabinet minister. The Bishop of London denounced the play, as did the ubiquitous Mrs. Hornibrook. The *Morning Post* critic had a more or less typical critical reaction to it. He said, "*Scotch Mist* is one of the worst plays I have ever seen." It was, nonetheless, a big commercial success.

As her personal following burgeoned, Tallulah began to feel

emotionally and financially secure enough to put down roots. She signed a ninety-nine-year lease on a flat-topped mews in the charming Mayfair section of London: 1 Farm Street. It was a cozy little house in the back of Berkeley Square, with two floors above and one below street level. A winding staircase—spinal column of rich dark oak—linked and dominated the floors, which were no more than twelve paces in either direction. Tallulah spend thousands of pounds decorating. Syrie Maugham supplied the last word in Mayfair tone. The house was all tarnish gold and silver woodwork. Tallulah's bedroom was done in soft pinks and gold. She insisted on a coal-burning fireplace.

She began to gather a ménage. As spoiled as Tallulah had been in America vis-à-vis personal services, she was even worse in London. At one time she had at least picked up after herself. It would not have occurred to her now to do anything about her personal maintenance. Dresses dropped where they fell. Bath water was prepared. Cars were driven. The anarchy of adolescence was unnaturally sustained: the cocoon was peopled with friends and servants. There was Mrs. Lock, a little lady who had been her dresser since *The Dancers*. Once in the house, she hired a couple, John and Mary: John to buttle, Mary to cook. Finally, there was Edie Smith.

Edie had been one of Tallulah's fans, as opposed to the Gallery Girls, a plump, dark-haired girl, about Tallulah's age, with marvelous teeth, rosy cheeks, and a quiet style. She saw Tallulah one day leave the theater with a British chain store magnate. Soon after, she asked Tallulah to put in a good word with him since she was planning to apply for a job in one of his stores. Tallulah obliged.

When Tallulah decided that she needed a live-in right hand, she invited Edie to work for her. Edie agreed. In no time at all, Tallulah was totally dependent on her new friend and factotum. During the General Strike in England in 1926, when everything stopped one day in May, Tallulah set out to walk to the theater for a performance. She did not yet have a personal chauffeur. Within half an hour she was on the phone summoning Edie to come fetch her; she was lost. Edie arrived and they both laughed helplessly at Tallulah's ineptitude. When Edie went away to the country once for several days, Tallulah telephoned her at three in the morning. One of Edie's manifold duties was to open Tallulah's cigarette tins. Consequently, Tallulah's cigarette-tin-opening abilities withered away. After an unsuccessful struggle, lasting about two and a half minutes, she was on the phone to Edie, childlike and importunate. "I'm dying for a cigarette," she said to Edie. "How do you open the bloody tin?"

Edie Smith had the kind of tolerance of waywardness that was absolutely essential if one was to survive around Tallulah. Tallulah took. She was demanding, undisciplined, neurotic, a creature of impulse and moods, expansive energies and rotten temper. But she gave, too, because she had the gift of life, the grace and vulnerability of a child, the generosity of a sailor. And that is good to be around.

She was incapable of maintaining what she had discovered to be a properly distant relationship with her servants because she could not relegate them to nonpeoplehood. She plied them with questions about what they wanted and where they were going and whether they believed in the life hereafter. She could also be unspeakably rude, abusive, and thoughtless. But she was never indifferent to the people about her.

The sight of a street beggar, for instance, might upset her for days. She didn't undertake any programs for social amelioration —indeed it was years before she ever cast a vote—but she would spontaneously give every bit of wealth she was carrying on her person.

She gave lavishly to her friends. She was the easiest touch in Mayfair, and a good deal of her spiraling salary was spent to entertain other people. At 1 Farm Street, a party was almost always in progress, with the best food and champagne that money could buy. Tallulah's parties were known to spin out for three or four days in a row.

One such marathon was held in honor of Ethel Barrymore. The actress was visiting London and staying with Tallulah. Tallulah decided to give Ethel a bon voyage party on the eve of her sailing. Cathleen Nesbitt was invited, left in the wee hours, bid farewell to Ethel, expecting naturally that that would be the end of it. She returned the next afternoon on her way to a performance and found the guests, many of them still in evening clothes, gathered about drinking, smoking, and laughing as though time had stood still. Tallulah, in crepe hostess pajamas, was fresh and bright, nicely high on wine, and being the perfect hostess. The doors opened, and Ethel Barrymore, in full form and also nicely high on wine, appeared. She said to Cathleen, "One of your English fogs delayed my sailing. We've alerted the party to suit."

That night, after giving the evening's performance, Cathleen returned to the lidless little house. She was greeted at the door by John, the butler. Casting his eyes heavenward as a gesture of petition and an indication of the state of the guests, he said, "The party, madam, is still in progress."

Actually, there was more to it than that. Not only was the party still going on, but another one was in progress. The fog had lifted, and Ethel Barrymore had finally left. Her farewell party, however, segued right into another which Tallulah had planned far in advance. She managed to sustain herself by taking a ten-minute nap before greeting the new arrivals, though several of the august bodies who started with her were strewn about napping on a variety of divans, chaises longues, and throw rugs.

To prepare for Sidney Howard's *They Knew What They Wanted*, Tallulah scoured the house of august bodies and dedicated herself to work. This was a prestigious and brilliant property. Under the auspices of the Theatre Guild, *They Knew What They Wanted* had been an outstanding commercial success in New York and won a Pulitzer Prize. The part of Amy, in the London production, was offered to Tallulah by Basil Dean, though neither the Theatre Guild nor Sidney Howard was very enthusiastic about his choice.

This was a radical departure for Tallulah. Since the beginning of her career in London, Tallulah had played only sex symbols, always exotic, usually rich, very glamorous, and exceedingly promiscuous. The plays were none of them any good. Increasingly, they were being tailor-made for Tallulah, written with Tallulah in mind as a hectic, sophisticated modern woman, wearer of beautiful gowns, smoker of cigarettes, pursued. Her phenomenal success with the "gods," the galleryites, was explained more and more in these terms. Hubert Griffith of the *Evening Standard* expounded this point of view in a column about Tallulah. He wrote: "Down there on stage she wears the clothes that would cost a year's earnings. She moves in expensive apartments, at Paris, Deauville, St. Jean de Luz. Young men in exquisite evening dress are rivals in love with her. Miss Tallulah Bankhead is on the stage what every woman in the gallery in some degrees wishes to be, the dream fulfillment made manifest."

There was no such manifest dream content in the Howard play. Tallulah was to play a waitress in a "cheap spaghetti joint" whose total onstage wardrobe cost an estimated six pounds. Her love rivals were an illiterate aging Italian immigrant and a drifter named Joe, "dark, sloppy, beautiful, and young." The play was set in the darkling home of the immigrant in the Napa Valley, California.

Here finally was a play of which she could be proud. Tallulah insisted repeatedly that she hadn't been happy with the previous plays, that she took them only as expedients. "You don't for a minute think I enjoy doing sex plays," she told a friend. "But when you're climbing, you've got to take what the gods offer." Hoping now to make the transition to quality, she worked hard and long, divesting herself of all the mannerisms she had picked up while doing plays that were essentially vehicles. She wanted to be very good, excellent as Amy—to prove to the snobby Theatre Guild, to Sidney Howard, to Somerset Maugham, and, not least of all, to herself, that she could play waitresses in cheap spaghetti joints in Pulitzer Prize-winning plays if she so chose.

They Knew What They Wanted opened in May, 1926. Its premiere was one of the most exciting events of the London season. Sam Livesey proved to be a vital, poignant Tony. Glenn Anders, who was to become a close friend of Tallulah's, repeated the role of Joe, which he had originated in the American production. Anders was a big, luggy, extraordinarily handsome and broad-shouldered blond. His Joe was one of the high-water marks of the theatrical year. He and Tallulah played the attracted couple magnetically. Her performance was a total success.

The press was ecstatic about this pure and fulfilling Tallulah Bankhead. James Agate wrote on May 23, 1926:

> One had read one's programme with, let it be confessed, something of a sinking heart, for it foreshadowed an actress whose successive incarnations had connoted a fallen angel, a green hat, and a scotch mist. Would this piece be yet another incredible farrago of maidens very far from loath, and epigrammatic noblemen too languid to pursue?
>
> One's fears were soon allayed. The curtain had not been up five minutes before we knew that Miss Bankhead was to play the part of an ex-waitress in a "spaghetti-joint" or cheap restaurant. Ten minutes later, the actress appeared wearing the cheapest of cotton frocks. At once she set about a piece of sincere emotional acting felt from the heart and controlled by the head, which set up a standard of accomplishment for this clever artist. Miss Bankhead made an instantaneous and a great success, and one would seize the occasion to say that to deplore the misdirection of talent is a very different thing from denying its existence. It would be ungenerous not to recognize that her performance in this piece is one of quite unusual merit.

St. John Ervine of the *Observer* commented:

> Miss Tallulah Bankhead played the part of Amy with a nervous intensity that I hardly suspected her to possess. Her agitation and restless excitement in the first act were superbly done. . . . Miss Bankhead's performance must considerably increase her reputation.

The *News* said:

> There were those who were not convinced by her performance in *The Green Hat* and *Scotch Mist* but last night she showed herself a fine artist. Miss Bankhead acted brilliantly.

That night she and Glenn went dancing at the swank Embassy Club. He was properly boutonniered and very handsome in his white tails; Tallulah wore a green gown and her hair hung loose. The Prince of Wales was watching. Anders peeked at himself and Tallulah in the mirrored ballroom and thought, "God, we dance beautifully together." Everybody was rich, successful, and twenty-five.

It was the summit of Tallulah's whole career—*They Knew What They Wanted*. And yet something was missing. Something was not quite right about it. Tallulah hit upon the gallery as the answer. Her girls, it seemed to her, were not as receptive as they had been in her previous plays. She experienced an abatement of excitement, a lessening in the intensity with which she personally was received by her audience. They no longer yelled, "Tallulah, we love you!" and that was a source of considerable concern to her.

Tallulah was overreacting to an understandable phenomenon. The very atmosphere of this play discouraged flagrant exhibitions from either side of the footlights. It was the custom in England for the stars to take individual curtain calls at the end of each act. This was eliminated now in the interest of the ensemble effect and the integrity of the play. This was, after all, Sidney Howard's play, not Tallulah's.

Although it was a solid hit, though the "gods" were filled to capacity every night, the Gallery Girls did not, in fact, like *They Knew What They Wanted* as much as they had liked *Scotch Mist*. These were unsophisticated, uneducated East Enders, and they preferred the bathetic, the second-rate. They wanted escape, not catharsis.

More to the point, they wanted their Tallulah back, their Tallulah as "dream made manifest." As Amy, she was as ignorant as they were ignorant. She was as poor as they were poor, as hardworking as they. They preferred her in the gawdy appurtenances of exhibition rather than in the austere garb of her art.

Tallulah, who could not brook abandonment on any level, was vaguely uneasy throughout the run of the play. She was delighted with her critical success, with her new prestige, but she wanted her fans back. She had neither the courage nor the faith to forfeit the archetypal chant "Tallulah, we love you!" for the less orgasmic tokens of approval. Consequently, *They Knew What They Wanted* was the last growth step she would take in London.

11

"If You Can't Sing 'Melancholy Baby'..."

A MAGAZINE called *The Sphere* asked the British public, in 1927, to choose the ten "most remarkable" women in the country. The winners' names appeared in alphabetical order. They were: Lady Astor, Tallulah Bankhead, Lady Diana Cooper, the Duchess of Hamilton, Lady Londonderry, Olga Lynn, the Queen, Claire Sheridan, Edith Sitwell, and Mrs. Vermet.

The Duchess of Westminster recollected the year 1927 in her autobiography, *Grace and Favour*. Her memory was spurred by turning over old press cuttings: "I find curious gossipy bits about fancy-dress parties. At one in 1927 everyone had to represent a living celebrity. Oliver Messel came as Tallulah Bankhead in 'her *Garden of Eden* dress.' A little later the same columnist reported him as being at an all-Ballet party wearing his Tallulah mask again, but it was a mistake. It seems he was really wearing the mask of 'a grotesque clown from 1840 designs for the Triumph of Neptune,' and what had caused the confusion was that they both had eyelashes which fluttered when a string was pulled."

She used sex with an increasing abandonment. Tallulah flew to Paris for a Sunday assignation with a married tennis champion. Late Saturday night, she was sitting in a darkened *boîte* with Edie Smith, drinking too much. She looked around the room. Her eyes feasted on a tall, thin, blond Austrian army officer, standing at the bar in full regalia.

"That is the most attractive man I've ever seen," she said to Edie. "Go get him."

Edie Smith replied, "I'm not pimping for you. Get him yourself."

Tallulah sat churlishly deciding what to do when Clifton Webb walked into the *boîte*. He immediately noticed the same Austrian officer, turned around, and left. He returned in minutes, wheeling a pushcart of roses which he had purchased hastily from a street hawker. Webb began tossing rose petals at the officer.

Tallulah took another sip of wine, stood up mightily, and disappeared into the street. She returned wheeling a similar pushcart. Stationing herself at the opposite end of the room, she began tossing whole flowers at the Austrian officer like some demented Carmen. She yelled to Webb, "This will be a fight to the finish!"

Webb threw several roses at a time; Tallulah hurled bouquets. The amused officer, crested with flower fragments, put down his whiskey, approached Tallulah, and escorted her out of the *boîte*. Webb nodded graciously. Tallulah missed her date with the tennis champion.

Tallulah wanted what she wanted when she wanted it; that applied to cigarettes, food, and bed partners. She astonished men with explicit invitations; if their response was negative, she was incredulous, wounded, and finally aggrieved.

There was a good deal of hostility in her sexuality. Basil Dean writes, in *Seven Ages,* of an episode that occurred during the rehearsal period of *Scotch Mist*. Tallulah had several torrid love scenes with Godfrey Tearle, in whom she had no genuine romantic interest. Tearle had a jealous wife, Mollie, however, who offended Tallulah. According to Dean, the jealous wife attended every single rehearsal of the play, never taking her eyes off Tallulah and her husband. When the question of dressing rooms came up, Mrs. Tearle, on Godfrey's behalf, accepted a very inferior location just because it was far away from Tallulah's quarters.

At the final rehearsal of the play, Tallulah decided that she would give the woman something to worry about. They rehearsed the hottest love scene of them all, and Tallulah played it with such sensuous ferocity she reduced Tearle's wife to tears. The curtain came down. Dean rose from his seat, was about to mount the stage when Tallulah poked her head through the curtain. She said playfully to Dean and Mollie, "Good thing I had me drawers on, wasn't it?"

Tallulah would leaven such incidents with bawdy and amusing one-liners. But there was, nonetheless, fierce bellicosity connected with such behavior. It was as though Tallulah, the scampering little fat girl, the bluff bully, had simply changed her weapons. There had been an element of this need to "show 'em" in her performance in *They Knew What They Wanted*. She ravished the critics. She proved she could do it. Somewhat slaked by the conquest, Tallulah returned, with a vengeance, to the kind of rubbishy vehicles that gave her the most immediate, most intense satisfaction, the kind to which her gallery responded rapturously.

They Knew What They Wanted was followed by *The Gold Diggers*. It was an extravagant comedic tour de force about show girls and how they land rich sugar daddies. In the play, Tallulah wore gold pajamas by Molyneux, cartwheeled, pretended to get drunk, and did a dance which turned out to be a sensation. One critic said that it combined "all the scandalousness of the worst can-can with all the grace of the best Charleston." In response to the persistent cheers of her gallery, Tallulah regularly repeated the dance five and six times a night.

Her first nights were beginning to make news even in the United States. The New York *Times* reported on the premiere of *The Gold Diggers*. Correspondent Charles Morgan commented: "Cheers began some time before her first entrance; when she entered they became deafening, mechanical and persistent; there seemed to be a reasonable possibility that the play would be prevented from proceeding further. Greeting of stars is, in any case, an objectionable practice that destroys the theatre's illusion, but tradition does offer some excuse for it when it is done in moderation. When it is exaggerated as at the first

night of *The Gold Diggers*, it becomes oppressive and disgusting."
The play was, nonetheless, a solid commercial hit.

In May, 1927, she opened in *The Garden of Eden*, a dark,
cheap melodrama adapted from the German by Avery Hopwood,
who also wrote *The Gold Diggers*. Tallulah played Toni Lebrun,
a dancer in a notorious café who loses her job because she would
not submit to the overtures of an amatory proprietress. She leaves
the café and becomes engaged to a rich and high-toned Monocan,
whose father is unfortunately opposed to the union. On their
wedding day, the old man impugns Toni's purity. Furious, she
stands at the head of a flight of wide steps and, with half the
population of the south of France watching, rips off her wedding
dress, stands arms akimbo in her camiknickers, and then self-
righteously departs.

Both the lesbian theme and the striptease were considered
rather daring for their time. One critic called *Garden of Eden*
"heavily vulgar as only the German mind can conceive." Another
remarked coyly on the reaction of the Gallery Girls to the scene
between Tallulah and the proprietress. "You can imagine the
details," he wrote, "and the self-conscious giggles from the audience." *Theatre World* commented, "Tallulah Bankhead has a
following and unfortunately is in imminent danger of offering
herself and her intelligence as a sacrifice to those adoring 'gods.'
Her performance may save *Garden of Eden* but the cost will be
too great to make it worth her while."

The critics' gibes did not interfere with Tallulah's close relationship with her fans. She regularly invited a contingent to her
house on Farm Street for drinks, though they were not asked to
stay on to socialize with her smarter, late-arriving friends. She
bought them gifts on Christmas. When she or Mrs. Lock appeared
at the stage door to bid them, "Come on, girls," they jammed into
Tallulah's dressing room, watching with shy adulation as she prepared to go on the stage or leave the theater.

When one of the girls elicited a new datum about Tallulah, it
spread through the ranks and was often transmuted into a chant.
They knew, for instance, that Tallulah consistently used a Coty
scent called Shypre. Many of them, like bloodhounds, knew she

was in the vicinity by the smell of it. So, while they raced in a herd, up the winding, endless stairs of the Lyric Theatre, they chanted en masse the name of the perfume. It came out "SHEEP! SHEEP! SHEEP!"

Presently, an argot developed, part of the private, underground line of communication between Tallulah and her Gallery Girls. "Bye-bye," as in "so long" became the code word for "beddy bye" as in "sex." Whenever Tallulah waved onstage or indicated that she was about to leave, the puerile gallery took leave of their senses. They howled with delight.

The hysteria reached a kind of crisis in 1928, when Tallulah opened in *Her Cardboard Lover*, the least undistinguished of the plays that followed *They Knew What They Wanted*, but not very good. Thousands of fans, most of them girls, mobbed the Lyric Theatre opening night. Traffic was stopped and then redirected. A phalanx of bobbies was assigned to keep order.

When Tallulah's newly acquired cream-colored Bentley approached the Lyric, the car was almost overturned. She was shaken so badly that she had to have a drink before going onstage, an infraction of her severest principle.

The stalls and the dress circle were amused at first by the tumult which transpired within the theater. But as the chantings seemed to be interfering with the beginning of the play, they began to shush the gallery. The gallery began to shush the shushers. The Lyric sounded more like a steam bath than a legitimate theater. Tallulah entered finally, wearing cream-colored pajamas, and more mayhem broke loose. Leslie Howard, who gave a miraculously good performance in spite of everything, was totally ignored. The applause and demonstrations for Tallulah after each act went on almost as long as the acts themselves.

Tallulah said very little publicly about the gallery. She confided to Hannen Swaffer once, "What can I do? They love to see me in my underclothes." When he printed the remark, she is reported to have slapped his face. As the thing got more and more out of hand, Tallulah was forced to say something. The press commented scathingly. Writer after writer called the demonstrations appalling and implored somebody—Tallulah, management, Scotland Yard —to do something about them.

But Tallulah would not renounce or attempt to mitigate the behavior of her audience. "I cannot pretend not to enjoy it," she said. "That would be hypocritical. I feel greatly complimented by these demonstrations. As far as my dishabille is concerned, when I take off my dress, it is because the play demands it, because it is a quite natural outcome of the plot of the play. There is nothing indelicate about it."

12

Diminishing Returns

DURING THE YEARS that Tallulah was becoming the most celebrated actress on the London stage, her sister, Eugenia, was Left Banking it in Paris with Morton Hoyt, her husband, and a coterie of rootless international celebrities.

Tallulah and Eugenia saw little of each other. They led entirely separate—which is to say, noncompetitive—lives. Their relationship was pleasant and nostalgic. Often when it was convenient to them both, they switched residences on short holidays, the Hoyts taking Tallulah's Farm Street house, Tallulah staying at their flat in Paris.

In 1928, Eugenia's second marriage to Morton was officially dissolved, and she crossed the Channel with some vague idea of radically altering her life. Under the name of Sally Hoyt, Eugenia made a brief appearance in a movie; but the klieg lights affected her bad eye, and she was temporarily blinded. Shortly afterward, her sight restored, Albert de Couville offered her a small part in his play *The Barker*, scheduled to open in London in the spring, starring Claudette Colbert. Eugenia accepted.

The debut of another Bankhead in London was an event widely covered in the British press. An article in *The People* began: "Walking about London—when she can resist the lure of taxicabs —is a charming and vivacious young woman who bears a remarkable resemblance to Tallulah Bankhead. She walks like Tallulah, has many of Tallulah's characteristics, speaks like Tallulah, and has the same husky voice."

Tallulah was sufficiently quieted by her immense popularity to treat Eugenia's debut with an amused curiosity. She attended the premiere, escorted by *Daily Mail* critic Alan Parsons, whose column the next day was all about taking Tallulah to see her sister's introduction to the London theatergoing audience. To deflect attention away from herself, Tallulah showed up at the premiere heavily disguised in a wig and glasses. This disguise was an absolute necessity by the late twenties, when Tallulah caused a sensation everywhere she appeared. At one particular opening night, the whole dress section, alerted to Tallulah's presence as part of the audience, stood up to get a better look at her. It was as though the band had suddenly struck up "God Save the Queen."

Eugenia had a tiny part in *The Barker*. She did a swift, artful can-can, and got off. Prince George subsequently commented favorably on the legs that she had displayed that night, but aside from that endowment, Eugenia was obviously no threat to Tallulah's meteoric success. Nor did she intend to be. In other areas, however, formidable problems arose between the two sisters.

Tallulah, when Eugenia came to London to flirt with the wicked stage, was in love with a tall, blond, hot-eyed Englishman, from a very distinguished family, named Tony Wilson. Tony somehow met Sister, took a shine to her, and Sister, unattached at the time, shone back. Sister would later claim that she knew absolutely nothing about his relationship with Tallulah at the time of their meeting and by the time she found out it was too late to end it— all of which Tallulah vigorously disbelieved. Tallulah, on the other hand, swore that she and Wilson were not just good friends but engaged when Eugenia came along and took him away—all of which Sister vigorously denied. The whole affair was exacerbated by the intervention of Sir Guy Francis Laking, who carried tales, missives, innuendo, and accusation from sister to sister. Eugenia, without giving any notice to the producers of The Barker, packed up and left for Paris. Tony Wilson followed her. It was years before Tallulah spoke to her sister again.

Tallulah's "engagements" throughout her London years covered a multitude of situations: from prolonged affairs to the Tony Wilson affaire, in which she used the designation probably to make what Sister had done seem worse; to liaisons which she formalized in order to shake up Napier Alington. Unfortunately, Naps was unshakable. His health, his sexual preference, his mother—all militated against marriage to Tallulah. When he did choose a bride, in 1928, she was Lady Mary Sibell Ashley-Cooper, the eldest daughter of the Earl of Shaftesbury. It was reasoned, most probably, that since Napier would never have an overwhelming passion for a woman, it would be folly to marry disadvantageously, rather like doing an unrewarding role for scale.

There was every reason now for Tallulah to consider not only an "engagement" but an engagement to marry. Naps, on whom she had had her heart set, was taken. She was furious at Sister and wanted to do her one better. She was twenty-six, and it was time. She was restive and wanted a change. And there was the matter of children; Tallulah adored them.

While on a short vacation in Brighton, she met Count Anthony de Bosdari. He was a short, dapper Italian with impeccable manners, a commanding presence, and dark hair waved in front like shallow water at low tide. He moved into Tallulah's house shortly after their return from holiday and began ordering her servants about with an appealing macho. He asked her one day to close her eyes, and when she did, he slipped a hulking but tasteful diamond necklace around her throat. It was the first present Tallulah had had since she had begun doing the buying. She felt compromised and excited. They decided to marry at Christmas, 1928, when she had three days off from the show.

Tallulah was enormously impressed with Tony, his background, his pedigree, his achievements, and his wealth. At twenty-eight, he seemed a veritable Florentine *Ubermensch*. He was, she discovered gradually: the London-born son of a former Italian official; a cousin to the King of Italy; a rich financier with interests in the German film industry; a graduate of Winchester, the oldest public school in England, where at sixteen, he won the king's gold medal for the best classical poem of the year and, at eighteen, headed the football team, the cricket eleven, and the dramatic society; a marvelous dancer; and a political aspirant.

She enumerated all these data to Daddy in an exultant letter, which ended:

> I'm telling you all these things darling so you will see I'm marrying a man that you will appreciate and love . . . and apart from all this I love him so there and within a decent space of time I hope to present you with a grandson because you know darling I'm getting to be a big girl now. . . . Anyway my sweet I'm frightfully happy. . . . But darling don't address your next letter to me as Countess Anthony de Bosdari yet because I hope to hear from you before Xmas and I won't be married until then. He has given me the most beautiful diamond necklace and a Rolls Royce for Xmas. He has one already but he is giving me a two seater Rolls so that I can get some fresh air and exercise at the same time. He also thinks it would be rather chic for me to pick him up at the office. Just a model wife you know. I don't have to give up the stage unless I want to but he thinks I will want to. He's usually right. . . . All my love to you all darling and don't forget don't tell. I'm marrying the 22nd of December at the Regent's Office as you are not here to give me away.
>
> I love you
> TALLULAH

The marriage was several times postponed. First, Tony asked Tallulah to make a film for the German company in which he had some interest. It was postponed again when Tallulah discovered that his divorce from the young daughter of a rich Chicago industrialist was not entirely kosher under English law. The clincher came from Sir Guy Francis Laking. Sir Guy, of course, resented any man in whom Tallulah had a romantic interest; when she had a lover, she was less in need of a court jester. Sir Guy, who was an expert in such matters, discovered and revealed joyously to Tallulah the fact that Tony had not paid for the diamond necklace he had so cavalierly given her.

Further investigation unearthed other flaws in the self-presentation of her Renaissance man. The engagement was broken in May, 1929. Tallulah remains listed in various British reference works as Countess Anthony de Bosdari. Most likely, she thought it a kick to fill out some biographical form with her imminent but still unofficial title. She had once similarly, impulsively, and prematurely sent out announcements to the papers of her engagement to Lord Napier George Henry Sturt Alington, third baron.

Whether or not the marriage to Bosdari could have worked, it might have provided, at the very least, the kind of divertissement Tallulah needed by the sixth year of her English reign. Instead, she toured with *Her Cardboard Lover*. The play was a phenomenal commerial success throughout the provinces and in Scotland, where it set Olympian box-office records. Nonetheless, Tallulah continued to experience a certain malaise.

She began to have a good deal of trouble falling asleep at night. She had always lived erratically and slept minimally, but she had nonetheless been able to call her own shots, to fall off to sleep when and if she chose. Now she seldom dropped off until the wee morning hours.

She took a long holiday in the south of France. There she gambled, drank, sunned, and sexed—all in large dosages. She was still troubled.

Tallulah resorted then to a very radical meliorative measure and, in doing so, began a pattern which she continued throughout life. She had some small plastic surgery done: this particular time on her nose. It was minor rhinoplasty; the bridge in front was narrowed minusculely. She wrote to Daddy that her nose was now perfect. "In fact, darling," she continued, "I have changed my type. I am letting my hair grow and wearing it off my face à la Greta Garbo."

Perhaps what bothered Tallulah was that things were simply not going as swimmingly for her as they had been. The auguries were multifarious and sometimes involved the slightest offsetting of a very delicate balance, but they nettled Tallulah nonetheless.

There was, for instance, the matter of money. Tallulah—profligate, generous, insular, and irresponsible—had never quite penetrated the pound-dollar ratio. She was, as she would claim in her autobiography, spending pounds like dollars. When she made 500 pounds a week—as she did consistently in the late twenties—she spent 600 just as consistently. That worked in the marketplace then, as it does now, so long as income is constant and there are no unforeseen economic upheavals. Unfortunately for Tallulah, that was not the case. With astonishing ignorance but no criminal intent, she had neglected for years to file an income tax return. When the British government finally made this remarkable discovery, she was already in debt for *thousands* of pounds.

Other trouble brewed. Regularly the yellow press in Britain began to turn the events of her life into highly publicized incidents. For instance, she and the returned prodigal, Tony Wilson, one Sunday drove into the country to pick up Tony's brother and another boy, who were both students at Eton. They were to lunch somewhere on the Thames. As it turned out, the boys—both in their late teens—had neglected to secure permission for the outing and were declared AWOL. As reported in the daily press, Tallulah's plays were thereafter off limits to all students at Eton. There was no such boycott, and Tallulah's solicitors petitioned the authorities at the school to issue a statement to that effect. Though she could at least try to deal with reportage, Tallulah could do absolutely nothing to check the rumors which grew out of the original story. Gossip had it that Tallulah was a sexual predator with a predilection for small boys. Eventually, it was said that Tallulah was deported from England because of the Eton incident. It was all unpleasant, insidious, and increasingly out of control.

She and Audry Carten went inpulsively to Albert Hall one afternoon to see the evangelist Aimee Semple McPherson, who was visiting England, preach a sermon. Along with Charles

Cochran, they went backstage to see Mrs. McPherson and were both rather fascinated with her. Later that week, Tallulah gave a farewell party for Beatrice Lillie. On a dare from Audry, Tallulah invited the evangelist, who accepted.

Bea Lillie was sailing to the United States. They were all a little tight when Tallulah suggested that it would be great fun to pile into a series of cars and take Bea to Southampton. Mrs. McPherson, Audry, Leslie Howard, Bea Lillie, and Tallulah all were in one car that broke down, once again in the middle of the night. It was foggy, of course, and they all sang Russian Volga songs while pushing the vehicle. A good time was had by all, until the papers somehow got hold of the story.

To make matters worse, Tallulah attempted to deny certain parts of the story which other members of the party confirmed. Everybody was telling the kind of half-truth which made them all look like fools. There were screaming headlines in the press such as: MRS MC PHERSON'S ALL NIGHT JOY RIDE and TALLULAH DENIES STORY OF MOTOR JOY RIDE.

This kind of story, two years before, would not have worried Tallulah. Between it and the Eton affair and her debt to the government, she had good reasons to be anxious. She was advised, too, to remember her alien status.

Her beloved England had changed somewhat since she first arrived in 1923. Many of the Bright Young Things had lost their money or their minds with the help of booze and drugs. Some had reformed. A few had even died. Sir Guy Francis Laking, for instance, was taken suddenly ill in August, 1930, and died shortly thereafter of diabetes complicated by a glandular dysfunction. Hannen Swaffer reported in the *Daily Express* that an autopsy disclosed: "a large gland which normally disappears in the average human being as he approaches his teens. This caused a condition of non-development of the brain, and, in consequence, poor Francis had the mentality of a boy of fourteen or fifteen. If those who frequently blamed the boy for his actions could know the truth of his condition during the past few years they would be more charitable in their judgment."

Francis had the last laugh on Tallulah, with whom he had been feuding bitchily for several months prior to his demise. He bequeathed "to my friend Tallulah Bankhead all my motor cars." His will was probated in October. The twenty-six-year-old retarded nobleman left unsettled property at the gross value of 872 pounds, and no motorcars at all.

There was a new austerity, a slackening of toleration, and a loss, not of innocence, but of naïveté. In late 1928 the Home Secretary requested Radclyffe Hall's publisher to discontinue publication of the celebrated lesbian novel *The Well of Loneliness*. And about the same time Tallulah's critics began analyzing not only the manifest but the latent dream content of her gallery appeal. A reviewer for *Theatre World* who signed himself VHF commented:

> No criticism of Tallulah Bankhead's plays is complete without reference to her display of lingerie. Personally, I find her more attractive in a jumper-suit than without one, and I am quite willing to take her underclothes for granted. I am told, however, that these rather feeble attempts at immodesty are for the benefit of the feminine element of the audience. Well, well, girls will be boys!

She took one last compensatory stab at impressing the natives, at proving once and for all that she was not only a serious actress, but a damned serious actress. She chose to do *The Lady of the Camellias* by Alexandre Dumas, the play in which Sarah Bernhardt had made a resplendent triumph.

The excitement surrounding the production was extraordinary. In spite of everything, Tallulah's insane popularity had not dwindled one iota by March, 1930, when she opened in the costume play at the Garrick Theatre. People at the time were talking about the controversial portrait that Augustus John had recently done of her. The bearded, colorful eccentric had sketched Tallulah first during a chance encounter at the Eiffel Tower restaurant and then asked her to sit for the full oil treatment. He intended to show the finished product at the Royal Academy Exhibit of British artists that year. Tallulah agreed to cooperate on condition that she be permitted to buy the portrait for 1,000 pounds after the show.

John's "Tallulah" was done in pale pastels. In the manner of El Greco, her head and body were stretched vertically so that she took on a baleful fragility. One of the judges at the exhibit said that the work was "the greatest portraiture since Gainsborough's 'Perdita.'" Lawrence of Arabia begged to have a chance to buy it. The Viscount D'Abernon wanted the portrait for the Tate Gallery. It was the sensation of the art world that year, and Tallulah kept the regretful Augustus John to his word.

At the Garrick Theatre on opening night of *The Lady of the Camellias*, the crowd was enormous and disorderly. Eleven cigarette cases were picked from the pockets of the elegant throng. Only the Derby and the Lord Mayor's Show approached a Tallulah opening in the abandonment with which the art of the light touch was practiced.

Her fans were in frenzy as she showed herself in the first of a series of lavish and crinolined period gowns. Out of respect, however, to the apparent solemnity of the Dumas play they quickly settled down. The applause at the end was deafening. Her curtain speech began, "I am aware that I have been undergoing a challenge. . . ."

Tallulah proved very little in *The Lady of the Camellias* except that she was not quite up to it. A creature of extremes, she had exorcised from her performance all the flamboyant mannerisms about which the critics had been carping for years. That left not purity, but *flatness*. James Agate summed it up: "I can promise anybody who visits the Garrick Theatre an interesting evening in which they will see Tallulah Bankhead make a gallant shot at a play demanding another kind of talent." And the public? According to Herbert Farjeon, "they preferred her as The Lady of the Camiknickers."

In the fall of 1930, Tallulah decided to accept an extraordinarily lucrative offer from Paramount Pictures which necessitated returning to the United States. She sold her house, threw a smashing party for herself, and left for the sailing, accompanied by Kenneth, Audry, and Dola Cavendish, a rich Canadian fan she had recently befriended. Edie was scheduled to follow shortly thereafter.

Swathed in a smooth, rich fur, looking almost as thin as she did in the John portrait, she read a prepared statement to the press which ended, "I've never had a good part yet."

In Southampton she cried like a child as Kenneth, Audry, and Dola prepared to leave the ship. "Oh, come with me! Do come with me," she begged all of them.

Audry and Kenneth disembarked and stood on the beach, watching half their life sail away. Dola was on board with Tallulah.

13

Marlene *Manquée*

TALLULAH ARRIVED in New York on January 13, 1931. Her homecoming was, of course, far less spectacular than her leavetaking of England had been. There she was and would remain a household word. In her homeland, however, she was simply an actress from a distinguished Southern family of whom followers of the theater page may have read occasionally. Impressing the image of Tallulah Bankhead on the great majority of Americans was up to Paramount.

Dressed in a simple black dress and soigné white hat, Tallulah stepped off the *Aquitania* followed by Mrs. Lock. Dola had disembarked at Cherbourg, her spontaneity dampened by an expired passport. Will and Florence were among the expectant coterie: hugs and kisses all around. Florence asked her excitedly to recite the death scene from *The Lady of the Camellias*. Such a request, under conditions of stress, would have ordinarily distempered Tallulah. But she looked at Will, healthy and happy, and she knew full well that Florence was largely responsible. While she didn't consent to do Dumas, she did keep her temper.

Tallulah went directly to the Elysee Hotel on East Fifty-fourth Street, off Park Avenue. She moved into a spacious and elegant twelfth-floor suite whose previous tenant had been Ethel Barrymore. The sofas and chairs were done in modish chintz; there were inlaid commodes and smoking tables. The grand piano was covered with a rich Chinese embroidery.

The staff of the Elysee, alerted to Tallulah's distinguished international reputation, were especially solicitous when they discovered that a call for ice, or bootleg liquor, or a pair of nylons was likely to bring a $20 tip. Tallulah kept them hopping, but they hopped eagerly. Messages, visitors, calling cards, bouquets of white lilacs—her favorite fresh flower—poured into the Bankhead suite. And the press came, too.

Paramount set up a series of get-acquainted interviews with all the important columnists in the city. They took to Tallulah straightaway. She had theories about everything: British satire in comparison to American; the charms of Lady Astor; the cachet of certain colors; her favorite movie stars, the political currents in the House of Commons. Her bastardized language and mutant free style, her gritty *brio* were unlike anything they had ever experienced. She was an original. They had merely to copy her words and imply her energies, and they had a story. These are fairly typical Tallulah quotes from that period:

"One can't be smart in a hurry. Last winter, when I opened a theater in London, I flew to Paris in the Early Bird, bought a dress at Worth's, fitted it, flew back that afternoon, and wore it that night. In spite of all the flattering remarks of the press, do you think anyone could persuade me that I looked as chic as—as Daisy Fellowes, for example, in one of those toilets of hers, for which she had wrap, scarf, slippers, purse, brassiere, girdle, lingeries, handkerchief, yes, even stockings and jewels made to order?— *Jamais!*

"In spite of all this ballyhoo about 'Tallulah—the Mysterious,' 'Tallulah the Exotic—the Illusive,' I'm just a good, healthy American girl with a husky voice and the strength of a horse."

She was due to report almost immediately to the set of the first of the five pictures she was contracted to make for Paramount, *Tarnished Lady*. There was time only for a weekend of rest. She visited torch singer Libby Holman at her home in Sands Point. Among Miss Holman's other guests that weekend was Louisa Carpenter, twenty-four, an iconoclastic, tough-talking aviatrix and a direct descendant of Alfred V. Du Pont. The guest list exceeded expectations, and servants were not readily available. So Tallulah, at one point, said to Louisa, "Dahling, would you draw my bath!"

Louisa looked rather stunned at the unusual and peremptory request. "I didn't mean to shock you," Tallulah added. "It's merely that I'm used to ordering women about."

"Not this woman!" Louisa replied.

They became great friends, and that same day, Tallulah asked Louisa to go for a walk with her through the countryside. It was a walk Louisa Carpenter would never forget. Tallulah first ordered her Rolls-Royce brought around. The touring car picked the women up in front of Miss Holman's house. There were two uniformed chauffeurs on board. The passenger cabin was appointed with a fully stocked bar and a portable phonograph on which Tallulah played Bing Crosby records continuously. The two women motored until the car reached the top of a hill.

"We get out here," Tallulah said, as the chauffeur brought the luxurious vehicle to a stop.

"I wondered when we were going to walk," Louisa said, following Tallulah out of the car. From the top of the hill, they walked briskly to the bottom, the Rolls inching behind, Crosby crooning audibly all the while. They reentered the car which proceeded to the top of another hill. The chauffeur opened the door; they disembarked and walked to the bottom. That went on for several hours.

That Monday, sufficiently exercised, Tallulah reported to work at Paramount East in Astoria, Long Island. They began to shoot *Tarnished Lady*, the story of a woman from New York who marries for money in order to save her mother from poverty. The screenplay was devised by Donald Ogden Stewart; George Cukor directed. It was Cukor's first solo directorial effort.

Tarnished Lady took ten weeks to film. Tallulah displayed her bad temper only once during that time, when she refused to don a rather shabby dress designed for the character's poverty period.

"I can't put this thing on," Tallulah said to Cukor.

"You've got to put it on, Tallulah," Cukor replied.

"Well, I won't," Tallulah repeated.

"You'll put the dress on *now*," Cukor demanded. She put it on, and the scene was shot.

For another of *Tarnished Lady*'s episodes, Tallulah was to be shown singing in a lowly cabaret. The cast and crew went on location to Harlem. Tallulah stayed on to socialize in one of the joints they hit, and the newspapers somehow picked up the story.

Distressed at the report of his fair Tallulah cavorting among colored people, Will wrote her a stern, disapproving letter. Tallulah was crushed. All her London escapades had been kept successfully from Daddy. Indeed, one of her primary anxieties about returning home involved the possibility of a disclosure such as this one. Will's displeasure continued to evoke in Tallulah a vague and agonizing guilt. Like a little girl requesting a verifying note in an adult handwriting, she had her producer, Walter Wanger, explain the incident, by telegram, to Will.

"Tallulah showed me your letter of February 14," the missive began. "I think it is scandalous that her sole trip to Harlem should be so misinterpreted. She was sent there with her director Mr. Cukor to see conditions as there was a Harlem nightclub scene in her present picture. But after a visit it was decided atmosphere was too vulgar. . . . I regret episode should have caused such misrepresentation.—WALTER WANGER."

In fact, Tallulah went to Harlem frequently in those days, and she soon became well known and well liked among some segments of the black community. It was not a matter of obtaining liquor because that could be purchased downtown, too, and she continued her nocturnal adventures well after Prohibition. Tallulah made the Harlem nightclub scene because she felt freer uptown to do and see and say. She could also get cocaine there from a black hunchback named Money. There was good jazz and fun smut and all varieties of sexual exhibitions which her natural curiosity impelled her, no doubt, to witness.

There was a quietude about Harlem that she also enjoyed. After repeal, she often went up to the Club Hotcha, for an early dinner. Eddie Steele, a blind black pianist, played for the casual diners, and Tallulah, in a mellow, Play-It-Again-Sam mood, leaned over the piano, requesting tunes and singing along. Sometimes she would press a $50 or $100 bill into Eddie Steele's hand.

"I'm sure your mother would like a new hat, Eddie."

"Thank you, Miss Bankhead."

She would lead blind Eddie to the floor, where they danced quietly together. Once or twice she and some friends went home with Eddie Steele to sit and chat with his affable mother. Tallulah introduced many of her moneyed and famous friends to the various pleasures of Harlem: John C. Wilson, Noel Coward, Cole Porter, and the first Charlie Knickerbocker. She became a friend to many black entertainers, Billie Holiday among them. More than once she bailed the legendary singer out of jail on drug charges.

If Paramount had only been able to utilize all the real facets of Tallulah's personality in the properties they created for her and in the image they very carefully promulgated, they might have made a very important motion-picture star out of Tallulah. But in 1931, Paramount and the nation had Marlene on their minds.

Since the movies had begun to talk a couple of years before Tallulah's return to the United States, the American public had manifested a strange and consistent fascination for the European woman—a category into which Tallulah was shoved because of her eight-year residency in London. Greta Garbo, who was under contract to MGM at the time, was one of the most emulated and commercial film stars in the business. Paramount's own Marlene Dietrich, by the very early thirties, was duplicating, indeed surpassing, Garbo's incredible appeal.

By 1932, Dietrich had made three films for Paramount, *Morocco*, *Dishonoured*, and *Shanghai Express*. They all were spectacularly successful, the last breaking all records at the studio by grossing

$4,000,000 at a time when admission price to a theater was still a dime. Paramount was hoping to turn Tallulah into another Marlene. The reasoning was simple arithmetic: If one Marlene could make $4,000,000, then two Marlenes should double the profits.

John Kobal, in his book *Dietrich,* commented on the emulative phenomenon of which Tallulah was a part: "Prior to the advent of Dietrich, studios had been scrambling for a Garbo in their backlot. Now they wanted a Dietrich as well. Browless, languid, chain-smoking creatures poured into Hollywood from every corner of the globe. If they weren't born with a foreign accent, they quickly acquired one. They appeared through screens of cigarette smoke and vanished into them as quickly as they arrived. . . . Hollywood talent scouts rummaged through Europe, returning with waves of exotics in their tow. In the search for substitutes many talented actresses were sacrificed." He cited Tallulah as the only threat, albeit temporary.

Because they wanted a second Marlene did not mean, paradoxically, that Adolph Zukor, Walter Wanger, and the other executives at Paramount wanted a second-rate star. Nor did they bother to obtain a surrogate Joseph von Sternberg to go with their surrogate Dietrich. They launched a fabulous, extravagant publicity campaign for Tallulah and *Tarnished Lady.* Enormous posters were emplaced in theater lobbies throughout the country, featuring a darkling, sinuous Tallulah, holding a cigarette between her mandarin-long nails, smoke billowing from her hands as though her fingertips were on fire. The bold print announced:

NOW THE PICTURE PRODUCERS WHO BROUGHT YOU DIETRICH BRING YOU ANOTHER WOMAN-THRILL—TALLULAH BANKHEAD. SHE ENTHRALLED A NATION. ENGLAND'S ADORED AMERICAN BEAUTY ON THE SCREEN. GET WITHIN RANGE OF HER RADIANCE—FEEL THE RAPTUROUS THRILL OF HER VOICE, HER PERSON!

On that same poster, a credo issued from the smoky Tallulah's mouth: "I pay as I go. My heart is slave to my head. Men are as pleasant and exciting to me as the lavish gowns I adore. I drink the sparkling cup of love because I know my heart will never betray me. I am TALLULAH the MODERN."

The Paramount Press Sheet, a trade publication which guided theater owners on the techniques of exploitation, came down hard on the electricity metaphor. They advised: "The Bankhead manner is the smart-world manner. But her entire attitude toward life is a charming and electrifying go-to-hell. She's like a *dynamo*. She's *shockingly* likable, *vibratingly* lovable."

To impress the electric appeal of Tallulah on their patrons, the Paramount Press Sheet suggested various possible lobby displays to the theater owners. The most elaborate was a simulated "third-rail episode," using toy trains. "Gap the tracks so they spark a lot," the publicity feed directed. Another suggested lobby display involved a sash cord devised to administer a minor shock to the curious. The cord was to be constructed beside the words: "This girl will shock you . . . her personality registers like a third-rail! Pull the sash and find out for yourself." The theater owners were warned, however, that the shock was to be mild. "If you're going to hurt anybody or make them feel the least bit of inconvenience," the Paramount Press Sheet concluded, "don't use the idea!"

Replete with electric trains and come-hither sash cords, *Tarnished Lady* opened at the Rivoli Theater in New York. The premiere was lush and touted. On the big stage before the picture began, Charles Ruggles introduced Morton Downey, Florence Eldridge, Ruth Roman, Barbara Bennett, and Buddy Rogers to the black-tie audience. Tallulah said a few tremulous words and then sneaked up to the executive offices on the balcony floor of the Rivoli to wait it out alone.

What she heard during the screening was not good. The audience laughed often, but in all the wrong places. They were restless and rude and talkative. She cringed. During this waiting period, Broadway columnist Louis Sobel walked in on Tallulah. "I can't bear to watch it," she said to Sobel, "I just can't. I wish I could stop them. I should have stayed in London."

The press lambasted *Tarnished Lady*, Cukor receiving a good deal of the blame. Tallulah, they agreed, was an interesting performer egregiously handled. Among the insurmountable odds cited was Paramount's lavish publicity campaign, "which suggested that her local appearance was an event comparable in importance to America's entrance into the World War or Lindbergh's conquest of the Atlantic." Richard Watts, Jr., commented that *Tarnished Lady* "might have been devised for Tallulah by her worst enemy in a particularly cruel moment."

Ironically, the engineers responsible for Tallulah's muddy, murky performance did enjoy victory of a sort. Mordant Hall of the New York *Times* wrote, "Miss Bankhead is not unlike Marlene Dietrich and she has the same deep voice." Thornton Delehanty of the New York *Evening Post* observed, "She gives a credible impersonation of Marlene Dietrich singing a song."

George Abbott was brought in to direct the next two movies Tallulah did for Paramount East: *My Sin* and *The Cheat*. Tallulah did succeed in compelling Walter Wanger to cease and desist all overt references to the "Berlin tart" in her publicity, but these two films were as Marlenicized as *Tarnished Lady*. The locales were exotic. Tallulah remained smoky-languid, playing humorless creatures with lurid pasts who gravitated to cabarets. The situations were invariably triangular, with Tallulah forced to choose between two men. She wore shady-lady gowns, stooped a little around the shoulders, and appeared decidedly uncomfortable. Abbott was obviously not her Von Sternberg. *My Sin* and *The Cheat* fared no better than *Tarnished Lady*.

In 1930 and 1931, Paramount was enjoying record prosperity. It had the capital and the faith to carry Tallulah until she scored. Wanger and Zukor buttressed her flagging spirits by blaming the failure of her movies on poor story material and lackluster direction. They continued to pick up her options and even raised her salary from $5,000 to $6,000 a week. They persuaded her, too, that she might fare better on the West Coast. She made plans to move in the beginning of 1932.

Just before the move, the faithful Mrs. Lock was forced temporarily to return to England. Tallulah had an opening in her ménage and made the mistake of telling Aunt Marie by telephone about the problems of recruiting good secretarial help. Marie subsequently applied for the position. She wrote her niece:

MY DEAR TALLULAH,

You may have forgotten but when you first started out in New York, you invited me to leave my family connections and be your secretary. I am situated so I can accept that position now in case you offer it to me and at as good a salary as I am getting. I have a salary of $4,000 a year and, of course, I would like to have $5,000 at least.

This is a hint and not an application. I will say that my five years experience in a newspaper office has made of me a first rate "publicity man"; my social experience has civilized me; and my love for you would warrant me in becoming a shock absorber between you and the clamorous public.

Marie told no one, not her son, not her daughter, Louise, not even her best friend, Mrs. Saffold, but she ached to become part of Tallulah's life, to experience some of the imagined glory and glitter. In her most ambitious imaginings she saw a position with her niece as a wedge from which she would be able to sell at least one of her romantic novels to the industry. But she would be willing to settle for less.

Marie carried on a hot and heavy correspondence with Adolph Zukor, the president of Paramount, from the time that Tallulah first signed with the company, suggesting various publicity gimmicks for more effectively selling Tallulah to the country. In a typical communication to Zukor she proposed that Paramount exploit the imminence of the George Washington bicentennial celebration. "You may have noticed in the paper," she began her letter to the executive, "that there are still living three women whose fathers were Revolutionary soldiers. One of these women is Mrs. Mary Priscilla Tillman, of Berkeley, California. Mrs. Tillman is a native born Alabamian and to have a newsreel feature showing Tallulah presenting this very ancient dame with a flower gift 'as one Alabamian to another' would be of National Interest."

Zukor's assistant responded to Aunt Marie's various brain storms with curt cordiality as a courtesy to their star.

With her naïve fecundity, her frequent letters of advice to Zukor, her unceasing attempts to have her literary works adapted for the screen, Marie became to the Bankhead ménage what Tallulah had been once upon a time to the heavyweights at the Algonquin: a fond and standing joke. Tallulah was not insensitive to Marie's poignant and closeted desires. She was always as gentle and lateral as she could be with the old woman without saying yes to anything. Permitting Marie to join her life was clearly out of the question, though, and Tallulah called to tell her so gingerly just before she left for the West Coast. Tallulah boarded the train while Marie began another romantic novel.

With Tallulah on the luxurious westward-bound Chief were her two favorite English playmates, Audry and Kenneth Carten, who, missing Tallulah as much as she missed them, had journeyed to the United States on what was conceived to be a three-week holiday. The holiday was slated to end several days before Tallulah's scheduled move to Hollywood. As the Cartens' departure drew nigh, Tallulah said to Kenneth, "I can't go out there alone. You and Audry are coming with me."

Much as the idea appealed to their hedonistic instincts, they demurred. Their strict Dutch upbringing mitigated against such frivolity. Unlike Dola Cavendish, they were not financially free to come and go and stay and live as they wished. Kenneth insisted that they could not go; Tallulah continued to plead.

"We'll cut the cards for it," she said. Tallulah called for a deck, divided the pack, and drew an ace. The Cartens prepared to travel west with Tallulah.

The four-and-a-half-day ride to Hollywood was a sybarite's fantasy. Tallulah had been instructed by her studio bosses to gain ten pounds for her next film, so she and the Cartens gorged on food and drink. They giggled a good deal and talked and played games. In between times, Tallulah did crossword puzzles. Edie Smith slept. Audry read Proust. And Kenneth tried to get a good look at Joan Crawford, who was also traveling on the Chief.

It was Joan Crawford finally who invited them to have dinner with her. In her commodious suite, they first dined and then endeavored to fill an evening. Kenneth suggested to Miss Crawford, who had taken out her crocheting and begun to make engaging small talk, that they all play a game of Truth. He explained to the star the simple rules: One was compelled simply to answer any question put to one. She agreed to play.

When it came time for Kenneth to elicit Truth from Joan Crawford, he asked the star whether or not she had ever been unfaithful to her husband. She raised her famous eyebrows, smiled wanly, and objected: "Since none of you are married, I don't think it proper to discuss the subject," she said.

"We're not *virgins* if that's what you mean!" Tallulah bristled.

The subject and the game were happily dropped.

Tallulah rented a fully furnished mansion from silent movie star William Haines on North Stanley Avenue in Hollywood. To staff the Haines mansion, she hired three black servants. She brought another Augustus John for her pine-paneled living room and another Rolls-Royce for her second garage. To impress the natives properly, she purchased thousands of dollars' worth of designer original dresses, though in fact she wore almost nothing but slacks.

Edie Smith admonished Tallulah about such lavish expenditures at a time when most of Hollywood was standing in doorjambs waiting for the economic quake, which was toppling almost every other industry, to hit the motion picture. Tallulah conceded that Edie was right and promised her not to spend any more money "for weeks and weeks and weeks." It was as difficult for Tallulah to cut expenditures as smoking. She finally consented to let Paramount place a good part of her salary in trust for her.

While she waited for her fourth picture, *Thunder Below*, to go into production, Tallulah lived a life of routine disorder. She walked every day for two hours, usually with the Rolls inching behind like some super elegant shadow. She slept a great deal, maintained her adored suntan, and entertained every night. It was less entertainment than constant open house with a group of regular guests. Dietrich was in and out, as was Ethel Barrymore, columnist Jack Cohen, George Cukor, Bobby Newton, Patsy Kelly, and a mystic named Charro.

Tallulah was obsessed with the idea of meeting Greta Garbo.

During many of their constitutional walks, she and the Cartens crept around in the vicinity adjacent to the Swedish star's en- walled and cloistered property. Armed with telescopes, they climbed trees and brooked brambles in an attempt to get a peek at Garbo. Kenneth caught colds, and Tallulah, as often as not, ended up furious and frustrated, catching neither hide nor hair of the mysterious actress.

Among Tallulah's frequent drop-ins were Berthold and Salka Viertel, who were intimate friends of Garbo's and reverential re- specters of her privacy fetish. Since the Viertels felt duty bound to divulge nothing about Garbo, they were made uncomfortable by Tallulah's persistent reference to her. Tallulah and ménage began, therefore, to refer to Greta Garbo as "that person." It was decreed in fact that anyone who uttered the cabalistic proper name would have to pay $1 to everyone else who was present at the time of the gauche utterance.

The Viertels finally did arrange a meeting between the two ex- otics. Tallulah and several friends—the Cartens among them— were invited to the Viertels' house in Santa Monica where Garbo was scheduled to appear. They piled into Tallulah's car, solemn and silent in their nervous expectations. Tallulah finally inter- rupted the baleful quiet. "You're all so damned unnerved," she said, "you'd think we were on our way to meet *Greta Garbo!*" For that she was compelled to shell out $5.

The inevitable happened. When Greta Garbo made her en- trance, ravishing in black crepe-de-Chine pajamas, Tallulah and Company burst into nervous laughter which almost alienated the self-conscious Swede. Tallulah pulled herself together, shook Gar- bo's hand, and pulled her eyelashes.

"Ow!" said Greta Garbo.

"I just wanted to see if they were real," said Tallulah Bankhead, putting up a fine show of insouciance. She turned away from Garbo, poked Kenneth in the ribs, and hissed, "Brandy. Get me some brandy. I'm so nervous I can faint."

By the end of the evening, however, Tallulah was relaxed, and she and Greta Garbo were getting on famously. Tallulah invited Garbo to her house for dinner; Garbo accepted enthusiastically.

Garbo possessed apparently the same somewhat elaborate, though puerile, sense of humor as Tallulah. When the dinner evening arrived, the Swedish star showed up at Tallulah's disguised in a black wig, mandarin dress, and Orientalized eyes. She told Tallulah in a thick and hybrid Sino-Scandinavian accent: "So sorry, but Miss Garbo vill not be able to join you. She send me instead."

Tallulah was no less eager to shock the Hollywood community than she had been to rock London, New York, Washington, Jasper, and Montgomery—and no more discreet about whom she alienated. She attended a party to which most of the important people of the motion-picture industry were invited and announced in the prime of the evening that she would like to sing a song dedicated to Louis B. Mayer. Mayer grinned widely and walked up to the piano, beside which Tallulah stood. She began her song, flirting tremulously with the key:

> Make my bed
> And light the lights
> I'll be home late tonight
> Bye, Bye JEW BIRD

Louis B. Mayer left, enraged.

Her language was as colorful as ever, and her homosexual humor, while it amused some, offended others mightily.

In her own living room or in other people's, she would frequently pick out the stodgiest-looking woman in the room, throw her arms around her, and whisper, "Surely, you must know by now that I'm mad about you!"

The quake arrived in Depression-proof Hollywood just about the time Tallulah had finished her fourth picture for Paramount, in March, 1932, *Thunder Below*. Charles Bickford and Paul Lukas completed the triangle in this one. The Paramount press boys tried more desperately than ever to pull people in to see the torrid Tallulah struggle against insurmountable odds somewhere in Central America: "Imagine her, the Exotic, the Sophisticated," they raved. "Imagine Tallulah Bankhead, the flower of a tropic camp, the only white woman on half a continent." Some of the press rallied on Tallulah's behalf, deeming her a potentially exciting star, but *Thunder Below* was dismissed rudely.

Paramount went into receivership. The president of RKO predicted that unless drastic economies were undertaken, the whole movie industry would be bankrupt in six months. Tallulah, along with most of the other contract stars, was forced to take a cut in salary. The cut came at a particularly inopportune time.

The government billed Tallulah for $15,000 in back taxes, she was overdrawn at the bank, and every day she received a plea for help from some relative who was hurting from the Depression. There was Aunt May, for instance, her mother's sister, whom Tallulah had never even met. Aunt May wrote to Tallulah, in care of the studio, a series of pathetic letters about the fall of the high and mighty Sledges. Aunt Marie wanted mortgage money so that she would not lose a little farm she had bought in Wetumpka, Alabama, for her old age. Eugenia, who was still in Europe, often needed financial assistance. Tallulah did what she could, wisely resisting the instinct to dig into her Paramount trust. The bleak financial news frightened Tallulah. Under ordinary circumstances she might have left Paramount to return to England or to a legitimate Broadway play, but this was clearly no time for experimentation.

Just before she began her last film for Paramount, *The Devil and the Deep*, Audry and Kenneth Carten chose to return to England. They too were smarting financially. Though they lived with Tallulah, Kenneth had been able to pay for many of his and his sister's living expenses by acting in an occasional Paramount picture. Now that the blight was upon the studio, work was scarcer and scarcer. What Kenneth did not know, however, and what he did not find out for several years, was that Tallulah had covertly *induced* Paramount to use him, that she had, in effect, paid his salary all along. What the studio paid to Kenneth Carten for his occasional and minor acting endeavors was taken out of Tallulah's pay. Tallulah would have continued the ruse, but jobs—even mock jobs—were no longer that plentiful. When the Cartens left, she asked actor Alan Vincent to move in with her.

In *The Devil and the Deep*, she played the wayward wife of a madding submarine captain, portrayed by Charles Laughton. The picture introduced Laughton to the American audience. Also among the crew were Cary Grant and Gary Cooper, who is torn between his love for Tallulah and his loyalty to the sub. The movie climaxes aboard the submerged vehicle with a magnificent mad scene by Laughton who attempts to drown himself, his wife, and her lover by unbattening the hatches. Tallulah, aided by Gary Cooper, escapes from the submarine by shimmying up a rope in high heels and a sequin dress. She and Cooper flee, à la *Morocco*, into a piece of desert located conveniently right on the edge of town. She says, "I want never to have been born." He answers, "There's magic out there. Do you want to kill it?"

The Devil and the Deep was well received, though it was Laughton's picture. Heartened by this small success, Tallulah asked for a raise when her contract came up for renewal. Paramount refused. Tallulah threatened to leave. The studio and Tallulah adopted a wait-and-see policy, and she was lent to MGM with the hope that a fresh approach by a new studio might indicate to Paramount what they had been doing wrong.

Actually, Paramount was watching for more than Tallulah's growth potential under optimum conditions. In 1932, there was blazing through the entire film industry a movement which Will Hays, the puritan deacon of the Motion Picture Code, likened joyously to "an avenging fire, seeking to clean as it burns." The Catholic Church, the Bank of America, the Presbyterian Mr. Hays, and thousands of organized watchdogs of American sexual morality were up in arms about the various excesses of the industry: the delineation of infidelity unpunished, miscegenation, gangsterism, dishabille, the frequent and favorable depiction in brittle comedies of smart-alecky New York types. They were upset about lurid, misleading advertising, licentious fan magazine stories, and the offscreen behavior of some members of the motion-picture community.

Hays even considered adding to the list of no-nos in the Motion

Picture Code, which had been formulated in 1930 but ignored for two years, a category called "verbal moral turpitude," the expressing of irreligious, un-American, and downright dangerous ideas by screen stars who were in a position—vis-à-vis their fans—to pollute, despoil, and lead from the paths of righteousness.

At a meeting of the Motion Picture Association in Hollywood, the Bank of America's Dr. A. H. Giannini, expressed dire concern over the low moral standards of the film community. Giannini, according to Will Hays' *Memoirs*, told the producers that "any convenience the Bank of America might extend the studios would become a moot problem of conscience in his own personal case unless a change of policy was quickly effected."

There was talk of state or federal censorship laws. Louella Parsons, in August, 1932, wrote approvingly: "We are in for an era of clean pictures unprecedented in the history of this industry."

While Paramount waited for the avenging fire, Tallulah gave to Gladys Hall of *Motion Picture* magazine a scoop which in the annals of journalistic *scandale* came to be called "the Tallulah Bankhead I-Want-a-Man-Story." The article, based on an interview with Tallulah, hit the stands in the late summer of 1932.

Miss Hall began the piece with an explanation of Tallulah's demimondaine status in Tinseltown. She reported that there was a legion of Hollywood hostesses, Marion Davies, Connie Bennett, and Bebe Daniels Lyon among them, "who prefer not to be home to Tallulah." The reason? "She disguises nothing. She calls a spade a spade. . . . She gives to all the functions and living and loving, of body and soul, their round Rabelaisian biological names."

"She has a romantic interlude," Miss Hall continued, accurately, "and, afterwards, discusses it with lurid details and complete unreserve. . . . She is said to dilate upon his ways and wiles, his abilities and disabilities, his prowess or his lack of prowess, with such consummate abandon that the unfortunate male, if present, can think of no recourse except immediate suicide."

Miss Hall then sallied into several direct quotes from her interview with Tallulah—an interview through which Tallulah smoked and paced in an appropriately "scarlet" pajama outfit, her page-boy flying. Edie Smith was in the next room, making mad cool-it gestures at her employer.

Tallulah first of all twitted the inaccuracy of reporting which made her out to be a madcap fool with no serious side. "I am serious," she objected. "I am serious about my work. I am serious about love. I am serious about marriage and children and friendship and the whole stuff of life. I pretend not to be.

"I am serious about marriage, too serious to indulge in it. . . . I know that once I get a thing, or a man—I'll tire of it and of him. I am the type that fattens on unrequited love, on the unattainable, on the just-beyond reach. The minute a man begins to languish over me, I stiffen and it is *finis*.

"I am serious about wishing I had children, beautiful children. I wouldn't care for the other variety. I love anything and everything that is beautiful. Perhaps beautiful is not the word. Personality is more like it.

"I'm serious about love. I'm damned serious about it now, of all times. I haven't had an *affaire* for six months. Six months! Too long. I am not promiscuous, you know. Promiscuity implies that attraction is not necessary. . . . I may lay my eyes on a man and have an *affaire* with him the next hour. If there's anything the matter with me now, it's certainly not Hollywood or Hollywood's state of mind. . . . the matter with me is, I WANT A MAN! . . . six months is a long, long while. I want a man!"

Tallulah was letting off accumulated steam. Throughout the filming of *The Devil and the Deep* and her first MGM movie, *Faithless*, she was on one of her recurring austerity kicks. She wasn't drinking, or smoking, or having *affaires*. She was going to bed early and leading what Alan Vincent referred to as "a nun's life." Gladys Hall had caught her on a heady, randy, soothsaying afternoon. Tallulah had gone on and on and on.

When the story finally appeared, it stirred up several hornets' nests. The Hays Office demanded that action be taken against *someone*—Tallulah, *Motion Picture* magazine, or both. Paramount advised Tallulah to deny that she had said any of it; that is what she did. To make matters much worse, *Time* devoted a column and a half to the story and its wake.

Will Bankhead saw the story, considered writing a censorious letter to his daughter, then decided against it. She was thirty years old and no longer his discipline problem. He did, however, dispatch various letters to friends of Will Hays, Will Rogers, Jr., among them, petitioning them all to put in a good word for Tallulah.

Marie, in Montgomery, almost went into cardiac arrest. She heard about the story from a friend who had, in turn, been told about it in the beauty parlor by a "snickering manicurist." After spending the night in tears, Marie wrote an excoriating letter to Tallulah, in which, among other things, she enumerated the possible consequences of such tawdry publicity. She seethed:

1. Your luster as a star has been tarnished.
2. Your employers would have every ground on that basis to discipline you, which means a cut in your salary.
3. Your enemies will have a festive time of Ha-Has, and
4. The best your friends can say is that Marlene's "dish of champagne" has made you drunk

She said elsewhere in the letter, "Your words sounded like the yapping of a hot canine locked up in the kennel. You don't need a secretary—you need an attendant."

Tallulah's primary concern was not Aunt Marie, but Daddy, to whom she had not written in several months because of her hectic schedule. Consequently, she was not sure if Will was in Jasper, Montgomery, or Washington. She telegrammed Marie immediately:

IF DADDY HAS READ IT PLEASE SEND HIM THIS WIRE I DON'T KNOW WHERE HE IS IF HE HAS NOT DON'T WORRY ABOUT HIM AND ABOUT IT HEREAFTER I SHALL REFUSE ALL MAGAZINE INTERVIEWERS I AM SO SORRY YOU BEING SO UPSET BUT PLEASE BELIEVE ME I COULD NOT AND WOULD NOT SAY OR DO ONE TENTH OF THE THINGS ACCREDITED TO ME IT IS ONE OF THE MANY DISADVANTAGES OF BEING IN THE PUBLIC EYE IN MY CAPACITY LOVE AND BLESS YOU—TALLULAH

Tallulah's MGM movie, *Faithless*, co-starring Robert Montgomery, was released during the *Motion Picture* melee. It was the picture that should have kept her in Hollywood. The new studio freshened, livened, and softened both her appearance and her "image." Her hair was fluffed, and a small bang took the hardness out of her face. She wore soft wools by Adrienne. Marlene was wholly exorcised.

Unfortunately, because of the reform movement in the industry, *Faithless* was cut to ribbons. The movie was the story of a spoiled rich girl who loses her fortune and becomes a better person for it. Originally the film's emphasis was on the comedy of wisecrack, on moments such as the one in which Tallulah's banker warns her of trouble ahead. "Do you realize," he tells her in the beginning of the movie, "that because you won't reduce your personal expenditures, I've had to cut everything else—even your charities—even your father's most beloved project—the Morgan Home for Girls?"

"Fine," Tallulah replies. "I don't believe in delinquent girls. Silly weaklings."

These comedic portions were followed by episodes of travail, redemption, and reform. Because of the Hays Office, however, and the moralistic demands being placed upon the industry, the spoiled rich girl was made to pay inordinately for her crimes against orphan girls and fine American values. The levity was minimized in the final print. Her dark travail was emphasized ruinously.

In spite of what was done to *Faithless*, the critics perceived in the snatches of comedy that remained a new, improved, and seemingly unburdened Tallulah. A reviewer on the Los Angeles *Herald* predicted: "Give this actress more sophisticated comedy and the same sort of excellent photography she receives in this picture and I'll venture to say she will double her screen following." There was general agreement that MGM had found Tallulah Bankhead's métier.

But it was too late . . . too late for that particular métier and too late for Tallulah. The studio talent scouts were home from Europe and rummaging now through Nebraska, not for exotics or drawing room comediennes, but for girls next door. They were glorifying the American girl and singing the praises of Nancy Carroll, who made a picture called *Honey* and then one called *Sweetie* and then one described as "Sweeter than Sweetie."

There was some interest at Paramount and at MGM in having Tallulah stay on, but not enough so that her salary demands were met. Louis B. Mayer, who hadn't forgotten the "Jew bird" incident or the *Motion Picture* article, called Tallulah into his office, offered her a contract and a long lecture on morality. She wasn't having either.

By mutual agreement, and after almost two years, Tallulah and the film industry parted company.

14

Helter-Skelter

DURING THE FINAL WEEKS of her Hollywood experience, Tallulah met Elsa Maxwell at a small party in Beverly Hills. She told Miss Maxwell that she was about to go east, where she would try her luck on Broadway. To bid farewell to the movie capital, Tallulah planned a party of her own.

"Won't you come?" she asked.

"I'd be delighted," Miss Maxwell replied.

As the rotund climber continued to circulate, Tallulah turned to George Cukor and whispered, "She knows that I'm not exactly riding the crest professionally. The bitch won't show."

And she didn't.

After the termination of her motion-picture contract, capped by a wild, albeit Maxwell-less soiree, Tallulah returned to New York in an attempt to find a producer for a play she had optioned, a sophisticated comedy about a bride jilted at the altar, *Forsaking All Others*.

Tallulah was never without Broadway offers. The problem was not quantity, but quality. As the scripts arrived, they were placed atop a monumental pile of similar entries which Tallulah never touched. Edie Smith screened them and passed them on to Tallulah if they seemed suitable for her hybrid, hothouse talents.

Tallulah liked *Forsaking All Others* when she read it first in early 1932, though she realized that it would require a great deal of fixing. The play was co-authored by a young man named Cavett who had been a cameraman on one of her Paramount pictures, and being part of that kind of upward mobility always enchanted her. Tallulah's career in Hollywood, however, at the time of her first reading was still somewhat promising, so she passed it on to her good friend Hope Williams. After Tallulah made her decision to leave the movies, finding nothing better than *Forsaking All Others* in the leaning slush pile, Tallulah bought it back from Miss Williams, who was otherwise committed.

Tallulah settled into the Gotham Hotel and attempted, without success, to interest Broadway backers in the play. It had, after all, been eleven years since Broadway audiences had seen Tallulah Bankhead on the legitimate stage. Her English success was well publicized through the efforts of the Hollywood press corps, but her movie career had turned out to be less than electrifying. Since the moneymen were unimpressed, she decided to dip into her trust fund and finance the play herself. That fact was kept from the public lest it undermine her professional status.

Though she picked Archie Selwyn, a gentle, darling man, as titular producer, it was Tallulah who hired, fired, and made most of the decisions. In the best tradition of the English theater, this made Tallulah Bankhead an actor-manager of sorts. She had a tendency to hire friends, but they were talented friends who did no disservice to the play.

She was daring and creative in choosing Fred Keating as her leading man. Keating, an eminent magician who specialized in making birds vanish, was down on his luck when Tallulah cast him in this, his first dramatic part. He was living at the Lambs

Club and had just declared bankruptcy, declaring his assets: "one canary worth $1; one canary cage worth $1,000." His liabilities amounted to $8,000.

Keating was one of life's amusing, compatible losers, one of many such types after whom Tallulah looked. He was picked up years later on some charge and put into Bellevue for observation. Tallulah at the time had just finished campaigning for Harry Truman. When she heard about Keating's inelegant incarceration, she fumed, "God damn it! If I can get Harry Truman into the White House, I can get Fred Keating out of Bellevue." She called the mayor's office. Keating was released.

She also cast Andrew Lawlor in an important part. Blue-eyed, wavy-haired, a graduate of the University of Alabama who, like Will, had sung there in the Glee Club, Lawlor was her concurrent escort and man-about-town. Ilka Chase, marvelous in the comedy of wisecrack, was chosen as Tallulah's love rival. Hattie Carnegie, Inc., designed Tallulah's clothes; Donald Oenslanger did the sets. Harry Wagstaff Gribble, whose name amused Tallulah, was assigned to direct the vehicle.

Unfortunately, Tallulah ran the production as she ran her household: wastefully and extravagantly. Jean Dalrymple, who was handling publicity for the show, had worked in John Golden's office before her stint with *Forsaking All Others*. Accustomed to the polish and professionalism of her previous employ, she was aghast at the turmoil and convolutions that attended every procedure. "Everything was terribly complicated and everyone seemed to take two steps forward only immediately to take three steps back," she recalled.

And like Tallulah's life, the show was characterized by impatience and impetuosity. Jean Dalrymple argued the point that *Forsaking All Others* was a vehicle of promise and sparkle not yet ready to go into production. Nobody listened. There were production meetings every afternoon and cast parties every night. The difference between the two was negligible. When the effects on her grievous inefficiency were several times made manifest, Tallulah had a tantrum and fired a director. Gribble had a breakdown. Cavett filled in temporarily, followed by Arthur J. Beckhard. He was replaced, days before the New York opening, by Thomas Mitchell.

Tallulah attracted the same kind of audiences on the American stage that she had attracted in London. When *Forsaking All Others* opened in Boston, the cheap balcony seats were filled with young women whose behavior astonished the orchestra section. They cheered Tallulah's entrance and hissed the fugitive bridegroom who abandoned her at the altar. There were similar demonstrations in Providence and finally in New York. Columnist Ward Morehouse commented: "The balcony can be heard shrieking her praises long after the orchestra has given up the pursuit."

On the other hand, there were the less vocal but very loyal Beautiful People of the day whom Tallulah knew and amused. In Washington, largely because of Will, the premiere performance was attended by the politically august. Alice Roosevelt Longworth sat in Row D; Will was in Row C. Senators, Representatives, and a prestigious gathering from the embassies all turned out. Will met and took a shine to Jean Dalrymple at a cast party in the capital. Tallulah, who was enormously sensitive to such things, watched Miss Dalrymple's evasive strategies with great amusement. She chided her later: "I just don't understand you, Jean. Daddy was obviously attracted to you. What have you got to lose?"

They moved into New York and played to an opening-night audience that included Amelia Earhart, AE Matthews, Philip Barry, Ruth Gordon, Rex Evans, Helen Menken, and Hope Hampton.

With all its failings, the play was probably as good as, if not better than, most of the vehicles Tallulah had ridden on the London stage. The audience in New York roared at the first-act curtain line. Tallulah, abandoned by her bridegroom, is comforted by the rector who was supposed to have performed the ceremony. He lasciviously invites her home. "Thanks," she replies, "I *know* Jesus loves me."

There was a speakeasy scene in which Tallulah had an abundance of deft, pungent lines which she delivered with inimitable comic shadings. When a young, hiccuping woman enters the cabaret, her clothes disheveled, Tallulah commented, "Probably hurled from a speeding car." And one of the highlights of the evening was the inevitable Tallulah cartwheel, followed by an energetic "Whoopee!"

Tallulah's personal reviews were outstanding, but the offstage whoopee took its toll. *Forsaking All Others* arrived in New York a concatenation of clever lines and Bankhead stunts. The work required to emend its dramatic failures had never been got to; it had not been rendered whole. About Tallulah, Brooks Atkinson said: "She is an amusing young lady with an individual and enlivening style of acting. She can underscore a line with true stage sagacity." The play he dismissed lukewarmly with the words: "It will serve."

Forsaking All Others did not unfortunately serve. Under the best of conditions the economics of the Broadway theater are more rigorous than the London stage. The American counterparts of Tallulah's Silk Hats and her Gallery Girls could not fill the Times Square Theater as the Lyric Theatre had been filled. There was simply too much of the American middle to whom Tallulah was not yet appealing. And these were not only not the best of times; they were the worst. The play opened on March 1, 1933, the day the banks closed. By March 6, Arch Selwyn announced in the newspapers: "Checks will be accepted at the box office or by mail for the duration of the bank holiday."

Hoping that the play would somehow catch on, Tallulah kept it running at a loss for fourteen weeks. She lost $40,000 before she decided finally to close it. Tallulah could not very well cast the blame for this wipe-out wholly on anyone but herself. She did manage, however, to inculpate Leland Hayward. Hayward was an agent at the time and apparently an unofficial adviser to Tallulah, a man on whom she relied. In her autobiography, Tallulah charges that he was "suffering from delusions of invincibility." According to Tallulah, Hayward hyped her hopes with false optimism. He promised her that with "one flourish of his magic wand . . . investors would stampede to my door. . . . Hayward proved one of the most elastic reeds I was ever to lean on."

There were two kinds of men in Tallulah's life: those like Arch

Selwyn, who took off for Florida in the midst of the out-of-town travail, like Fred Keating and numerous others from whom Tallulah would brook anything. She seemed to expect nothing more from them than good company and dependable dependence. Then there were those from whom she expected a certain degree of infallibility. When *they* failed her, she reacted with a vengeance.

Back in London, Sir Gerald had decided to take a vacation from *The Dancers* after it had been playing but six weeks. This infuriated her. She made inordinate, overweening demands on the actor, insisting on a salary hike and a two-week holiday for herself. She had the insight, regarding this incident, to write: "I had a recurrence of the pangs I experienced when Daddy denied me the picnic." By the time Leland Hayward disappointed her she was too far removed from the source of her anxieties to recognize the transference phenomenon.

Fortunately, she recouped some of her losses when MGM bought *Forsaking All Others* for Joan Crawford. With Joe Mankiewicz healing its dramaturgical wounds, it was a far better motion picture than it had been a play. Tallulah, as it turned out, had excellent taste in picking the raw materials of successful screenplays. Every one of the plays she elected to do on Broadway during the early thirties was bought by Hollywood. And all of them made excellent vehicles for other actresses.

Hoping to forge a dramatic career on Broadway as she had done in London, she jumped almost immediately into another play. Two months after the demise of *Forsaking All Others*, she was rehearsing *Jezebel* by Owen Davis under the direction of Guthrie McClintic. It was scheduled to open in September, 1933. Tallulah had been in rehearsal for ten days when she began to experience excruciating pains in the abdominal and pelvic regions. Her personal physician, Dr. Mortimer Rodgers, the brother of Richard Rodgers, put her into Doctors Hospital for observation.

Bulletins were issued at the end of August. The malady was described variously as a "slight illness," "an undiagnosed abdominal complaint," "kidney stones." She remained in the hospital for nine weeks. When she was up to it, the actors came to her and rehearsed at her bedside. McClintic was set on Tallulah and kept the company intact at great financial loss. Most of the time, however, Tallulah was in no condition to work.

Tallulah's primary concern was Daddy. Every ruse was employed to prevent him from undertaking the trip from Alabama to New York. He had suffered his first heart attack that April, while making a speech on the floor of the House. The stress of worry or the strain of travel could have been disastrous.

Benumbed with codeine, she returned to the play for a couple of days only to be recommitted—this time to Lenox Hill Hospital —with a soaring fever. There was a bowel stoppage. The three doctors who were by then in charge of her case decided to perform exploratory surgery. On November 3, 1933, a hysterectomy was performed on Tallulah. She was thirty-one years old.

Tallulah had had sexual relations some months before with a very well-known movie actor. From him, she had contracted gonorrhea. The gonococci had invaded her uterine cavity, ascended up into the tubes and ovaries, and finally into the membrane lining of her abdominal cavity. Her body was ravaged with pus by the time of the operation; she was down to seventy pounds. Only by removing all her reproductive organs were the doctors able to save her life.

Her condition was touch and go for days after the operation. She remained in the hospital for several weeks. By December 1 she was back at the Elysee with Edie Smith and a registered nurse. The fact of the hysterectomy was never withheld from friends or family, most of whom assumed that Tallulah had had some kind of malignancy. Only Edie Smith and Stephan Cole were told about the real cause of her condition. Of that, Tallulah was profoundly ashamed.

For weeks, she would see no one. After the physical pain was gone, she descended into a Stygian melancholia. She would tell a friend, actor George Hyland, years after: "Normal women get terribly melancholic when they have a hysterectomy, and I was pretty normal for an abnormal woman."

She had conceived and aborted repeatedly because the timing had always been wrong. Nonetheless, she spoke always of her desire to bear "beautiful children." She cosseted the notion of her underlying normality and felt an overwhelming admiration for women who could determine themselves biologically, as well as artistically. Whether or not she would eventually have borne children is beside the point. Tallulah must have considered her incapacity a cruel and woeful denial.

Because of her weight loss and her depression, Tallulah took on the emaciated look of the Augustus John portrait. She cried often and for no apparent reason. Her mood swings, which had always been erratic, were exacerbated. She stayed with the euphoria-producing opiates long after she needed them to slake her physical discomfort.

By the Christmas holidays she was well enough to travel. Though the doctors advised a warmer climate, she elected to spend some time with Daddy in Alabama. She had not seem him in two years. They had what Will described as "a grand old time." At Daddy's request, she made an appearance at a local movie house in Jasper and almost suffered a relapse from the exertion. Back in New York, she went back to bed for several weeks to recuperate from the activity.

Tallulah made no grand plans, but she did take stock. She broke her trust to pay for her illness; and she was in real financial trouble. There was no getting around the fact that between Hollywood, her hysterectomy, her financial wipe-out Tallulah's repatriation had been a dismal failure. She decided, in the spring, to return to England. She hoped, at the very least, that the change would lift her spirits.

In March, 1934, she sailed on the *Bremen* and was cheered immeasurably to receive her first fan letter from a particularly resourceful English fan when the ship docked at Cherbourg. She was afraid her fans had forgotten her. At Waterloo Station, mobs gathered to welcome her back. Mammoth placards read: TALLU-LAH RETURNS! And SHE'S BACK.

Her long hair down to her shoulders, wearing a tweedy long coat and a brown hat with a dash of enlivening feathers, she stepped into the Waterloo mob. "I've been ill for five months," she explained. "I want to take in some plays, see old friends, and just vacation."

She checked into the Hotel Splendide and then took over Dola Cavendish's splendid digs in Regent's Park. The Marquess of Donegal commented that she was "a more serious and poignant Tallulah than the one we used to know." But she began making the party rounds, doing a fair amount of drinking and doping, however, and the old Tallulah reappeared.

Charles Cochran held a party in his flat at the top of the Aldwych Theatre: a posh affair with red carpets, Prince George, and a security system which should have rendered it as uncrashable as Alcatraz. Tallulah was invited by Douglas Fairbanks, who at the last minute was unable to attend. She telephoned the young man who accompanied her to England.

"I haven't got a gink," she told him, "gink" being Tallulah talk for date, eligible 'male, one-night-stand, or swain. "You're going to take me to the party."

"The party's uncrashable, Tallulah."

"We'll see about that," she said.

After a nerve-shattering drive through a green English fog, they arrived. Tallulah's friend somehow gained admittance. They stood together at the top of a staircase waiting to be presented to Prince George. After several minutes, the prince approached Tallulah. They chatted amiably. Tallulah laughed: "I got my gink in with no trouble at all. Something should be done about your security system."

At a party of her own, which wasn't taking on the organic fluidity which characterizes successful gatherings, she whispered to Ivor Novello: "Ask me to do my impressions."

"What?"

"My impressions."

Novello walked into the center of the room, held up his arms for attention, and shouted toward Tallulah, "Tallulah, won't you do your impressions for us?"

"Please, dahling," she said, "I've come to England to get some rest, and I don't intend to perform."

There followed a wave of solicitous noises. Tallulah conceded with great reluctance, began with an impression of Elisabeth Bergner in *Escape Me Never,* and remained center stage for more than half an hour, bringing the party together.

At yet another party, she sat regally in a chair with a group of young men literally at her feet. Among them was black impresario Jimmy Daniels. Several other black people had been invited to the gathering. One of them, a very prominent society woman, entered the room carrying a platinum vanity case encrusted with a coruscating array of large and precious stones. Tallulah, who always knew precisely the right thing to say, except when she chose to say precisely the opposite, eyed the case and mumbled, "Probably given to her by some dirty nigga." Tallulah leaned over, kissed Jimmy Daniels, and toasted with her champagne glass: "To my grandmother. If she could see me now, she'd roll over in her grave."

Rested, partied, and exhibited, Tallulah began to look around for "the right play." As a sort of warm-up exercise, she did a benefit for the Indian Earthquake Fund and toured the music halls for five weeks in a sketch written by Audry Carten and her sister Waveney. She would have stayed on except that she received an excited transatlantic call from her friend Jock Whitney. Tallulah had been seeing a good deal of Whitney since her return from Hollywood. He was a handsome, dashing sportsman, whose father, Payne Whitney, who died during a game of tennis in 1927, had left him the largest gross estate ever appraised in the United States up until that time. Except that he was already married, the possibility of marriage to Jock appealed enormously to Tallulah. On the telephone, he told her about a play called *Dark Victory,* which he wanted to produce in New York with Tallulah starring. She left England straightaway.

In her book about the problem called *Marty Mann Answers Your Questions About Drinking and Alcoholism,* Miss Mann, founder of the National Council on Alcoholism, discusses various traumas that can precipitate changes in the behavior patterns of the inveterate drinker. To the question "Can alcoholism suddenly develop after many years of normal drinking?" she replies, "Yes, it can. Usually this can be traced to some kind of shock—a physical shock from a severe illness or an accident, or a psychological shock such as the loss of a wife or child."

Tallulah's drinking appears to have become a more serious problem during this period. Whether she ever crossed a Maginot Line into alcoholism depends upon which definition of the disease one accepts. But her hysterectomy can be considered both a severe illness and a severe loss. Following the operation, the alcohol she consumed seemed to have an increasingly dramatic effect upon her behavior.

She was rehearsing *Dark Victory,* a play about a Bridgehampton socialite who develops cancer of the brain and changes her lifestyle. She was staying at the Gotham Hotel and one night entertained a coterie of actresses that included Estelle Winwood, Laurette Taylor, and Gladys Henson. After midnight one of the ladies happened to mention that Sybil Thorndike, who was in New York appearing in *The Distaff Side,* was staying at the same hotel.

Tallulah, high on champagne, insisted that the distinguished English actress be rung up immediately, in spite of the unanimous implorations to the effect that Dame Sybil had very likely retired for the night. Tallulah would not be moved. She called her on the telephone and invited her in for a drink.

Dame Sybil entered the suite attired in a gunnysack robe roped in the middle, looking vaguely like Joan unrepented. Tallulah rose from her chair, knelt at her feet, and began a knowledgeable, though somewhat logorrheic, paean to the pure majesty, the utter brilliance, the dazzling star quality of the visiting actress. The obeisant Tallulah, still on her knees, ended the panegyric with a heartfelt "You fucking old miracle—what'll you have to drink?"

Dame Sybil responded, "You're terribly sweet. A sherry, please."

Dark Victory opened to disastrous reviews, its demise expedited by the fact that Tallulah became ill once again—this time with a rare head infection begun when she squeezed a pimple on her lip. The part Tallulah originated went to the same movie actress who finally did *Jezebel* in its screen version: Bette Davis.

That Tallulah had none of the commercial magnetism for the American theatergoing public that she had for the English was demonstrated dramatically by the fate of the next play into which she leaped, John Colton and Clemence Randolph's adaptation of Somerset Maugham's *Rain*, the very same property which ten years ago had almost driven her to suicide or a reasonable facsimile.

Producer Sam Harris had been instrumental then in suggesting Tallulah to Basil Dean. He was eager to revive it in 1935, but only on condition that Tallulah agree to do it. Tallulah was undecided. On the one hand, she felt that the property had rendered her miserable enough for one lifetime, that she would have to play in America to an audience who had seen Jeanne Eagels' interpretation, suffering the inevitable comparisons; on the other hand, there was the challenge of the role and the possibility that she could finally and supremely vindicate herself vis-à-vis Mr. W. Somerset Maugham.

Her self-confidence, always as low as a dachshund's belly, was closer to the pavement than ever. Sam Harris, in an attempt to convince her, promised, "I'll give you the Music Box Theater. It has never had a flop yet."

"Don't worry," Tallulah rejoined. "I'll fix that."

She agreed finally to do it and even convinced herself that it had been a good thing that she had not portrayed the prostitute ten years ago in London. She told a friend, "I was such a natural mimic then I couldn't have done anything else but give a good imitation of Jeanne Eagels."

Sam Forrest was to direct. The scenery was built to resemble, as closely as possible, the set on which Jeanne Eagels had worked in 1923; some of it, in fact, was from that original production. To facilitate matters for Tallulah, the character was modified just slightly to hail from Texas, though Tallulah put more magnolia than cactus in her dialect.

In the out-of-town tryouts, she was fearsomely nervous. She entered in a whory red dress with bangles dangling. She shook so that the bangles not only dangled, but dingled. She pulled herself together and portrayed Sadie as a far less vulnerable creature than Jeanne Eagels' prostitute had been. Though the playing was riddled with weaknesses and lack of definition, there were moments, such as the one in which she talks to Sergeant O'Hara about her religious conversion, which impressed many as brilliant, vivid, indeed memorable. The audience in Philadelphia went a little bit crazy with huzzahs. She was forced to make a curtain speech and said, "When I came here tonight, I felt more as though I was coming to an execution than to an opening. But through your reception, I feel as though I were reprieved for the time being."

The reviews, many of them, were glowing. The Philadelphia critics assumed that the performance would be tidied up before the play arrived in New York. Edie was instructed to clip each of the reviews, mount them neatly, and send them on to Mr. Maugham in England.

Alas, the performance remained unfinished. Tallulah never acquired the faith, or the strength, or the technique from her director to fashion an organic rendition. Once again, the critics in New York commended Tallulah on her promise. Her first-night audience was riveted. Marlene Dietrich banged so hard on the arm of her chair she almost broke it off.

Withal, the reviews should have evoked more interest than they did. Next to her London notices, they read like paeans. The fact was that Tallulah could not get away with riding vehicles or pulling stunts on the Broadway stage. She did not have the drawing power, the following, or the charisma for it.

She tried just once again in this attempt to replicate her English feat. The play was *Something Gay*, and it was the worst of the lot.

By 1935 Tallulah's plight, rather than her achievements, was becoming grist for the Sunday drama sections. John Mason Brown summed it up in the New York *Evening Post*:

> Tallulah Bankhead is so obviously an actress of uncommon possibilities that it is a pity that plays which are worthy of her talents do not seem to come her way. She has a personality that is arresting; a face that is pliant; a body that she uses gracefully; eyes that give instantaneous projection to the meaning of a line; and an unquestionable aptitude for the

nuances of comedy as well as a sure command of many rapidly shifting moods. But what she needs above everything else just now is, first of all, to find a new play that is in any way equal to what she has to bring to it, and then to discover a director who can control her in her many moments of wasteful restlessness.

Gone with the Wind

IN 1936, David O. Selznick read the long galley proofs of Margaret Mitchell's *Gone with the Wind* and, on July 30, bought the film rights for $50,000, a record sum for a first novel. There ensued the search for an actress to portray Scarlett O'Hara, the proud, gritty, and quintessentially Southern heroine. The "Scarlett Derby" became the most ballyhooed and expensive competition in the history of casting.

The blockbuster was delayed for almost two years while national nooks and crannies were scrutinized. More than a thousand candidates were interviewed, four hundred auditioned, and twenty finalists screen-tested: 140,000 feet of black-and-white film, 13,000 Technicolor seared with eager Scarlett types. There were brand-new faces, relatively new faces, stars' faces, and even the instantly recognizable faces of superstars who tested in absolute secrecy lest their public, and their competitors, find out. With the possible exception of Hope Emerson and Maria Ouspenskaya, there was hardly an actress who was not considered or who did not fervently consider.

As much as she had ever wanted anything in her professional

life, Tallulah Bankhead wanted that part. Hollywood had treated her shabbily by supplying her with cheap properties and attempting to push her into a European mold for which she was unsuited. And nothing was happening on the stage to approach the Matterhorn of her English success. *Gone with the Wind* would make the difference.

For a time, it appeared that the part was hers. From the Gotham Hotel she wrote to Will in Washington: "I have many excellent movie offers but as you have probably heard I may do *Gone with the Wind*. I am the top candidate. Say nothing but pray for your little girl."

Even Eugenia, who rarely took an interest in Tallulah's dramatic options, felt that there was some fated relationship between her sister and the tempestuous heroine of the Mitchell novel. She wrote to Tallulah from Italy: "There is only one person to play Scarlett in America. *Who but you who were born in that briar patch!* . . . Make them let you do it. And cable me the minute you know."

The GWTW promotion, which proliferated in the daily press, made it eminently clear to the motion-picture audience that their letters would help Selznick International determine the winner of the competition. Aunt Marie, in Montgomery, went to bat for Tallulah. She began a "Tallulah for Scarlett" campaign that pyramided into a nettlesome lobby.

Marie, who took over as official state historian after the death of her husband, had just bullied Alabama Governor Bibb Graves into funneling a big chunk of WPA funds into the construction of a mammoth building to house the state's historical archives. (The Montgomery Archives would comprise a proud and extensive collection of Alabamian articles and artifacts. As its assiduous boss lady, Marie Owen was naturally Bankhead-oriented. She kept the flame roaring even to Senator John Hollis Bankhead's chamber pot, prominently displayed during her tenure.)

After the victory over Graves, Marie was naturally feeling her oats. She wrote letter after letter about Tallulah to anyone she thought might have something to do with casting the movie. Only one week after the property was bought, Ronald Colman, who had been mentioned for one of the leads, received a missive from Marie. "I wonder if you had thought of Tallulah Bankhead as a suitable actress to take the role of Scarlett O'Hara?" she began. "Miss Bankhead is now in California playing in *Reflected Glory,* and if this suggestion interests you, I am sure you could see her." She threw out another idea to Colman: Would he perhaps have any interest in taking the lead in a possible film version of her yet unpublished novel *Yvonne of Braithwaite,* "with the title changed, of course, to show that it was the hero and not the heroine who had the leading role in the book?"

Then she addressed David O. Selznick himself. She reminded him that he had turned down the very young Tallulah Bankhead for a part when the actress was just starting out in New York. The implication was that it would be folly to make the same mistake again. "Tallulah has made an international reputation as an actress," she observed, "and her friends are most anxious to see her take the part of Scarlett."

At the behest and under the aegis of Marie Owen, Selznick International received communications from the Alabama Public Service Commission and the National League of American Pen Women; a Tallulah-for-Scarlett petition with thousands of signatures attached; a copy of an editorial in the Montgomery *Advertiser,* pro-Tallu, of course; and a copy of a letter addressed to the *Atlantan Georgian* in which Marie pseudonymously replied to an earlier letter which suggested that Tallulah Bankhead was "too old to play Scarlett." Marie's answer pointed out heatedly that while Scarlett may have been in her teens at the opening of the book, by the last chapter she had passed through three marriages, borne an equal number of children, survived the siege of Atlanta and the calumny of Reconstruction. Certainly a woman of maturity was required to fulfill the dramatic demands of such a part.

The Tallulah-for-Scarlett campaign was capped by a telegram sent to Selznick International by poor, put-upon Governor Bibb Graves: WHY DON'T YOU GIVE TALLULAH BANKHEAD THE PART AND BE DONE WITH IT.

While Selznick continued his search for Scarlett, Tallulah starred in *Reflected Glory*, a play about an American actress who flounders between a brilliant career and giving it all up for marriage. It was a mild success though the press bemoaned the fact that George Kelly, *Wunderkind* of the American theater who had been responsible for *The Torch Bearers*, *The Show-Off*, and *Craig's Wife*, had this time written a somewhat banal property. Because of Tallulah's great love and respect for Kelly, who also directed the production, she played well and professionally. It was the best of the vehicles with which she had been supplied since her repatriation.

But she was bored. She was disgusted with the critics who claimed still that she had yet to fulfill her great potentials as an actress, and she was broke, which was not the least of her reasons to pray for the chance to play Scarlett.

In 1937, a warrant was issued by the New York State Tax Commission which levied upon Tallulah's personal property a lien of $3,296, the amount of her still-unpaid taxes for the year 1931–32. The debt was, of course, paid, but the alien and frightening severity of the demand shook Tallulah.

The theater just about paid Tallulah's bills. Every five or six years, however, she needed some kind of supplementary windfall to maintain her profligate style of living, to ease her mind, to permit her professional options, and to enable her to continue to handle family responsibilities. Though the nation was emerging from the worst of the Depression, there was still that one-third of the nation to whom President Roosevelt referred as ill-clothed, ill-housed, and ill-fed. There were several Bankheads among them.

A cousin with whom she had grown up needed, at the very *least*, Tallulah's old clothes to keep his family warm. Aunt Marie continued to rely on Tallulah to help with the yearly mortgage on her farm. And Eugenia was often in need. She sent Tallulah a telegram once which read: DEAR SISTER STOP PLEASE SEND $2500 STOP LOVE SISTER. Tallulah read the message and screamed for Edie Smith.

"Take a cablegram, Edie," Tallulah said, pacing with agitation. "It's to read: DEAR SISTER STOP I DO NOT HAAAAAVE $2500 STOP LOVE SISTER. Read that back to me."

Edie, in her proper and measured English tones, read: "Dear Sister Stop I Do Not Have $2500 Stop Love Sister."

Tallulah was furious. "That's *not* what I said," she reprimanded Edie. "You know perfectly well that I *have* twenty-five hundred dollars. What I want to convey to Sister is that I do not *HAAAAAVE* twenty-five hundred dollars."

Sister's needs were as voracious as Tallulah's, but less vocational. Whereas the younger Bankhead girl sought mob love, mass approval all of her life, had found it once in England and was seeking the same kind of success in her native land now, the elder, Eugenia, had more modest desires: She wanted to find The Right Man who would give her a family. By 1936, she had tried six times —very nearly seven—to fulfill that dream.

Eugenia had married Morton Hoyt for the *third* time in 1929. His drinking problem had not abated any, and she divorced him that same year to marry a professional football player, named Wilfred Lawson Butt. The union was annulled. In 1930, she entered into a ten-day marriage with an aviator, Howard B. Lee.

By 1931 she had left yet another husband, whose name presented a formidable problem to both the newspapers and Aunt Marie.

An item, datelined June 30, 1931, on the subject of this latest Bankhead marriage, read: "Court records revealed today that Edward Ennis White and not Ennis Smith became the fifth husband last Saturday of Eugenia Bankhead. Mr. White is a New York business man."

The marriage was terminated before Marie was able to determine whether Eugenia had made another mistake with a Mr. White or a Mr. Smith. She wrote to Edie Smith: "I suppose you saw in the newspapers that Eugenia has left her last husband. I do not know whether his name is Smith or White but he seems to have used both. I think he is somewhat of a scoundrel. Poor, foolish Eugenia! What a pity she doesn't look into these husbands before she marries them and then she would not have all of this newspaper sensation which is a humiliation to Tallulah and her father to say nothing of what the rest of the family feels."

Marie was more diplomatic in her communications with her beloved brother, Will. She drafted and then tore up a note which read: "I notice in the paper that Eugenia has married again. There is one thing to be said about it and that is that she certainly does know how to get husbands. We will just have to take it in a light vein and not feel mortified about it."

She decided, in the final draft to Will, to strike a more jubilant pose, accentuating the positive: "Well, Eugenia has married again!" she began. "There is one thing you can say about it, she certainly does know how to get husbands. That is more than a lot of folks can claim. She is also adept at getting rid of them and that too is more than some folks can accomplish. Hurrah for Eugenia!"

Mr. Smith-White turned out to be the last of Eugenia's husbands for a while, though in the fall of 1933 she came very close to the altar in London with a certain Mr. McConnell. The Associated Press ran a story under the headline HER SEVENTH MARRIAGE, but Eugenia called off the ceremony at the last minute.

In spite of her disapproval, and more on Daddy's account than Eugenia's, Tallulah had always tried to assist her older sister financially. And in 1936, Eugenia was in particularly desperate need. While Tallulah waited for word on the casting of *Gone with the Wind*, Eugenia was fighting for her life in Corsica.

She had caught what Mamma Bankhead used to call "the dread pneumonia" while living on that Mediterranean island. She was so deathly ill that the people with whom she was residing had alerted an embalmer and purchased her coffin. Eugenia came out of the crisis stage, but the pneumonia debilitated her so that she contracted tuberculosis of the right lung and was forced to recuperate in a cozy, magnificently located sanatorium in Ortisei, Italy, close to the slopes on which Benito Mussolini skied bare to the waist. Impressed with the ambitious politico, Eugenia struck up a friendship with him. She convalesced for a year there, passing through a period of heady reassessment.

Tallulah sent her $100, most of her used clothing, and a bunch of books, including *Gone with the Wind*. She actively missed Eugenia for the first time in years and tearfully read her acknowledgment for the books. Referring to the Mitchell novel, Eugenia wrote:

With our old childhood habit, I am saving the biggest and the best bite until the last. It's too bad I didn't cling to that habit a bit more closely in the years since childhood fled. Wouldn't it be fun to know that the biggest and the best bite was still ahead? For you, darling, I sincerely believe it is.

If I am lucky and get cured, I want to come home. Not to be a nuisance to you and Daddy, but to live quietly in some small mountain town and hear American spoken again. I get so homesick among all these bloody Latins. That plan however is in the future and in God's hands. For the present I am all right and happier than you will ever know because of the sure proof that you have given me that neither the years nor my many stupidities have changed your love for

SISTER

When Tallulah first heard from John Hay Whitney, chairman of the board of Selznick International, that she was being considered very seriously for the Scarlett role, that, in fact, David O. Selznick himself had caught her in a performance of *Reflected Glory* and wired to Hollywood WE'VE GOT OUR SCARLETT, she sat down and read the behemoth, 1,037-page novel in one sitting. She was certain then not only that she would play the hell out of the role but that she was somehow ordained to do it. About the novel, about Scarlett, and about the South that they embodied, she had intensely proprietary feelings.

There were elements of almost cabalistic ethnicity in her regional loyalties. She could never have lived there again. Indeed, her short, rare visits were infused with a warm but impatient agony. She felt, however, that only a Southerner could know the South. Only a Southerner was capable of understanding and interpreting Southern caste and class and outrage and sensuality and pride. And only a Southerner, knowing what only a Southerner could know, had the right to despise the South.

Tallulah's Southernness was a strange and sometimes misleading mix. While she was on the road with *Reflected Glory* in 1936, she was visited in Detroit by a black woman, Mrs. Pickney Bankhead. The black Bankheads, now of Detroit, and the white Bankheads, still predominantly of Alabama, went, it seemed, a long way back together. Mrs. Pickney Bankhead invited Miss Tallulah Bankhead to a fried chicken lunch at her home, and Tallulah accepted enthusiastically.

She crossed the tracks with Stephan Cole, a handsome, curly-haired Colorado boy whom she had met through Edie Smith several years before and who had since become part of the Bankhead ménage. She waxed prolixly en route on the idyllic nature of her childhood in Alabama and the charms of the black folk who had all but reared her.

The afternoon was a memorable one for Tallulah; she spoke about it warmly for years afterward. At the home of Mrs. Pickney Bankhead, she met Barbara Bankhead, who was one of Mamma Bankhead's house servants in Jasper and had helped pick up after Eugenia and Tallulah. Then there was John Quincy Bankhead, who remembered pushing the sisters around in a wheelbarrow when Tallulah was five and he nine years old. Tallulah fixed her gaze on John Quincy, and so did Stephan Cole. Stephan thought that he bore a remarkable resemblance to Will Bankhead, but Tallulah knew that it was Granddaddy he really looked like, blue eyes and all.

She wrote to her father about the visit. For Tallulah, the letter was anomalous: it struck a strange, literate, almost canny tone. After regaling Daddy with jolly anecdotes about the afternoon, she concluded, "I thought you'd like to hear about it because they were really old-fashioned, respectful negroes, religious, proud, and dignified."

While she may have handpicked those adjectives to please Will, those qualities in Negroes also pleased and comforted Tallulah. They made her full and nostalgic and tender. With absolute delight, she commented to Stephan upon leaving the Pickney Bankhead residence, "It's as though the Civil War had never been fought."

Several times in that same letter to Daddy, Tallulah pointed out with some subtlety the physical resemblances between the two Bankhead lines. Of John Quincy, she wrote, "He looks exactly like Grandfather. Both he and his mother look more like Indians than colored. One of them said, 'All of the Bankhead men, both colored and white, was always tall.' "

This last was an epistolary device endemic among Southerners: the encapsulation, by means of quotation marks, of everything and anything *of color*, whether it be the name of a shantytown, the name of a colored man, or the too precious mispronunciations and grammatical errors of the colored folk—the more colorfully igno-rant, the better.

Letters between the Bankheads never say about a black man, "He decided to walk down the street." The idea, more likely, would be expressed: "Mr. Will, I think I is gonna take these hea' feet and walk 'em down the road." It's a habit which cossets and separates. It's the bulwark of Southern ethnic humor. It imbues the black world with a darling and childlike otherness.

When Will Bankhead replied to his daughter's letter that there was in fact a consanguinous link between the two families called Bankhead, that, after all, boys would be boys, his daughter laughed lustily. Tallulah was, where she lived, basically a Southerner. Sober as she had remained with the Detroit Bankheads, she was a gra-cious but rather *grande dame* who was called by last and replied with first names. Drunk, she was a funky fraternizer who went to Harlem to see and play dirty. She could be touchingly loyal and tender to individual black people, but if they transgressed, if they got proud, uppity, and arrogant, Tallulah went south.

She went west, in 1937, to make a Technicolor screen test for Selznick International. She was relaxed, assured, and buttressed in her optimism by the presence of George Cukor, a warm, good friend who was at the time engaged as the director of the South-ern epic and who directed Tallulah's test expertly.

The newspapers were issuing daily reports on the Scarlett search. The favorites included Tallulah, Bette Davis, Katharine Hepburn, Margaret Sullavan, Miriam Hopkins, Norma Shearer, Carole Lombard, Paulette Goddard, Frances Dee, Joan Crawford, Claudette Colbert, Joan Bennett, and Jean Arthur. After seeing the result of Cukor's direction of her test, Tallulah was more cer-tain than ever the part was hers.

Her happy little Hollywood stay was spoiled only by an item

which had appeared in Louella Parsons' column the day before the test. "Tallulah Bankhead breezed into town last night to take a test for Scarlett O'Hara in *Gone with the Wind*," Louella wrote. "George Cukor, her friend, is going to direct. Jock Whitney, another friend, is backing it. So I'm afraid she'll get the part. If she does, I personally will go home and weep, because she is not SCARLETT O'HARA in my language, and if David O. Selznick gives her the part, he will have to answer to every man, woman, and child in America."

Louella's world view was, as usual, a combination of small-time cynicism and silly putty. At the time that Tallulah was such a serious contender for the role, it was expected simply that she would be the best of all possible Scarletts. George Cukor, who was about to direct what could have been the most important film of his career (he was, as it turned out, replaced by Victor Fleming. Selznick felt that Cukor's direction lacked sufficient scope and sweep for the outdoor scenes), was not about to present the plum role to Tallulah like so much Steuben glassware. If a gift it was to have been, Hartford's own Katharine Hepburn was an even closer friend to Cukor.

John Hay Whitney was the principal stockholder of Selznick International and chairman of the board. Selznick was much indebted to him since Whitney had, in 1935, supplied the first million dollars which permitted the producer to start his own company. But Whitney remained the moneyman; in matters of final esthetic judgment he yielded to the primary voice of David O. Jock Whitney's position at the studio helped, but it was no guarantee for the eager Tallulah.

Moreover, by 1937 the relationship between Tallulah and Whitney had cooled. There are a multitude of stories about what happened between them. Tallulah's version, the one she told throughout her life, implicated his status, her cherished freedom, and the incompatibility of the two. As usual, she expressed the idea cryptically and humorously. "How would it have looked?" she asked friends, holding her small hand up to indicate an imaginary marquee: "MRS. JOHN HAY WHITNEY IN . . . . . . 'RAIN'!"

Though Whitney and Tallulah would remain friends for life, by 1937 the idea of marriage was probably no longer considered.

Marriage to *someone* appears to have been uppermost in Tallulah's mind in her thirty-fifth summer. She took a quick trip to England, where she rekindled her relationship with Lord Napier Alington. Alington's wife, the daughter of the Earl of Shaftesbury, had died the year before. Cecil Beaton, in his excellent *Diaries*, made this entry, dated May, 1937: "A quiet dinner at Sybil Colefax's, followed by Tallulah's Walpurgis night. Marian Harris, mad as a march hare, sang. Tallulah danced frenziedly, throwing herself about in a mad apache dance with Napier Alington. After he left, she wept and bemoaned the fact that he had never married her. Then she threw off all her clothes, performing what she called 'Chinese classical dances.' In the midst of these outrageous situations, one had reluctantly to drag oneself away."

By the late summer of 1937 Tallulah was in-between ginks and plays, on the rebound from Whitney and Alington, and fairly certain still that the Scarlett role was just a matter of time. She was vacationing on Langdon Island, a small island near Connecticut, with Stephan Cole and Edie Smith. Tallulah and Company were on a health jag: swimming, riding bikes, and drinking only lightly.

She was tanned, relaxed, and looking as lovely as she would ever look in her life. The sun and sand had helped reduce her beauty to its basics: tight, clear, flawless skin; bones out of an El Greco; gray-blue eyes; long, tawny, and sun-dappled hair. Like cheap buttons off a quality garment, the flushed and flossy, rather cherubic look of her early youth was gone.

She, Stephan, and Anna May Wong went one evening to the Country Playhouse in Westport, Connecticut, to see a production of an English whodunit called *Busman's Holiday*. Tallulah was fascinated with the Barrymorish leading man, John Emery, and asked to meet him.

He went home with Tallulah that night. The next day, he moved out of his small Manhattan apartment and in with her. Tallulah asked tasteful Stephan Cole to take John to R. F. Tripler's, where she had him completely outfitted. The one "perfectly terrible" green suit that John had owned was discarded forthwith.

Tallulah's ménage naturally assumed that Emery was just another gink until several days later when she announced frothily to one and all that they were going to be married.

16

"Because I Love Him"

THE GAME was called "pleasing Daddy." While Will was alive, it was the affective epicenter of Tallulah. She had played it as a child when she turned her cartwheels or sang her risqué songs on the dining-room table in Jasper. To please and appease Will, she took a husband. Jock Whitney would have been the perfect choice, but Emery would do. Marriage was the right thing for Will Bankhead's daughter at this particular time.

In June, 1936, Joseph W. Byrns of Tennessee, Speaker of the House of Representatives, died suddenly in his hotel apartment. Less than twelve hours afterward William Brockman Bankhead, in a white suit and rimless glasses, his hair thinning and receding, his body bowed in grief, stepped up to the Congressional rostrum to be sworn in as the forty-eighth Speaker of the House. He was renominated by acclamation during the 1937 session.

As a loyal lieutenant to President Franklin Delano Roosevelt during his second term, Will was an essential instrument by means of which the President obtained from Congress the billions of dollars still necessary to prime the national pump. Both Will and his brother, John, who was reelected to the Senate in 1937, were dedicated to the ideals of the New Deal: preservation through reformation.

John Bankhead that term introduced the progressive Farm Tenancy Bill, enabling thousands of tenant farmers in the drought-plagued South to secure cheap loans from the federal government and thereby starve on land which was theirs. Tallulah was especially proud when Daddy, sitting in a box at the premiere Washington performance of *Reflected Glory*, signed the Relief Deficiency Bill just before the curtain rose.

A class act—the Bankheads.

Politically, her discipleship to Will was fervid and complete. She sat for hours and listened to his florid assessments of the issues of the day. She was attentive and obedient. Will taught her, among other things, that the most insidious threat to the survival of the nation was Communism, that vigilance and intelligence were the best weapons against this enemy of democracy. As the Speaker's daughter she had to be doubly chary in her judgments.

During that period, she allowed her name to be used in the sponsorship of something called National Sharecropper Week. Alerted to Tallulah's titular involvement, Will dispatched an immediate admonition to her. "I dislike to make the suggestion to you," he wrote, "but it is my opinion that this organization is composed largely of Reds and Communists, and while it purports to be organized in the interest of white and colored tenant farmers, its leaders are subject to very grave suspicion, and they are not entitled to be sponsored by your name. I am enclosing the literature which came to me on the subject. I hope that this is a matter upon which you will take my judgment and act accordingly."

There was no necessity to read the literature. Daddy's judgment in such matters was the last word for Tallulah. She wrote to the organization: "I have reason to believe from information that has come to me from unimpeachable sources, that many of the heads of your organization are Reds and Communists. I, therefore, wish my name to be withdrawn immediately from any connection with your organization."

She sent a copy of the note to Daddy and scrawled across the bottom: "Hope this meets with your approval."

This marriage to Emery was on various levels of Tallulah's consciousness as solicitous and deferential as the note. Throughout her life Tallulah possessed an abiding sense of style, taste, and appropriateness. Her lapses were outrageous and destructive, but they were nonetheless variances from a norm which she recognized and respected. Just as it behooved Tallulah to remove her name from the list of sponsors of a politically suspect organization, so it *behooved* her, as the daughter of the Speaker of the House, two steps removed from the highest office in the land, to finally enter into a state of holy and respectable matrimony.

After Tallulah proposed to John Emery, she called Daddy to tell him about their marriage plans. Will was stunned, incredulous, and delighted. He listened while his daughter apprised him of the arrangements, arrangements to which John had, of course, acceded. They were to be married in Will's rambling house in Jasper. No fuss. No cousins. Only Florence, Will, Edie Smith, and Stephan Cole were to be present at the actual ceremony. There would be a small reception afterward to which Aunt Marie, Uncle John, and his daughters would be invited. An Episcopal ceremony, in honor of Mother, would be performed with simplicity and decorum. The marriage plans, their itinerary—all to be kept in strict confidence.

Will organized everything. And in a matter of days Tallulah and John took off for Alabama. Louisa Carpenter, the Du Pont heiress whose Uncle Coleman had staked Tallulah on her voyage to England in 1922, lent the couple her private plane and the services of her pilot, the first man to fly nonstop from the United States to Denmark. The marriage party planned originally to fly directly to Birmingham, thence motor to Jasper, but rough weather forced the pilot to put down several times en route.

Tallulah wore silk hostess pajamas on the trip, blinked her nervous blink, and erupted from sheer nervousness at the slightest bit of frustration. She drank constantly, the effects of the alcohol exacerbated by the state of her nerves. At each unscheduled stop, Tallulah refueled. Between the tantrums, which she directed at the elements, Tallulah sat on John's lap and behaved in a way that embarrassed even Edie and Stephan, who were accustomed to seeing her at her worst. John, several times, almost slapped her. By the time they arrived in Birmingham the press had somehow been alerted. Reporters crowded in as they disembarked. Tallulah, ruffled and unprepared—according to Lily Mae Caldwell of the local paper—"lost control of her emotions."

By sheer will and in spite of a monumental imbibition of brandy and champagne, Tallulah was sober and becalmed by the time the group reached the Tutweiler Hotel in Birmingham. The Tutweiler was the first hotel that Tallulah had ever been in. Daddy had taken her there to recuperate after a tonsillectomy. At the Tutweiler, she had heard a lady called the Birmingham Lark sing entirely unsuitable songs. Will roared, and Tallulah copied him. It was there now that she changed into her simple wedding ensemble: tailored brown Hattie Carnegie suit, poke-bonnet hat, the pearls John had given her as an engagement present.

They drove from Birmingham to Jasper. Tallulah held her groom's arm all the way and waxed knowledgeably on crops, industry, and local problems. The Speaker met them at the door, embracing his daughter and imminent son-in-law. Will liked John immediately, as most people did. He was a gentle, charming man, rapturously handsome, with a velvet, cultivated voice, which he used sparingly offstage, as a boxer, fooling around, pulls his punches.

Will asked John whether he had procured all the health certificates required for marriage in the state of Alabama. Tallulah, still holding possessively to the arm of her lithe bridegroom, replied on his behalf, "Oh, John doesn't need any further certification, Daddy. He was examined on the way down."

Tallulah's wedding day, August 31, 1937, went, more or less, according to the master plan she had elaborated. The one hitch was the ceremony. Because of John's previous marriage to actress Phyllis Calvert, the local Episcopal bishop refused apologetically to permit a religious ceremony. The marriage vows were exacted instead by a close friend of Will's, a local judge. The Speaker gave his daughter away. Stephan Cole functioned as best man. Edie duplicated the role to which she was very well accustomed: lady-in-waiting.

The couple exchanged gold bands; the one Tallulah gave to John was a family heirloom worn by Grandmother Bankhead for the fifty-two years of her marriage. It was already suitably inscribed: Tallulah Brockman Bankhead. They stood opposite a portrait of Florence Bankhead painted by Howard Chandler Christy. Florence, unhappy with the way in which her lips had been rendered by the artist, had retouched the offending feature with her own lipstick shade especially for this occasion. Immediately after the civil ceremony, Speaker Bankhead stood over the couple and read the twenty-third Psalm. Tallulah and Will wept silently.

The solemn part accomplished, Tallulah led John down the garden path, from which they waved royally to a huge cordoned gathering of fans, press, and citizens. Tallulah joked Southern with some old acquaintances while John shied back. All questions from the press were addressed to and fielded by Tallulah.

"Is this your first marriage?"

She smiled. "My first—and last."

"Is Mr. Emery an actor?"

"Yes, and a damned good one."

"Why did you get married, Miss Bankhead?"

"I married for love. Isn't it ridiculous?"

And she was no doubt, at that brimming moment, as seriously in love with John Emery as she was with the idea of marriage.

The event in Jasper profoundly shocked various theatrical communities in New York. In Harlem, Gladys Bentley, a sort of black Mae West who dressed in men's clothes and played piano anarchically and sang dirty songs, composed and performed an anatomically absurd lesbian song about the fact that the notorious Tallulah had married a man.

Michael Mok, New York *Post* feature writer, reported the reaction of the downtown crowd. "Broadway was all a-flutter today," he wrote, "when the news of Tallulah Bankhead's marriage to John Emery reached the street. You could have knocked the boys over with a pair of passes. They were amazed to learn that the theatre's saltiest sophisticate had fallen for a tall, wide-shouldered, narrow-waisted stage lover like any mooning matinee girl."

The man for whom the theater's saltiest sophisticate had fallen at a time when she was ripe for marriage came from a long line of actors. John Emery's progenitors included six generations of English and American stage notables.

An aunt of his, Winifred Emery, had been married to Cyril Maude. John's grandfather, Sam Emery, was the first interpreter of Charles Dickens on the London stage. His mother created the part of Little Eva in *Uncle Tom's Cabin*. And about John's father, Edward Emery, Jed Harris once said, "He could wring tears out of a stone." Edward Emery had a distinguished stage career as leading man to Mrs. Fiske, Ethel Barrymore, and Margaret Anglin. He was in his early forties when his only son, John, was born in 1904.

John Emery spent a lonely boyhood at LaSalle Military Academy on Long Island while his parents trooped around the country. He was a sensitive, delicately blue-eyed youngster who applied himself assiduously to mastering the manly arts of boxing and fencing. For a time he even considered becoming a professional boxer.

When he was eleven, John was left in the care of John Barrymore, who was then married to Katherine Harris. A strong and enigmatic bond developed between the two men. When Emery was way into his adulthood and Barrymore was a sad old alcoholic, the latter tried desperately to communicate with his erstwhile charge. Emery refused adamantly to see him. "Once he is permitted in my house," Emery told his third wife, "he'll never leave. I know him."

Throughout the years of his marriage to Tallulah, the rumor was rife that John Emery was the illegitimate son of John Barrymore. There was indeed a startling resemblance, and Tallulah, who had a thing about the Barrymores, was undoubtedly first drawn to him because of the likeness. Emery had the same outlandishly handsome, almost epicene profile, a matinee mustache, that velvet, stagy voice, and all the characteristically broad Barrymore mannerisms.

With his face at rest, unposed, John Emery looked far more like Edward Emery than he did John Barrymore. If Emery came to resemble Barrymore, it happened most probably in the same way that adopted children begin to look just like their adoptive parents: through that sincerest kind of flattery, imitation. The rumor would appear to be untrue.

John's imitative instincts, however, were out of favor with time. His Barrymore as-if was extremely destructive to his acting career. Though he played opposite Katharine Cornell in several fine plays —*The Barretts of Wimpole Street* among them—and was a distinguished Laertes in John Gielgud's *Hamlet* of 1936, he was stiff and uncomfortable out of costume plays.

He was a reticent man whose surface charm and suavity covered many small wars waging inside him. He appeared to be content, for instance, as a kind of decorative appurtenance beside his bride, Tallulah, but he was actually a man of great ambition. "He wanted his star right up there with his father's and with John Barrymore's," one of his several wives, actress Tamara Geva, commented. He was accident-prone. On the brink of some big and ameliorative professional step he broke bones or injured an eye. He had, in fact, just finished a major motion picture which many of his friends considered an important breakthrough for him, when he met, became infatuated with, and married Tallulah Bankhead.

They were like kids on their return from Jasper, full of ambitious and exultant plans. John's movie was called *The Road Back* and was based on the Erich Maria Remarque novel about postwar adjustment. This was the vehicle that was expected to transport him from the profile school of acting into a more naturalistic mold. He'd even taken a crew cut for the part. And there was yet another film in the offing with Orson Welles. During this same marriage week, *Variety* reported that Selznick had finally made his mind up and Tallulah Bankhead was definitely slated to play Scarlett in the filmic blockbuster.

They honeymooned at Tallulah's house on Langdon Island and then moved into Tallulah's suite at the Gotham with Tallulah's entourage. They began to rehearse Tallulah's play, into which she brought John: a fantastically expensive production of Shakespeare's *Antony and Cleopatra*. In her first flush of connubial exultation, Tallulah envisioned herself and John working together as a Lunt-like acting team. Dashing, suave John Emery. Glamorous,

unpredictable Tallulah Bankhead. Performing only in quality vehicles. The Speaker's daughter. This scion of the distinguished
Emerys. The pain, the responsibility, the loneliness, the burden—
shared. *Antony and Cleopatra* was a new beginning.

As a sort of dry run for the Broadway production, she played
Viola opposite Orson Welles in a radio performance of *Twelfth
Night.* Her classical acting was wanting. Indeed, she had trained
to interpret the demanding Bard only very early on—in childhood
performances of the balcony scene from *Romeo and Juliet* opposite Daddy. Concerned with her lack of training, both Ethel
Barrymore and Constance Collier offered diplomatically to coach
Tallulah for the part of Cleopatra. Her refusal was less a matter
of foolish pride than the not uncommon fear of the intuitive artist
to muck around with the tenuous calculus called native ability.

Antony and Cleopatra opened in New York on November 10,
1937. Rowland Stebbins produced. Conway Tearle played Antony. John enacted the part of Caesar. It was a complete extrav-
aganza, bulging with elaborate sets, panoplied with sphinxes,
mottled with a variety of acting styles that ranged from Richard
Mansfield to Leslie Howard—with Tallulah's own interpretation
running the gamut. Stephan Cole, who stage managed the production, complained to Tallulah that there simply wasn't enough
room on the stage to put everything.

Aunt Marie, of whom John and Tallulah made a kind of pet
during this period, was in the audience opening night, beaming
and stiff in Tallulah's $18,000 silver mink. Marie objected to the
play for its concentration on what she called "Egyptian politics,"
but thought her niece was a magnificent Queen of the Nile. The
critics demurred, though one or two took special pains to pick out
moments of excellence in her performance. If Tallulah Bankhead
had done or said nothing else during her years in the public eye,
she would have been remembered for the reviews which her performance evoked.

Brooks Atkinson was kindest. He said merely that Tallulah "was
neither Cleopatra nor Tallulah, which amounts to a vacancy in
two good houses." The critic of the New York *Sun,* Richard Lock-
ridge, liked Tallulah's athletic death scene but observed that, until

the moment of her death, Tallulah's "Cleopatra bears a strong family resemblance to Sadie Thompson."

The two classic zingers came from Richard Watts and the South's own John Mason Brown. The former said she was "rather more a Serpent of the Swanee than of the Nile"; the latter wrote: "Tallulah Bankhead barged down the Nile last night as Cleopatra —and sank."

The Emerys billeted themselves at the Gotham. John, whose performance had been reviewed quite favorably, suggested that they stay billeted, perhaps call room service for some cyanide; Tallulah insisted that they go out and party. If ever there was a need to go out and party, surely it was then. John's drinking was heavy and routine; during his marriage to Tallulah it grew heavier and more routine. They remained loaded for several weeks until Tallulah decided that it was time to snap back again.

In Hollywood, production had long since begun on *Gone with the Wind*. Tara, the quintessential Southern plantation, was erected and tenantless. They were shooting around Mistress Scarlett, even to the burning of Atlanta.

Selznick's last statement to the press revealed his dilemma: "I still hope to give the American people a new girl as Scarlett, a girl whom they won't identify with a lot of other roles. But to find an unknown actress who has the talent for it is almost impossible. And to find an actress of sufficient experience who is, at the same time, convincingly young—well, that's a job."

In late 1938, Vivien Leigh flew to the United States to visit Laurence Olivier. Myron Selznick, the agent brother of David O., saw Miss Leigh and knew that *this time* they really did have their Scarlett. He arranged for Miss Leigh to be on the set on December 15, 1938, while his brother was supervising the burning of the military supplies at Atlanta. The story goes that Myron, standing beside Miss Leigh, tapped David on the shoulder and said, grinning, "Hello, I want you to meet Scarlett O'Hara."

The beautiful green-eyed English actress, who had just turned twenty-five, was tested the following day and signed immediately. Tallulah's optimism had been on the wane for some months before the entrance of Miss Leigh. While the test Tallulah made was very good and though she was certainly not identified in the minds of the American public with any other role, she was probably simply too old for the part. George Cukor would surmise in a gentlemanly fashion, "Tallulah just wasn't fresh enough."

These were hard times for Tallulah. Her new role, as the Speaker's Daughter, was a hindrance rather than a help. She felt she could no longer do the kinds of plays that she had done in England or the kinds of movies she made for Paramount. After the closing of *Antony and Cleopatra*, Edie Smith wrote to Aunt Marie: "The plays that look like anything at all are usually full of sex and its perversions, which might be all right for some coming star—but *Miss Tallulah* has set up a certain standard and she feels it would be dangerous to attempt anything that is in the least risqué. . . . But just between you and me, I don't know how much longer we can hold out."

Tallulah finally hocked a star sapphire that Jock had given to her and some of the Bosdari gifts—which she had ended up paying off herself. It was Tallulah who continued to bear the financial responsibility and even to provide John with his pocket money. There simply wasn't any choice since he had nothing at all. John never presumed to be head of the household, but his status was made painfully and succinctly evident to him by a remark that he himself made. To a friend who inquired what he was going to do that evening, Emery responded, "I guess I'll go up to Tallulah's."

Tallulah was determined to continue to work with John, but they were forced now to take more or less what they could get. *Antony and Cleopatra* had scourged both their reputations. John's *Road Back* was indeed regressive. The picture received very bad reviews, and he was almost totally ignored. The couple of movie offers which he subsequently received he was unable to do because of his commitment to the Orson Welles film—which was never made.

John and Tallulah toured together in *I Am Different* by Zoë Akins. Tallulah throughout was despondent, disappointed, and drinking heavily. John several times had to carry her on and off trains. Though her drinking did not at the time directly disable her perfomance in this rather old-fashioned comedy, her despair and disgust did. When the play opened in Hollywood, most of Tallulah's West Coast friends either left before the curtain came down or avoided coming backstage to see her.

Glenn Anders, who co-starred in the vehicle, was responsible for injecting a little bit of levity into the proceedings. Tallulah never had to prepare or get into the mood for a performance. She simply went onstage and did it. Consequently, she was often engaged in animated and totally irrelevant conversations with stagehands or fellow actors while her plays were going on. One particular night she and Glenn were talking just before he was to make an entrance. This entrance, according to the script, followed a gunshot. He was to come onstage, discover a woman with a smoking pistol standing over a supine John Emery. His line? "I heard a shot." Examining the body, Anders was then to say, "It's only a flesh wound."

Discombobulated, he ran somewhat late onto the stage fresh from conversation with Tallulah. "I heard a flesh wound," he yelled excitedly. Emery's stomach began to bob with impacted laughter, and Tallulah could be heard, from the balcony, howling in the wings. All three of them dissolved when Anders, pursuing the logic of his error, leaned over the body and observed, "It's only a shot."

Passing through Montgomery, Alabama, on tour with the play, the couple was feted by Dr. Brannon Hubbard, the town's most distinguished surgeon. Tallulah, in an ankle-length silver fox, arrived with John and Fritzi Scheff, the former musical comedy star. At three in the morning, Tallulah rolled up the rugs and toasted her husband: "To my husband, Sir," she insisted:

> May you live as long as you want to.
> May you want to as long as you live.
> If I'm asleep and you want me,
> Wake me.
> If I'm awake and I don't want to,
> Make me.

If their sexual relationship was ever any good, it had become, as they entered their second year of their married life, decidedly lackluster. Sometime after the dissolution of the union, John Emery was asked to leave a prestigious theatrical men's club because of his disparaging references to Tallulah as lover. The consentient and vulgar evaluation of Tallulah's amatory performance was that she "talked a good lay"; even more perturbing to Emery and to others was the fact that she talked before, during, and after *ceaselessly.*

She was oral, aggressive, and fascinated with male genitalia, which she would describe scrupulously to anyone within earshot the morning after. She told a friend once that she enjoyed men sexually only during their climax. John apparently failed somewhere. Tallulah's evaluation of his masculine prowess was as opprobrious as his dismissal of her.

How, indeed, could it have been otherwise for these two ebbing careerists? A great respecter of power, Tallulah had a husband who was, at this point in his life, wielding absolutely none. And John Emery was a sensitive man. His sexual powers would have had to reflect the fact that he was not having his way with the world in general, that he was residing in Tallulah's house, living Tallulah's life among Tallulah's people.

She had never altered her life-style one iota on John's behalf. He was never able to be a total environment for Tallulah. From the time they first moved into her house on Langdon Island, there were always other people about. He would complain, late in the marriage, that he and Tallulah might have been able to make a go of it if only they had some time to themselves. "I'm not married to Tallulah," he complained. "I'm married to Tallulah and Edie Smith and Stephan Cole."

When the money was very short, they were forced for a time to move out of the Gotham into a furnished apartment in the East Seventies. When some funds began to come in again, Tallulah decided to return to her favorite hotel, the Elysee. In between undistinguished tours they lived a late night life of cabarets and wags and jags, of room service and impulsive telephone calls at two and three in the morning.

One such call was made to Marc Connelly, the distinguished playwright, who lived in the apartment underneath Tallulah. Orson Welles had come in from Philadelphia where his ambitious production of *The Four Henrys* was in danger of closing if $25,000 was not raised that night. Connelly showed up, fresh from sleep, in a robe and slippers.

"Marc," she said, "Orson needs twenty-five thousand dollars. Will you lend it to him?"

"Tallulah," Connelly replied, "I don't have twenty-five thousand dollars."

"*Someone* must have twenty-five thousand dollars," she said impatiently, the telephone, like some McLuhanized Pandora's box, cradled in her lap. "I'll call Sherman Billingsley."

The Stork Club proprietor, who responded faithfully to all kinds of requests from Tallulah, was at the Elysee in minutes, a magnum of champagne tucked under his arm.

"Sherman, this is Orson Welles. He's a genius. If he doesn't get twenty-five thousand dollars by tomorrow his absolutely brilliant Shakespearean adaptation will be closed."

Neither Welles' credentials nor his collateral were sufficiently impressive for Billingsley. He didn't give Welles the money. The champagne was served. Tallulah, Orson, Connelly and Billingsley began to swap stories. And within minutes the plight of *The Four Henrys*—which never did get to New York—was temporarily forgotten.

Tallulah was drawn to the Elysee for many reasons. Most important, the management was permissive and the soundproofing maximal, though apparently not perfect.

Connelly was more amazed than annoyed at the noise which emanated from Tallulah's suite. He recalled sardonically, "About three in the morning, Tallulah and the gang were, I suspect, throwing safes at each other. It certainly sounded that way."

One day Dorothy Gish, who also lived at the Elysee, stopped Glenn Anders as he was on his way up to Tallulah's red-carpeted suite. "Glenn," she pleaded, "for heaven's sake, can't you tell Tallulah to keep it quiet? Everyone's at the windows, including me, and we're hearing foul language and all kinds of personal things at all hours of the night."

Not only were there friends in Tallulah's suite at night, but often there were strangers. To John's continual perturbation, Tallulah, when she was full and high and disastrously egalitarian, had a tendency to pick up people in the street. During one graduation season, she was smitten with the freshness, youth, and beauty of a group of four youngsters who were out on the town after their high school prom. Tallulah stopped them, engaged them in conversation, and invited the group back to her suite for a nightcap. They were, of course, delighted.

Tallulah, John, Glenn, and the kids played a game of charades. Tallulah drank throughout. John's inability to guess a frantic mimic clue of hers led to a bitter argument between them. John slammed out of the suite. Puffing with fury at being abandoned, humiliated, and wrong, Tallulah grabbed a glass off the living-room bar, announcing, "I gotta piss." She lifted her dress, filled the glass with urine, and toasted in the direction of the door: "To Rabelais!"

The next morning, she made her tearful, rueful apologies to one and all—except the prom kids, whose identities she had not ascertained.

The intimate Monkey Bar at the Elysee was among their favorite haunts. Tallulah and John were leaving the piano bar one night when John stopped to light, à la Paul Henried, two cigarettes: one for his wife and one for himself. As he lit Tallulah's cigarette, John overheard an insulting remark about his wife muttered by a drunk at the bar. He deposited the mystified Tallulah at the elevators, ordered her to stay put, returned to the scene of the crime, and flattened the man.

They were on their way up to their suite, John rouging with manly satisfaction, when Tallulah inquired, "What did he say, John?"

"It's not important."

"You've got to tell me what he said."

John repeated the contumelious utterance.

Tallulah coiled in anger. "Why, that son of a bitch! You should have killed him."

And, with frenzied, unsatisfied fury, Tallulah lashed out and punched John Emery in the eye.

17

The Little Foxes

PERHAPS SHE WAS MADE for bigger things. It took, in any case, a classic American drama and a burgeoning world war in Europe to revitalize Tallulah. After her succession of Broadway flops, Tallulah received a copy of *The Little Foxes* by Lillian Hellman. Miss Hellman had already established herself as a skillful, excoriating playwright with *The Children's Hour* (1934), though her *Days to Come* (1936) was far less successful. Her third play, *The Little Foxes*, which was scheduled for production in 1939 under the aegis of Herman Shumlin, was a lean and powerful melodrama set in the South at the turn of the century. The part offered to Tallulah, that of the Machiavellian land grabber Regina Giddens was a lollapaloosa. Tallulah agreed to do it for 10 percent of the gate.

These were epochal times for Tallulah as they were for the rest of the world. It was the wake of Munich, the dawn of Poland, and the day of the secret Nazi-Soviet Nonaggression Pact. Under Daddy's tutelage, because of her reverence for Winston Churchill and Franklin Delano Roosevelt, and because of her heartfelt love for England, Tallulah became vitally interested in the gathering storm in Europe. She listened and read with more focus and intensity than she had ever applied intellectually in her life. By the time she went into rehearsal for *The Little Foxes* in the last months of 1938, she had a very definite set of ideas about the world situation.

The play itself was not without political significance. Underneath its melodramatic pyrotechnics, *The Little Foxes* was, of course, a parable about the rise of the mercantile class in the South, as represented by the rapacious Regina and her brother Hubbards. Late-blooming capitalists, they are like walking catfish that *shlepp* out of the delta mud to connive, lie, steal, and finally murder. It was a bitter and controversial indictment. Dorothy Thompson, in a 1940 Valentine column, itemized maliciously: "To the Communist Party of America—'The Little Foxes.'"

Because it was known generally that Tallulah was a fierce anti-Communist, it was assumed by many that she simply didn't understand the play's political ramifications. A marvelous story was told by Maurice Zolotow about Herman Shumlin, the producer-director, turning to Miss Hellman during one of the rehearsals to whisper, "If Tallulah ever finds out what this play is about, we're all in a hell of a fix."

Shumlin may or may not have uttered the line. Since neither he nor Miss Hellman will at present consent to talk about Tallulah Bankhead—so bitter did their relationship with her finally become —it is unverifiable. If Mr. Shumlin did, in fact, assume that Tallulah was unaware of the political underpinnings of *The Little Foxes* or that, knowing them, she would have found them inimical, he was grievously mistaken.

Like Will and largely because of Will, Tallulah was a fervid New Dealer who came to believe in preservation through modification, in the curtailment of the power of land barons like the Hubbards, in the rights of the little man. Like Will, who had recited "The Man with a Hoe" tremulously when speechifying on behalf of his lend-lease program in Congress, she could be emotional and bathetic. And like Will, she would never have considered an indictment of irresponsible capitalism an unpatriotic act.

In a landmark address in 1937, Will Bankhead had impressed his daughter with these words: "The progress of the world depends upon our adopting new ideas and discarding old ones. . . .

Look at our recent legislation and then consider how a majority of the people but a few years ago would have regarded it. Our entire outlook, both social and political, has broadened. When I first entered Congress the most liberal leaders of the day would have hesitated to propose some of the measures for which the conservatives now vote. Old-age pensions and unemployment insurance for example are adopted by everyone as reasonable. In my early days they involved dangerous dogmas."

The play, in any case, appealed to Tallulah as an actress, not as an ideologue. Tallulah knew, when she first read the script—before Miss Hellman had finished the third act—that the part was the best thing that had ever been offered to her. It was her theatrical *Gone with the Wind*, except that this one was definitely bagged. It was a classic, serious role in a stunning drama, and she knew it could have a tremendous impact on her career as an actress.

She was petrified, of course, to be found out, frightened that her lack of training and technique would be discovered in this demanding role. She tried walking through rehearsals—saving her "performance" for opening night. This was her usual ploy. It meant that she could hide effectively like some sea-shy vessel nosing close to the safety of shore. On opening night, compelled by the high wind of nerves and adrenaline, she would permit herself to be carried out to sea: to sink or swim or bobble. Shumlin would not permit her to cop out. He wanted to *rehearse*.

They disagreed about the interpretation of a line. Shumlin criticized her harshly at one point. It had been a long, hard day. She ranted a bit at her stern taskmaster and then fled, in tears, to her dressing room. Shumlin followed her there and closed the door. Maurice Zolotow, in *No People Like Show People*, gave this account of what transpired:

> "Listen, Tallulah," Shumlin said, "when you're out on the stage and a certain power comes out of you, you hypnotize people. If I don't criticize you any more I know that on opening night you'll give a sensational performance. But you'll do it on instinct and nerve. I want you to bury Tallulah in Regina Giddens. Then you'll know *why* you do the things you do and

you'll be sensational on opening night and every other night."

She sighed. Then she said softly, "You're right. It's always been that way. I've lived on my nerve. From the second night on, every part I have ever done has been torture to me."

From then on during rehearsals, she would point at Shumlin and say, "There sits teacher."

Besides encountering the strongest and most effective director she would have in all her years in the theater, Tallulah aligned herself, during *The Little Foxes* experience, with Richard Maney. He was working as a press agent for the show at the time and for half a dozen others running concurrently. Tallulah took an immediate liking to the florid Irishman whom Russel Crouse once described as resembling "a boiled leprechaun." Maney was the best and certainly most literate press agent in the business at the time. He loved language and liquor, and he understood actors. "Press agentry," he said once, "is no business for people with nerves. But it can be a gay life for one with detachment, with sympathy for the deranged, and with an understanding of why the theatre's children behave the way they do."

He and Tallulah became barroom buddies and permanent allies. Each of her contracts from *Little Foxes* on, with the exception of those negotiated with the Theatre Guild, made two peremptory demands: footlights and Maney. She was enormously impressed with his erudition, his competence, and the fact that he had signed articles which appeared in the New York *Times*. That, in Tallulah's eyes, made him more than a press agent. He was an artist.

Handling Tallulah's press relations was a formidable task. As often as not, Maney was called upon to appease the offended. During the rehearsal period of *The Little Foxes*, for instance, he set up an interview between Tallulah and a very important female feature writer, a priggish, shockable sort who was diffident at first even to consent to meet with the terrible Tallulah. Her attitudes showed. She and Tallulah were cordial but cool in their twenty-minute interview at the Elysee. Tallulah did not like the writer any better than the writer liked Tallulah.

When the interview came to an end, Tallulah offered uncharacteristically to walk the woman to the elevators. Interviewer and interviewee ambled together down the long corridor. Tallulah made some smallish talk and pushed the button. The elevator arrived loaded with people. The reporter stepped in, smiling wanly, embarrassed even to be seen with the notorious Tallulah Bankhead.

As the doors of the elevator began to close, Tallulah waved cheerily. "Good-bye, dahling," she said, "as I already told you, you're one of the *nicest* lesbians I've ever met."

Tallulah left the Elysee in January, 1939, to journey to Baltimore for the out-of-town premiere of *The Little Foxes*. She was somewhat run-down with worry and in her weakened state developed a nasty bronchial cold. Her nervousness manifested itself as well in her mouth, which parched so badly that her lips stuck to her teeth. Edie stood by with a bottle of petroleum jelly to wet the inside of her mouth.

The opening in Baltimore was ragged. In spite of all of Shumlin's preachments, Tallulah lapsed into a lot of her old tricks. The audience was unenthusiastic. And the third act, Tallulah thought, was fifteen minutes too long. She argued with Patricia Collinge, who played the brutalized Birdie Hubbard brilliantly, about the temperature of the theater. Miss Collinge wanted it warm; Tallulah claimed that the steam heat suffocated her. Will Bankhead was at the premiere with his brother, John Bankhead. So were Lillian Hellman, Dorothy Parker, Dashiell Hammett, and Sara and Gerald Murphy.

Gilbert Kanour wrote of Tallulah's performance: "She encourages the suspicion that she is confusing Regina and Shakespeare's Lady Macbeth." *Variety* contended, "The character does not hold up generally." As indeed it did not. Everyone's worst fears, most pronouncedly Tallulah's, were direly confirmed.

There was a little party after the opening at which several people drank too much. Lillian Hellman would claim in a New York *Times* piece about that night that Will and John Bankhead harmonized; Tallulah in a subsequent *Times* essay would contradict her flatly. Hammett and Hellman argued about a waiter. Tallulah, who had soothed her ragged nerves with bourbon, gallantly invited the black waiter who was serving drinks to sit down and join the party. He beat a frightened retreat from the room. Hammett contended that the invitation was folly; Hellman contested his argument.

Lillian Hellman wrote about that night: "I was entirely in agreement with Tallulah and I had a sharp argument with Hammett who, having been born in Baltimore, was trying to explain to both of us that a Negro in an edge-Southern city had possibly even more reason to be frightened of our liberalism than in her Alabama or in my New Orleans."

Miss Hellman apparently had her own repetitive symptomatology. According to a *New Yorker* profile of Lillian Hellman, she had argued with Hammett, too, after the disastrous opening of *Days to Come*, two years before, in the wake of which he told her frankly that the play was no good at all. Frightened and shocked, she reminded him that he had claimed, after reading it, that *Days to Come* was the best play he had ever read. Hammett got up, put on his hat and coat, and replied, "I have changed my mind."

Fearing perhaps that *The Little Foxes* would be another *Days to Come*, Miss Hellman took off for parts unknown and stayed there for several weeks in spite of the persistent efforts of Shumlin and his associate, Kermit Bloomgarden, to reach her.

Tallulah was furious, of course, but at the same time strangely buttressed. Lillian Hellman's reported apostasy drove Tallulah closer to Herman Shumlin, which is precisely where she should have been. She had been feeling somewhat left out of the close professional alliance between the playwright and the producer which went back many years. Shumlin managed to help Tallulah conquer her worst fear: that she was not good enough.

The play opened in New York at the National Theater on Forty-first Street, on February 15, 1939. It was sixteen years to the day since the first performance of *The Dancers* in London. Her mouth slicked with Vaseline, she stepped onto the stage, where she garbled and wobbled her first lines. She went dry, resorted to a Tallulahism or two, and floundered a bit. Shortly, however, calling on a last modicum of faith, saliva, and technique, she took command.

The performance—her greatest performance—was *there*. She played with an utter magnificence. *The Little Foxes* was a triumph of play and players.

Her reviews were unlike any she had ever received. Brooks Atkinson, writing in the New York *Times*, raved:

> Sometimes our Tallulah walks buoyantly through a part without much feeling for the whole design. But as the malevolent lady of *The Little Foxes*, she plays with superb command of the entire character, sparing of the showy side, constantly aware of the poisonous spirit within. . . . It is a superb example of mature acting that is fully under control. . . . Her Regina Giddens in *The Little Foxes* is not only the finest thing she has done in this country but brilliant acting according to any standards.

John Anderson of the New York *Journal-American* extolled:

> As the vulpine lady, Miss Bankhead is a fox out of hell, sultry, cunning, and vicious. The sight of her condemning her husband to death is a moment to parch the scenery; her crafty outwitting of her desperate brothers has the suavity of merciless laughter. Her performance, cloaked lightly in the buoyance of her comedy manner, suggests a combination of trade marked Southern charm and the spirit of the Borgias to breed a carbolic acid sugarfoot. She is Cindy Lou and Mme Dracula, honeysuckle and deadly nightshade, all done in a magnetic performance that is brilliantly sustained and fascinating.

The important critics, virtually all of them, agreed. John Cambridge of the *Daily Worker*, under a picture of Lillian Hellman looking utilitarian in Russia, wrote:

> Of the players, Tallulah Bankhead gave perhaps the best performance of her career as Regina Giddens, a greedy, unscrupulous and heartless woman. In the beginning, Miss Bankhead indulged in a few of her characteristic mannerisms, which seemed a hangover from the long course of whisky sodden trollops on which she dissipated her talents for so many years

in England. Afterwards, however, she settled down to a fascinating portrait of an evil spirit.

One of the most satisfying commendations came from Will Bankhead, who had always been just a little apologetic about the kind of properties in which Tallulah chose to play. "I have been gratified and pleased beyond measure," he wrote to Tallulah, "to have seen so many favorable notices and I believe now that you have a play worthy of your talents that should have a long and successful run. I implore you, however, to not overtax yourself and to get every possible moment of rest and relaxation now that the strain of the opening is over. You live practically upon your nerves and there is a limit, of course, beyond which you cannot call upon them."

The second performance of Miss Hellman's play, Thursday evening, February 16, was bought out entirely by the Friends of the Abraham Lincoln Brigade for the benefit of the ninety-two Americans, many of them wounded, who had recently returned from Spain. Miss Hellman had been in Spain in 1937 and had been deeply moved by what she experienced there. She was profoundly anti-Fascist, pro-Loyalist, and a sponsor of the Lincoln Brigade.

Though Tallulah was strongly anti-Fascist and sympathized with the Loyalists, she did not become as involved with Spain as she did with various other causes of the late thirties. The fight in Spain had preceded her real politicalization, and by the time she jumped on the bandwagon most of the good seats were already taken. It's possible also that the liberal American flank of the Loyalist cause was simply too far left for her. Though Tallulah was happy to play the benefit for the Abraham Lincoln Brigade, the degree of her commitment to this particular cause was best exemplified by her behavior at another pro-Loyalist function several months hence. At the Second Annual Village Fair for the benefit of refugee Spanish Republicans, which was overseen by Dorothy Parker, Tallulah appeared wearing a milkmaid's uniform. She, Gypsy Rose Lee, and Helen Hayes were among the many celebrities slated to be introduced to the gathering in New York's Greenwich Village. To complete her motif, however, Tallulah was expecting that the fair officials would have a cow on hand for her. When they failed to produce one, she left in a huff without waiting to be introduced.

In the fight to maintain the WPA Federal Theatre Project she was an uncontestable star. Herman Shumlin called her the "Joan of Arc of the WPA" and that pleased her enormously. In January, 1939, Congressman Martin Dies convinced the House of Representatives to pass a funding bill for the WPA which entirely liquidated the Federal Theatre Project. The Dies Committee report, filed in the House of Representatives on January 31, 1939, stated: "We are convinced that a rather large number of employees of the Federal Theatre Project are either members of the Communist Party or are sympathetic with the Communist Party." One particular Congressman inveighed that the project did not produce one single work in which "organized labor does not have the best of the other fellow."

Tallulah led the fight to head the bill off in the Senate. Though "dirty Communist" was her favorite expletive, when it came down to actually putting people out of work—of putting *actors* out of work—Tallulah rankled. After a summer matinee in June, she was presented with a huge bouquet of flowers and a scroll bearing the signatures of hundreds of Federal Theatre Project employees. Five days later, accompanied by Blanche Yurka, Philip Loeb, Herman Shumlin, Frank Gillmore, and Donald Ogden Stewart, she went to Washington to implore the Senate to restore the funds. The meeting involved a public confrontation with her Uncle John, who had announced his opposition to continuing the project. Daddy was there and squarely in Tallulah's camp.

While flashbulbs popped snappily in the Senate corridors, Tallulah entreated her lanky uncle with kisses, cajolery, and rhetoric.

"Uncle John," she said, "you'll vote to do something for the unemployed actors?"

"No, I don't think I will," he replied. "Those city fellows in Congress never vote to do anything for farmers. Sol Bloom and the whole crowd always vote against the farm bills."

Tallulah exhaled, "Sol Bloom will do *exactly* as Daddy tells him and he'll vote for the farmers. Anyway, we actors shouldn't be punished for what Sol Bloom does. We give benefits for the farmers all the time. We'll give one right now."

Tallulah filed into the committee room. Until the hearing was called to order, she sat on a Senatorial desk with her legs crossed, lobbying flirtatiously. When it came time to read her statement, she sat demurely with a script and a water pitcher like something out of *Woman of the Year*. She cleared her throat. In a voice shaking with emotion, she read: "I *beg* you, from the bottom of my heart, not to deprive these people of the chance to hold up their heads with dignity and self-respect, which is the badge of every American. Shakespeare lives in the hearts of men, but who can remember the name of Shakespeare's bookkeeper?" Her voice began to break as she continued "Actors are people, aren't they? They're people. . . ." She broke down; the gallery applauded.

Though Uncle John changed his vote, the Federal Theatre Project was ended by an act of Congress on June 30, 1939. In the wake of its demise, a Representative named Lambertson from Kansas, a member of the House Appropriations Committee, got into the act. In a statement read into the *Congressional Record*, he blamed the death of the project on Actors' Equity. He contended that "deserving actors and actresses all over the country" were being deprived of relief because the Communists had taken over "key positions" in the union. "There will be no WPA theatre project as long as this condition is permitted to exist."

Several months before Lambertson's tirade, in a most uncharacteristic burst of activism, Tallulah had run for a minor position in the governing council of Equity and lost. Her victorious opponent for the office was Sam Jaffe. Using Tallulah's defeat as "evidence," Representative Lambertson described Jaffe, according to a New York *Times* piece of July 9, 1940, as an "avowed Communist," who was elected "in preference to an outstanding American actress, Tallulah Bankhead." He admonished Equity to "clean house," to rout subversives from their organization. Lambertson went on to name the "Communists and fellow travelers" who were in control of the actors' union. His list included: Sam Jaffe, Philip Loeb, Hiram Sherman, Alan Hewitt, and Edith Van Cleve. They all denied the irresponsible charges against them, petitioned, and were denied an opportunity to defend themselves to the Congress.

Edie Van Cleve, who was at the time chief production assistant to George Abbott, was a close friend of Tallulah's, a steadfast bridge partner, a good listener, and a sage counsel, whose advice on contracts and money Tallulah was more and more inclined to heed. She would subsequently head the theatrical office of MCA. Edie's politics lay considerably to the right of most of the other people on the Lambertson list. The Congressman would appear to have picked her name off a roster of guests invited to an Algonquin luncheon given by Helen Hayes on behalf once again, of the Loyalist cause. But these were hysterical times during which many producers hung signs on their doors that read: COM-MUNISTS NEED NOT APPLY.

Edie was completely stunned by Lambertson's accusations when she read them in the morning newspaper. Ben Washer, who was a newspaperman at the time, called Edie to ask her whether she wanted to make a statement in response to the Lambertson attack.

"Why should I have to defend myself! The charges are absolutely ridiculous," Edith Van Cleve railed.

"You should make a statement," Washer advised.

Edie decided to walk over to the Elysee and ask Tallulah for advice. It was four in the afternoon when she arrived. Tallulah was sitting in a long silk robe having her morning coffee. She and John were still living together at the time, but he was out bright and early.

Edie Van Cleve showed Tallulah the newspaper story. "I don't know whether to dignify these charges with a statement," she told the star. "What do you think I should do?"

Electrified with mission, Tallulah rose from the table, grabbed a cigarette, and began to pace the room. "You've simply got to make a statement, Edie," Tallulah fumed. She yelled for Edie Smith and asked for a pad and pencil. She pummeled the paper with repeated jabs of her impatient, rushy handwriting, seething with outrage, and reciting as she wrote: "I would like to know where Representative (what the hell is his name) Lambertson received his erroneous and, to my mind, libelous information. I *demand* either proof or public retraction of his statement, as I feel this accusation not only severely impairs my professional and personal integrity but is an outrage to my belief in and loyalty to my country."

Tallulah picked up the telephone, dialed Ben Washer, and read Edie's statement to him. Her statement was printed by the Associated Press along with the statements from the other Equity members pilloried by Lambertson. Tallulah settled down; Edie joined her in a cup of coffee.

Tallulah rattled on about political footballs, the situation at Equity, and the laws of libel. She interrupted herself in midstream, looked over her coffee cup at Edie Van Cleve, and said, "My God, I never thought to ask. Here I've written this brilliant, passionate, outraged statement for you, and I don't know whether you're a Communist or not."

Edie laughed, "Well, I've never really paid much attention to politics, Tallulah. My whole family were Republicans. My father is a Republican, and I guess I've always considered myself . . . a Republican."

"A Republican," Tallulah gasped. "*A Republican.* That's worse then being a goddamned Communist!"

In the final analysis, people came before politics to Tallulah, emotion before reason.

She was profoundly moved by the plight of Finland during the so-called Winter War which started in November, 1939, when Russia, without provocation, attacked its tiny neighbor. At the time of the invasion, *The Little Foxes* was in its eleventh month, still hale and hearty, with Tallulah's performance a beacon of vigor and brilliance. Her relationship with Herman Shumlin, to whom she was and remained enormously grateful, was cordial. Lillian Hellman visited her regularly backstage. They too had a casual but amicable relationship. The Finland *affaire* would change that.

In considering the Russian invasion of Finland the brutal act of a bully, Tallulah was no different from a majority of the sentimental people of the theater. Tallulah attended yet another Algonquin luncheon in January, 1940. Plans were made for a general fund-raising drive on Broadway for the benefit of the thousands of refugees who were made homeless by the invasion. Former President Herbert Hoover, sitting beside Tallulah, told her that by the end of that week 700,000 Finnish citizens would be dependent upon relief funds. To the distinguished rostrum of guests, including Katharine Hepburn, Eddie Dowling, John Golden, and Helen Hayes, Hoover proclaimed, "We are fighting the battle for civilization."

The first week in February was designated Finland Week in the Legitimate Theatre. A Tin Can Brigade of attractive young Finnish girls would move up and down Broadway soliciting money. Plans were made for special benefit performances. Lee Shubert promised, at that luncheon, "You can have all my theaters, anything I've got." Tallulah, Alfred Lunt, Lynn Fontanne, Gertrude Lawrence, and all the distinguished luncheon guests promised to do anything they could. Tallulah just assumed that she would be able to make some kind of arrangement with Herman Shumlin, her producer, that there would be a benefit performance of *The Little Foxes*.

She was shocked to discover that neither Herman Shumlin nor Lillian Hellman was sympathetic with the Finnish cause. Miss Hellman contended, in a statement to the New York *Times* of January 21, 1940, that aid to Finland would merely "fan the war flames," increase the likelihood of the United States becoming involved in a general European war. Shumlin reasoned, rather petulantly, that the money raised for the Finns would be put to better use supporting the actors who were out of work because of the dissolution of the Federal Theatre Project. He was suspicious of the fervor that the Finnish invasion provoked and embittered that the Spanish Civil War had not generated as much sympathy in the United States. All these sentiments were included in a letter written by Shumlin which appeared in the New York *World-Telegram* on April 20, 1940. The letter concluded, "I feel that if Franco, Hitler and Mussolini had been defeated in Spain, the present war would not be going on. But it is on now and I want no part of it and I hope America takes no part in it."

Every show on Broadway, with the exception of *The Male Animal*, *Life with Father*, and *The Little Foxes*, held special benefit performances for Finland. Tallulah donated money privately to the cause and contributed her services wherever she could. She appeared at Gertrude Lawrence's benefit performance of *Skylark*—in which both husband, John, and friend Glenn Anders were employed. She was accompanied by a thirty-six-year-old midget named André Ratoucheff. Ratoucheff did an imitation of Maurice Chevalier at the party afterward. "That was the year," Stephan Cole recalled, "that we were up to our asses in midgets."

Tallulah was furious at both Shumlin and Hellman. By the time Finland Week was over Tallulah had simply stopped talking to either of them. Essential professional missives were carried between them by Dick Maney. Political argumentation was covered, rather prominently, in the press. The dispute was big news for a couple of days. Lillian Hellman made a statement almost identical to Shumlin's about the Spanish Civil War, to which Tallulah replied publicly: "I am confused. By what reason can she come to that conclusion? Were not Hitler and Stalin, those murderous monsters, already deeply imbedded in power before the war in Spain?"

And she rebutted Shumlin's ratiocinations thus: "I question Mr. Shumlin's reasons for not wanting to give a benefit for Finland. Mr. Shumlin had no hesitancy in donating his time, mental activities and monetary contributions to the Loyalist cause of Spain and to the cause of China. It is on the record that I, too, gave freely. Human sufferance has nothing to do with creed, race or politics.

"Mr. Shumlin's reasons for not wanting to give a benefit for Finland are not my affair and I would be the last to try to convince him otherwise. But I do ask for an honest reason. I ask that he hide behind no smoke screen of Americanism."

Tallulah intimated in the press that the Shumlin-Hellman team refused to consent to the Finnish relief benefits because of a bias in favor of Soviet Russia; privately she was more direct in her dismissal of the both of them as "goddamned Communists."

The team of Shumlin and Hellman had, however, provided Tallulah with the greatest property of her career. And Shumlin, in his direction, had taught her how, in a way, to separate life from art. She had the good sense to press on professionally, never allowing the Finn-de-siècle to interfere with her playing.

After a year of *Little Foxes*, righteous causes, and Richard Maney, Tallulah Bankhead emerged with the favor and prestige for which she had always yearned. It was the busiest, proudest, and most related year of her life. And, after 408 performances, she took the show on the road.

18

Will's Death

A COUPLE of months before she left to travel with *The Little Foxes*, Tallulah described her marriage to Elliott Arnold of the New York *Telegram*. "We're no Darby and Joan," she said, referring to the ideally happy couple in the popular song classic "The Folks Who Live on the Hill." She insisted, however, that she had found a "place" and a "content" which she had never experienced before. "I'm in love and I'm married to the man I love and I'm in a successful play. If John could only get work." John happily got work soon afterward in *Skylark*. By that time, however, Tallulah was off with the national company of *The Little Foxes*, and the marriage was rendered more meaningless than ever.

She and John seemed to have hit upon some kind of arrangement at that juncture. She began to see a great deal of an English actor, a lanky blond named Colin Keith-Johnston. Emery was smitten with the Russian ballerina and actress who was once married to George Balanchine, Tamara Geva. Divorce never occurred to Tallulah. She had said and meant that John Emery would be her last husband. He was a very convenient appurtenance, whose existence pleased Will enormously. Certainly, too, if it behooved the Speaker's Daughter to get married, it behooved the daughter of the possible next President of the United States of America to stay married.

It was Tallulah's dream someday to be the President's daughter, and that was not completely beyond the realm of possibility. In 1940 the florid Southern Speaker was at the height of his popularity and power. There had been, the year before, a move in Alabama to send Will Bankhead to the White House. That was months before the Presidential convention and prior to the time that FDR announced that he would accept a nomination for a third term. Will was not among those for whom votes were cast in the single ballot that named the President, but he was decidedly in the running for a Vice Presidential candidacy.

FDR had promised Will to leave the selection open if the Speaker threw his weight and his influence behind him. Will delivered the keynote address at the convention. But in a sly and surprising political maneuver, FDR refused adamantly to accept the nomination unless Henry A. Wallace was chosen to be his running mate. Will was the runner-up, receiving 329 votes to Wallace's 627. He felt betrayed and never quite forgave the President. He continued, however, to support him loyally.

"Everybody I have seen in Montgomery is seething with indignation because the President let you down at the Convention," Marie Owen wrote to Will.

And Will replied, "Except for the President's intervention I might have been nominated but, frankly, I had no assurance of it. I shall, of course, do everything in my power for the success of the ticket."

To his bitter constituents, many of whom threatened to vote for Willkie, Will replied with earnestness: "The Republican party has never been the friend of the South since the Civil War, and it is not even now interested in our development and prosperity. I have seen a great many times on the floor of the House when bitter sentiment against the South has been expressed by the Republicans, especially by their votes in matters in which our people were deeply interested. The South has gotten more actual benefits and consideration from the Roosevelt administration than we can ever expect to receive from Mr. Willkie if he should be elected."

Will's vigorous and unselfish campaigning for FDR took a ruthless toll. He was not a well man and had not been since 1933, when he suffered his first heart attack, followed, in 1935, by a severe coronary thrombosis. Weeks before he sojourned to the Chicago convention, he had what was diagnosed to be an attack of internal influenza. He vacationed in Florida for a month to prepare for the rigors of the campaign season, but he never completely regained his strength.

In September, 1940, he was in Maryland to open the Democratic campaign there. His doctor had cautioned him against this kind of activity; his answer had been, "Come on, Doc, you know I can't let the boys down." On September 11, minutes before he was to deliver the address, he was found unconscious on the floor of his hotel suite. Will's predecessor, Joseph Byrns, had been discovered unconscious in similar circumstances during a campaign year. Will would be the third of FDR's Speakers to die in office. When he awakened in the hospital, Will was told that he had suffered a painful attack of sciatica; in fact, the artery of his abdomen had ruptured.

At the time of the Speaker's seizure, Tallulah and Eugenia, who had abandoned bellicose Europe the year before, were gathered around the radio waiting to hear Daddy's address. Tallulah never missed a speech of Daddy's or any other political event that related to his career. She hissed like a goose at any guest who stirred or coughed in competition with Will's mellifluous oratory. News of Will's illness came first over the radio. Before she could leap to the telephone, the call arrived. It was Will's driver. He had been taken to a hospital in Baltimore; she and Eugenia were advised to come. Tallulah chartered a plane, and they flew to Baltimore. His daughters stayed at Will's bedside for several minutes; a longer vigil would have alarmed him. They chatted. Tallulah asked him where his pain was. "I don't play favorites," he chuckled, "I scatter my pain." She leaned over then and spoke her last words to Will: "Daddy, do you still love me?"

They returned to New York. Daddy was well enough to be moved from Baltimore to a better-equipped hospital in Washington. Tallulah pressed on. *The Little Foxes* was scheduled to begin the second lap of its national tour in Princeton, New Jersey, that Saturday. It was a solid hit in every regard.

Tallulah and Stephan Cole were in Princeton on Saturday. In the late afternoon, Stephan was unable to find Tallulah. He said to Colin Keith-Johnston, "I'm going to the theater. If anything is wrong, Tallulah will be there."

She was, in fact, backstage, staring out at the empty house. She turned as Stephan approached her and said plangently, "Daddy's dying." Uncle John had called to tell her that Will had lapsed into a coma, that it looked very bad.

Tallulah functioned tearlessly and efficiently. She made arrangements, contingency plans, decisions. She was gentle but stern with Sister, who was inclined to show her feelings. Sister was to go on ahead. A hired car would take her to New York, where she would catch a train to Washington. Tallulah would follow after the performance. When Eugenia objected, Tallulah replied, "You don't just leave a show like *Little Foxes*. A great many people are depending on me."

Eugenia rode the train to Washington alone, gazing out at a new moon. "It was a tiny baby new moon," she recalled. "I kept saying to myself: 'I wonder whether Daddy will be alive when that moon rises tomorrow?' He wasn't."

Tallulah played the play to a hushed, respectful audience who knew about the gravity of the Speaker's condition. She numbed herself to lines like: "Grief makes some people laugh and some people cry. It's better to cry, Alexandra." With Stephan, Tallulah boarded the Washington train. She drank a little and talked softly about what she would do to impress upon Eugenia the importance of control. She was still on the train at 1:35 A.M. when Will Bankhead, sixty-six years old, died. Eugenia was at his bedside along with Uncle John.

The rest was black cars and a series of well-choreographed dignified national steps. Heavily veiled, Tallulah took her place at the state funeral on Monday, September 16, in the House Chamber. Will's colleagues of the House of Representatives had already taken their places in the chamber when the Senate filed in, two abreast, followed by representatives of the Supreme Court and the diplomatic corps. His widow, Florence, followed, immediately preceding Tallulah, Eugenia, and Will's brothers, John and Henry. The President entered just before the services began at 12:35, leaning heavily on the arm of a military aide. He was led to a chair near the family members, who described an arc around the coffin, which was banked handsomely with lilies, asters, and gladiola wreaths.

Tallulah had admonished Eugenia before the ceremonies, "Sister, if you want to cry, cry your heart out. But do it out of view. It behooves us to behave with dignity." She sat to Eugenia's left throughout.

The funeral was opened by the Reverend James Shera of Montgomery. "O blessed Lord God," he intoned, "the memory of this scholarly Christian gentleman we will not knowingly allow to die out of our aching hearts. He loved the good, the beautiful, and the true and he saluted a greater future for his brother man."

Eugenia was about to break down when Tallulah applied pressure to her arm. "Shhh, Sister," she said firmly. "If you cry, I'm gonna stick a pin in you." Eugenia regained a proper composure.

Will was to be taken to Jasper, there to be buried among his closest kin in the family plot. A funeral train was due to leave Washington on Tuesday with a distinguished assemblage of passengers, the President among them.

To the chagrin of her disapproving family, Tallulah decided not to board the Southbound funeral train, but to return to her play. She was needed there. And at this time in her life, she needed to be needed and to be kept occupied. The state funeral had been a suitable modality for her grief and for her sense of decorum. The proceedings in Jasper would have been a lugubrious tautology for Tallulah.

On the Wednesday of his interment, business and municipal

offices in the little Alabama town were closed. Sixty-five thousand people jammed into Jasper to pay last respects to Speaker Bankhead and to be among the great who mourned him there. Services were held at the First Methodist Church with Roosevelt, Morgenthau, Ickes, Rayburn, and Justice Black in attendance. To the left of the pulpit and above where the President and other dignitaries sat, a row was reserved for the seven black servants of the Bankhead family.

He was taken to the little cemetery outside Jasper and interred beside his parents, who were buried in a common site, with the epitaph: "Here lies the man who inaugurated Federal Aid for Highways." Will had expressed a desire to be there, rather than next to Ada in Huntsville. His second wife, Florence, who had fished with him, and supported him, and nursed him through ill health for twenty years, would be laid to rest beside him in 1952.

Tallulah visited Daddy for the first time four months after his death. She went alone, leaving in the very early morning from her Birmingham-destined company train. She was pleased with his headstone: "Good night, Sweet Prince, and Flights of Angels Sing Thee to Thy Rest." He had always been her Sweet Prince. She wept and returned to the train.

In November, 1940, only a month after Will's death, Tallulah suffered another significant loss. Napier Alington, who had enlisted as a fighter pilot in the Royal Air Force, was killed in action during the Battle of Britain. He was forty-four years old. He left a daughter, Anna Sibell Elizabeth Sturt.

Alington was one of too many. During the late summer and early fall of 1940, the British lost one-fourth of all their available pilots. Britain was taking an egregious trouncing, and Tallulah was appalled at her own country's appeasement policies. Just hearing the name Hitler made her crazy. "God," she sizzled, "if I were a man. . . ."

Will Bankhead had been an early advocate of preparedness and a strong air defense for the United States. His memory, Naps' death, and her own passions impelled Tallulah to involve herself intensely with the burgeoning interventionist movement. She and Maney fashioned statements which fell stylistically somewhere between Rooseveltian vainglory and Will Rogers at a Liberty Bond sale. A typical Tallulah statement went: "I don't pretend to understand world politics, but I can understand that if Hitler were to win this struggle our own situation would be in a pretty serious way. That is why I favor giving all we can to Britain. . . . You can't take away people's freedom of thought and religion without going back to the Dark Ages, and the world won't stand for that."

Tallulah became an active and concerned member of the Committee to Defend America by Aiding the Allies and spoke at several of its rallies. On July 14, 1941, 76,000 people gathered in the various boroughs of New York to hear a series of speeches which emanated from the Rainbow Shell at Oriental Beach. Navy bombers dropped fluttering American flags. Telegrams were read from the various leaders of the armed forces. The pledge of allegiance was recited. In a voice quivering with nervousness and anger, Tallulah read a prepared address. "This mortal enemy of every American principle is threatening us with the most vicious and destructive forces of evil ever to be visited upon mankind, in spite of what all the isolationists and appeasers are trying to hoodwink you into believing," she exhorted.

Referring to "Lucky" Lindbergh, she continued, "Let me say here and now that one flier and his cohorts, who are in a position to command respectful attention, are in their blind ignorance more detrimental and destructive to our American way of life than all the subversive elements put together."

Though they were tinged with the melancholy of recent loss, these were proud, fine, and invigorating times for Tallulah. After Dunkirk, she swore that she would not touch a drop of liquor until the Allies had settled Hitler's hash once and for all. She cheated sometimes, feigning an upset stomach and sipping brandy out of a paregoric bottle. However, she had no need to cheat very much; her life was still too full and busy for alcohol to present any serious problem.

With all her activities, she still had time and energy to develop a brand-new and, for a short time, obsessive interest in baseball. Once again, the trait was Barrymore-derived. Ethel was a fervid baseball fan with an astonishingly encyclopedic knowledge of the game, a nonpartisan who could discuss its history and lore with anyone. Tallulah was incapable of neutrality and never acquired the in-depth understanding that her idol possessed.

The Giants became Tallulah's team. What she lacked in knowledge and rules and records she made up for in lung power and passion. Particularly at the beginning of her interest in the sport, Tallulah made some whopping judgmental errors. Before she realized that the teams traditionally change uniforms when they go on the road, Tallulah visited Ebbets Field, where her beloved Giants were playing the Brooklyn Dodgers. She assumed that the guys in white were her own Giants and that the handsome devil sporting the number 4 on his back was none other than Mel Ott, a particular favorite. Throughout the entire game, therefore, she cheered lustily for Brooklyn Dodger Dolph Camilli, though she could never quite reconcile herself to the fact that he was playing first base.

She had a box at the Polo Grounds and attended every game she could. Among her proudest possessions were two shares of Giants' stock which had been given to her as a gift. They paid an average of $20 a year.

She claimed to hate the Yankees. "How could I possibly root for a team with a name like *that?*" she maintained. But that was publicity stuff. Less public were her frequent visits to Yankee Lou Gehrig when he was stricken with a fatal form of infantile paralysis. She several times dined with him and his wife and did her best to buttress his spirits when Gehrig was living out his last days in White Plains, New York.

Dick Maney exploited the Bankhead baseball mania with consummate skill. "The press agent's role," he said, "is to foment publicity, *i.e.*, free publicity, and fan it once it starts to glow." He fanned Tallulah's interest in the national pastime into a roaring conflagration. The anomaly of the glamorous Tallulah Bankhead munching hot dogs at the ball park (Tallulah bites dog), cheering on and cavorting among her beloved Giants, became big feature news. Baseball-oriented Tallulah stories such as "Why I Love the Giants," featured in the *New York Times Magazine,* and "Tallulah Goes to the Ballgame," which ran in the *Woman's Home Com-*

panion, were typical. No Tallulah interview for the next thirty
years would be complete without her comments on the baseball
scene. Her passion for the game became an integral part of the
Tallulah image.

Central to that image too was candor: Tallulah as soothsaying
iconoclast who told on herself and others, who had no secrets,
who held nothing back. The image did not quite jibe with the
reality. She used dirty words. She dwelt obsessively on the intimate details of the sexual act. Because of this predilection, she
came to be considered a completely open person. Actually, where
the bones were buried deepest, Tallulah was absolutely secretive.
She never told anything close to the truth about the dissolution
of her marriage to John Emery.

John Emery had met Tamara Geva first after one of the pyro-
technic arguments with Tallulah of the sort which brought Dorothy Gish to her window. Miss Geva, who also lived at the
Elysee, was having a small party for about twelve people in her
suite when Vernon MacFarlane, the corpulent designer who
striped El Morocco, rang her bell. MacFarlane was a friend of both
the Emerys and Miss Geva.

"Look, Tamara," he said, "Tallulah and John Emery are having one of their fights. Why don't you ask them to break things
up by inviting them to your party?"

Miss Geva, who knew Tallulah casually, agreed to call them.
They came to the party, though they spent a great amount of
time and a good deal of Miss Geva's money making long-distance
telephone calls in her bedroom. She remembers Tallulah literally holding onto John "as I have never seen a woman hold onto
a man."

More than a year later, Tamara was sitting alone in her suite
when she heard again from Vernon MacFarlane. MacFarlane
asked her if he might come over for a drink.

Miss Geva replied that she would be delighted to see him. On
his way to her suite, MacFarlane encountered John Emery, who
was drinking by himself in the Monkey Bar, angry and depressed
after yet another fight with Tallulah. MacFarlane went on to Miss

Geva's apartment and suggested they invite Emery. She recalls, "So John came up, and he hardly left."

In the summer of 1941, after the tour of *The Little Foxes* had ended, John asked Tallulah for a divorce so that he could be free to marry Tamara Geva. She consented as she might not have done had Daddy been alive. Tallulah left for Reno where she was to have resided for the mandatory six-week period. Stephan Cole accompanied her.

En route to Reno, however, Tallulah had welling, resentful second thoughts. She stopped over in Hollywood, where she talked to George Cukor about the situation. Emery was summoned to Cukor's house. He and Tallulah met in the director's den.

On the verge of tears, Tallulah told her husband, "I'm not going to Reno and I'm not going through with this divorce unless you give me your word as a gentleman that you will not remarry for at least a year."

Tallulah got her way. She went to Reno with Stephan Cole and established her required residency there. It was not, of course, an uneventful six weeks. Having passed through her early midget period, Tallulah began a collection of exotic and attention-provoking animals, the first of which was a ring-tailed marmoset. She paid $3,000 for the small, blond, bushy-tailed monkey, which had the torso of a squirrel and the head of a diminutive lion. It hailed from central Brazil and sang like a canary bird. Unfortunately, the animal was extraordinarily tone-sensitive and took an immediate dislike to Tallulah, probably because she did not sing like a canary bird. The marmoset clung to Stephan and could not be entreated into Tallulah's waiting arms. Enraged by yet another rejection, she told Stephan to keep the goddamned thing.

She and Stephan then went to a circus. During the performance, the electricity failed, and the ringmaster, in order to hold the audience's attention, told about the recent birth of three lion cubs to their prize lioness. After the show, Tallulah went back to see the cubs and fell in love with one: a tawny, blue-eyed beauty. She bought it and named it Winston Churchill. Happily, the cub took to Tallulah. She toured with it in *The Second Mrs. Tanqueray*, took her calls with it on a leash, and walked it up and down Fifth Avenue. She parted with it tearfully when Winston's size made its frolicsome disposition a danger to life and limb.

The grounds for the divorce from John was mental cruelty, to which this time there was an element of legitimacy. In a prepared and overwritten statement, she lied to the press: "There is no third party involved on either side. We choose rather to put the blame on that 'Old Debbil' career which through force of circumstances has separated us for the better part of our marriage. This will in no way affect our mutual esteem and great friendship for each other."

She made reference to a "sealed financial agreement" negotiated between herself and John, which implied that he would settle a certain amount of money on her. At the time of her broken engagement from Count de Bosdari in England, there was widely disseminated the rumor that Bosdari had settled $500,000 on her. Of course, the count had given her nothing but some unpaid-for trinkets. Similarly, it is extremely unlikely that Tallulah either asked for or actually received any money from John Emery.

Where money and men were concerned, Tallulah had a convoluted sense of propriety and appearance. Though it was she who most often paid the way, it was the man who did the actual *passing* of currency. It was a matter of his pride and her vanity. In public places, she did not want it to appear that she was purchasing companionship. Where official relationships were concerned—and that including the severing of same—gentlemen paid their way in and out. To dower was to impart value, to endue with the deference befitting a Southern lady.

Tallulah's versions of why she had married and why she then divorced Emery would undergo extensive alterations through the years. She commented to a friend once, "I married John Emery because I loved him; and I divorced him because I loved him." She implied darkly that he was on the verge of suicide before their breakup and that that despair was related somehow to her as the elusive, indomitable object of his love.

There was an element of truth in the story. Emery despaired for a time because he could not live with or without Tallulah. She stopped somewhat short of the real truth, however: that finally she had lost him to another woman, that he had ultimately abandoned her because he was miserable being her husband. By insisting that he wait a year before he remarried, Tallulah was making absolutely certain that no third party would *appear* to be involved.

She would never reveal to her friends or to her public what she herself could hardly endure: that quite simply another woman had taken a man away from Tallulah Bankhead. Her candor was a red herring. The only "Old Debbil" at work here was a stark and rather poignant example of her own female vanity.

John married Tamara Geva on June 13, 1942, exactly one year after Tallulah's divorce was final.

19

Windows

TALLULAH COULD BE brilliantly intuitive, savvy, witty, and even sage. An intellectual pioneer she was not! She accepted the role of Sabina, the eternal woman, in Thornton Wilder's radically structured, megaview play about the resilience of the human race in spite of the fact that it rather confused her on first reading. When Tallulah, as Sabina, her hair long and cascading, in high stockings and a mini maid's uniform, wielding a feather duster and looking like a debauched cheerleader, addressed the audience audaciously, "I hate this play and every word in it. As for me, I don't understand a single word of it, anyway—all about the troubles the human race has gone through, there's a subject for you. Besides, the author hasn't made up his silly mind as to whether we're all living back in the caves or in New Jersey today, and that's the way it is all the way through," she was speaking a kind of truth.

She agreed to do the play because both Stephan Cole and Estelle Winwood implored her to do it. And she did it because, in 1942, she wanted nothing so much as a home, a place in the country. She had bought a magnificent place in Rockland County, New York, during the road tour of *The Little Foxes*. But it had burned to the ground before she had a chance to live in it even one day.

Before signing to do the play, she had dinner in the Cub Room with the producer Michael Myerberg into whose hands Thornton Wilder had put *The Skin of Our Teeth*. Wilder was serving with Army Intelligence for the duration. Myerberg, a swarthy man with teacup ears who had recently crossed over from the concert field where he had managed Leopold Stokowski, was waxing enthusiastically about the brilliance and profundity of the play when Tallulah barreled into the heart of the matter. She always negotiated her own contracts in the theater and prided herself on her business acumen. "How much are you going to pay me?" Tallulah asked.

They were interrupted by the entrance of critic George Jean Nathan, who shook hands with Myerberg and kissed Tallulah. "Is the play any good?" he asked Michael Myerberg.

Winking at Tallulah, Myerberg answered, "It's the play everyone hoped Saroyan would write."

Nathan had a reputation for squiring around town very young and exotic women of various races and nationalities. He was, this particular evening, alone. Tallulah chided him: "What no Japanese? No Chinese? No fledglings out of the nest?"

It was decided that Tallulah would be paid $1,500 a week, plus 10 percent of the gross, exactly what Fredric March, her co-star, previously signed, had agreed to take. They shook hands, possibly the last friendly gesture to transpire between Michael Myerberg and his star.

By the early forties Tallulah's terrible tempestuousness was notorious along Broadway. What set Tallulah off? What indiscernible offenses made her disrupt and boil and wreak havoc on the people for whom and with whom she worked? She could be a pussy cat or a tiger, depending on how she felt about what she was doing and how much *control* she felt she was exercising over her environment. She made inordinate demands on the people around her—demands for attention, approval, and deference. Her ragged ego required constant cosseting; she had to feel good about herself. If she was injured, slighted, threatened—which could be caused by the most innocuous behavior—a chain of incredible responses was set off within Tallulah. Hell had no fury and the Broadway theater hardly any comparable phenomenon.

When she did *Clash by Night,* just before *The Skin of Our Teeth,* the basic problem was her part. Under optimum conditions, the Bankhead style could be accommodated so that she was believable and brilliant within a certain limited range. There were certain *kinds* of women she could play, certain sensibilities she could render convincingly. But Stanislavski himself would not have been able to shove the forty-year-old Tallulah Bankhead into the skin of a slatternly Bronx housewife who is passionately involved with a *lumpen* movie projectionist. By the time Tallulah realized this it was too late for disengagement; she was stuck with it. Her entirely justified insecurities manifested themselves in tears, bellicosity, rage, insult, and manic intractability.

She had been wonderfully cooperative all during the rehearsal period. The problems started out of town, in Detroit. There, Lee J. Cobb, one of her co-stars, received glowing reviews from the critics; Tallulah, they said, was simply all wrong for the part. "That," recalls Robert Ryan, who was playing the juvenile lead, "was when the shit hit the fan."

To Cobb's absolute astonishment, Tallulah stopped talking to him. His long onstage method pauses, which had annoyed her from the beginning, were now intolerable. As he scratched or stared or ruminated before uttering a line, she hissed and muttered under her breath, "Get on with it!"

She fought constantly with Billy Rose, the producer, which was not difficult to do. During one technical rehearsal, Rose was out in the auditorium, shouting orders at the electricians through a megaphone. It was a crass procedure which began to get on Tallulah's already frayed nerves. She screamed at Rose to stop it. According to Polly Rose Gottlieb's biography of her brother, Billy Rose responded, "My mistake. I thought you were just running the scene for the lights, not the words."

"My mistake," snapped Tallulah, "was being in this play."

Cobb, nettled by Tallulah's behavior toward him, interjected: "Your mistake was not realizing that my part steals the show."

When Tallulah left the theater that day, she saw for the first time the marquee that Rose was planning to use, to wit: BILLY ROSE PRESENTS TALLULAH BANKHEAD IN CLASH BY NIGHT.

She was furious. Her standard contract stipulated that her name had to be first and foremost in any advertisement. She rechecked her contract and demanded that the showman take down or redo the huge sign. He obeyed. The neon lights on the Belasco Theater were changed to read: TALLULAH BANKHEAD IN CLASH BY NIGHT.

It was Rose, however, who had the last laugh. He rented some space on the rooftop of an adjacent building and erected there an enormous electric sign which capped the sign at the Belasco. It read: BILLY ROSE PRESENTS.

Tallulah spewed out her feelings for Rose all over town, her favorite phrase for him being "that little bully." When Tallulah's words came back to him finally, he objected: "How can you bully Niagara Falls?"

The trouble in *The Skin of Our Teeth* might have begun when Tallulah somehow learned that she had been a lukewarm third choice for the plum starring role. That in itself wouldn't have been enough to set her off, but it was certainly the kind of thing which she stored up for future use. Finland had been the final and most important reason for the rift between herself and Lillian Hellman, yet she never forgot or really forgave the fact that Miss Hellman had had certain doubts in the beginning about her ability to play Regina.

For the part of Sabina, Thornton Wilder and Elia Kazan wanted Ruth Gordon; Myerberg could not see Miss Gordon as essentially a sex symbol. He suggested Helen Hayes, who loved the play and held onto it indecisively for months. When she did finally return it, Miss Hayes commented, "I'd love to play it. But I couldn't even walk on the stage my way without feeling that I ought to be walking Tallulah's way. She's the girl for you."

Then there was the question of directors. Tallulah had entered negotiations with the hope that she could somehow convince Myerberg to use Orson Welles. But Myerberg remained loyal to his first choice, Elia Kazan, the intense, brilliant young director who had recently distinguished himself with the Group Theatre. Tallulah proceeded to make life hell for Kazan, who at that time was relatively inexperienced in the care and feeding of superstars. She stormed out of rehearsals frequently, refused to take direction, requisitioned lines for herself which had been originally written for other characters to say. She fought about dressing rooms, tore at her costumes, ripped at the set, vilified, cried, slugged, shouted, and divided the company into allies and enemies. She asked Myerberg to remove the first five rows of the orchestra section so that she and Fredric March would have more room to perform one of their scenes. When the producer refused, she grabbed a screwdriver and attempted to unloose the seats herself. One story tells how Kazan came to Tallulah's hotel, literally tied and gagged her, and proceeded to catalogue to Tallulah what she was doing to herself, to the rest of the company, and to the play.

At one point, Kazan, Fredric March, Florence Eldridge, and Isabel Wilder, the playwright's sister, who was looking after her brother's interests in his absence, all issued a Tallulah-or-Us ultimatum to Michael Myerberg. The producer thereupon decided on a radical and somewhat megalomaniacal course of action. Playing parlor psychologist, he decided to redirect Tallulah's free-floating animosities entirely upon himself, to become her one and only personal antagonist. All during the pre-Broadway tour, Myerberg devised various and sundry ways to needle Tallulah, to make his very presence offensive to her. He succeeded in offending not only Tallulah, but several other members of the company. By the time the play reached Philadelphia, Kazan and Fredric March had aligned themselves with Tallulah against Myerberg—so cruel and unjust did his behavior appear. Tallulah, who was moved and touched always by protection and fealty, began to respond to her director and her leading man as never before.

By the time the play left Washington *The Skin of Our Teeth* had coalesced. There were two benefit performances scheduled in New York before the official opening at the Plymouth Theater on November 18, 1942. All the actors had come into New York comfortable with the play, happy with their performances, and fairly certain that they were involved with a hit. Their attitude worried the producer. He reasoned that if the benefit performances went too well, his company might be too complacent for the Wednesday opening.

The Skin of Our Teeth opened with a costumed band marching down the theater aisle to take their places in the pit. Myerberg intentionally sabotaged the first benefit performance. The band's outfits were lost and mismatched. While they were frantically hunted down by the production staff, the audience was kept waiting out on the street for more than half an hour. The frazzled actors played to a hostile house; the first performance did not go well. Myerberg recalls, "By Tuesday, they were all out there with egg on their faces working very hard. On Wednesday, they were ready. Things like that don't happen accidentally; they have to be planned."

Myerberg's behavior was so bad that Thornton Wilder finally wrote him a letter and asked him to lay off. He did, though Tallulah was never to forgive him. The mention of his name was enough to evoke a torrent of imprecation. Indeed, she would not say his name, preferring to refer to him simply as "Static Slime."

Tallulah was a gamy and altogether luscious Sabina. Her performance won the Critics' Circle Award. *The Skin of Our Teeth* was a *succès de curiosité* which became a classic of the American theater. The opening-night *détente*, however, was temporary. She disliked Florence Eldridge particularly. Miss Eldridge, Fredric March's wife, had an important part in the production.

As Mrs. Antrobus, Florence Eldridge spoke a long, difficult speech about the human race after which the curtain was dropped. On several occasions, Miss Eldridge was perturbed by Tallulah's presence during the speech. "Would you mind not moving during my speech? It's very difficult for me to concentrate," she asked Tallulah. Her request became less and less polite. One night, Tallulah replied, "I haven't moved a goddamned eye!"

"Now, Tallulah," Florence Eldridge replied, rather patronizingly, "be a good girl."

"I'm sick of being a good girl, and I'm sick of your fucking frustrations," Tallulah ejaculated. Miss Eldridge blanched. Tallulah turned her back, sauntered over to one of her allies, and said, out of the side of her mouth: "Frustration—that'll get her every time."

Tallulah remained with the play through June, when her contract came up for renewal. She wanted to renegotiate and take the play on tour; Myerberg needed her desperately. But they each played a game of intrepid bluff. By the time Tallulah indicated a willingness to make certain concessions Myerberg had signed another actress. In the last weeks of her association with The Skin of Our Teeth Tallulah was as difficult as she could be. While she was applying her makeup one night, Danny Stein, the company manager, stole quietly into her dressing room and put down a box. Tallulah cast a reflective glare over her shoulder.

"What's in the box, Danny?"

"It's your bathing suit, Miss Bankhead. We're having it copied for Marion Hoffman at Brook's."

"You mean she had it on."

"Well, I suppose. . . ."

Tallulah drew herself up. "How dare you come in here and take a costume of mine without my permission! How do I know she's not diseased. Well, I've had it. I'm not going on tonight."

As Tallulah sat back down at her vanity table and began violently to wipe her makeup off, Danny Stein got down on his knees. "Miss Bankhead, I'll give you anything. A case of liquor. A pound of dope. Please, please, go on. Do it for my sake. For Danny Stein."

After Stein's departure, Tallulah began to rectify the minor damage she had done her maquillage. She laughed her Regina Giddens laugh and said to Morton Da Costa, who'd been there quietly throughout, "Those fucking idiots. If they'd read their contracts, they'd know I have to go on."

Despite the play's kudos and publicity, despite Wilder's distinguished reputation, *The Skin of Our Teeth* was, in the public eye, Tallulah's play. On tour in Boston, the management had to give tickets away to get people into the theater.

In her autobiography, Tallulah wrote, "I have three phobias which, could I mute them, would make my life as slick as a sonnet, but as dull as ditch water: I hate to go to bed, I hate to get up, and I hate to be alone."

Tallulah's inability to cope with solitude, as she entered her fortieth year, was becoming a more and more palpable phenomenon. From the time she left her service flat in the beginning of her London career, she had never lived and very seldom been alone. There were servants. There was Edie. There was a lover or a houseguest. There was even a husband. There was sometimes a friend, often an actor down on his luck, who would live with Tallulah for a time. They constituted her ménage, a permanent institution in Tallulah's life.

The lovers were less of a constant now than the male friends who resided with Tallulah. There was a series of such men in her life and, at the suggestion of Richard Maney, they came to be called caddies. In show business, where loneliness is endemic, livelihood precarious, and rootlessness generalized, it is not uncommon for friends to function in a service capacity for periods of time.

In Tallulah's case, such functionaries were required to be handsome or at least attractive, charming, dedicated, and generally *serviable*. They were sometimes but by no means always homosexual. They needed bridge skills, alcoholic capacities, and a kind of bohemian adaptability. They were boon companions, psychoanalysts, escorts.

There was no clearly defined line between service and friendship. People around Tallulah were expected to do for Tallulah, in return for which they received the various perquisites of being part of the star's life. The allocation of work was exceedingly egali-

tarian. Once a proud and rather arrogant young actor bristled in
Tallulah's company when she asked him to mix some drinks for
herself and some people. Tallulah boomed at the reluctant young
man, "If Jock Whitney can caddy for me, goddammit, so can you!"

Stephan Cole had been the first full-time in-residence caddy in
Tallulah's life, though lovers, fiancés, ginks, co-stars, and sundry
unclassifiable ménage members had always waited on her. When
Stephan joined the American Field Service in 1942, she needed a
replacement and chose Morton Da Costa, a robust, blue-eyed,
redheaded actor who had had a minor part in *The Skin of Our
Teeth*. It was especially important that she have someone with her
now. Her newly purchased country home was waiting.

She chose Da Costa because he interested her, because he was
unfettered and because he rather resembled Stephan. Except when
her directness was absolutely shocking, Tallulah's indirection was
elaborate and protective. She played almost ritualized courting
games with men—whether or not she had sex primarily in mind.
She simulated issues, evinced a tempestuous anger—which always
came as a complete shock to its object, but, if the object reacted
properly to Tallulah's erratic behavior, which is to say, with élan
and humor, she would munificently forgive and warm. With Merv
Griffin, who worked with her as a band vocalist in the 1950's when
she was playing Las Vegas, she took fatuous issue with the fact
that he had got unavoidably sick and was forced to miss a couple
of performances. With Da Costa, in 1942, inexperienced and very
much in awe of Tallulah Bankhead, it was a matter of flowers.

They were both in the wings, during the run of *The Skin of Our
Teeth*, waiting to go on. They were not friends. They had not exchanged a word previously except when Tallulah okayed him for a
very minor role in the play. Da Costa was minding his own business, trying, in fact, to stay out of the Unpredictable's way.
Tallulah had received a basket of flowers from a group of technicians.

"Very sweet of you, dahlings. Very sweet," she said to the crew.
And then she glared at Morton Da Costa, "Not like *some* people I
know!" Several days later Da Costa had reason to approach the star.
He had heard that she was making the rounds of the Third Avenue

antique shops, furnishing her new home in the country. He asked her to alert him if she happened to see a Victorian sofa frame.

"You'll go shopping tomorrow, Morton," Tallulah said matter-of-factly. He went home with Tallulah the next night. On their way to the country, she said to him, "I've decided that you're going to take Stephan Cole's place in my life." And that was that.

Each one of Tallulah's residences reflected in some inverse Gothic way what she had in mind during the period in which she lived there. The Algonquin offered hope, excitement, the chance to see and mostly to be seen. The mews in London was elegant, tony, and chic. The Elysee Hotel permitted her great freedom, an abundance of service, and ready accessibility. The country home to which Da Costa moved temporarily was for peace, gracious living, security. "Everyone I know is buying land," she explained to a reporter. "In these unsettled times, I think people feel that urge to own a little piece of dirt they can call their own."

This particular piece of dirt comprised sixteen acres in Bedford Village, New York. She called the spread Windows for its ample fenestration. The house which stood on the knolly land was a whitewashed brick Tudorish castle which had been built in the 1930's. She was able to purchase it for $25,000 because the war made country living most impractical and turned the marketplace into a buyer's paradise. The house was professionally decorated, though Tallulah hinted darkly and probably came to believe that she had done it herself. She sent for her English furniture, which had been stored at Daddy's house in Jasper, and set up housekeeping.

Tallulah invested a small fortune in her new home. Her eighteenth-century dining room was perhaps most emblematic of the tone she wanted. The walls and ceiling there were white. Mimosa-figured draperies hung at the windows. The dining table, which Tallulah insisted remain uncovered at mealtime, was of Italian holly. Her lighting fixtures were Continental crystal and bronze; wall sconces delicately governed the lighting ambience in the room. Her only ornaments were a pair of exquisite candelabra. She served on unmatched antique porcelain which she had collected over the years and old Irish silver. An extensive service of Waterford glass was displayed in a cabinet alongside an enormously expensive set of Steuben glassware. These were glasses, valued at $90 apiece, for every conceivable potable liquid. They were called the Hitchcock Glasses in honor of the director who had given them to Tallulah.

When Morton Da Costa woke up a little after ten o'clock on his first day at Windows, he put on a pair of trunks and walked out onto the veranda to soak up some sun. Tallulah appeared at noon, naked in slingbacks and carrying her robe. She lay down next to him, riffling through a stack of magazines. She talked constantly about her plans for the house, bolted up to stomp on some ants, lay down again and perorated on the killing of ants, called Edie for her cigarettes and a mint julep, and offered herself to the sun.

She and Morton were talking lazily when a Macy's truck pulled up to the house. Two men got out, each with a chair over his head. Tallulah, dressed in her nicotine stains, pointed the carriers in the direction of the front door and continued her conversation. Morton watched as the Macy's men did their double takes, shrugged their shoulders, and were admitted to the house.

At dinner that night, Morton was introduced to the rest of Tallulah's household. "This," she said proudly, "is Morton Da Costa. He's a poir-fect gentleman. This morning, we were lying on the veranda, I broke wind, and he never raised an eyebrow."

The Bankhead ménage varied from year to year. She needed people about all the time. People to do the multitude of mechanical, banal things she had simply ceased doing for herself. She needed people to drive her car, cook her meals, fluff her pillows, run her bath, make her bed, lock the doors, open the doors, keep her books, dial the phone, reach for objects, emplace her toothbrush, pick up the bridge cards which she would regularly hurtle across the room, open her mail, answer her letters, mix her drinks, do her shopping, keep her fireplace roaring, distribute tips, and, most important, keep her company.

Some of this was servants' work, but the more conventional breed would not have stood for the waywardness of Tallulah's household, for the drinking, the nudity, the unpredictable arrival of guests at all hours, or the flamboyant temperament of Mistress Bankhead. Tallulah hired and managed to retain, however, servants as unconventional as the house in which they worked. There was a black couple at Windows who were responsible for cooking, serving, and light housekeeping. They had once been in vaudeville. Tallulah often stopped the progress of a dinner party to ask them to perform one of their old song-and-dance routines.

When she hired her chauffeur, Robert Williams, a burly, handsome black man, he did not yet have his driving license. But Tallulah took an immediate liking to him and insisted that no one else could drive her car. Within the confines of Bedford Village, there was an understanding reached between herself and the police; when Robert was forced to drive outside the district's borders, she convinced the local police to escort them on motorcycle, thereby precluding the possibility that they would be stopped en route by alien traffic enforcers.

Estelle Winwood, Tallulah's oldest and closest friend, lived at Windows from 1942 to 1944, when she left to marry her third husband. Tallulah viewed the grave and antic English actress with a loving mixture of admiration and incredulity. She consulted Estelle about virtually every important decision in her life. She called Estelle "her sibyl" and trusted her completely. Tallulah never forgave or forgot a lie, though the truth sometimes made her furious. Estelle never lied to her.

Estelle and Tallulah were completely different. Estelle eschewed publicity, talked very little, continued to believe that the personality of a "theatrical artist" should be supplanted by his or her characterization. She had a felicitous, self-contained quality which fascinated Tallulah, who had no inner resources at all.

At Windows, one night, Estelle reminisced fondly about a period in her life when she lived on a farm in New Zealand with one of her husbands. There were no roads, no automobiles. They had neither a telephone nor a radio.

"How could you stand it, Estelle?" Tallulah asked.

"We were perfectly happy, Tallulah, because we were so much in love."

Tallulah just stared. She was fascinated but incredulous.

In the two years that Estelle lived at Windows, she and Tallulah had only two arguments. The first was about the dogs' dinners and happened during the Christmas season. Tallulah, who adored animals, had a surge of energy one evening when the servants were off and decided to go into the kitchen to feed the menagerie. Estelle got there first. When Tallulah marched in, Estelle was bustling around like the Henri Soulé of Bide-a-Wee.

"I'll do that, Estelle," Tallulah said.

"Don't be silly, Tallulah, you don't know how to fix the dogs' dinners."

Tallulah chose to think of herself not as incompetent but as lazy. She entertained the notion privately that there was nothing she could not really do if she wanted to, and she expected all her friends to appreciate that. In fact, most of them did. If she cooked, it was great food. If she painted, it was great art. If she negotiated a contract, she was a shrewd businesswoman. Tallulah was adjudged like the proverbial three-legged dog: The wonder was not that it walked well but that it walked at all.

Tallulah resented Estelle's patronizing manner. "Of course I know how to fix the dogs' dinners," Tallulah answered. "Any idiot can fix the dogs' dinners."

"The fact remains," Estelle replied, crossing from cupboard to work area, "that you do not know how to fix them."

Tallulah seethed at Estelle's imperturbability. "You think you're something, don't you? You're running my house, and I don't care for it."

"Well, someone's got to run it, Tallulah, because you're not."

"I wouldn't stay in anybody's house if I felt that way about them," Tallulah bellowed.

Estelle packed her bag and left. Several days passed. It was New Year's Day. Estelle had moved in with an ex-husband in New York City who convinced her to telephone her dear friend Tallulah. She picked up the phone, dialed Windows, and said, "Hello, Tallulah. Happy New Year!"

Tallulah said, "Happy New Year, Estelle. You must be back by Wednesday."

By Wednesday Estelle was settled into Windows once again.

The second argument followed a short trip into Bedford Village. Estelle's car needed some repairs, and Tallulah decided to ride into town with her. Tallulah was wearing a pair of old slacks and hadn't bothered to comb her hair or apply any makeup. She fretted about her appearance on the way into Bedford Village and expressed the hope that she wouldn't be recognized. At the garage, Tallulah was not recognized, the mechanic, in fact, appeared to be utterly oblivious to her as he discussed labor costs with Estelle. Tallulah thereupon took out her compact, smeared a coat of her favorite lipstick, Elizabeth Arden's Victory Red, on her face, combed her legendary hair, and emerged from the automobile. She flopped around the garage glamorously. The mechanic continued his conversation with Estelle, still unaware of her presence. Out of the blue, Tallulah asked the automobile mechanic if he would like her to send him an autographed picture. He agreed politely. Estelle, by this time, was seething quietly at her friend's foolishness.

There was a bridge game every night in Windows. The game was one of the few continuing divertissements in Tallulah's life. During the bridge session that followed their trip to the mechanic's, Estelle, out of nowhere and in the middle of a tricky play, said to her friend, "Do you know what the matter is with you, Tallulah? You're a showoff."

Tallulah was taken totally by surprise. "How can you say that about me?"

"I'll tell you how I can say that about you," Estelle explained, not lifting her eyes from the cards in front of her. "You said this afternoon that you wanted to go into town, that you didn't want to put on any makeup, and that you hoped you wouldn't be recognized. When we got to the garage, you forced yourself and a picture on a poor man who didn't even know you. I call that showing off."

Tallulah replied, "Of course he knew me, Estelle. Don't be ridiculous."

Estelle turned to her bridge partner and added, "The man said to me, 'Who is she?'"

"He knew who I was," Tallulah said, punching out her cigarette. "He'll know who you are when he reads your signature on the picture and not before," Estelle rejoined.

Once again, the argument heated up. There was an exchange of rudeness, but this time Estelle did not leave Windows. She and Tallulah simply stopped talking to each other for the duration of the night.

The next afternoon Estelle passed the living room. Tallulah and Dola Cavendish, who was also staying there at the time, were sitting and getting solemnly drunk. Estelle looked in at the mute and inglorious scene. Tallulah glared at her. Quietly, Estelle left the house and drove into town. She returned shortly, entering the living room with a little brown bag in her hands. "What's in the bag, Estelle?" Tallulah asked coldly.

Estelle replied softly, "*Mushrooms*. I thought I'd liven things up a bit."

Tallulah threw back her head and laughed so hard she almost sobered up.

Dola Cavendish, the wealthy Canadian Gallery Girl who had impulsively boarded the ship on which Tallulah left England, had been in and out of the star's life since their first meeting in 1924. At that time Dola made her interest in the colorful actress apparent to several of their mutual friends. Though she was too shy to ask to meet Tallulah, she queried frequently, "Is she all right? Does she need any money? Can I help her in any way?" It was Tallulah who insisted on being introduced to her mysterious and generously intended potential benefactress.

A poised, though laconic, young woman, Dola was the youngest of eight girls born to the Honorable James Dunsmuir, who had been the lieutenant governor of British Columbia. Her mother was Laura Surles, who hailed from the Deep South and was one of the numerous descendants of the famous Byrd family of Virginia.

During the Second World War Dola's considerable funds were frozen in Canada, but she was in the United States and wanted to remain. She moved into Windows, where, in return for bed and board and Tallulah's company, she helped keep the household functioning. She shopped, helped with the mail, traveled with Tallulah, ran Tallulah's morning tub, scrambled eggs for her at three o'clock in the morning, and listened adoringly when the actress, who was experiencing an increasing amount of difficulty falling asleep at night, wanted somebody to talk to until dawn.

Edie left for a time in the forties. She and Tallulah argued about a group of misplaced scrapbooks. Before that, however, Dola's presence had caused a certain amount of tension in the house. Edie had apparently felt somewhat undermined by Dola's eagerness to take over many functions that had previously been hers.

Few people who had eyes for such things missed the undercurrents in Dola's worshipful attentions to Tallulah. Tallulah, who had grown very sensitive to her own reputation, made it a point to explain to one and all that Dola was there for the duration of the war because she could not get any money out of Canada. Dola stayed on, however, long after her funds were available to her.

In fact, Dola was repressed and Tallulah uninterested. Tallulah told Glenn Anders once, "I know what people think, Glennie, but I've never even seen Dola in a slip."

Dola dressed in staid black velvet and quietly expensive pearls. She drank warm gin in abundance and suffered from a blotching hivelike affliction which made Tallulah furious. She and Dola argued constantly, their mutual hostilities released by alcohol. Their fights were almost ritualized. Dola taunted or nettled Tallulah until Tallulah slapped her, at which point Dola would walk to the butler's pantry unsteadily and pretend to call for a cab, her hand pressed down on the receiver. "That bitch isn't calling anyone," Tallulah would growl.

Tallulah knew how Dola felt and why she could not leave. She used her, and she knew she was using her. That knowledge infused Tallulah with guilt and anger which booze unloosed. Tallulah held onto Dola, however, because she needed her. Company and help were becoming increasingly difficult to snare. And Dola would always be there.

Glenn Anders was around and about but not actually living at

Windows. He liked to putter in Tallulah's garden, was a welcome
escort and dinner companion. Paula Miller, who would become
the wife of drama teacher Lee Strasberg, did secretarial work for
her and, for a time, lived at Windows. Ruth Mitchell, who is now
a very successful Broadway producer, was also staying at Windows.
Ruth was eighteen when she sneaked into a theater in Philadelphia where Tallulah was rehearsing *The Second Mrs. Tanqueray*.
Tallulah thought Ruth was with the theater management; the
theater management thought she was with Tallulah. She made herself generally useful and became part of the Bankhead ménage.

Tallulah had many lovers during her years at Windows, but seemingly no important love affairs. Her sexuality had always been a
complex and elusive phenomenon. As she grew older, it grew increasingly elusive. During these early forties, she was most tender,
most loving toward the male homosexuals who surrounded her.
She propositioned each and every one, always after an evening of
drinking, when she was feeling high and full and needful.

"You and I are going to bed," she advised one of them.

"Tallulah, that's the most romantic proposal I've ever had, but I
don't think so," he replied.

She was hurt and almost childlike. "You won't mind," she assured him. "It won't be so bad."

With heterosexual men, she was a rather cold, predative Don
Juan. She selected, seduced, and disposed. When she had her
sights set on someone, her personal maid was advised to prepare
her negligee, dose the bedroom with Coty's Jasmine, treat the environment kindly with candles, and lay on plenty of liquor.

Sex had always been conquest and acquisition. As she sailed into
her forties, she needed men increasingly for reassurance. The
younger they were, the more reassured she appeared to be. Tallulah was particularly proud of her liaison with a young man who
had social position and a glorious body. He was the father of a
small boy.

Tallulah summoned several of her close friends up to Windows
to show him off. By the time the entourage arrived Tallulah was
in the process of ending the affair. They were arguing about an
earlier affront to Tallulah's sense of decorum; the young man, dur-

ing a night out on the town, had called John Hay Whitney Jock. The worst of the fireworks had passed, and the wrestler was looking for his coat. Tallulah asked him coldly, "Where shall I send your little boy his Christmas present?"

"My address is in the register," he said arrogantly.

"I beg your pardon," Tallulah snapped.

"My address," he repeated, "is in the *Social* Register."

"Oh, I don't have that fucking thing around here," Tallulah replied. "All I have is *Burke's Peerage*."

The wellspring of her life outside the theater, however, was not sex but something Iris Murdoch has called "the metaphysic of the drawing room." Few things in life gave Tallulah more satisfaction than the good company of colorful and intelligent people. That, in a way, was what Windows was all about. There was hardly a person of stature in the entertainment world who did not, at one time, spend an evening with Tallulah at her home.

At her best, Tallulah was an attentive and marvelous hostess. Every visitor, right off, was given a grand tour of the house, the gardens, and the land. She developed a litany which went with every object, every painting. When Eugenia visited in the early forties, Tallulah stopped in front of a picture of Will Bankhead and said, "This is my beloved Daddy."

"Yes, I know, Sister," Eugenia replied. "He was my beloved Daddy, too."

Tallulah pleaded with playwright George Kelly, a painfully shy and reclusive man, to come to see Windows. He consented only when she promised that just Estelle Winwood and Edith Van Cleve would be there. After dinner, they filed into the living room and Tallulah coaxed Kelly to talk about his experiences as a vaudeville performer. He gradually loosened up; Tallulah was still mute and enthralled, when, at five o'clock in the morning, he began enacting, at her request, the entirety of his play, *The Torch Bearers*.

Guthrie McClintic, an ace anecdotalist, was another of Tallulah's favorite guests. She was thrilled and excited, too, when Katharine Hepburn drove in from Connecticut and admired her gardens. Tallulah had a very special admiration for Kate Hepburn, though they saw little of each other over the years. She teased Miss

Hepburn about being a "prim New England spinster," but she knew better. Miss Hepburn's waywardness, her honesty, her intelligence, and the great fun she derived from the part she played in life delighted Tallulah.

Aunt Marie, who seemed to grow fatter with the passing years, waddled in from Alabama at a time when one of her niece's servants was in jail on a morals charge. Tallulah donned a maid's uniform and served the meal herself. Maison Bankhead featured its specialty: vichyssoise, Southern fried chicken, champagne. Tallulah had great fun always shocking her Aunt Marie. When she telephoned the old woman in Alabama to invite her up to Windows, Tallulah went on and on about her new beau, how handsome and fine and intelligent he was.

"He sounds just glorious, Tallulah," Marie said.

"I knew you'd think so, baby. Would you like to talk to him? He's right here in bed next to me."

After the visit to her niece, Marie Owen returned to the Montgomery Archives with hours of fascinating stories. Marie, like Tallulah and the rest of the Bankheads, was not above punching up an episode to give it more drama. She described Windows, the beauty of the gardens, the lay of the land, and the artistry with which Tallulah's living room had been decorated. "The only things I took exception to were the lepers," Marie recounted. "The place is full of lepers." In truth, there had been but one leper, the young man through whom Tallulah had begun to take a special interest in the disease.

Actually, Tallulah was less interested in the disease itself than in helping dispel all the ugly and disastrous myths about it. She had visited the federal leprosarium in Louisiana, was the financial kingpin of its newspaper, and made it a point to be photographed touching the victims. During Marie's stay, Tallulah threw a party to which she invited the afflicted young man. Tallulah—quietly and unostentatiously—kissed him as he was about to depart for the evening. Fortunately, Marie did not see *that*, though apparently Estelle Winwood did. After the gathering was over, Tallulah passed Estelle's bedroom. Hearing quiet sobbing emanating from within, she poked her head inside.

"What are you crying about, Estelle?" Tallulah asked.

Estelle replied, "Because, Tallulah, you can be so marvelous when you want to be."

Like Estelle, the guests, the caddies, the prodigies, the servants, the visitors to and the boarders at Windows were there because they loved Tallulah. Those who left did so because Tallulah was increasingly a difficult and draining experience. She gave with prodigality: food, lodging, liquor, clothes, money, opportunity, fierce loyalty, the feeling of being part of a feisty, free, and glamorous life. Like most desperately lonely people, however, she exacted.

"Tallulah is an awfully demanding friend," Estelle Winwood told profile writer Maurice Zolotow. "She's very possessive. Woe betide you if she calls and you do not come."

After Morton Da Costa drifted away, Glenn Anders ran into him in New York and knelt before him on the sidewalk to say with admiration, "You got out." And it was Howard Dietz, the librettist, who proclaimed, "A day away from Tallulah is like a month in the country."

She was most exhausting when she drank, and at Windows, she drank a great deal of the time. And she was more and more into pills: barbiturates to help her sleep, codeine for relaxation. The pattern and effect of these combined chemicals depended on her mood.

When the apple blossoms were in full bloom one weekend, she invited Cathleen Nesbitt up for the weekend. Miss Nesbitt was given the full treatment: chauffeured limousine ride from Manhattan, house tour. Tallulah planned a formal dinner. Glenn Anders was invited. Fred Keating was asked to entertain.

Anxious perhaps about pleasing Miss Nesbitt, for whom she had tremendous admiration, Tallulah had begun to drink before the actress' arrival. Withal, she was still heady, risible, and entertaining as the group was ushered into the eighteenth-century dining room. The champagne served at her clothless holly table pushed Tallulah over the line. She became loud, garbling, and obstreperous. She passed out between courses and had to be carried, her hair matted with soup, to a chaise longue.

Miss Nesbitt and Keating left Windows on the first morning

train, long before Tallulah's awakening. Glenn bought them parlor car seats back to New York so that their exit could be more
gracious than their stay. Tallulah called Miss Nesbitt full of regrets
and apologies.

Tallulah thought and talked about her drinking, but she derived
great comfort from the fact that she was not, in the taxonomy of
the day, a classifiable alcoholic. There were no lost weekends in her
life yet. There continued to be periods when she didn't drink at
all. She was buttressed in her optimism by articles she read in sundry magazines.

One night Edith Van Cleve was tiptoeing past Tallulah's bedroom very late at night. "Eeeeee-die," Tallulah called. Miss Van
Cleve stopped. Tallulah was sitting up in her enormous bed, surrounded by magazines, a spray of little down pillows. Her fireplace
was roaring, her radio blaring, there was a half-finished crossword
puzzle at her feet; the room was dimly lit save for a spot thrown
by her overhead reading lamp.

It was test time. Tallulah rested a magazine on her chest, opened
to a piece entitled "Are You an Alcoholic?" The piece ended with
twenty questions. Miss Van Cleve sat on the bed while Tallulah
read the questions to her and carefully checked the yes or no boxes.
Edie, whose alcoholic intake never comprised more than two mar-
tinis a day, answered all the questions obediently. The test over,
Tallulah carefully calculated her friend's score. Her eyes scanning
for the verdict, Tallulah roared with delight. "Just as I thought,"
she said to Edie, "you're the alcoholic, not me!"

In 1944, Tallulah found herself one day without company at
Windows and decided impulsively to call Eugenia in Alabama.
Eugenia, at the time, was married to her seventh husband, a marine
named Bill Sprouse. Sprouse was overseas for the duration, and
Eugenia had elected to turn Marie's little farm into a boardinghouse, opening it only to couples with children. The idea was
inspired by the difficulties she and her marine husband had encountered in Alabama when they sought lodgings for themselves
and their infant boy, William Brockman.

Since her first marriage to Morton Hoyt, Eugenia had tried unsuccessfully to conceive. In 1921 she had some minor corrective

surgery performed. The operation had resulted in a bad case of septicemia, the disease that had killed her mother. She was advised that she would be unable to bear the children she had always wanted so desperately. "I prayed in every church in Europe for a baby," Eugenia recalled.

William Brockman, called Billy, was an adopted child. He was fair-haired and blue-eyed. Tallulah, among other things, was eager to check out the child who bore her beloved Daddy's name.

"What are you doing?" Eugenia asked Tallulah on the telephone.

"I'm here by myself drinking a mint julep," Tallulah said. "What are you doing?"

"I'm running a boardinghouse," Eugenia replied.

"I'm in no mood for jokes, Sister. Why don't you and the baby come up here and stay with me for a while? I've never even seen that brat of yours."

Eugenia traveled north with Billy. She and Tallulah had a joyous time for days, laughing, sunning, and catching up. Tallulah fell in love with the boy and volunteered to look after him while her older sister returned to Alabama to close up her boardinghouse.

Tallulah's speculations about what kind of mother she would have made ranged, depending on her mood, from the realistic "hideous" to the maudlin "wonderful." Over short periods of time, however, she was splendid with other people's children. She combed and fussed over Billy, took him on buying excursions to FAO Schwarz, read to him, danced with him, and sat for hours just stroking the back of his neck while she whispered to him. She swore to her friends that Billy was really hers. "Why do you think I live in the country, dahlings?" she laughed.

She was especially sensitive to youthful feelings. Some days before Eugenia's return, Tallulah was sitting on her patio, relaxed in the sun and talking to Mildred Dunnock. Billy threw a hard ball at her, yelling gleefully, "Catch, Sitter!" The ball hit Tallulah squarely on the nose. She buried her head in her hands and sizzled with pain. Alarmed, Miss Dunnock asked Tallulah if there was anything she could do. Tallulah smiled on Billy's behalf. "Don't let him see that he's hurt me," Tallulah muttered.

Billy loved his aunt, but he missed his mama. At one point during his visit he took to his room, hugged his old teddy bear and rocked in his new rocker. "I want my maaa-ma. I want my maaa-ma," he repeated. Tallulah tried charm, coquettry, chocolate, and finally sternness. Billy would not be moved. Tallulah was concerned and not a little wounded. "Thank God you're back," she said to Eugenia as she walked through the door. "I adore him, but I couldn't do a thing with him."

That night, the sisters Bankhead had a couple of drinks, spoke of their childhood, their beloved Daddy, and their respective lives. Tallulah asked Eugenia how long it had been since they'd played Marion and Elizabeth. Eugenia conjectured: thirty-five years.

"Well, Elizabeth"—Tallulah smiled—"how has life treated you?"

Eugenia narrowed her eyes. "Marion, I can't begin to tell you. I have a perfect marriage to the man of my dreams and a house in the country full of beautiful children. What about you, Marion? Didn't you want to be an actress?"

And Tallulah said, "Oh, I've become a legend in my own time, Elizabeth. I'm rich, famous, an accomplished theatrical star. I just couldn't be happier."

They burst into tears and had another drink.

20

Lifeboat

TALLULAH SPENT a lifetime ducking her chivying professional energies. Back in her early Hollywood days, she told a reporter, "Do you know what my ambition is in life? To be without ambition. As far back as I can remember I've been absolutely hag-ridden. I'd like to attain the state of mind that the Indians call Nirvana. That, for me, would happen if I were free of ambition."

At Windows, Tallulah was looking for an alternative life-style or at least a suitable environment to enrich the interim grace periods. When the company was good at Bedford Village, she came close to achieving the state of relatedness that existed for her otherwise only in acting.

By the mid-forties, however, the company was no longer so good. Because Tallulah ended too many evenings with her head in the soup, many people simply stopped coming to visit her in the country.

One quiet summer Sunday, only she and Glenn Anders were there. Glenn, handsome and sturdy in rolled sleeves and old dungarees, was snipping and pulling in the gardens, when Tallulah passed him in a sun suit. He watched as she ambled down the road.

Tallulah seldom walked on her own land, never strayed off it on foot and certainly not alone. Contrary to her typical behavior, however, she headed in the direction of Janet Cohen's house. Miss Cohen was a literary agent who was that day entertaining a group of prestigious people of the theater, including playwright Elmer Rice and his wife, Betty Field. They all were gathered around Miss Cohen's pool, splashing, laughing, eating, and drinking. Tallulah hung back in the bushes and watched.

She wandered back to Windows, passing Glenn on the way to her own empty house. Glenn stared at her over the jaws of his gardening shears; she swung her arms playfully, looking young and bumptious. As though she had just solved some weighty problem, she said in childlike meter to Glenn, "Someday I'm gonna have a pool so people will come and visit me."

It was not so simple. Tallulah had already sunk a small fortune into Windows, and her financial condition was precarious. Her accountant and her lawyer—those advisers on practical matters whom she respected and resented at the same time—cautioned against getting the pool. The water at Bedford Village was scarce, the lay of the land tricky, the vicinity rocky, and Tallulah's taste always deluxe. The swimming pool would have to *really* cost.

But Tallulah had to have what she wanted as soon as possible. A financial killing was clearly indicated; the movies were the answer.

Between 1943 and 1945 Tallulah made three motion pictures. The first, *Stage Door Canteen*, had more to do with the war effort than with her desire for fast cash and plenty of it. Tallulah was very active on behalf of the USO. She worked closely with Mrs. Roosevelt, raising money to open the first canteen in Washington. She claimed she was the first major star to dance with a serviceman at a USO function. *Stage Door Canteen* was a concatenation of big names gathered together: Isn't-that-George-Jessel-coming-in-the-door? And-look-there's-Selena-Royle-dancing-with-a-buck-private! Tallulah had one of sundry cameo roles.

The real movies recalled her that same year, 1943. Her old friend Alfred Hitchcock wanted a strong, sophisticated, and mature actress—but a relatively unexposed *film* face—to portray Connie Porter in *Lifeboat*. For $75,000, Tallulah agreed to be set adrift on a 40-foot-raft—a glamorous, materialistic journalist who has survived torpedoing by a German submarine.

Tallulah, as Connie Porter, is first seen alone on the raft, her hair and makeup fastidious, clad in the kind of mink that becomes a legend, surrounded by the appurtenances of her craft: typewriter, camera, and case of jewels. She is joined shortly by John Hodiak, a seaman with Marxist leanings; William Bendix, a burly Brooklynite who remembers Roseland; and Henry Hull, a proto-capitalist; Canada Lee, a Negro. Hume Cronyn, Mary Anderson, and Heather Angel complete the patchwork quilt of characters, representing the democracies. They rescue Walter Slezak, a very smart Nazi, who manipulates them all and takes advantage of the discordance among them.

To prepare for her central role as the cosmopolite journalist, the only passenger aboard able to communicate with the crafty Nazi, who pretends not to speak English, Tallulah's most formidable problem was learning German. In this area, Paula Miller was a great help. She drilled Tallulah in her foreign lines. Tallulah picked them up phonetically and rendered them by rote satisfactorily.

Though the picture was shot by the process of rear projection, against the background of Florida sea and skies, the characters several times had to appear soaking wet. Tallulah was drenched repeatedly and came down, during the shooting, with another case of pneumonia. She blamed in on the soaking and the sweating in her mink. But there was hardly a professional event in her life not attended by a major illness.

For her performance in *Lifeboat*, Tallulah received the coveted New York Screen Critics Award as best actress of the year. She was proud of her work in the movie and bitter at not being nominated for an Academy Award.

Actually, the film was not a very big success nationally. *Lifeboat* made money primarily because cosmopolitan audiences flocked to see it. There were problems in middle America, however. The picture was said to be somewhat subversive.

The *Lifeboat* controversy was begun by Bosley Crowther and Dorothy Thompson, both of whom objected mightily to the rather favorable delineation of the film Nazi, an accomplished, wily, and masterful man. In stark contrast with him, the representatives of the "democracies" came across as squabbling fools. Crowther wrote: "Unless we had seen it with our own eyes, we would never in the world have believed that a film could have been made in the year 1943 which sold out democratic ideals and elevated the Nazi superman."

Tallulah was dumbfounded by this thesis. She believed, as did Hitchcock, that the picture should serve as an admonition to the Allies: Germany would triumph unless they pulled themselves together and presented a united front.

In their own febrile, jingoistic terms, the critics of *Lifeboat* had a point. The German emerges as an eminently civilized, rather remarkable man, who resorts to perfidy only to save his own neck. The other characters *are* fools. They manage not to outwit but finally to outnumber the wily Teuton. In a scene of primal violence, they turn their backs to the camera, literally close ranks around him, and pummel the man to death. Their skyward fists are photographed against a vast expanse of darkening sea.

Tallulah expected to discuss the *Lifeboat* controversy when she met with the press in the Louis XIV room of the St. Regis in January, 1944. She sat in a chair, sipped cocktails, and fielded questions. The conference was just getting started when Tallulah espied a new face among the reporters and commented cheerily, "Here's someone I haven't met."

The journalist identified herself as a representative of *PM*. In an instant, Tallulah's mood swung violently. Clutching the arms of the chair on which she was sitting, lowering her head, she hissed through clenched teeth, "My Gawd. If I'd known. . . .

"Of all the filthy, rotten, Communist rags that is . . . the most . . . the most vicious, dangerous, hating paper that's ever been published."

Another reporter attempted to explain to Tallulah the difference between Communist and liberal.

"Liberal my eye," she yelled. "It's a dirty Communist sheet. I loathe it. *Loathe it.* I wouldn't even touch it with my hands. It's cruel, unfair, and rotten."

Still another reporter had the temerity to attempt to quiet Tallulah before she had ventilated all her fury. She stood and flung out her hand. "Don't shush me. This isn't your cocktail party. If you don't like what I'm saying, get the hell out."

Tallulah had another drink, paced around a bit, and pulled herself together. She addressed herself once more to the *PM* staffer. "I'm sure there are perfectly lovely people working on the paper," she said. "I'll tell you what I do love about your stinking little paper: *Barnaby.* I love darling *Barnaby.* I think that's the most *enchanting* comic strip in the world. I have my maid bring the paper to me with *tongs,* but I do adore *Barnaby.*"

There was general, relieved laughter at the St. Regis. And at the end of the press conference, which never touched any of the questions of *Lifeboat* and its political ramifications, Tallulah strode over to the hapless *PM* reporter and took her hand. "Dahling, I do hope I haven't hurt you," she said. Then, taking a very good look at the woman, added, "You know you look just like a dear friend of mine." The reporter smiled, began to leave. Tallulah yelled across the room, "*She committed suicide!*"

Tallulah's tantrum had far less to do with the politics of *PM* than with a certain four-page story which the newspaper had featured about her in its Sunday issue of December 27, 1942, more than a year before the swank press party for *Lifeboat*.

Written by Bob Rice, published after Tallulah had made a great critical success in *The Skin of Our Teeth*, the story was totally unsupportive of the Bankhead image, which she and Dick Maney had worked so hard and long to promulgate.

It questioned her baseball expertise, suggested that her work with the Stage Door Canteen was not wholly unconnected with a desire for publicity, and cited two anonymous sources: one of whom claimed she had argued a great deal with her late father, the other, referring to her marriage, expressed sympathy for Emery. "Poor John," the quote went. "It was like living with a puma."

All these disclosures, with their varying degrees of insight and accuracy, would have naturally upset Tallulah. But they took a simmering second place to Rice's references to Tallulah's drinking. The *PM* story was sneaky in this regard since it used the old journalistic device of negativity.

Rice began, "No longer is Tallulah's public primarily concerned with her capacity for liquor. . . ." Later on in the article, he referred to another "friend" who reported to him that Tallulah had polished off an entire bottle of champagne before going onstage to play a performance of *Dark Victory*. The article maintained that Tallulah, in spite of the imbibition, was "cold sober" for the performance. That addition did not mitigate the seriousness of the charge in Tallulah's eyes.

In yet another place, Rice reported that Tallulah had been abstemious since Dunkirk, that she would remain so "until the British won the war." He wrote: "She sticks to Coca-Cola, though there is a sinister rumor afoot that she puts aspirin in it."

The central theme of the article—that Tallulah was now on the wagon—did not make it any more palatable to her. To be on the wagon in the second place required that one had to have a problem in the first. Tallulah was aggrieved and humiliated by the charge. In 1942 one did not refer to a woman's drinking habits in the press, not even and perhaps especially to Tallulah's.

It would be many years before the proud Tallulah Bankhead became inured or at least more accustomed to that kind of publicity.

Several years hence the problem recurred with the profilist Maurice Zolotow, who planned a major and, as it turned out, a professionally valuable piece about her for the *Saturday Evening Post*. Tallulah asked Zolotow if she might see the copy before publication; he demurred. When the *Post* photographer arrived at Windows to take her picture for the piece, she used all her wiles to seduce him into showing her the copy. She finally plied him with enough brandy; he allowed her to see what Zolotow had written. The article several times referred to Tallulah's alcoholic capacity.

Furious, she telephoned Ben Hibbs of the magazine, demanded myriad changes lest her reputation and the honor of the entire Bankhead family be ruinously besmirched. She cried and begged and screamed and finally threatened legal action. The *Post* stuck to its guns, agreeing to make only one or two minor deletions.

When the piece was published it was a major success, drawing more mail than any other *Post* profile that year. Tallulah was placated but not appeased.

Her life was riddled with fine distinctions. They were of supreme importance to her. Though she minimized the seriousness of it and vaunted her capacity, she never attempted to hide her drinking from anyone in the *private sector*. Tallulah laughed uproariously when she heard stories about Jane Cowl, who, rather than leave empty champagne bottles behind in a hotel, packed them in her luggage and disposed of them with stealth. Tallulah would never have thought to do that since hotels and their managements fell into the private sector.

The *public sector*, on the other hand, comprised everything and anything which made the papers or hit the airways. That was entirely other. So the *PM* story hurt and aggrieved her. Her press conference at the St. Regis, one year after its publication, afforded her the first opportunity to retaliate. She was not yet ready publicly to be limned drinker.

Tallulah's prestigious exposure in the Hitchcock film led, in 1944, to another Hollywood offer. She was offered, for this one, considerably more than she got for the Hitchcock film, $125,000, enough to sink a pool on the lunar surface. The volatile and gifted director Ernst Lubitsch wanted Tallulah to star in A *Royal Scandal,* a stylized farce about the life and loves of the tempestuous Catherine the Great of Russia, a part with which many actresses had dallied. Lubitsch himself had directed Pola Negri in an earlier version of the vehicle, *Forbidden Paradise* (1924), and Mae West, the year before Tallulah, had portrayed Catherine in a stage comedy characterized by a series of solicitatious offstage raps in response to which Miss West undulated, "Entah!"

After Tallulah had signed her lucrative contract, Ernst Lubitsch suffered a heart attack. Though he was well enough to function as producer for Twentieth Century, his young assistant, Otto Preminger, was assigned to direct in his stead. Tallulah was fond of Preminger; she had, in fact, been instrumental in securing citizenship papers for his entire family in 1939, when Europe was beginning to ignite. She respected his talent and was undeterred by the change in directorship. Her fealty was reinforced by Preminger's faith in and loyalty to her.

At the very beginning of the production, Lubitsch summoned Preminger excitedly to his office. "I have extraordinary news," he told Preminger. "I had dinner with Garbo last night. I told her the story of the picture, and she wants to play the part."

Lubitsch naturally expected that Preminger would jump at the opportunity to direct Greta Garbo, who had not made a movie since *Two-Faced Woman* in 1941. But Preminger objected. "Ernst," he replied, "we have a contract with Tallulah."

"Buy her off," said Lubitsch.

The two rather high-voltage Europeans sparred for a time, but Preminger would not be moved. He issued an ultimatum: "Tallulah is a friend of mine. She's been very good to me and to my family, and while I would love to make a film with Garbo, I will not double-cross Tallulah. If Garbo gets the part, I will not direct your picture."

Lubitsch might have opted for Garbo over the Bankhead-Preminger package, except that, oddly, neither Darryl Zanuck nor his sales department in New York was that enthusiastic about Garbo. Lubitsch screamed that they were all out of their minds and resented Tallulah from that day on.

Tallulah learned of Otto's loyalty and functioned magnificently on his behalf. But the set was, nonetheless, rife with tensions. Tallulah had a multitude of reasons for hating Anne Baxter, who played her lady-in-waiting. There was Anne Baxter's personality—which simply rubbed Tallulah the wrong way. There was her age, twenty-two—which simply rubbed Tallulah the wrong way. There was her politics—Republican—which simply rubbed Tallulah the wrong way. And there was the *deference* paid directly and indirectly to the younger actress, especially by Lubitsch, which was the most offensive phenomenon of all.

Miss Baxter's grandfather, architect Frank Lloyd Wright, visited the set one day, causing a great deal of excitement. A scene was scheduled between Tallulah and Miss Baxter, and Wright had come to observe the filming. Tallulah walked over to Preminger and told him that she would not and could not work with the architect on the set. It was the middle of another Roosevelt campaign and Tallulah used as her excuse the fact that both the old man and his grandchild were "black Republicans."

"He's a very famous man, Tallulah, and he asked if he could watch his granddaughter act."

"Well, I'm not his granddaughter, and I will not act in front of him."

A master of compromise at least where Tallulah Bankhead was concerned and keenly tuned into her odd and proud distinctions, Preminger asked if she would *rehearse* in front of Wright. To that she agreed. Wright watched the same scene run through more than twenty times, became bored, and left. Filming was then resumed.

Ernst Lubitsch went, one afternoon, to view the rushes of one particular scene between Tallulah and Anne Baxter. It was Miss Baxter's most important scene, one in which Preminger had directed Tallulah, at one point, to close her eyes, a gesture used sometimes by one actor to deflect attention from another. Lubitsch stormed out of the screening room and castigated Tallulah. "That poor girl has one scene in the whole movie and *you* stole it from her," he yelled.

Tallulah was dressed in one of Catherine's voluminous satin gowns, her hair piled high and capped with rococo ringlets. She allowed Lubitsch to speak his piece, her mouth opened in a chasm of incredulity. When he finished, she reviled him with a barrage of scurrility that might have shocked Henry Miller, turned on her pumps, and walked off.

"What's going on here?" Preminger asked, as he walked onto a starless set. Lubitsch told him about the rushes. "I directed her to close her eyes, Ernst."

"She doesn't close her eyes in the script."

"I changed the script. The script was wrong."

Tallulah, after the exchange, had stormed into the tent which had been set up for her in place of the usual portable trailer. She ripped off her dress, hurled her wiglet against the canvas, and sat down on the floor. She was in her crinolines, brushing her hair furiously when Preminger entered.

She cried, her voice thundering out over the entire sound stage, "I'll give them back their goddamned money. I'm through with the picture. Nobody in my life has ever said that to me. Never in my thirty years of acting has anyone accused me of stealing a scene from another performer. Does he think that I have to steal scenes from that little nobody? Who the fuck does he think he's dealing with!"

Otto Preminger hunkered down to Tallulah's level, gentled his voice to an avuncular whisper. "Listen, Tallulah," he said, "you know Ernst isn't well. You know he doesn't mean half of what he says. I can't finish the picture under these conditions, and he's too proud to admit he was wrong. If you really want to do me a favor, you'll come with me to his office and we'll try to talk things out."

Tallulah heaved a tremendous sigh, thought for a minute, and agreed to Preminger's proposition. Lubitsch had settled down somewhat by the time they arrived but never, over the course of the meeting, admitted to having been dead wrong about the scene. Nonetheless, on Otto's behalf, and with great humility, she apologized for the violent temper she had displayed. The picture was finished not without incident, but at least without another major upheaval.

Lifeboat would survive as a minor film classic. It was the first one-set motion picture in the history of the medium, and its confining physicality demonstrated, once again, the early-middle virtuosity of director Alfred Hitchcock. It was the best screen performance of Tallulah's career. In spite of the nettlesome effects of the German *Übermenschlichkeit*, the righteous rhetoric of the Americans aboard the raft remains a fascinating demonstration of how we sounded when God was on our side.

A *Royal Scandal* has less to offer to posterity. It is a witless, chaotic, low-camp spectacle, too turgid for *opéra bouffe* and too undeveloped of characterizations to succeed as modern comedy. Tallulah looked magnificent, but magnificence has never been a particularly successful motion-picture commodity. She used all her tricks as Catherine: undulating, underscoring, raging, pacing. They were entirely appropriate, but spent abortively.

Lifeboat, however, should have endowed Tallulah with more than one chance to fail. It did not, and she did not make another motion picture for more than twenty years. She was not then, nor would she ever become, an actress who could captivate a mass movie audience. She was, in all regards, simply too big for the medium.

Frank Lloyd Wright could have stood and watched Spencer Tracy, for instance, on the set of a movie and never known whether Tracy was discussing a shot, relating to his co-workers, or actually filming a scene—so low-keyed and natural is movie acting at its best. Film acting is a symbiotic and open-ended art. The camera feeds and is fed; the audience relates to their stars by completing in a sense the cool, low-definition characterizations offered to them. Only by such a relationship is identification possible. Tallulah's performances were too highly stylized for such a phenomenon to occur.

Nor was she a screen beauty. Though she could be photographed so that she looked great, she was not in the classic sense photogenic. Many of the screen's most ravishing female stars are merely very pretty women *in vivo*. By a rare and miraculous kind of synergy, a marriage of features, contours, lights, and shadows they emerge enhanced: ravishing, interesting, or mesmeric. She returned to Windows in 1944 proud of her performance in *Lifeboat* and solvent temporarily on account of A *Royal Scandal*. The pool was built—a round affair, enwalled in part so that Tallulah could reach it naked from her bedroom door. She hoped now to stock it with fascinating people who would change her life.

21

Private Lives

THE PROFESSIONAL INTERSTICES in Tallulah's life she had filled since the beginning of the forties with summer circuit and touring productions. In her various forays into the hinterlands, Tallulah had always cleaned up, earning four and five times what she made on Broadway with no risks involved. When other names were making $500 a week in summer theaters or on tour, and other stars powerful enough to demand a piece of the action $1,500, Tallulah demanded and got $3,000 and $4,000 a week. Usually, the deal involved a guaranteed salary, plus a percentage. Richard Aldrich, the husband of Gertrude Lawrence, numbered among the producers who were appalled by Tallulah's demands. "My God," Aldrich muttered as he signed one of her checks, "that's more than I pay my wife."

Tallulah was an experienced tourer and rather enjoyed it. Traveling, in the summer of 1941, in Pinero's *The Second Mrs. Tanqueray*, she had pioneered the first complete package deal in theater history. Instead of relying, as was the custom, on local talent for minor acting assignments and on local artisanship for sets, lights, and sound, the Pinero revival came complete. It irritated the talented natives but resulted in a far more professional package. As usual, necessity mothered invention; Tallulah could never have tolerated a sustained relationship with amateurs. She had trouble enough with the pros.

Since summer theater was still considered somewhat infra dig Tallulah defended her choice as though besieged. Several stories, bearing her by-line, but *actually written by Dick Maney*, appeared in the *New York Times Magazine* in the mid- and late-forties. One read in part: "I work in the summer theatre, as do most of the other members of my sorority, be their bracket high, low, or indifferent because I'm prodded by economic necessity. . . . I work in the summer theatre because I'm usually only two jumps ahead of the Sheriff." But crying poor was not sufficient. She idealized her decision. Broadway audiences were spoiled and boorish and pseudosophisticated! The long run was a bore! The short run, a waste of time, money, and energy! In the Citronella Circuit—the term she used for the barns which weren't barns at all—people were appreciative, well mannered, responsive. The theaters were comfortable and modern. The experience was a comparative joy.

What Tallulah did not write was the more salient truth that summer theater was the only medium which afforded her the opportunity to be virtually sovereign. She had options about everything. She was the boss lady. As such, she could do her best to prevent or eliminate the vicissitudes which obtained when she was forced to deal with egos as bulky as her own—with the Kazans, the Myerbergs, the Lillian Hellmans, and the Ernst Lubitsches.

When her new pool failed to attract the kind of company for which it had been intended, she elected to return to the Citronella Circuit. Now she had another material goal in mind: an annuity for her old age, a fund for that future time when she might no longer be able to work as a performer. The play which she chose as a battering ram against eventual insolvency was Noel Coward's *Private Lives*.

She had been involved in several productions of the comedy, the first, in 1944, at Gus Schirmer, Jr.'s theater in Connecticut. It was an undistinguished but lucrative stint.

In 1946, she did *Private Lives* again, but the difference was Donald Cook, who played brilliantly opposite Tallulah. Dark, handsome, one of the last of the high-comedy matinee idols, Alfred Lunt called him "the only leading man in America," an endorsement which Tallulah cited frequently. They played for two weeks in Connecticut and went on to do a quick series of one-night stands through Canada.

Cook was one of the few first-rate talents with whom Tallulah was able to work. He was known in the theater for his amorous involvements with his leading ladies. Tallulah felicitously was known for her fervent pursuit of her leading men. They became and remained lovers.

The production was a prodigious success. Summer theater boomed after World War II. Gas rationing had just been lifted, the production of automobiles resumed, and the restrictions which remained on travel abroad kept the kind of people most likely to go to the theater in the country. All that and Tallulah, too. There were hundreds of turnaways at every stop in the tour.

Will Bankhead's youngest brother, Henry, with whom Tallulah had lived for a while during her lean, early days in New York, was a career diplomat stationed in Ottawa. When Tallulah and Company came through, he was naturally overjoyed at the prospect of showing off his famous niece. The rotund attaché planned a quiet buffet for her and the cast at an elegant hotel in Ottawa. He invited an assortment of Canadian VIP's.

Tallulah called together her little company: Donald, Mary Mason, Alexander Clark, and Alice Pearce. She lectured them gently on diplomatic protocol, begged them to be on their best behavior as Americans and as representatives of their often maligned profession. It was, however, Tallulah's behavior which was less than decorous. She got drunker than she intended to at Uncle Henry's buffet, took off all her clothes, and ran naked up and down the corridors of the hotel. The next day she called together her company once again. She made no overt reference to the gala event of the night before but told her fellow actors firmly that for the remaining weeks of the tour they were *all* going on the wagon.

Several thousand dollars richer, Tallulah left *Private Lives* to return to Broadway in March, 1947. The play was a Cocteau drama which had fared well in Europe called *The Eagle Has Two Heads*. For her leading man, she set her sights on the young and yet unsung Marlon Brando. They worked together for a while. He was replaced. She would claim in a press interview that Brando drove her to distraction picking his nose, pausing too long, and scratching himself. The chemistry was unfortunate; the havoc that prevailed made a Tom and Jerry chase sequence seem Chekhovian.

Eagle Has Two Heads was a prolix tract about a Bavarian queen who falls in love with the man who is hired to assassinate her. The play had enormous appeal for Tallulah. In the first act, she had a marathon speech comprising 20,000 words. In the last act, after she was shot, she toppled climactically down a vast flight of steps.

Despite a $50,000 advance, which testified to Tallulah's growing magnetism along Broadway, *Eagle* flopped after twenty-nine performances. She threw up her hands, turned down Orson Welles' offer to play Lady to his Macbeth in Utah, and returned to *Private Lives*. This time she intended to exact from the vehicle the best of both worlds. An exhaustive countrywide tour was planned with a Broadway terminus. She would make lots of money in the minor leagues and garner the prestige of the majors as well.

Now that the stakes were larger, she endeavored to make certain adjustments. Though taxonomy had not yet caught up with Tallulah's drinking problem, Donald Cook was by anyone's standards, his own included, an alcoholic. One drink could and frequently did set him off. His drinking on the prior tour had been tolerated, but no more. Tallulah forbade him to drink at all and warned that he would be fired "summarily" for even one lapse. Their affair was severed at the same time, perhaps because either one or both of them realized that an emotional involvement with Tallulah was incompatible with extended sobriety. Tallulah, in her role as hard-nosed queen bee, was fully aware of the good sense of this arrangement. She needed a leading man of Donald Cook's caliber certainly more than she needed a lover.

John C. Wilson, an old friend of Noel Coward's and a talented man of the theater, was recruited to produce this more ambitious *Private Lives*. Martin Manulis was chosen to direct. But it was Donald and Tallulah who made all the important stylistic decisions about their performances.

This play with which Tallulah was becoming so lengthily involved had been written by Coward during a three-day spell of influenza in Bangkok. It is about two insufferably civilized ex-lovers, Elyot and Amanda, who meet in the south of France after each has chosen another mate and promptly decide that, though living together was difficult, living apart was even worse. The play is characterized by such lines as Amanda's: "I believe in being kind to everyone and giving money to old beggar women and being as gay as possible." It is a metronomic ronde of bon mots and high comedic sighs. Noel Coward played it first, in the United States, opposite Gertrude Lawrence. That production was a very English, rather fluty thing whose style Donald and Tallulah never chose to emulate. They turned *Private Lives* into a romp: vital, American, somewhat athletic, and frequently divine.

Rehearsals were held almost without incident at Windows. Donald and Tallulah had a wonderful rapport throughout. He knew, for instance, that her temperamental explosions were due frequently to the fact that she was simply *unable* to communicate with her director. It was the age of the acting school. Problems had names. Acting had a vocabulary. But Tallulah refused to use that vocabulary. So she was in rehearsal like a child who could not ask for what she wanted. Coupled with Tallulah's hauteur, the consequences could be disastrous.

Cook's sensitivity was averting. At one point she said to Martin Manulis, "What am I doing?" She meant that she did not understand why Amanda behaved as she did at one moment in the play. Manulis couldn't help; he didn't understand the question. She groaned at John Wilson. "What am I doing, John?" He replied, "You're doing just fine, Tallulah." "*Donald!*" she implored. Donald Cook knew precisely what she meant, and together they worked on the problem.

Therese Quadri, the Frenchwoman who had played the maid in the original *Private Lives* with Noel Coward, was chosen to repeat her performance. The part is minuscule, but Miss Quadri was and continues to be almost an institution in the part. Auditions for the second leads, male and female, were held at the Belasco Theater with Tallulah, of course, presiding.

Phil Arthur, a good, sturdy, pleasant-looking fellow with a flair for high, dry comedy was picked to play Amanda's present husband. He had toured successfully with Lucille Ball, Ruth Chatterton, and Sylvia Sidney, was known to be cooperative, quiet, and nontemperamental. The ideal touring actor. When a group of strangers is impelled to live together for months, sometimes years at a time, these qualities are as important as the dramaturgical ones.

In choosing Sybil, her young female rival, Tallulah auditioned hundreds of ingenues. Blond, fluffy, twenty-year-old Buff Cobb was her final choice. Buff, who had had a bit of experience in radio and movies, read with facility. As important, she was the granddaughter of Irvin S. Cobb, the humorist, and the daughter of Elizabeth "Buff" Cobb, whom Tallulah had known for years. The young Buff had recently married William Eythe, Tallulah's co-star in *Royal Scandal*. She was, therefore, a known commodity, obviously a girl of breeding and good manners. She would defer, and she was no threat.

"My granddaddy saved your granddaddy from drowning once," Tallulah yelled to Buff from the darkened auditorium. "Or was it *your* granddaddy who rescued my granddaddy?"

With the play cast and rehearsed, the *Private Lives* company played Westport, Connecticut, for several weeks to get the kinks out. From Westport they were scheduled to go on to Chicago and hence to ten or so major cities before coming into New York some time in the spring of 1948.

Opening night in Westport, July 14, 1947, Tallulah was being zipped into a sensational midnight blue Mainbocher by her theater maid, Evyleen Cronin, when she overheard a conversation taking place next door in Buff Cobb's dressing room. Buff had been unable to get into New York City because of the hectic rehearsal schedule to have her hair done as she would have liked. The ingenue's mother, also called Buff, had come back to see her daughter just before half-hour. "My God," she said to the young actress, "you're not going on like *that*."

Tallulah barked: "Buff!"

"Yes, ma'am," young Buff said, appearing obediently at the threshold of Tallulah's dressing room.

"Not you. Buff!" she repeated, at which time the elder, intrusive Buff came smiling.

Tallulah hurled her pointed right hand, "Get out," she yelled. "Get *awt* and don't come back until after the performance."

She called for Stephan Cole, who was stage managing the production. Stephan had returned to Tallulah's life after his time away with the American Field Service. Tallulah informed Stephan that the backstage area would henceforth be out of bounds to the ingenue's family. Her quidnunc's instinct, developed in the service of her natural curiosity and her desire to control absolutely, made Tallulah, at her best, a tough, effective and protective company manager. She knew everybody's business all the time.

They went headily on to Chicago, where the opening was an hysterical success. Buff Cobb remembers, "It was like nothing I have ever experienced, terrifying in many ways, very much like a title bout at Madison Square Garden. The audience was not just applauding; they were pounding, kicking, and cheering. The play was an absolute knockout, like Benvenuti's first fight. Tallulah was magnificent." The run they knew would exceed the original estimate.

Tallulah settled into a commodious suite at the Ambassador Hotel. There she entertained her *Private Lives* company almost every night. She regularly wore a string of perfectly matched pearls, baggy Hattie Carnegie slacks, and a dippy top which showed her shoulder blades to their best advantage. She rather liked her shoulder blades as she did most of her bones. She was fond of saying, usually while exploring her facial contours in the mirror, "I'll never grow old because I have a marvelous bone structure." She had less faith in her breasts, which were beginning to sag with age, and even in her naked escapades she had taken of late to wearing a bra.

She paced and chafed and talked constantly, telling all her old stories to new people. At three or four in the morning, a combination of bourbon and sleeping pills would cut into her tensions and she turned from chattering neurasthenic to garbling sybarite. Then someone would help her to get to bed. There was a tacit understanding among the company that someone had to stay and be with Tallulah until she fell asleep. The job went alternately to

Buff, Dola Cavendish, who was traveling with her, Stephan Cole, or Dave Garroway, who was very much around during that Chicago stint. Everyone came to Tallulah's suite in the evening, except Phil Arthur, who kept to himself. His diffidence made Tallulah angry.

The real nemesis, however, entered the picture after the Chicago opening. She was Barbara Baxley, Buff Cobb's nineteen-year-old understudy, an intense, gifted actress with a dancer's back and alarmingly wide Bette Davis eyes. Donald Cook was immediately interested.

Tallulah would admit, years later, that her animosity toward Barbara was the pure and simple jealousy of an older woman toward one much younger. Tallulah was furious at Donald's attraction to the girl. That he was no longer Tallulah's lover was irrelevant.

Tallulah used a complicity of other factors to justify her jealousy. They were not bogus but probably secondary. There was Barbara's training, her manners, her standoffishness, and her arrogance. Tallulah resented the whole package.

Barbara was straight out of Sanford Meisner's acting classes. Tallulah disapproved of all acting schools, Meisner's, Kazan's, and Stella Adler's especially. She lumped them together with the Group Theatre. Where the enemy was concerned, she was not a keen individuater. To Tallulah, these were all alien institutions that produced politically susceptible, theatrically abhorrent specimens of mumbling, stumbling, psychoanalyzed actors, like Cobb and Brando, who were invariably trouble.

Tallulah couldn't fault Barbara's acting. It was too good. But she did wait for her to do something ridiculously "method" in preparation for the part. And when Tallulah heard that the understudy had gone to the zoo to find an animal to serve as an archetype for the part of Sybil, that she had discovered that animal in the hummingbird, Tallulah turned into a veritable Vesuvius. "*Hummingbird,*" Tallulah screamed, and began to pummel the nearest table with her open hand. "*Hummingbird!* There's a beat to this play, and you say your lines!"

Tallulah also objected to Barbara for her political involvement.

Those were fiercely partisan times. Paul Robeson was being scrutinized lest his low notes topple General Motors. The Hollywood Ten were hauled before J. Parnell Thomas and the House Un-American Activities Committee. The Navy refused to allow its personnel to view a motion picture called *Crossfire,* which was about nothing more than the deranging effects of anti-Semitism and ended with a brotherhood speech delivered by a pipe-puffing Robert Young. With Helen Hayes in the forefront, Equity was attempting to desegregate legitimate theaters in Washington, D.C.

Barbara *and* Buff were active and concerned. They went to rallies, attended benefits and luncheons, and tried generally to behave like responsible citizens. Tallulah demanded manifestos. She accepted Buff Cobb's involvement, once explained, as the activities of a liberal, humanitarian, intellectually curious young artist, dismissing her with the admonition: "Don't be bamboozled by those goddamned Reds." Barbara's activities were somewhat more liberal and therefore eminently more suspect. When Barbara walked into the theater with a copy of *PM* under her arm and announced to one and all that she was an atheist, Tallulah's suspicions were confirmed.

Tallulah was fanatical about what she called "theater manners," amenities among actors. She said "Good evening" to one and all when entering and leaving the theater and expected the courtesies to be reciprocated. Barbara failed in this department as well. She was corrected. When she did try to greet the star, however, Barbara ran into additional problems. If she said, "Good evening, Miss Bankhead," Tallulah objected, "Damn it! Why don't you call me Tallulah?" If, on the other hand, she said "Good evening, Tallulah," she was told: "You're to call me Miss Bankhead."

Barbara passed Tallulah's dressing room one night and said nothing. Tallulah yelled out, "Why don't you say good evening?"

"I just don't feel like it, Tallulah," Barbara replied.

"I insist on certain amenities in my company," Tallulah said. "Now will you say, 'Good evening, Miss Bankhead'?"

Barbara did not answer.

"Very well," Tallulah replied. "I'll say it for you."

Tallulah began to pummel her dressing table, repeating: GOOD

EVENING, MISS BANKHEAD. GOOD EVENING, MISS BANKHEAD. GOOD EVE-
NING, MISS BANKHEAD. GOOD EVENING, MISS BANKHEAD.

Tallulah was not crazy, merely manic sometimes. Barbara
could have got to the star, with humor, or deference, or vulnerability, or loyalty. Tallulah, on the other hand, could have fired Barbara any time she pleased, but she had too much pride in her
professional rectitude to indulge in that kind of caprice. Also, she
may very well have begun to enjoy the game.

After turning down many of her invitations, Barbara Baxley
consented finally to attend one of Tallulah's evenings at the Ambassador East. The gathering was small. It included Stephan Cole,
Dola, Donald Cook, Buff Cobb, and William Langford, a Canadian actor who was understudying Phil Arthur. When Barbara
entered, Tallulah was telling one of her favorite dialect stories
about Daddy and the Colored People. The story concerned Will's
return to Jasper, Alabama, after several triumphant years in Washington. The town turned out to give him a hero's welcome. A band
played. Signs of greeting were hoisted aloft. Into this general state
of excitation, an old colored man walked. He scratched his head
and inquired about the hubbub.

"Mr. Will's back!" he was told.

And the old colored man said, "Mr. Will's *back!* Where's he
been?"

Tallulah was drunk. Barbara had barely time to settle in when
Tallulah walked up to her and inexplicably pushed her. "Awfully
sorry, dahling," she said.

Barbara smiled wanly. "That's all right, Tallulah."

Tallulah circled the room, came up to Barbara again, and
pushed her for the second time.

"Awfully sorry."

"I wish you wouldn't push me, Tallulah."

"I know just how you feel. I don't like to be pushed either."

When she pushed the young actress a third time, Barbara took
one of Tallulah's shoulder blades in each hand and hurtled her
across the room. Tallulah fell on top of the bar: shattering glasses,
spilling liquor, upsetting flower arrangements, and squashing caviar.

Barbara went home that night and waited for the call. She simply assumed that she would be fired. When no call came, she showed up at the Harris Theater the next evening and shuddered as Tallulah approached her.

Tallulah said only, "Quite a party, wasn't it, Barbara?"

Withal, Tallulah and the *Private Lives* company continued to function magnificently. The production was kept finely honed and totally controlled. If a laugh came on the wrong beat or not at all, the problem was discussed at length and usually solved. Tricks, jokes, indiscipline were kept very much within limits, though here Tallulah was less pristine than Donald Cook. He would not tolerate kidding onstage and was irate when Tallulah tried occasionally to break Buff up in the middle of a scene by lowering her long, beaded eyelashes seductively and gazing out from beneath them. During the World Series, she asked Donald *sotto voce*, in the middle of a love scene, "What's the score?"

He glared. "Concentrate!"

In September, Tallulah's acting underwent a gradual process of miniaturization. It was an astonishing reversal. Tallulah, as a rule, became broader in her playing as time went on. The reason was Noel Coward. She had been informed that he was due in Chicago to attend a performance of the play. His permission was required to take *Private Lives* into New York. Tallulah realized that the slightest bit of overplaying would offend him. By the time Coward arrived in Chicago all the performances were toned down. Coward was pleased and agreed to the Broadway revival.

According to his biographer, Sheridan Morley, the playwright had reason later to regret that decision. But, at the time, he found that Tallulah's *Private Lives* worked "astonishingly well."

Several seams split open, but they were promptly closed. In October, Tallulah began to suffer severe pains in her right shoulder. Proud of her professionalism and her ability to withstand physical pain, she continued to play. One night she appeared at the Harris Theater stooped and frail with pain. She stood at the head of the steps backstage clad in mink and cradling her offending arm.

She barked at Evyleen Cronin to get Stephan. Stephan ran up

the steps and tried to assist her down. She howled helplessly as he inadvertently touched the sore arm. Barbara Baxley, who was waiting around for Buff to break an arm, quietly motioned Stephan away. Facing Tallulah, the understudy supported her frontally around the hips. They made an agonizingly slow descent. Tallulah closed her eyes with each move, the tears dropping mute and reluctant. By the third step Barbara was crying with her. Unable to make her characteristically defensive, quick, averting gestures, Tallulah looked stunned and quizzical at Barbara's sympathetic tears.

Tallulah took a breath and regained her composure at the bottom of the steps. Evyleen Cronin helped her into her dressing room with Barbara close behind. Tallulah sat at her dressing table, her head in her arms. "Get the child out of here," she said gently to Evyleen. Once Barbara had left, Tallulah began to sob.

Tallulah had had an attack of neuritis. The show closed for two weeks while she was put into traction. The hiatus gave Donald Cook a chance to go away and dry out. After months of abstinence, Cook was beginning to weaken. He had had several rather sodden nights, and he realized that it was time to pull himself together.

His drinking had begun as a result of Tallulah's breach of their sensible nonaggression pact. Just before her neuritis attack, however, she was alone with Donald and very drunk. He made a motion to leave, and she begged him, "Stay with me. Please stay with me." He pulled away, and she pressed a glass of liquor into his face. He pushed her and the glass away, shaking with fear and rage. Within several days, he was drinking again.

They pressed on. Tallulah healed. Donald forgave. After seven months of playing to capacity audiences in Chicago, enduring even a sizzling heat wave which crippled or killed less healthy shows, they set out on their cross-country, pre-Broadway tour. By railroad, for half a year, they jiggled east and west, west and then east again, with fantastic, record-breaking successes in St. Paul, Minneapolis, Cincinnati, Buffalo, Rochester, Cleveland, Pittsburgh, Indianapolis, St. Louis, Cedar Rapids, Kansas City, Joplin,

Tulsa, Pueblo, Des Moines, Seattle, San Francisco, and Los Angeles.

Tallulah's physical stamina was herculean. The rest of the company was not so lucky. Buff Cobb left the show permanently as a
result of a virus that she had picked up in the sub-zero tempera-
tures of the Twin Cities. She was replaced by Barbara Baxley,
who was herself felled temporarily. The company shared a private
railroad car. Tallulah had her own bedroom; Donald his own. The
rest of the people slept in uppers and lowers. Tallulah talked constantly, loudly and all night. In an attempt to get to sleep in spite
of the star's vociferous verbal barrage, Barbara took a sleeping pill,
mixed it with a beer, and literally fell on her face.

Before they arrived in Los Angeles, Tallulah took William Langford, a long, lanky twenty-five-year-old, as her lover. She fired Phil
Arthur so that Langford could take his place. This was against all
the precepts to which Tallulah tried to adhere, but she was desperately lonely at this point in her life. Stephan Cole was appalled
by the action and lectured Tallulah about professionalism and common decency. Tallulah knew she was wrong, and that knowledge
exacerbated her anger. She and Cole argued fiercely. He left the
show, thereby dissolving a friendship of many years.

The tour, which terminated in Los Angeles, had grossed $970,-
000 in a year and a half. Over that period, Tallulah's salary aver-
aged about $7,000 a week; she took another 15 percent off the top,
plus 25 percent of the profits. The annuity was begun.

Tallulah talked to columnist Ward Morehouse just before the
play came into New York. She was at the Ritz Carlton in Philadelphia, wearing a yellow blouse and black slacks, balancing her para-
keet, Gaylord, on her finger, sipping a mint julep while Dola
rushed about freshening drinks.

"I'm Tallulah in the play and I'm not a bit ashamed of it. Just
Tallulah and that's all. Have a sandwich. Have a bunch of grapes.
Don't just sit there. That darling Jack Wilson sent flowers every
week. . . . We went to Chicago for six weeks and stayed seven
months. I lived on vichyssoise and a couple of daiquiries for a
whole month, dahling. Chicago heat. I love my little company.
Alfred Lunt said Donald Cook is the ONLY leading man in
America."

Culver Pictures

The Bankhead home in Jasper, Alabama, was called Sunset.

Tallulah's paternal grandmother, the first Tallulah Brockman Bankhead.

Courtesy of Mrs. Sam Rice Baker

Five generations of
Bankhead women
(*left to right*): Mrs.
John Hollis Bankhead,
Sr. (Mamma); Great-
grandmother McAuley;
Aunt Louise (standing);
in the foreground,
holding her own baby,
is Aunt Louise's
daughter.

*Courtesy of
Mrs. Sam Rice Baker*

Captain John looks
justifiably proud of his
three sons (*left to
right*): the colonel,
the Senator, and
the Congressman.

*Alabama Department of
Archives and History*

Right: The Bankhead sisters, Tallulah and Eugenia, at a Washington finishing school, *circa* 1916. Tallulah had already begun her lifelong practice of crash dieting, "starving for my art."

Below: The five children of Senator and Mrs. John Hollis Bankhead, *circa* 1916 *(left to right)*: William B. Bankhead (Daddy); Aunt Marie Owen; John Hollis, Jr.; Aunt Louise; and Uncle Henry. John was the most level-headed. Of the other Bankheads, a contemporary descendant would recall: "They all had visions. Not of grandeur, but of another kind of life."

Alabama Department of Archives and History

By the mid-1930's Will Bankhead's several heart attacks had aged him considerably. Tallulah's stepmother, Florence, stood by faithfully.

Culver Pictures

Who Is She?

The young lady whose photograph is printed above has been chosen by the judges as a winner in our Screen Opportunity Contest. But who is she? We do not know. Her letter, containing her application blank, with her name and her address, was lost among fifty thousand other letters and packages, and her identity remains a mystery. But the judges, resolved to retain the utmost fairness in their decisions, did not put another in her place among the winners. Will the lady of mystery, who is having the door to success in filmdom held open until she arrives, kindly communicate with the editor of PICTURE-PLAY MAGAZINE immediately upon seeing this?

Culver Pictures

Katharine Cornell appeared opposite this Tallulah in *Nice People*, 1921. Miss Cornell remembers Tallulah as "highly amusing, smoldering with talent, and very beautiful."

Culver Pictures

Tallulah rocked London audiences in her first appearance there in *The Dancers*, 1923. She called this getup an "Alabama version of Minnehaha!"

Tallulah would eventually choose comfortable over chic, but in this portrait by Dorothy Wilding—done in 1930—she was the very model of Mayfair elegance.

Mrs. Morton Hoyt ("Sister") and Tallulah return from Europe together. Tallulah once unleashed a chain of expletives about Eugenia which ended with the modifying ". . . but she's good company."

Culver Pictures

Her engagement to the elegant Count Anthony de Bosdari was broken in 1929, when she learned that there was a great deal less to him than met the eye.

UPI

Tallulah posed with eccentric Augustus John in front of her famous portrait.
After her death, John Hay Whitney purchased the painting from Parke-Bernet
and gave it to the National Gallery in Washington. It hangs there opposite her
beloved Adlai Stevenson.

Tallulah played shady lady in her third picture for Paramount, *The Cheat*, 1931.

Tallulah scrawled, in late 1960's, across this early movie production still: "Who the hell is she (shawled crone, left) except Die Die my Darling."

A

GALLER

OF

SCREEN

ROLES

Tallulah was the only survivor in *Lifeboat* (1944) who could communicate with the devious Nazi, played by Walter Slezak. Of her performance, for which she received the New York Screen Critics Award, she said: "I was simply divine!"

Culver Pictures

Charles Coburn, William Eythe, and Tallu in *A Royal Scandal*, 1944.

Culver Pictures

On this production still from her last movie, *Die! Die! My Darling!*, she wrote with resignation to friend Cal Schumann: "Who dat? Not me. Oh well. Tallulah."

Flanked by Charles Laughton and Cary Grant in *The Devil and the Deep* 1932. Laughton never forgot Tallulah's greeting: "Dahling, I hear you're going to be in MY picture."

Culver Pictures

In this lovely Dorothy Wilding study, Tallulah wears the lingerie that caused England's Gallery Girls to shriek.

In 1935, Tallulah finally got her chance to do "the tart's part" in *Rain*.

Culver Pictures

Culver Pictures

Eugenia Rawls played Tallulah's daughter in the touring company of *The Little Foxes* (1939).

Culver Pictures

In 1950, Donald Cook wound up three years of supporting Tallulah in *Private Lives*. "I've been in and out of hospitals ever since," he told an interviewer. "With Tallulah, a leading man has an exhausting time offstage."

On the road with *Here Today* in 1962, she lunched with co-star Estelle Winwood and Shirley Booth. During a performance, the stage phone rang accidentally. Tallulah ad libbed: "Answer the phone." Estelle glared at her, picked it up, and replied: "It's for you."

Craig Studio

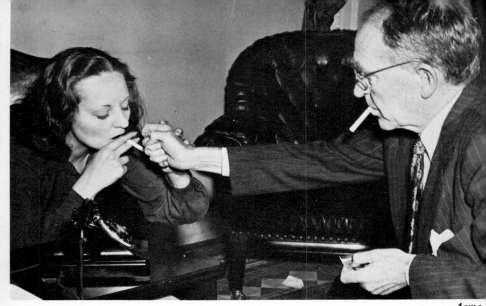

Acme

She went to Washington in 1939 to appeal for restoration of WPA theater projects. Tallulah hated to have her cigarettes lit for her; but Daddy, by that time Speaker of the House, was an exception.

In 1946, with nephew Billy Bankhead.

Acme

The Big Show

The Big Show

Culver Pictures

Tallulah in 1951 moiled through the sensational trial of her check-kiting maid, Evyleen Cronin. Photographers snapped frenetically when Tallulah, quite by accident, ran into Evyleen in court corridor.

Acme

Barrymorish John Emery never quite recovered from his four-year marriage to Tallulah. He commented on that phase of his life: "It was like the rise, decline, and fall of the Roman Empire."

Culver Pictures

Tallulah was interviewed at the Elysee in the mid-1940's. The costume is typical, casual Hattie Carnegie. She is surrounded by the bare necessities: bourbon, cigarettes, comb.

Culver Pictures

She made one of her last television appearances in *Batman*. One of her caddies encouraged her to do it: "It will be a camp, Tallulah," he said. "Don't tell me about 'camp,'" she replied. "I invented it!"

In Chestertown, Maryland, on Saturday, December 14, 1968, Tallulah Bankhead is carried to her final resting place in casket covered with white mums. *Background*: William Bankhead, Jr., Donald Seawall. *Foreground (left to right)*: Bus Roe, Cal Schumann, Bill Nicholson.

Cal Schumann Collection

Autographed portrait of Tallulah was inscribed on the back: "Love life and people."

Private Lives opened at the Plymouth Theater on October 4, 1948. Brooks Atkinson wrote about Tallulah: "She is a fabulously interesting trouper with a worldly style based on a fine Southern upbringing and a cavernous voice that shivers the galleries. . . . Dressed as expensively as possible, she gives an exciting and hilarious performance. 'Ferocious' might be the word."

Though many of the other critics objected to the ferocity that Atkinson rather admired, the show had a healthy Broadway run. And it was a rather remarkable example of art imitating life.

Donald Cook played Tallulah's ex-husband.

William Langford portrayed her current mate.

Barbara Baxley enacted the part of Tallulah's young competitor.

Holding On

BY LATE 1948 Tallulah's fame reached a peak. Two weeks after the New York opening of *Private Lives*, at the request of David Dubinsky of the International Ladies Garment Workers Union, she introduced the incumbent Presidential candidate, Harry S Truman, to the nation. The occasion was a major campaign address. The speech was sponsored by the ILGWU, or, as Tallulah put it, "paid for by all the little garment workers pooling their salaries." The *Private Lives* curtain was raised ten minutes early so that Tallulah, between acts in her dressing room at the Plymouth Theater, could accommodate the demands of live radio.

She was supremely honored to be chosen. Democratic politics, loyalty to Daddy's party, continued to play a special role in her life.

There was nothing she would not have done on behalf of the national organization. Her small, garishly polished hands shook as she sat in her dressing room, surrounded by sound technicians and their confettilike equipment. She read from a speech prepared with the help of Dick Maney.

"There were Alabama Bankheads in one or another of the houses of Congress for sixty consecutive years," she began. "My father was Speaker of the House for four years, served with that body for twenty-five. My grandfather, John, sat in the Senate for thirteen years. My Uncle John spent twelve years of his life in the Upper House. They all died in harness. I would be outraging their memories, I would be faithless to Alabama, did I not vote for Harry Truman. Yes, I'm for Harry Truman, the human being. By the same token, I'm against Thomas E. Dewey, the mechanical man. . . .

"My Dewey is trim and tidy, but is he human? I have my doubts. I have no doubts about Harry Truman. He's been through the wringer. And by the wringer I mean the 80th Congress. That 80th Congress which ignored his passionate pleas for veteran's housing, for curbs on inflation, for legislation to aid and comfort the great mass of our population. . . .

"What is Mr. Dewey for? Well, he has come out for one thing that, by his standards of caution, is revolutionary. Again and again he has said that he is for Unity. Will all the candidates for *disunity* please stand? Come, come, Mr. Dewey. Act like a grown-up. The next thing we know you'll be endorsing matrimony, the metal zipper, and the dial telephone. If Mr. Dewey has any genius it lies in his ability to avoid expressing an opinion on any controversial subject. Mr. Dewey is the great neutral. Harry Truman is the great partisan—the partisan of our troubled millions.

"In my lifetime I've enjoyed many thrills. I'm about to enjoy my greatest one. For now I have the distinguished honor to present to you the President of these United States."

After Harry Truman's election, Tallulah was sent a pair of tickets to the inaugural ceremony. The tickets placed her in the official reviewing stand among the top-echelon government officials. She was decorous and attentive, deviating only once by leaning on

Secretary of State Dean Acheson's shoulder to boo Dixiecrat Governor Herman Talmadge of Georgia as he passed in review. She departed before the ceremonies were over to catch the four o'clock train back to New York and the evening performance of *Private Lives*. Her credentials were scrutinized by a policeman before she entered the reviewing stand and as she left. For the impertinence, she gave the cop a volatile piece of her mind.

She was horrified when she read the New York *Times* report the next day of what had transpired between her and the cop. The story implied that Tallulah had had no ticket, that she had somehow followed the parade and entered the reviewing stand when she was recognized by an influential friend, that she had, in short, "crashed" the inauguration. To be even misquoted angered Tallulah; to be made, by the New York *Times*, to appear an intrusive *outsider* when she had practically cinched the election for Harry Truman, was intolerable! She called on managing editor Edwin L. James and demanded a retraction, threatening to fight to "my grave" lest she receive vindication. Her demand was successful and the *Times* subsequently reinterpreted the events at the inaugural ceremonies.

Tallulah was similarly appalled when *Time* magazine, which she detested for a multitude of injustices it had inflicted on her over the years, contended that she had at some point during the campaign sat on Harry Truman's lap.

And the *Daily News* made a tabloid mockery of her reverence for the salty Missourian when they ran a front-page picture of her kissing his hand at a Madison Square Garden rally under the headline: HE'S HER MAN.

For neither of these indignities was she entitled to legal redress. But 1948 and 1949 were, nonetheless, litigious Bankhead years. It was Donald Cook's valet who told Tallulah first of the shampoo jingle, suffusing the airways:

> I'm Tallulah, the tube of Prell
> And I've got a little something to tell.
> Your hair can be radiant, oh, so easy
> All you've got to do is take me home and squeeze me.

I'm Tallulah, the tube of Prell
And I'll make your hair look so swell
It'll shine, it'll glow so radiantly
For radiant hair, get a hold of me
Tallulah, the tube of Prell Shampoo.

Tallulah was outraged. Over the years, she had turned down offers involving thousands of easy dollars because she refused to endorse any commercial product. It was a hard-and-fast rule, based on her concept of dignity. Now Prell, without securing permission or paying her a peso, was not only impugning her morals but linking her intimately with their sticky green product.

She brought a million-dollar suit against BBD&O, Procter and Gamble, and the two radio networks that had played the nefarious jingle. The defendants claimed, of course, that they had used only a first and not a surname and that, therefore, the verse could refer to any Tallulah. The gist of Tallulah's case was contained in one sentence of her lawyer's brief: "The name Tallulah gained widespread fame and publicity because of its unique identification with plaintiff."

The suit was not without publicity value. *Life* magazine did an amusing piece about it. When the *New Yorker* came to visit, she made it a point to tell them that she never used anything but cleaning fluid on her hair. "Everybody in the world knows that Tallulah is me," she said. "Max Beaverbrook once said that I'm one of the few people in the world whose first name instantly means them. . . . Everyone else in school was always called Virginia."

The litigation was successful. Prell and Tallulah settled out of court, but more important, BBD&O was forced to discontinue the use of the offending jingle. Tallulah proved that the bizarre, mellifluous concatenation of the eight letters T-A-L-L-U-L-A-H, on which she had paid a fair amount of dues, were hers and hers alone.

With these various publicity bonuses, Tallulah's play drew vigorously at the Plymouth Theater. People came to see the phenomenon about which they were reading more and more: the unpredictable, the energetic, the supersophisticate, the "only volcano dressed by Mainbocher."

By March, 1949, she had been involved with *Private Lives* in some way for five years; she was in it exclusively for two. That was decidedly the longest gig in Tallulah's professional life.

She hated long runs and groused frequently about being goddamned tired of the play. She told *Variety* that she had no intention of continuing with the show beyond the end of that theatrical season. She was of a mind, she insisted, to pull out immediately, that minute, to complete the season by taking a short Southern tour, where she was bound to clean up financially, and bid adieu to Amanda by the spring. It was landlord Lee Shubert, she said, who was keeping her in New York. Her contract stipulated that the play was to remain on Broadway for as long as the play grossed a minimum of $14,000 a week. They were still taking in at least $15,000 when Tallulah talked to *Variety*. Not until May of that year did the show dip below the stop-limit line and close.

Contract or no, Tallulah had always been able to disengage herself from a distasteful vehicle. Despite her public protestations, Tallulah seemed to be clinging to *Private Lives*. For good reason. The Coward comedy was more than a play to her. It had provided Tallulah with one of the most suitably ordered environments in her life. The part was perfection. Amanda challenged without straining or threatening. The act of touring had afforded Tallulah just enough mobility to stave off rut, with fresh rushes of love at each stop along the way. She was working, all through the tour and into the Broadway run, under the aegis of an adoring management, which sent her red roses every week and knew better than to attempt to manage.

And she had, in a sense, trapped company in her company, with none of the vicissitudes of a purely social order. During the tour, though Donald Cook went away at night, at least he didn't go home. After the tour, Bill Langford moved in with her. He reminded Tallulah that, at forty-six, she was still a desirable woman, though their relationship too was contingent, as it turned out, upon her professional largess. With Buff Cobb, she had been almost maternal. Barbara Baxley, whom she could have fired at any time but didn't until the very, very end of the *Private Lives* experience, was the nemesis without whom Tallulah never ordered her little worlds. Everyone had a function vis-à-vis Tallulah.

The Southern tour began after the Broadway closing in May, 1949, and was extended into the New England territory.

In July, the company played Marblehead, Massachusetts. Tallulah rented an old eighteen-room mansion on the ocean's edge for herself and the cast. She hung a "Gents" sign on her bedroom, gave Gaylord the run of the house, issued a fiat that all the lights were to be kept on all the time lest he become frightened and lonely, and mightily offended the owner of the house, a Mrs. Blaisdell, by calling her Mrs. Bloodshot. It was to be a week of easeful work and relaxing intimacy, enjoying this brackish and beautiful New England resort.

After one Saturday night performance, she had a party for her company and for the local summer theater management. By three the next morning various residents of Marblehead, among them the "Bloodshots," had complained to the police about the commotion emanating from the house. The police, checking out the complaint, were greeted by a swacked and naked Tallulah. She assured them that she was perfectly all right; they countered that it was not her benefit about which they were concerned. The exchange pyramided, and Tallulah struck one of the cops.

She and the manager of the summer theater were arrested and booked. Tallulah was jailed for the brief period of time it took to raise the bail. She was asked to leave town at her earliest convenience. While travel arrangements were made, she took a small $25 room in a back-street boardinghouse. She left during the night to avoid being recognized on the street.

Tallulah claims in her autobiography that she continued to play Amanda out of necessity "to escape debtor's prison," that it was the only part offered to her. It was not the only part offered to her; it was the only part she could cut.

In August, 1949, a month after the incident at Marblehead, she was contacted by Warner Brothers. A movie was about to be made of *The Glass Menagerie*, the brilliant, tender Tennessee Williams play in which Laurette Taylor had made her comeback of legend. Tallulah was to test for the part of the mother, an aging Southern belle with grandiose delusions about her past and present life.

The test and the picture were to be directed by Irving Rapper, a gentle man with a talent for appeasing tempestuous actresses. Rapper had directed most of Bette Davis' famous Warner Brothers epics in the thirties and forties. Davis had been his first choice. She turned him down because she felt that she was too young for the part. Tallulah's vanities were more complex.

Tallulah was at Windows when Rapper telephoned. He had just flown in from Hollywood. Though they had never met, Tallulah was prepared to like Irving Rapper. She had gingerly elicited information about him from Mildred Dunnock and Glenn Anders, and she had been told good things. Tallulah, however, said nothing to either one of them about the test. As far as it is possible to tell, Tallulah kept her involvement with *Glass Menagerie* a complete secret from everybody, including Estelle Winwood.

Was her secretiveness a matter of humiliation at having to test at all? Probably not. She had made no secret about her test for *Gone With the Wind,* and she had absolutely no pretensions about her status as a motion-picture personality. It was a matter, more likely, of the stupendous importance of this particular property at this particular time. It was four years since *Lifeboat,* seven since *The Skin of Our Teeth,* and almost a decade had elapsed since *The Little Foxes.* Though *Private Lives* had enriched her considerably and caused her only a minimum of pain, her reputation as a serious actress had certainly not been enhanced by it.

Glass Menagerie must have seemed right to her. The part itself is one of the finest in theatrical literature. She had always felt such a keen rapport with the characters of Tennessee Williams. Added to this was the mystique of Laurette Taylor—the epitome of second chance. Tallulah was talking more and more about the alcoholic actress.

In keeping the test for *Glass Menagerie* quiet, in dealing with it herself, she was on one level, of course, precluding the possibility of public failure. On a more essential level, she was making a kind of Lental bargain, a throwback to her days at the convent. In return for success she had agreed to silence and sacrificed the comforting reassurances of her closest friends.

"Where are you, dahling?" she asked Rapper on the telephone.

"I'm in New York at the Warner Brothers office. I just got off the plane."

"Where are your bags?" Tallulah asked.

"Under my eyes," Rapper replied.

Tallulah roared an approving laugh. "I love you already. Come out here this instant."

The director spent the whole day out at Windows. Only Robert Williams, her manservant, was about, fixing lunch and coffee and then dinner. Tallulah, that afternoon, was candid, intense, and heavily sober. She confided to Rapper how critical she thought *Glass Menagerie* could be to her flagging career as "a serious actress."

"I come from the South," she told him. "I was born there and I understand it. I know this dialogue, that woman, better than Tennessee."

With the test just a couple of days off, Rapper became a kind of lifeline for Tallulah. She insisted that he accompany her to Brooks to pick out a costume for the test. On his arrival, Rapper was directed to a back dressing booth, where Tallulah awaited him. He knocked. She opened the door. Only her head was covered.

"How do you like my hat, dahling?" Tallulah asked.

Rapper recalls: "I tried very hard to look at her hat. She wasn't any longer that slim."

For the whole testing experience, preparation and execution, Tallulah had moved into the suite that she continued to maintain at the Elysee. The night before the test, she telephoned Rapper as he was about to meet some friend for dinner. Tallulah's voice was high and strained. She asked him to come to the hotel; he made his excuses. She burst into tears. "You've got to come here, Irving," she said, "or I won't do it at all."

Tallulah was alone when he arrived. They sat together on her couch. She sobbed. "I'm afraid I won't be any good."

Rapper talked to her about talent, insecurity, and the consanguinity between the two. "All great actresses are afraid all the time," he said. "Tomorrow will come, and you'll be frightened. But you'll be marvelous, Tallulah. Believe me. I know that."

He stayed for only an hour but in that time managed to bolster her spirits and banish her tears.

The test was shot in a tiny, depressing New York studio during a scorching August day. Though she was ordinarily hypersensitive to heat, Tallulah seemed oblivious to anything save the part. They filmed first the scene in which Amanda, the mother, comes to the cruel realization that life has somehow passed her by.

Rapper was perched near a camera, about to call "Action," when he checked the opening shot of Tallulah through the viewer. He saw a miniaturized, absorbed, optimumly primed professional, right and real. He had had his doubts about Tallulah's intrinsic strength overpowering the birdlike character of Amanda, but now those doubts were dissolved. "All the tragedy of that woman—of both women—was in that frame," he recalls. "I shall never forget it."

All the key moments from *Glass Menagerie* were filmed. On the third day of testing, Tallulah did the scene in which the mother hems the skirt of her lame daughter, who is preparing to meet the gentleman caller. The scene called for her to get down on her knees, lift the daughter's hem slightly, and confront the brutal reality of her own situation as she sees, for the first time, the withered leg of the girl. A choke overwhelmed Tallulah. It stilled and moved profoundly both Rapper and his crew. She gave a powerful account of herself.

The fourth and final day of testing should have been a cinch for Tallulah. She was scheduled to do a scene with Ralph Meeker, a young Broadway actor who had recently received rave notices in William Inge's play *Picnic*. The test scene was primarily his. Tallulah had merely to feed him a couple of lines. She worked through the morning and took lunch alone in her dressing room. There she finished a fifth of liquor.

The light and sound equipment were set up for the afternoon session. Meeker was in place. Tallulah was summoned. She reeled onto the set, swaggering, cursing, and demanding to direct the scene herself.

"Goddamned Ralph Meeker 'ill be better than Jack Barrymore. I'll direct this goddamned movie scene so that goddamned Ralph Meeker 'ill be better than Jack."

Tallulah would not win.

This new environment was not, unfortunately, ordered to protect her. Like all studio bosses, Jack Warner maintained an information network which conveyed information such as this to him in minutes. And within minutes, Warner was calling from Hollywood. Rapper pleaded with him not to be too harsh.

"I swear to you that she hasn't touched a drop in all the days I've been with her," Rapper said. "She's been brilliant. She thought that she wouldn't have to exert herself today. It won't happen again, Jack, I guarantee it."

Warner's reply was final and flinty. "I had enough with Errol Flynn," he said. "Go to the next girl."

Gertrude Lawrence was signed in September for the part. Tallulah called her *Private Lives* company together again, pushing the test, her humiliation, and her disappointment out of her mind. They opened in Boston, went on to Baltimore, and then headed into Tallulah's heartland: the South. By the early months of 1950 *Variety* was no longer referring to *Private Lives* as a "revival" but as an "oldie." Tallulah, who had simply ceased to give a damn, was going south in more ways than one.

She began to do what people had been accusing her of doing all along. *Private Lives* became a circus. She mugged, grunted, played tricks on fellow actors, turned suggestive lines into lewd possibilities, and drank enormously. The scraps she had on stage with Cook were frequently and embarrassingly real. In Alabama, to Donald Cook's disgust, she waved the Confederate flag and turned Amanda into a Southern belle so drawly that she was barely understood even by the natives.

Tallulah's machinations hurt the box office not at all. People apparently wanted to see her in spite of what she did and no matter how seriously she was breaking her faith with the profession. In Charlotte, for instance, the 1,500-seat house was bought out on the same day that the first *Private Lives* newspaper advertisement appeared. The additional demand for tickets was so overwhelming that the mayor and the Chamber of Commerce implored Tallulah to play an extra performance.

This tour was grimier, grimmer, and more hectic than the others. Because most of the performances were literally one-night stands, Tallulah and Company not only traveled by railroad car but actually lived aboard, disembarking only to shower and change before a performance.

Tallulah was plumping with booze, relaxing with marijuana and an assortment of opiates, and behaving so impossibly that Donald Cook was sent by the rest of the company to talk to her about the destruction she was doing to herself and to her fellow actors. She would stop periodically. Once she said to Donald, "I'm going to start drinking again, Don, because when I'm sober, I don't think anybody likes me."

Her remark was prophetic and self-fulfilling. On the *Private Lives* car, the company had taken to playing a constant game of cat and mouse with the star, boarding early to avoid her, stealing past her door, and running to the toilet when she was distracted. "*You,*" she screamed at Barbara Baxley, who was in the act of stealthily slipping past her door one morning at 2 A.M. "Come in here!" Being caught meant playing word games with Tallulah until after dawn.

They all had been together for more than three years. By the end of the *Private Lives* tour Donald hardly spoke to her at all. Barbara Baxley was sending notes. Bill Langford, who hadn't begun to learn to act, was chafing to get away, and Evyleen Cronin, Tallulah's loyal theater maid, was kiting madam's checks rapaciously.

23

"And My Name, Dahlings, Is
Tallulah Bankhead"

DURING THE RUN of *Private Lives*, Stephan Cole and Donald Cook sat up one night drinking and talking about Tallulah. Cole asked Cook what he thought would happen to the star. "She'll end up like Jack Barrymore," Cook replied, "a caricature of herself."

The process began with *The Big Show*, a radio program conceived by the National Broadcasting Company as a sort of last-ditch effort to deflect some of the fugitive advertising dollars from television back into radio. The point was to dazzle and seduce by assembling gaggles of superstars on Sunday evenings from six to seven thirty. NBC invested up to $50,000 on each program, a staggering venture and almost unprecedented in its day. Tallulah was to be mistress of ceremonies. The show was to premiere in November, 1950.

The weeks before were hell for Tallulah and all the people around her. As usual she was terrified, but in this case, Tallulah just did not understand what her *function* would be. She couldn't conceive of herself as a comedienne—which is leaps and bounds away from an actress in comedies—and radio announcer wouldn't do at all. That she was, on *The Big Show*, engaged to be somehow *herself* eluded and perplexed her. She neither trusted nor understood the role, nor did she have any way of evaluating its importance. The NBC showcase antedated the era of the television panel personality. Actors then acted. Singers sang. Comedians amused.

Entertainers did not, in 1950, drop in on Dick Cavett or Johnny Carson to approximate "being."

Tallulah's contract gave her the opportunity to get out after four weeks. She had got "in" first because the money was good and the work easy. Now all her doubts were heightened. She had every intention to exercise that option. She wrote in her autobiography: "I walked through the rehearsal like a woman under water, numb with humiliation."

During this period, she slept hardly at all, though by this time she was conditioned to sleeplessness. Tallulah was paying doctors hundreds of dollars a week to venture out to Bedford Village to give her injections of Demerol, an opium derivative one step away from morphine and two from heroin. Even with the Demerol, she would be up until dawn, reading, talking, doing crossword puzzles, listening to all-night radio programs, calling for Edie Smith, who had rejoined her life, for a frankfurter, or a malted, or an order of bleenies.

In those weeks before *The Big Show* went on the air, she called producer Dee Englebach all day and all night. She wanted out. She wanted new writers. She wanted better billing. She wanted *reassurance*. Edie Smith reminded her once, at half-past three in the morning, that she had called Englebach four times since midnight.

"*Die Donner*," Edie pleaded, "let him rest." Die Donner was the name Edie had taken to calling Tallulah. It was said variously to derive from the German for "the thunder," the French for "young roast turkey," or "The Dam-ah," which is what Hope Williams' maid called her mistress.

"Don't argue with me," Tallulah thundered. "Get him on the phone."

Tallulah haggled about lines with head writer Goodman Ace. Of one of her guests, Tallulah was to say, "No schmo, he!" She didn't understand what the word "schmo" meant.

"Is it anything like schmuck?" Tallulah asked.

"Don't worry about it, Tallulah."

"It's not funny."

"It'll get a laugh. You'll see."

She wanted to know, at that point, what "schmuck" *really* meant. Tallulah had an incredible capacity for tangents, time wasting, and getting off the track. She worked at two speeds: dolorous and frantic, the latter neurological, as well as compensatory, to make up for time frittered away.

During an ensuing rehearsal, a half hour before air time, she sat next to Lauritz Melchior, while the ninety-man West Point Military Academy Choir ran through "The Corps." Tallulah, of course, raised goose bumps, stood up in the darkened auditorium, and said to the cadets, "Be angels and sing *Alma Mater*." Englebach reminded her, over the talk-back system, that they were in rehearsal and not in concert. She had requested. Now she demanded. The song was sung.

The first program began with the standard opening. "Ladies and gentlemen," Ed Herlihy intoned over the kind of solemn silence that only a hot medium can contain. "You are about to be entertained by some of the greatest stars of all time on one big program." Meredith Willson, in steel-rimmed spectacles, led a mammoth conglomerate of instruments and choral voices into a sweet, exultant Brahms-like theme. The stars of the program introduced themselves. They included: Fred Allen, Jimmy Durante, José Ferrer, Ethel Merman, Paul Lukas, Danny Thomas, Russell Nype, and Frankie Laine.

In a hushed and humble and honeycombed voice, the mistress of ceremonies introduced herself. "And my name, dahlings," she said, "is Tallulah Bankhead."

The first program was more or less typical of the early *Big Shows*. Presented live from the immense, newly rebuilt Center Theater in New York, it was a swank, lushly produced showcase, just a mite ragged around the edges for the erosive effects of Tallulah's tantrums and time wasting. Ethel Merman sang a good deal of the score from the erstwhile Broadway smash *Call Me Madam*, following subtle cues from Tallulah like: "Now tell us, Ethel, how you became the hostess with the mostest?" José Ferrer recited the "Nose" speech from *Cyrano*, which was about to be released as a movie. There was a tribute to George M. Cohan, during which each of the guests—singers or no—sang one of the composer's songs. Tallulah crooned "Give My Regards to Broadway" incredibly.

All this was more or less filler. It was Tallulah's presence—her personality—that unionized this confederation of segues and superstars. Her voice, her style, and the material tailor-made for her by Goodman Ace, Selma Diamond, George Foster, Mort Green, and Frank Wilson gave the show what is called in the music business today "a sound."

The sound comprised the caustic comedy of insult, still nascent and somewhat tame in the first couple of programs. The insult had to do with advancing age, diminished sexual appeal, drinking, and androgyny. Tallulah's advancing age. Tallulah's diminished sexual appeal. Tallulah's drinking. And Tallulah's rather androgynous *ambiente*. One of the biggest laughs in the show was garnered by Portland Hoffa when she addressed Tallulah as "Sir."

"No schmo, he!" did get a laugh, as Goodman Ace predicted it would. That line typified the literate, sometimes cryptoliterate quality of the show, which abounded in puns like: "Did your mother see me?"/"She never could." . . . "No mews is good mews." . . . "Tannhauser. It used to be called Fivehauser, until inflation set in."

Television was the butt of much of the humor, spawning at least one classic line, uttered by Fred Allen and written by Goodman Ace: "I've decided why they call television a medium. It's because nothing in it is well done."

And still another:

ALLEN: I've been dabbling in something which for want of a better name we shall call tee vee.
BANKHEAD: Please, dahling—people are *eating!*

Tallulah's diction correlated with her sense of security. If she was getting a laugh, she slowed down, enunciated, imploded her consonants with clarity and professionalism. If she blew one line or somehow lost faith, there followed a soft, garbled torrent of slurred sound, a rhythmic straight line with neither peaks nor troughs. Often Tallulah "got" a joke for the first time while she was reading it on the air. She exploded with laughter. It added great charm and spontaneity to the show.

Tallulah's fears were assuaged when the reviews of the premiere appeared. The broadcast critics raved. John Crosby of the New York *Herald Tribune* wrote: "It was in practically every respect a perfectly wonderful show. . . . NBC's biggest gamble may have been Tallulah Bankhead, an unpredictable volcano who has been known to sweep away whole villages when she erupts. As mistress of ceremonies, though, she was sharp as a knife and succeeded somehow in outshining even the most glittering names on that glittering roster."

He had two reservations: first, Tallulah's singing voice, which Crosby described as having "more timbre than Yellowstone National Park," and second, Tallulah's addiction to the word "dahling." Crosby was reflecting a consensus.

Tallulah had a standard line about Eugenia's tone deafness, which appeared to run in the Bankhead family. "Sister," Tallulah commented, "stands up whenever she hears any music just in case it turns out to be 'The Star-Spangled Banner.'" Tallulah herself learned the song which was to become most intimately identified with her, "May the Good Lord Bless and Keep You," only when Meredith Willson sang it directly into her ear. But she adored singing, insisted upon doing it whenever possible, and enjoyed the sound of her own voice immeasurably.

According to Crosby's count, Tallulah employed the word "dahling" either 422 or 425 times on that first show. Though the number was facetious, Tallulah did overuse the word on the premiere broadcast, a symptom of her understandable nervousness. It was the verbal analogue of her theatrical gestures, to which she also resorted when her mouth went dry.

Tallulah, who didn't know how or what to think about the show before the reviews appeared, was jubilant. She abandoned any plans to leave when her four-week option came up. It is part of the "indestructible Tallulah" myth, perpetuated by herself and swallowed whole by the idolatrous even among those who claimed to know her intimately, that Tallulah cared not one whit about her press. She cared passionately.

She could recite word for word every important review of her performances from *The Squab Farm* to *Private Lives*. When, in later years, a columnist wrote that an important television star had refused to appear on a stage with Tallulah because of her drinking, she took to her bed for a solid week: staring, fasting, crying. Her manservant, Robert Williams, forcibly had to lift her out of the bed so that the linens could be changed.

The Big Show was more than a critical success. In the days when television was burgeoning, it managed miraculously to knock several points off the Trendex figures of its visual competition. Tallulah became a Sunday institution in millions of American homes. Hers was the classiest and certainly the most-talked-about event of the 1950 broadcast season.

The production had one of the tightest rehearsal schedules of any major network show. In spite of her enormous success, Tallulah remained a medium snob. Her allegiance was to the theater. Her roots and her self-respect resided therein. This was still radio, and she denied it any more than three days of her week. Rehearsals were limited to Friday afternoons and the weekend. Tallulah tore through in her standard shovel-seat slacks by Hattie Carnegie, cardigan, wedgies, her badly smudged horn rims perched on her head. She smoked all the time, knitted feverishly, stopped talking only to cough or laugh.

When she arrived back from her lunch breaks on Sunday afternoon, the ticket line at the Center Theater often spilled up the entire block. Glenn Anders was instructed by Tallulah to sneak servicemen in through the side door. Men in uniform—like black people, unemployed actors, and the memory of her parents—made Tallulah cry. George Cukor, on his way by automobile to pick up Tallulah and take her to the theater, stopped to give a young serviceman a lift. Tallulah was fetched, chatted at the young man about Korea, calling him "sergeant, dahling." He was taken to his destination, hopped out of the car, and wished Tallulah good luck. She blinked her eyes, closed them, and burst into tears. "Imagine," she said to Cukor, "he's going off to Korea and he wishes me good luck."

She developed a protective, almost seignorial attitude toward her production staff. She referred to Meredith Willson, Goodman Ace, Dee Englebach, and associate producer Bud Barry as "her boys." When several of these staff people were sent to negotiate a guest appearance with a very young Jerry Lewis, he apparently treated them quite shabbily. He subsequently did agree to appear on a *Big Show*, but Tallulah never forgave a slight to herself or to any extension of herself.

Lewis was late to a rehearsal. Tallulah prowled the stage of the Center Theater in leonine fury, the script crumpling in her grip. He appeared shirtless and mugging, with an electric shaver tied around his waist to indicate that he had been shaving. Tallulah broke his comic spirit and almost his jaw—slapping him across the mouth with the script, right to left and then left to right. "That," she explained, "is for treating my boys so badly."

Though it had not yet begun to interfere seriously with her performances, Tallulah continued to drink heavily. After a *Big Show* broadcast from Hollywood, she attended a small dinner party with her agent, Phil Weltman of William Morris. Her plane was scheduled to leave for New York at 11 P.M. At 9:30 Weltman hustled her out of the party onto the veranda while he went to get the car. Tallulah was, at that point, drunk but not running amok. While Weltman was pulling the car up to the house, one of the male homosexual guests at the party persuaded her to take one for the road. The game was called getting Tallulah swacked, and the gay guys, some of them, adored it.

The last slug seemed to make the difference. Weltman made her wait in the car while he checked her in at the airport. As she flapped up the ramp in her mink, the captain spotted her. It was, unfortunately, the same captain on whose flight she had previously fallen asleep with a cigarette in her hand. He refused to take her. Weltman cozened her down the ramp with a story about bad weather and impossible flying conditions. She saw Meredith Willson, Bud Barry, and Dee Englebach walk up the ramp and get onto the plane. She stood in the middle of the airfield, waving her arms and shouting, "If the boys are going up, I wanna go up. If the plane goes down, I wanna go down with my boys."

She awoke at two the next day in her bungalow at the Beverly Hills Hotel, called Weltman, and asked him how bad it had been. He told her. Tallulah then telephoned each one of "her boys" in New York to apologize for any embarrassment she had caused them.

Tallulah's most opprobrious label continued to be "common." She hated it in others and deplored it in herself. Will Bankhead, dead or alive, functioned as Tallulah's ubiquitous alter ego. Back in England she had frequently commented, as she appraised her luster, her money, her accomplishments, and the quality of her friends, "I wish Daddy were here. Wouldn't he be proud?" She had occasion now to utter more and more often: "Thank God my blessed Daddy isn't alive to see this."

Ironically, the conscience she introjected came complete with all the regional, middle-class Southern sensibilities of its prototype. The bad behavior, which could be excused and even expected in front of servants and some friends became intolerable when it was held up to the humiliating light of public scrutiny. The events of the following year were to be the most painful and emotionally debilitating of Tallulah's life.

24

The Trial

EVYLEEN CRONIN ENTERED Tallulah Bankhead's life as a wardrobe mistress in 1946, during the short and unhappy run of Jean Cocteau's *The Eagle Has Two Heads*. Evyleen worked her way up to maid-secretary and keeper of the Bankhead checkbook.

An ex-vaudevillian, Evyleen was an anomaly in Tallulah's household. She was a sluggish, middle-aged woman with turgid ankles, henna hair, and no bridge skills. She had neither panache, pizazz, title, money, innocence, nor wit. Between October 8, 1949, and April 11, 1950, Evyleen bilked Tallulah out of at least $10,000. She did it by raising the amounts on checks disbursed for incidental expenses.

Mrs. Cronin was discovered in April, 1950, attempting to pass a check endorsed to her, which she had kited from $200 to $1,300. An alert signature clerk in the A-BRA section of the Guaranty Trust Company in New York noticed the difference in ink color and brought the matter to the attention of Tallulah's accountant, Benjamin Nadel. Nadel investigated and found a legion of similarly altered checks. He called Tallulah; Tallulah called her friend and lawyer, Donald Seawell.

The matter seems then to have been taken out of Tallulah's hands. Or, more accurately, she threw up her hands. On April 23, 1950, Nadel confronted Mrs. Cronin in an upstairs area of Tallulah's Bedford Village estate, Windows. Downstairs, the actress smoked and chafed and paced. Seawell reportedly forbade her to see or talk with Evyleen. At six o'clock that evening, Evyleen Cronin was dismissed from service and ordered out of the house. No complaint was made.

Except for Tallulah's braggadocio, the matter would probably have ended then and there. But Walter Winchell ran an item with the bare facts of the bilking, congratulating the great lady for being big enough *not* to press charges. District Attorney Frank Hogan apparently followed Winchell's column. Tallulah was impelled to press charges or compound the crime.

Throughout the trial, around the courthouse and among Tallulah's intimates, there was loose talk of blackmail. Mrs. Cronin, it was claimed, had warned Tallulah either to drop the charges or not to press them—which one is not clear. The story goes that Mrs. Cronin threatened to tell "all"—and that "all" included blackmail about her personal life.

The blackmail ingredient, however, did do a service to Tallulah. She was reared on rhetoric and she needed it for self-preservation and self-presentation. Although she had perfectly legitimate reasons to bring Mrs. Cronin to justice, she now had a slogan. She could tell the press and herself, "I would not capitulate to blackmail."

Tallulah's heart was selfish, but it was big. She screamed and ranted and often took deadly aim. But it seems unlikely that she, who could not tolerate being in a room with a closed door, would have voluntarily set in motion a group of forces that could have imprisoned another human being for a period of years. It wasn't in her repertoire. Once the forces were set in motion, however, Tallulah's anger and righteousness were exacerbated by inconvenience, lies, and the humiliation of public scrutiny.

Before the trial began, Tallulah and her lawyer ran into Mrs. Cronin and hers, while they all waited for a municipal elevator at the district attorney's office. Tallulah approached Evyleen and implored: "I know you have the money. You have it buried somewhere. Go and dig it up and we can forget this whole bloody mess."

"I don't have it buried," Evyleen pleaded. "But I'll get a job and pay you something every week."

"I don't want it in fives and tens," Tallulah said, and stepped haughtily into the elevator.

The trial began on December 11, 1951, in General Sessions Court at 100 Centre Street, with Judge Harold Stevens presiding. Mrs. Cronin was represented by Fred G. Morritt, a long-faced, bow-tied Senator from Brooklyn who had once sung baritone on radio's *Lucky Strike Hour*. For the people: Assistant DA Jerome Kidder.

The eighty-five-seat courtroom was full and giddy. More than 100 people were turned away, and phalanxes of fans stood outside and around the building waiting for a glimpse of the fabulous and unpredictable. Fred Morritt's opening remarks set the tone of the proceedings. It became immediately apparent that Tallulah Bankhead's life and not Evyleen Cronin's crimes would be the subject of the trial.

It was Morritt's defense that his client was forced to kite

checks in order to pay for Tallulah Bankhead's enormously profligate ways. He never denied that Evyleen had monkeyed with
her employer's disbursements. "Reluctantly and with great regret,"
he said in his opening remarks, without a trace of either reluctance
or regret, "we will prove to you that the lady [Tallulah] was never
sober or rarely so. That she spent a fortune, enough for you to
send your kids to college . . . on cocaine, marijuana, and booze
and scotch and champagne."

He mentioned, promised to produce, and never did: "a very,
very celebrated radio and tv star [who] brought loose marijuana
to Tallulah Bankhead, which Tallulah Bankhead used to refer to as
tea." He maintained that she "taught Mrs. Cronin how to roll
marijuana cigarettes and, after a great deal of difficulty, Mrs. Cronin became rather adept at rolling marijuana and, in four or five
hours, was able to roll 98 of them." The press had great fun with
that last tableau. He also referred to a savings account that had
been opened by Tallulah in the name of William Langford.

None of this was gratuitous or vindictive, but crucial to Evyleen's defense. Evyleen, he said, was compelled to disburse the
money to keep this inferno in fire and brimstone. Mrs. Cronin's
duties included the disbursement of money for incidental expenses. Liquor and drugs, the lawyer maintained, were among
the incidental expenses in the household of Tallulah Bankhead.
Mrs. Cronin allegedly was compelled by fear, brutalization, and
stupidity to add a couple of figures to the checks involved in order
to reimburse herself properly. She had tried once to go to Tallulah
and tell her what she was *really* spending every week, and Tallulah, according to Morritt, had ranted, "Don't speak to me about
money. It's for my comfort." Tallulah, the defense maintained,
beat Evyleen "unmercifully . . . not once but at least fifty times."
Mrs. Cronin, in her fashion, was just trying to keep peace in the
family.

During these opening remarks, Tallulah, the prosecution's
chief witness, wrapped in a brown Hattie Carnegie dress and a
simple strand of pearls, sat toward the back of the courtroom,
flanked by Seawell and Bill Langford. She dug her nails into
Langford's arm in an attempt to maintain proper composure,

swallowed her bon mots, and blinked back tears of rage. She was warm, uncomfortable, and wanted desperately to smoke. She was unused to the stringent rules of courtroom decorum. When she was decorous, she picked the time and the place. Earlier in the proceedings, she had thrown open a window in an anteroom and a guard told her to close it. She reared around. "*I want it open.*" "It isn't what you want around here," the guard answered. "It is what I want," she screamed.

The flagrancy of the beating accusation was too much for her, and she began to lose control. She took the deepest breath of which she was capable and emitted a tremulous, sepulchral sound—one of what somebody once called her "Liberty Bell in heat" noises—and shuddered, loud enough for the press but not the judge to hear: "Next thing they'll have me vivisecting my dog without an anesthetic."

From then on, until she was evicted from the courtroom, it was all sails. With coughs, grunts, Liberty Bell in heat noises, and mini press conferences which she began holding in the hall outside the courtroom, Tallulah was fighting back or, at least, reacting. The phenomenon enraged Morritt, who became aware of certain noises in the rear of the court. Morritt was saying, "My client begged and pleaded and did everything but get down on her knees to Donald Seawell, Miss Bankhead's. . . ." He turned: "Was that Miss Bankhead who just laughed? May I ask the Court to admonish the complaining witness not to make any remarks when I am addressing the jury?"

"I coughed, your honor," Tallulah said. Soon half the courtroom was coughing sympathetically with Tallulah.

The picture that the newspapers used to illustrate the "I Coughed, Your Honor" story, typified all the press coverage. It was obscenely ugly, her face chalky, thick, and suddenly old, her huge Elizabeth Arden, Cupid's-bow mouth twisted in coy apology.

The picture was run in *Time* and the *Daily News*. In the *News*, she shared the front page with Franchot Tone, who had just received a forty-day suspended sentence for spitting in the face of sob sister Florabel Muir. The New York *Mirror* ran six pictures of Tallu on its front page and even co-opted its back sports page for the trial. The subheadline, underneath HST WILL CLEAN HOUSE, read: COUNSEL FOR MRS. CRONIN TOLD THE JURY TEMPERAMENTAL TALLULAH TAUGHT HER TO ROLL REEFERS. She objected most strenuously to the front-page coverage in the prestigious New York Times.

Publicly, her attitude was self-righteous and indignant. Semipublicly it was gamy. At a rehearsal of The Big Show, the writers and the guests, including Phil Silvers, Merv Griffin, Sarah Vaughan, and Ethel Merman, sat around the big horseshoe conference table at the Center Theater, nervously awaiting their mistress of ceremonies. She entered, walked up to the orchestra pit in which the entire NBC orchestra sat, and roared, "Has anyone got a reefer?" Privately, she was mortified. She shook through most of the trial and said to Glenn Anders, "Thank God my blessed Daddy isn't alive to see this."

Morritt's case hinged on a dynamic: the enormous evil of Tallulah Bankhead as opposed to the harassable, pitiable innocence of Evyleen Cronin. Tallulah knew that Evyleen had danced in vaudeville, and she even had some vague recollection of burlesque. But Tallulah was not a listener, and of the particulars she was unsure. Just before the trial began, however, Tallulah, Edie Smith, Dola Cavendish, and Glenn Anders were sitting around Tallulah's red-carpeted suite at the Elysee Hotel, where she had moved for the duration of the proceedings. Glenn had met Evyleen first in 1913, when she was dancing with Six American Dancers. Evyleen had even confessed to Tallulah, in the beginning of her employment, that she had had a crush on the elegant actor. Tallulah loved the whole idea of it and, with the kind of grand sensitivity she had in abundance, arranged it so that Evyleen, in the performance of her sundry duties, never had to serve Glenn.

Glenn, boutonniered and pouring himself some gin, had an idea about determining the nature of Evyleen's show business background. "Listen, Tallu," he said. "There are these two old birds in Bridgeport, Connecticut, who used to cartwheel with Evyleen to 'The Dance of the Hours.' They call themselves the

Lovenberg Sisters, and they're bound to know something juicy about Evyleen."

Tallulah dispatched Glenn to Bridgeport. He found the residence-dancing school of the septuagenarian Lovenbergs. A white-haired old lady in a colorful tutu, Annabelle Lovenberg, answered.

"Why, Glennie Anders," she said.

"Annabelle Lovenberg," he answered. "I just happened to be in the neighborhood visiting a fraternity brother and I saw your sign out front."

"Glennie Anders!" she said.

Annabelle's sister was banging an upright piano while a small class of prepubescent girls danced on a long board. The class was dismissed while Glenn and the Lovenbergs went out on the glass-enclosed porch to reminisce over tea. Glenn, who had to catch the seven thirty out of Hartford, had to work with less savoir faire than he would have liked.

"What ever happened to little Evyleen Cronin?" he finally asked.

Annabelle's sister was surprised by his naïveté. "Haven't you been reading the *papers*, Glennie? She's involved in a big trial with Tallulah Bankhead. Evyleen is supposed to have stolen some money from her."

"Do you think little Evyleen would have done such a thing?" Glenn asked.

The sisters exchanged knowing looks, and finally Annabelle spoke up. "Well, I don't know about that, Glennie, but last time we saw Evyleen she came to Bridgeport in a burlesque show and invited us to come see her. Glennie, do you know what a G-string is? That's all she had on. We were so surprised we just left."

The trial lasted for thirteen days. Tallulah for two. On the second day, Judge Stevens excluded all witnesses from the courtroom. Since Tallulah was the only witness in the courtroom, the intent was obvious. Tallulah never reappeared in court until the day she was called to testify. Glenn became Tallulah's window on the courtroom. He attended each day and returned to the Elysee at cocktail hour to enact for Tallulah the entire day's proceedings.

Though Morritt never kept many of his initial promises, he and Evyleen—despite repeated and vociferous objections from the prosecution and the bench—managed to drag in a whole lot of sensational data on the life-style of Tallulah Bankhead. He claimed repeatedly that this was not a collateral and gratuitous attack but relevant to Mrs. Cronin's motivation and state of mind when she raised the checks. "I don't care in the slightest whether Tallulah Bankhead smoked a Chesterfield or a marijuana, drank one case of bourbon or a thousand, used cocaine or Coca-Cola. That's her business. We did not attack for the sake of attacking. It had to come out because that's what the lady spent the money for."

By hook or crook or in contempt of court, Morritt and Cronin had obviously conspired to catalogue as graphically as possible every vice, excess, or peculiar circumstance of Tallulah's life with the hope that the jury would conclude that a woman capable of A, B, C, and D was certainly capable of E—*viz*, beating Evyleen into abject terror. And, more important, that a woman capable of A or even C really deserved anything she got. The trial was Gallicized with a vengeance:

MORRITT: Did you know William Langford?

CRONIN: Yes, I did.

MORRITT: Who was William Langford?

CRONIN: He was first an understudy with the company. Then he became the second leading man in place of Phil Arthur.

MORRITT: And do you know how old William Langford was, about?

CRONIN: Well, he told me he was 27.

MORRITT: Do you know how old Miss Bankhead had told you she was?

CRONIN: Yes, she was 48.

MORRITT: Was William Langford continually in the company of—

KIDDER: Objection.

MORRITT: For the purpose of the record I will ask these questions. And don't answer them, Mrs. Cronin, until the District Attorney is given a chance to object: Do you know whether or not Bill Langford was Miss Bankhead's lover?

KIDDER: I object.

COURT: Sustained, Mr. Morritt.

MORRITT: I warned my client not to answer.

*   *   *

CRONIN: We went out to this place supposed to be a cabaret. When we got there it was a private home. There was a living room, a dining room, and a kitchen. They served us drinks first. It was very dreary, very dark. Then they served us some spare ribs. Then they brought us some marijuana cigarettes and each one took a puff of it, except Josie, the valet, and I.

MORRITT: Who took the puff?

CRONIN: Miss Bankhead, Mr. Langford, Earl Smith. And they took deep breaths of it. Miss Bankhead told Mr. Langford: "Why do you take such a deep breath?" He said, "You get more."

*   *   *

MORRITT: Did you ever tell Miss Cavendish that you raised checks?

CRONIN: No.

MORRITT: Why?

CRONIN: Well, because Miss Cavendish was never quite herself. She drank a lot and was always so frustrated and upset about Miss Bankhead. She worried about Miss Bankhead all the time.

MORRITT: Is there anything else you want to tell us about Miss Cavendish? This is your opportunity, Mrs. Cronin.

CRONIN: Only that if Miss Bankhead would go out she would scream and carry on in the hotel, carry on so we would have to go on up and get her.

*   *   *

MORRITT: Tell the Court and jury your conversation with Miss Bankhead before you wrote your first check.

CRONIN: I told Miss Bankhead that she was spending a lot of money. I said that she was spending a lot of money and Mr. Nadel spoke about it and I said that—

MORRITT: What did you call her?

CRONIN: I called her, when I was alone with her, I called her baby, because I felt. . . .

MORRITT: And when there were people around what did you call her?

CRONIN: I called her Miss Bankhead. I told her, I said, "Baby, I think you are spending too much money." And she said to me, "Evyleen, I don't want you ever to talk about money again. Never. That happens to be my business." And she hit me right here on the breast and said, "I will give you cancer of the breast."

MORRITT: Did she call you any names the time she hit you on the breast?

CRONIN: Yes.

Morritt solemnly asked for a conversation with Kidder before the bench, maintaining that filthy language was involved which struck at "the very essence of the case." The raising of checks, it seemed, was induced by another of Mrs. Cronin's phobias: the fear of obscene language. The courtroom was cleared. Mrs. Cronin was instructed to write down what Miss Bankhead had said, whereupon the paper was handed to the judge, the attorneys, jury, and court stenographer. At one point, Fred Morritt held the paper, allowed his mind to ramble, and quite unconsciously doodled on the exhibit. He proffered this explanation to the court: "I inadvertently made an arrow, doodling on the original record. I didn't know the Court would want it as part of the record, so I would like the record to indicate that that arrow was doodling, which means nothing. I did it, not knowing. The witness did not know it."

To this day, scrupulously emplaced in the official file of the Cronin case, is a tiny, ragtag piece of white doodled-on paper on which Evyleen Cronin penciled cacographically: "I will give you cancer of the breast goddamn it. It isn't your money and I don't want it ever mentioned again, you old cunt."

On this question of fear—and fear of obscene language—Mrs. Cronin's background and character were extremely relevant. Morritt did everything in his somewhat limited power to have her emerge as a kind of *Billboard*-reading Whistler's Mother. He stressed the fact that she had once adopted her best friend's daughter—a girl named Josie, nineteen at the time. Morritt put Josie on the stand. "Who is Mrs. Cronin?" he asked tenderly.

"That's my mother," said Josie.

"Not your real mother, is she?"

"No, sir. But she's real to me."

Mrs. Cronin testified that she had been born in a trunk, had snatched a bit of education when she could, and as a youngster played Oliver Twist and Little Lord Fauntleroy. To the question of whether or not she had ever been arrested or officially charged with a crime, she answered no.

Assistant District Attorney Jerome Kidder, no doubt aided by Glenn Anders' revelations, began his cross-examination thus:

"You mentioned having played in Oliver Twist and Little Lord Fauntleroy. I take it, as you progressed in years, your parts became a little more sophisticated, didn't they?"

Mrs. Cronin admitted that she had gone into vaudeville and then into burlesque as "a soubrette."

KIDDER: Were you also a stripper at one time?

CRONIN: . . . not stripped way down as they did afterwards. I stripped down to a bra and panties, as they are doing in Broadway shows today.

KIDDER: So by the time you went to work for Miss Bankhead, four-letter words were not unknown to you or particularly shocking to you?

CRONIN: No, they weren't.

KIDDER: I don't think you mean to convey that because somebody used four-letter words in a dressing room that gave you an excuse to raise seven or eight thousand dollars worth of checks, do you?

To make Mrs. Cronin's familiarity with pure Anglo-Saxon even clearer to the jury, Kidder read into the record a letter from Josie's real mother addressed to Josie and Mrs. Cronin in which she referred to them as "two shits."

"Just a minute," said Mrs. Cronin, "my breath. I can hardly breathe."

Mrs. Cronin's story was demolished. She could produce no bills and hardly a witness to her lavish expenditures. In a dull, disappointing, and rather coquettish half hour on the stand Tallulah testified that she paid for almost everything by check, checks made out directly to liquor stores, or to restaurants, or to drugstores, or to the hotels where she did her omnibus living on the road. Solid verification was produced. Incidental expenses came nowhere near the amounts Mrs. Cronin overreimbursed herself with.

Tallulah did lash out physically at people. And, with women, she invariably went for the breast. But it is most unlikely that she ever administered a beating to anyone. What Cronin did was to reorder, reattribute, and grossly exaggerate the facts of Tallulah's life. The phrase "cancer of the breast" was probably overheard. It was a piece of black humor between Tallulah and Edith Smith. Cash disbursements for marijuana were very rare. And only on one or two occasions did she have Evyleen buy cocaine for her. On the subject of bought sex, Tallulah was particularly vehement. "I haven't stooped *that* low yet," she told the press.

As part of his elaborate defense, Fred Morritt hit upon something very significant. He pointed to the sloppiness of Mrs. Cronin's adulterations, to the long period of time that elapsed before she was apprehended, and submitted that "the lack of criminal intent cries aloud to the world." He maintained that Mrs. Cronin had "fair grounds for considering that she had authority to raise checks." His claims were not legally germane and Judge Stevens, a terse and brilliant logician, struck them down.

Morritt was implying—and still believes—that Tallulah knew what Evyleen was doing. In the sense that Morritt meant it, she did not. She did not know, for instance, that Evyleen hiked her own birthday check from $50 to $250 and used the difference as a down payment on a Buick. That between March 20, 1950, and April 11, 1950, Evyleen Cronin drew checks which totaled $1,700 after kiting. Tallulah would have been outraged at such fiduciary chutzpah.

But Tallulah knew certain other things at various levels. She knew from her youthful success to the time of her death that people were stealing from her. She was *reared* to expect that servants would steal. If she handled her checkbook sloppily, perhaps she was, in a larger sense, protecting herself.

Tallulah allowed for what she called "totin' rights." "I'm earning it and they're totin' it away," she would say. Totin' rights is a very Southern concept, dating back to the plantations and endemic among people who cannot afford to have the service trades professionalized. One way to maintain the nigger-ness of niggers was to give them every opportunity to act like niggers, occasionally to catch and to forgive, thereby adding gratitude to opportunity. By the very nature of their service, they know everything about their employers, so the totin' game maintained a balance of sorts. One has servants who are, at the same time, consorts. It's a game that can be played North, as well as South, and between members of any races.

Tallulah knew that Evyleen Cronin was a thief. In their travels around the country, Evyleen was picked up several times for "totin'" from department stores. Tallulah got her off each time. The stores discreetly dropped the matter, and Mrs. Cronin was able to testify at the trial that she had never been arrested or charged with a crime. Evyleen told Stephan Cole once that she was in the process of teaching Helen Hayes' theater maid how to shoplift. During the run of *Private Lives,* Evyleen tried to sell several thousand dollars' worth of what she claimed was hot jewelry to Tallulah. And Tallulah was interested. Cole, however, had a dream about "paste," argot for phony stuff, and advised Tallulah against the purchase. The jewelry turned out to be fake.

But the totin' game—with Tallulah—required moderation, humility, prudence, and strict privacy. Mrs. Cronin blew it. She toted too much, too often, and too blatantly. Her many stupidities invited the crass intrusion of nonplayers like the Guaranty Trust Company, Frank Hogan, and Donald Seawell.

Without offering various kinds of perquisites, Tallulah never

could have expected or afforded the kind total service she required
from the people surrounding her, many of whom could not have
found a job anywhere else, some of whom would not have worked
for anyone else. To Edith Smith, she gave a life-style. To Dola
Cavendish, she gave her presence. And in front of Evyleen
Cronin, she dangled possibilities.

Mrs. Cronin was found guilty of grand larceny in the second
degree. She was sentenced to one to two years. But because of
age, infirmity, and a strong plea for mercy from Tallulah, her
sentence was suspended. Tallulah, once again, got Evyleen off.
The wonder was that she didn't take her back.

"... Is Tallulah Bankhead, Tallulah Bankhead"

WHILE *The Big Show* was still a roaring success, a young playwright had a dream about Tallulah. The dream was reported
dutifully to a prominent New York psychoanalyst. The psychoanalyst speculated that Tallulah Bankhead was probably the most-
dreamed-about woman in the world, symbolizing to the dreamer
a kind of joyous emancipation from restraint and guilt.

By 1951, however, after the one season, the radio show began
to totter. The causes were varied. In the first place, the pull of
television was far too strong for anything on the radio to combat
effectively for very long. And, in the second, a little bit of Tallulah—onstage, as well as off—went a long way.

Like Ravel's *Bolero*, the Tallulah of the fifties never developed; it just got louder and louder. The jokes, the *shtick*, the image began to cloy. Tallulah needed control, enrichment, a firm hand. But she repelled all hands strong enough to control. She built for herself, out of inertia, fear, and insecurity, a professional cul-de-sac.

Her excesses were typified in the first broadcast of the second season, for which Tallulah traveled to London. A very big deal, the show was presented conjointly by the British Broadcasting Corporation and the National Broadcasting Company on its Silver Jubilee, as an "expression of unity between the two countries." Tallulah's return to England was front-page news there.

Thin, taut, and tanned, she stepped onto the stage of the Palladium Theatre in London and drew gales of laughter with her opening lines: "Bless you, dahlings. Now let's see. What was I saying when I left London sixteen years ago—oh, yes—make mine a double!"

She fell back into the fiat Bette Davis-Tallulah Bankhead feud, conceived, perpetuated, promulgated exclusively by Tallulah and stoked at fever pitch since the release of *All About Eve*. "Don't think I don't know who's been spreading gossip about me and my temperament out there in *Hollywood*, where that film was made: *All About Me*. And after all the nice things I've said about that *hag*. When I get hold of her I'll tear out every hair of her mustache."

There were multitudinous references to Tallulah's desperate aggressiveness, her advancing age. "I've decided," she said to guest George Sanders, "to grow old gracefully." To which he replied very dryly, "And have you?"

To climax the show, Tallulah and guests read from Gene Fowler's mawkish poem "Jervis Bay," a tribute to the men of a British frigate who went down with their ship while fighting the Germans. Meredith Willson led what sounded like hundreds of choral voices. Tallulah read in a mushy, quivering tone. She went straight from the paean to "This earth, this realm, this England" to "May the Good Lord Bless and Keep You."

A couple of the British papers liked the show. The majority

hated it. The lachrymose "Jervis Bay" became a *cause célèbre* in London. The English had, by then, ceased to celebrate war or death in that tone of voice. The *News Chronicle* called the poem and the reading a "most regrettable breach of taste."

Reaction to the show at home was exasperated. Robert Lewis Shayon of the *Saturday Review* wrote: "Miss Bankhead begins her season as the Big Show's Mistress of Ceremonies still billed as the 'glamorous and unpredictable.' She is definitely no longer the second. Her vain, rude, and temperamental role has worn very thin. She would be well advised to try something fresh."

After the demise of *The Big Show*, Tallulah toured the country in a series of lucrative, one-shot lectures for women's clubs. At the McFarlin Auditorium in Dallas, Texas, she drew a capacity crowd of 3,000 people. She trundled onstage from the wings swinging her Mark Cross pocketbook and shouting, "Hello, dahlings."

She told stories about Daddy, Aunt Marie, Grandmother, Grandfather, recounted her desire to go on the stage, her early days at the Algonquin, her introduction to Gerald Du Maurier. She sang her songs without accompaniment and did impressions.

She chain smoked and referred to the glass in her trembling hand, hoisting it at the audience. "I bet you think it's gin. I wish it was." It *was* gin, and it was garnished with orange peel and lemon. John Rosenfield of the Dallas *Morning News* wrote, under the headline NOTHING BUT PERSONALITY ON LOOSE AS TALLULAH BANKHEAD TAKES A TRICK: "Miss Bankhead showed the lecture world a new trick. There are two types of attractions, one with a message, and the other to stalk personality. Hers is an ideal formula for projecting celebrity. She gave the paying customers what the lecture committee ordinarily reserves for itself in a post-performance cocktail party."

Meanwhile, back at Windows, Tallulah was learning to talk into a tape recorder. There was the inevitable autobiography. Harper's had guaranteed her $30,000, a very large amount in 1952 for a show-business memoir. Richard Maney ghosted the book, but she was encouraged to turn on the machine whenever she had night thoughts. She ranted and raved that she couldn't talk into any goddamned machine. When her outbursts were played back to her the next day, she roared with laughter.

The book, called *Tallulah*, was typical stylistically of Maney: arch, florid, literate, abounding in *jamaises*, and totally supportive of the Bankhead legend. For 1952, however, *Tallulah* was pretty hot stuff. It broached the questions of sex, drugs, and drinking, but it was filled with half-truths and untruths. The book seethed with self-vindication, epigrammatic attitudes, reverence for family and poets and English peerage, and contempt for self-analysis that is finally serious. She cried poor, claimed the theater didn't matter to her a jot, and emerged triumphant from all her famous feuds.

On the latter, she parried with legalisms and often missed the heart of the matter. She devoted two pages, for instance, to Elia Kazan. Ignoring the personality problems they encountered in *The Skin of Our Teeth*, she *got* the director on a technicality. *Tallulah* cited a newspaper story about the feud between them. The story ended, "Tallulah swung hard, but Kazan cut her down, and the play eventually went on as he wanted it. He and the star haven't exchanged a word since." Tallulah, via Maney, wrote: "A pretty story, *mesdames et messieurs*, but it has a single flaw. It isn't true. . . . So Kazan and I hadn't exchanged a word since the opening of *The Skin of Our Teeth* on November 18, 1942, eh?" She disproved that contention by pulling out a letter from Kazan written to her *after* November 18, 1942.

By 1952 *Tallulah* was the best-selling book in the nation. It was serialized in thirty American newspapers, bought by Lord Beaverbrook's London *Express*, and excerpted as far away as Tasmania, where a headline read: TALLULAH TOPS THE BIBLE.

At the height of this personal success, Tallulah was offered more money than she had ever earned in her life—$20,000 a week— to perform a cabaret act at the Sands Hotel in Las Vegas. The money was too good to turn down. She prepared to leave for the desert.

Patsy Kelly accompanied her there. Patsy, who had fallen on some hard times, was part of Tallulah's household during this period. She answered phones, helped Tallulah dress and undress, ran tubs, made drinks, drank along, and listened attentively. Her favorite line about Tallulah's helplessness was: "She dropped an egg and stood aside."

Edith Smith, who had cleaned up Tallulah's eggs on and off for twenty years, was beginning to tire. She had a series of accidents, the last of which left her with a slight limp. And Glenn Anders, faithful and loving, had also by this time apparently taken a certain amount of stock in himself.

Tallulah was about to leave Windows for Vegas after a particularly riotous going-away party. The house was a mess. Neither Edie nor Glenn had consented to accompany her. Glenn took Tallulah's arm to escort her to an awaiting limousine. They walked together over the bucolic lawn at Windows.

"I wish you were going with me, Glennie," she said.

"I can't, Tallu. We've been through that," Glenn Anders answered. "What if the Ray Millands or some other friends of mine should come into the casino? How could I explain what I was doing just kind of hanging around? It makes a pimp of me, Tallu."

As Tallulah pulled away with Patsy Kelly, Glenn strolled back to the house. Edith Smith was sitting in the living room, her ample chin resting against her fist, surrounded by a sea of empty glasses, cigarette butts, dirty plates, unwashed skewers. There were several additional burns on the carpet and the remains of a bouquet of white orchids brought by Louisa Carpenter, who had flown in from Delaware in her private plane.

"Edie, do you mind if I take these orchids for a friend of mine?" Glenn asked.

"Oh, darling," Edie said, heaving a mighty sigh, "take the whole damned place."

At the Sands, Tallulah knelt down before the picture of her mother, said her customary "Please, God, don't let me make a fool of myself out there," stood terrified in the wings, screaming at Patsy, and finally walked out onto the floor. She wore a white, low-cut gown, long black Hildegarde gloves. The audience was well dressed, too, since Tallulah had demanded that Entratter impose more rigorous shirt-and-tie requirements on the patrons.

She entered to tumultuous applause. Her opening line, after a long, suggestive, and heavy-lidded gaze around the room, was a tremulous and galvanic "OHHHHHHHHHHHH, MY GAAAA-AAAWD!" The audience laughed hysterically. At what, Tallulah was never quite sure, but she cozied up to the microphone and relaxed somewhat.

"Now listen, dahlings," she continued. "I want to correct the impression that this is my first time in a nightclub. I've spent half my life in saloons. But this is the first time I've ever been *paid* for it."

The audience continued to respond very favorably as Tallulah went into the body of her act: a mélange of special material, much of which had been tried and proven true on *The Big Show*.

The quintessential Tallulah monologue had been written for *The Big Show* by Goodman Ace. In it, Tallulah copes barely with a New York taxicab strike. She is forced, for the first time in her life, to take a subway. She hands the man in the booth a check and asks for a Pullman to 125th Street.

In Las Vegas, she performed a routine very similar to that classic piece of material. The theme once again was: Tallulah in Wonderland, Wonderland being anything outside of the narrowest but most sophisticated New York purview. The alien métier was now *gambling*, in relationship to which Tallulah is the sophisticated innocent. The gambling monologue has her walk up to a table, roll a seven, and yell indignantly: "I *what?*" And there were lines like: "I'm faded? What do you *mean* I'm faded?"

She did impersonations, danced the black bottom, sang her standard songs, and read aloud from Dorothy Parker's "The Waltz." The latter was included to remind the Sands' patrons that they were in the presence of an actress. In spite of "The Waltz," Tallulah's saloon act was hugely successful.

Since her mammoplasty, Tallulah had taken to displaying her firmer, higher, more youthful-appearing breasts in the same casual manner as one would an engagement ring or a particularly well-done pedicure. She had pulled one breast out at the Stork Club for Otto Preminger. She had asked an all-night radio personality called Big Joe Rosenfield if he would like to touch. Stories of similar exhibitions are legion. Appearing on the bill with Tallulah in Las Vegas was a young singer named Merv Griffin. "How do you like them, dahling?" she said, as Griffin tells the story. "It's not plastic, you know. It's me."

Tallulah was apparently interested in the handsome, blue-eyed singer and evinced her interest with a series of antic strategies, which had become almost ritualized by the early fifties.

Following the bust-baring incident, Griffin tells how she invited him to her dressing room between sets. Knocking on her door, he heard a voice which summoned him to enter. It was Tallulah's voice, but there was no Tallulah in sight as he entered the dressing room.

"Where are you?" Griffin asked.

"In here," she answered.

"Where, Tallulah?"

"Here," she repeated.

He followed the voice into the bathroom, where Tallulah was squatting on the toilet. Griffin jumped back, startled.

"What's the matter? Are you *chicken?*" she laughed.

On the second day of the show, Griffin lost his voice. It was a temporary condition called "desert virus" and happens to most singers who are unused to the climate. When he returned the third night, the stage manager advised him to stay away from Tallulah, because she was furious at him.

Griffin went to his dressing room. Tallulah and retinue passed, as they did every night. He called. She did not respond. Several minutes later, she passed again. He said, "Hello, Tallulah"; she didn't answer. When it happened a third time, he yelled insistently, "Hello, Tallulah!"

"Son of a bitch," she growled, from behind a moving cloud of smoke.

"Wait a minute, Tallulah," Griffin said, walking out to her. "What's the matter?"

She stood in full makeup, her arms akimbo. "You know very well what the matter is."

"Tallulah," Griffin said, "if you're referring to the fact that I wasn't here last night, I just couldn't make it. I could hardly talk, no less sing. What did you want me to do? Drop dead on the floor?"

"You know perfectly well that I can't *stand* hearing about other people's illnesses. Immediately, I think I have it. I have merely to hear Jimmy Durante or Louis Armstrong speak and my throat goes bad. If I'm around a stutterer, I stammer. If I hear about an automobile accident, I feel bruised all day."

"What happens when you hear about a rape, Tallulah?"

"I masturbate, dahling." She roared at her own joke and walked off.

At 2 A.M. one Sunday morning, Griffin and Tallulah decided to go to the casino. They had been drinking daiquiries and were rag-doll drunk before they got there. They went to the blackjack tables, shoved out money, and miraculously began winning thousands. Tallulah chastised the dealer with every new hand, "Son of a bitch"; she rolled. Griffin concurred: "Son of a bitch." This went on through the night. They got drunker, raunchier, and richer. By ten o'clock the next morning a crowd in bathing suits was gathered around, listening and watching.

Jack Entratter, a mountain of a man physically, was told about the scenes his star was making. He came up behind them, grabbed and cashed their chips, tucked Bankhead under one arm, Griffin under the other, ascending a staircase that led out of the casino. Tallulah looked down at the gathered crowd of hotel guests. Dangling like a puppet from beneath Jack Entratter's arm, she yelled, "Well, isn't anybody gonna fuck me tonight?"

Stories of Tallulah's startling behavior circulated widely, as can be expected. Bowdlerized versions appeared in the newspaper columns frequently. Her friends told it like it was, most of them marveling at the spontaneity and utter lack of inhibition which Tallulah seemed to them to embody, typical assessments being,

"She just didn't give a damn," "Tallulah was a totally free human being," "She was the first of the Aquarians."

Certainly there were aspects of Tallulah's unconventional behavior which might be dismissed as simply robust iconoclasm. She knew that getting suddenly and insouciantly naked was very funny, and she used it as a device to liven up parties and to amuse individuals.

Sometimes at Windows, at the end of a party, she sprawled across the top of her piano, wearing only a strand of pearls, singing "Bye-Bye, Blackbird." Estelle Winwood came in upon such a scene one night and chastened her firmly with her standard assessment: "Do you know what your problem is, Tallulah Bankhead? You're a showoff." Miss Winwood took another approach to Tallulah's nakedness when, in reply to a serious query, she puzzled, "I just don't understand her. She has so many pretty frocks."

There was nothing pathological in Tallulah's preference for swimming and sunning in the nude among consenting adults in the privacy of her own backyard. In this regard, she deferred sensitively to the feelings of others, especially the very young or the very old.

Mildred Dunnock, for instance, telephoned Windows one summer afternoon and asked if she might visit and swim there with her preteen daughter, Linda. Tallulah was delighted and offered to retrieve her bathing suit from the attic if her nudity would be likely to embarrass or offend the child. Miss Dunnock replied that Linda had had a very progressive upbringing and would not be bothered at all by the sight of the human body.

There are examples of Tallulah's behavior which were so delightfully outrageous that they simply ought to be out of bounds to the sour dicta of conventional psychiatric scrutiny.

In the mid-fifties, Tallulah befriended a young actor named Jimmy Kirkwood, Jr., the son of James Kirkwood and Lila Lee. Tallulah asked Jimmy to name the three people in the world that he would most like to meet. One of Jimmy's choices was Eleanor Roosevelt. Tallulah said that she would arrange it.

Tallulah called Mrs. Roosevelt and invited her to tea with herself and Jimmy. They all three sat on a sofa. Mrs. Roosevelt was warm and responsive. Tallulah was charming. Jimmy was enchanted. In the middle of a conversation about the state of the Democratic Party, Tallulah rose to say, "Wait a minute. I've got to pee. But I don't want to miss a word of this."

She scrambled down a long hall, toward a bathroom which was completely visible from the sofa, unbuttoning the trousers of her yellow slack suit as she moved. Mrs. Roosevelt and Jimmy continued their conversation. Tallulah, with the door open, talking all the while, lowered her trousers and sat down on the toilet. Jimmy looked at Mrs. Roosevelt, who shrugged just slightly and spilled less tea than he.

After Mrs. Roosevelt had left, Jimmy turned to Tallulah to say incredulously, "Do you know what you did! You peed in front of Eleanor Roosevelt!"

"So?" Tallulah asked.

Jimmy repeated, "You *peed* in front of *Eleanor Roosevelt.*"

"Oh, don't be ridiculous, Jimmy," Tallulah said. "She didn't mind. Eleanor Roosevelt has more important things on her mind than my bathroom habits. I'm sure she didn't even notice. She pees herself, you know."

It has been said that Tallulah always left her bathroom door open because she suffered claustrophobia. That was true. Still another explanation proffered is that she could not bear to be left out of things. And that, too, was true. But too many significant people in Tallulah's life met the actress for the first time when she was on the toilet or in the bathtub to validate either of these explanations.

That a kind of exhibitionism had always been involved in all of Tallulah's extremes is undeniable. But earlier in her life there had been a certain psychical utility in the way she acted. Attention had to be paid, and she behaved in such a way that it was paid. Her cartwheels, her language, her nudity, her public tubbing all made a kind of survivalistic sense and, in the long run, paid off.

Increasingly, however, the quality of her behavior changed.

More and more she dispensed with all the frippery and got down to basics—which is to say that she exposed herself.

In the strict psychiatric sense, exhibitionism is the intentional exposure of the genitals to a member of the opposite sex. Dr. Leonard Blank, writing in *The Journal of Sex Research*, commented that neither he nor Kinsey "in an intensive review of the literature . . . was able to find a single reported case of female exhibitionist."

Once again, Tallulah broke all the rules.

She set up situations in such a way that specific genital exposure was inevitable. There was neither displacement nor accident involved. She raised her dress to display a bandage on the upper thigh. She arranged seating so that she was elevated. Invariably she was in the dressing room, in the bathtub, or on the toilet when she met her new directors.

The most frequently uttered comment about these various episodes is that they seemed to have had no seductive quality. Tallulah didn't like her flabby and trunk-dominated body and said so. She used it in a way that could be violent, contumelious and self-deprecating, with more contempt involved than come-hither.

When she was feuding with a well-known actress during the run of *The Skin of Our Teeth*, she appeared in a bra and pants and said jocularly to the actress' husband, "I think I'll go on like this." The other actress replied, "Why don't you?" Tallulah turned to her, ripped off her underwear, and growled, "Because they might see my scar."

Morton Da Costa went backstage to see her in *Private Lives* when she was playing in Pittsburgh. He was accompanied by a seventeen-year-old boy, the son of a rich and influential family. Because he had not liked her performance, Da Costa focused on the hat she had worn. "About that *hat*," he said disapprovingly. "Your taste is in your mouth," Tallulah answered. She had been wearing a precariously hung wrapper and as Da Costa introduced her to the boy, she let it drop, stood stark naked, and extended her hand. "Hello, dahling, *terribly* nice to meet you."

She had pulled a comparably hostile stunt back in the thirties when a producer, whom she loathed, sent an aspiring and virginal ingenue backstage to see her. He had begged Tallulah to treat the eminently shockable young woman gingerly. Tallulah did not. During the meeting, Tallulah dropped a bead in her crotch, fetched it, described what she was doing as she was doing it, and flailed the girl for her embarrassment.

Certain parallels can be drawn between her sexuality and her performances. The Tallulah of *The Little Foxes, The Skin of Our Teeth, Lifeboat,* and *Rain* had been garbed austerely in the garments of her art. The Tallulah of the camiknickers, playing to her Gallery Girls, and the Tallulah of *Private Lives,* romping with Donald Cook, was a joyous, spontaneous exhibitionist loosely appareled but respectably covered. The Tallulah who trundled onstage swinging her pocketbook and shouting, "Hello, dahlings," the Tallulah of Las Vegas—this Tallulah was publicly, aridly, and increasingly bead fetching.

In an essay called "Creativity in the Theatre," Philip Weissman wrote, ". . . excessive reliance on exhibitionism assures a communication to the audience which will be artless and superficial. The actor's appeal to the audience is then personal (often sexualized) and the audience's response to the actor is equally personal. Artless theatre, like the striptease, is often intended as mutual seduction between actor and audience. It is a meeting ground of the voyeur and the exhibitionist."

Some dragon somewhere Tallulah never slew, and perhaps it was at least partly traceable to the incident on the dining-room table when Will lifted Tallulah up in her nightgown and approved warmly when she did high kicks and sang risqué songs. On the one hand she hung tenaciously to that time by continuing to exhibit all through her life, only seldom covering herself with the introduction of formal theatrical structure, only seldom transmogrifying her basic cry of "Look at me" into something more meaningful and ultimately more fulfilling to performer and audience. On the other hand, she exhibited with undercurrents of resentment and hostility as though she were saying to Will, "I will do anything for your approval, but I don't like the terms."

26

The Queens' Queen

IN 1956, during the bidding of a conventional game of bridge, Tallulah heaved a tremulous sigh. "If I have to go out on a stage once more and say 'Hello, dahlings,' I shall go stark, staring mad," she complained. She asked Jean Dalrymple, who was then director of City Center, to find her something serious to do.

This was a transitional time for Tallulah. Edith Smith, devoted friend and handmaiden since England, had left for good. She took a nine-to-five job in the book department of Marshall Field, in Chicago.

William Langford died, at thirty-five, of a lung disease. He had left Tallulah two years before his death to align himself with actress Signe Hasso, with whom he made a movie in Sweden and toured in a play. Tallulah would refer to Langford as the last man she ever loved, though she boasted darkly of an affair with the most prestigious television journalist of the day.

She sold Windows, to which it was becoming increasingly difficult to attract company. Just before her decision to sell she was asked what she did way out there in the country. "I take care of old actors," Tallulah answered. She bought a four-story town house at 230 E. Sixty-second Street and told herself she was going to get out more. The town house had twelve rooms, six fireplaces, a latticed garden, and sycamore trees. She hung the Augustus John portrait of herself over one of the fireplaces and built a cozy kind of conversation pit around it. Richard Maney wrote, under her by-line in the New York *Times*, "It is to this house, if I may jostle Thomas Gray, that 'I may hie, at evening's close, to sweet repast and calm repose.' "

Robert Williams continued to provide the repast and several New York doctors, for a price, the repose.

The play which Jean Dalrymple found for Tallulah—who had stepped out of caricature into a character only once since 1949 in *Dear Charles,* a drawing-room comedy—was a revival of *A Streetcar Named Desire,* whose writing Tallulah had originally influenced. Tennessee Williams suggested Tallulah to Irene Selznick soon after she had optioned the young playwright's work. He told Mrs. Selznick, "While I was writing this play all of the speeches seemed to be issuing from the mouth of Miss Bankhead." Selznick vetoed the suggestion. Tallulah, she said, would demolish "the moth-like side of Blanche."

The personal relationship between Tennessee and Tallulah was mercurial, violent, full of bluff, envy, anger, and role playing. Tallulah considered Williams' Southern background inferior to her own. He bought her once a very expensive, engraved black Mark Cross bag. She held it up to the light, squinting with scrutiny. Unable to find any minor imperfection, she flung it at him across the room. "How dare you bring me this?" she yelled. "A lady *always* travels in brown. But I suppose it's impossible for *you* to understand what a lady is."

Herbert Machiz was chosen by Williams to direct the revival, which was slated to open at the City Center for a limited run following a four-week Florida tour. This would be Machiz's Broadway debut.

Tennessee Williams brought Herbert Machiz to Tallulah's town house, introduced his mercurial star to his director, and left. After a quiet dinner, Machiz read *Streetcar* to Tallulah.

"I can just tell that you're going to be a great director," she beamed, swiping her lips with a fresh coat of Elizabeth Arden's Victory Red. He brimmed with evangelical fervor. She talked constantly about England, Daddy, the frustrations of her career as a "personality." She read him several letters she had kept, written by important people and attesting to her talent. It was as though it were she who had to impress the fledgling director.

For the production, Tallulah gave up booze and cigarettes. Machiz read her the play only one more time, and she had memorized the part. Tallulah could still ingest enormous hunks of material by simply listening twice to the material.

The owner of the Coconut Grove Theater, at which the revival was to premiere, turned his enormous house over to Tallulah, and the cast rehearsed there in a mammoth, high-beamed foyer. Rehearsals went very well. Tallulah listened to her young director with almost pained intensity. She wanted this very much.

Acting remained, for Tallulah, completely intuitive. She had no method and inveighed against actors who verbalized theirs. She certainly never discussed Blanche as Blanche, as another woman with biography, ideas, delusions, ideals, a special set of demons. In working with Tallulah, Machiz used a subtle method of indication.

"She wanted to know what everything meant," he recalled. "But she didn't want to be *told* what something meant as though she were too stupid to understand. When Tallulah didn't understand something, she wouldn't admit it. She had a way of saying, 'How would *you* do that, Herbert? Why don't you do that for me?'"

Rehearsals were smoothest when Tennessee Williams, under whose aegis the production was supposed to be done, chose, as he often did, to absent himself. He rankled Tallulah terribly during one run-through when he said to her, about her interpretation of the part, "This isn't Mayfair, y'know."

At the Florida premiere, a strange phenomenon became apparent. Certain lines were suddenly construed to be enormously funny. Tallulah, as Blanche DuBois, was getting laughs where none were intended. The delicate emotional balance of the play was shattered.

Tennessee Williams, who had always considered *Streetcar* his finest work, was furious. Sober, he blamed Machiz for his inability to direct Tallulah. Drunk, he blamed Tallulah for being Tallulah and threatened to cancel the whole production.

Tallulah was bewildered. She had no idea what the audience was laughing at. Machiz suggested that they found her *manner-*

isms amusing: her tremulous voice, the whiplash movement of her head as though drying her hair, the staccato, bronchial laugh. She turned on him. *"That's me. I'm Tallulah Bankhead. What can I do?"* As usual, the violent shout was a plaintive cry, and this time, a legitimate question to which she had the right to expect an answer.

It was Jean Dalrymple, who had been in the audience opening night, noting every explosion of inappropriate laughter onstage and in the audience, to whom Tallulah listened. She invited Jean to come to her house that night and work with her. Together, they tried to exorcise from Tallulah's performance every one of the mannerisms that had hardened sclerotically over the years. Tallulah worked exceedingly hard.

Over the course of the Florida run the performance improved, and the laughter disappeared. Tallulah was tanned and content and having minimal sleep problems. At the end of a night's work she was inexplicably exhausted. Estelle Winwood said to her, "That, my deah gurl, is because you're really *playing* it." Exhausted or not, Tallulah was by this time habituated to soporifics and made a public display of their use. Tennessee Williams recalled a gathering in Florida at which Tallulah announced, "I'm going to take a suppository, and do not become alarmed at anything that might happen. I will soon become incoherent and leave the room, but let the party continue."

The production moved into City Center to a huge advance sale. It was scheduled to run from February 15, 1956, to February 26. Tallulah's opening-night audience was exultant, elegant, and primarily male homosexual. They came because they had received word through the grapevine that the performance was a "hoot."

That she had exorcised from her performance all the mannerisms which were wrong for Blanche did not matter. The gay guys were there to laugh at their burgeoning goddess, and they did from the time she said, "Somebody told me to take a streetcar named De-sigh-ah." When she pointed stage left and said archly, indicating the liquor cabinet, "I spy! I spy!," there was an uproar in the house. Tallulah had used her life as art for too long.

During a crucial scene with Mitch, her last-chance beau, she looked out at the audience and said, as Blanche, "I'm looking for the Pleiades, the Seven Sisters, but these girls are not out tonight. Oh, yes they are. There they are. God bless them! All in a bunch, going home from their little bridge party." There were more than seven sisters in her audience that night. And when Tallulah uttered those lines of Tennessee Williams, pandemonium ensued.

Tallulah, in recounting that terrible night to Jimmy Kirkwood, said subsequently, "I wanted to stop the performance and beg them all to give me a chance. But as a professional I couldn't do that."

Nor did Tallulah allow herself to be seduced into playing *Streetcar* for comedy. Opposite an inadequate Stanley and a merely adequate Stella—eliciting insane responses—she went through the play steeled somehow and undeterred. Tennessee Williams rushed up after her performance to bow before her and kiss her hand. He subsequently apologized in a letter to Tallulah for his behavior in Florida. She did not acknowledge the letter.

Tennessee Williams was of two minds with respect to Tallulah and his play. In an *Esquire* profile of September, 1971, he told writer Rex Reed, "The *worst* Blanche DuBois in the world was poor Tallulah, although I must say she was amusing. I'm sure the attack on Blanche being a drag queen started when Tallulah played her."

Writing for the New York *Times*, however, just after *Streetcar* closed, the playwright focused on Tallulah's inner struggle and on the difficulties she faced with her audiences. "I doubt that any actress has ever worked harder," he commented, "for Miss Bankhead is a great 'pro,' as true as they make them. I think she knew, all at once, that her legend, the audience which her legend had drawn about her, presented an obstacle which her deepest instinct as an artist demanded that she conquer . . . she set about this conquest with a dedication that was one of those things that make faith in the human potential, the human spirit seem far from sentimental. . . . When the play opened at the City Center, this small, mighty woman had met and conquered the challenge. . . . To me, she brought to mind the return of some great mata-dor to the bull ring in Madrid, for the first time after having been almost fatally gored."

After the opening-night performance, there was a party for Tallulah. John Emery and his wife, Tamara Geva, were invited. The first newspaper notices were bad. Brooks Atkinson, for whom Tallulah had particular respect, was unimpressed. The Emerys were leaving early, soon after the Atkinson review appeared. "The clothes were upstairs in the bedroom," Miss Geva recalled, "and I walked in there and saw Tallulah on a chaise longue weeping. It was a rather frightening picture to see her weep, sobbing very quietly, trying not to be heard. That was the only time I saw something human in her."

In later notices, there would be not only praise, but, just as important for Tallulah's sake, justice. *Cue* magazine wrote: "Each passing reference to anything stronger than Coke brought forth gales of uproarious, pseudo-sophisticated laughter. These gay lads had come to see a travesty and, despite Miss Bankhead's sturdy refusal to commit one, they applauded, as though by their actions they could call it into being. Such response must have completely baffled and enraged the actress. It is likely that it would have floored a weaker personality. As it was, one could only admire Tallulah's restraint in not stepping out of character and roaring out something like, 'You idiots! Be *quaht* or leave the theatre!'"

The *Saturday Review* called hers "a surprisingly disciplined performance," also commented on the audience, and said: "In those scenes where the play allows her to express her feelings about youth and age, or to recount the story of the boy she drove to suicide through a self-centered failure to understand his problem, she is right back in the top rank of American actresses."

And William Hawkins of the New York *World-Telegram* called Tallulah's Blanche "one of the most extraordinarily shattering performances of our time."

There was nothing new, to be sure, about Tallulah's strong appeal to certain homosexuals. Her Gallery Girls, back in England, if not outright lesbians, were undeniably homoemotional and strongly so in their vociferous reactions to Tallulah. But there was an innocence about those girls in terms of what they didn't know about themselves and in regard to what they worshiped in Tallulah. They took her very seriously as a person, even when they laughed at her lines. She symbolized youth, beauty, idealized wealth, opportunity, mobility, freedom.

Tallulah's appeal to the guys who flocked to see her was of a different sort. They were upper-class, hardly innocent, and they wanted not the best but the worst from Tallulah, which is to say the utter extreme of her personality playing.

What they relished in Tallulah was the kind of atrophy, the kind of triumph of form over content, that makes a drag ball terribly, terribly funny. They wanted sham, and Tallulah gave it to them. She was configurational rather than substantive. Her lip-line had ceased, for instance, to have anything to do with the shape of her mouth. Her clothes were almost but never quite right; they were *about* glamor rather than glamorous. The style of her hair was still Mayfair-Veronica Lake. Had Tallulah cut it or brought her *maquillage* down to her face, had she permitted herself to be *seen*, they probably would have stopped laughing.

Tallulah moved and talked the way gay men do when they imitate the female animal. One of Tallulah's secretaries analyzed her fetishistic appeal to them this way: "She was doing onstage what they all did when they played dress-ups with their friends. Hers was *their* kind of talk, *their* gestures. She was a highly identifiable creature. They identified. They grooved."

By the time Tallulah did *Streetcar*—after years of exploiting nothing but the personality with which the boys identified—she was firmly in the ranks of the queens' queens. Garland was their singer. Bette Davis their actress. Dietrich, Mae West, Joan Crawford ranked among their other favorites. Tallulah became—sadly at times—their comedienne.

Tallulah had other qualities that were attractive to them. Especially to the gay world, Tallulah projected availability, and she was, indeed, to many of them available.

She made their kind of mistaken-gender jokes dating back to *The Big Show*. They had, all of them, heard rumors about Tallulah's homosexual or, at least, bisexual predilections. That made her one of the gang. And, if there was any misogyny in all of this adulatory hysteria, Tallulah's self-destructiveness was part of her appeal. Drunk, sad, lonely, dependent, she was more proximate, more theirs forever.

Would she be the queens' queen or a working actress? Atrophy or move? Enlarge herself through her art or entrap herself in her narcissism?

She seemed to be searching desperately for answers in 1956 and 1957. After *Streetcar*, which like some great love afforded profound pain and great satisfaction, she reverted to the exploitation of the Tallulah image.

The Ziegfeld Follies, a revue capitalized at half a million dollars, starring Tallulah as Tallulah, failed to reach Broadway.

Tallulah had been unhappy with much of the material originally submitted to her and furnished her own. Again, she read Dorothy Parker's "The Waltz." Again there was a sketch modeled after the highly successful subway routine; in this case, Tallulah's maid took the day off and the Wonderland with which she was forced to cope was Domesticity: "Now if I can just find where she keeps the kitchen." Also included in *Follies* was the inevitable baseball sketch for which Tallulah donned baggy pants and hoisted a bat incompetently. Jerry Gehegan of the Philadelphia *Daily News* wrote: "It's the kind of musical you walk out whistling the settings."

The press blamed *Follies'* failure on the paucity of material. One of the show's writers explained, "It's hard to write for a legend."

For the first time since *The Skin of Our Teeth*, Tallulah, in *The Ziegfeld Follies*, had been provided with an understudy. Tallulah was beginning to experience symptoms from the forty to a hundred unfiltered English cigarettes she smoked daily. She experienced difficulty breathing, and climbing steps was increasingly burdensome to her. The producers of *Follies* provided her with two dressing rooms, one of them right offstage so that she would not have to exert herself between numbers. She was also guaranteed, by the terms of her contract, a twenty-minute rest period between scenes.

She took an extrapolated version of the show into summer stock and called it *Welcome, Darlings*. It was through this vehicle that she met Jimmy Kirkwood, who was then in his mid-twenties. He was sent to her house by the producer of *Welcome, Darlings* for an audition. At the time, he was appearing regularly in the television soap opera *Valiant Lady*. He was told to be at her house at one thirty, prepared to do at least a half hour of comedy material. He sat nervously downstairs, while Tallulah, who had just arisen, pulled herself together upstairs. He heard slight movements and some coughing. Tallulah appeared at the head of the staircase. Jimmy rose. Tallulah said, "Don't get up. I see you almost everyday on *Valiant Lady*. You've got to tell me all about it. Is your sister really such a bitch? Do you have to pick the shit out of your eyes every morning? I do."

She sat down next to him, proceeded to explain every piece of material in the revue to him, stopping only to catch her breath. After almost an hour of monologue, during which time he had the opportunity to utter not one line of conversation or audition material, she said to him, "You're hired. You're absolutely perfect. You're charming, attractive; you have background, class, and talent." As Kirkwood tells it, she then hoisted herself around, swung her legs on to his lap, and continued, "What about those ankles? Aren't they the best you've ever seen?"

Tallulah was no less terrified of a summer circuit opening than she was of a Broadway premiere. Jimmy Kirkwood recalls the first performance of *Welcome, Darlings* in Maine. The star was to appear first to the audience standing at the head of a long flight of steps, which she then proceeds to descend, all the while singing "Welcome, Darlings." She and Jimmy were backstage, waiting for the curtain to ring up, about to assume their places. Tallulah was at the bottom of the steps and needed assistance getting to the top. Her hands were icy. She looked haggard and as stiff as peanut brittle. As the curtain rang up, however, perched atop the stairs, she threw her shoulders back and galloped down the stairs, completely renewed by the presence of an audience.

Throughout the Citronella Circuit, with her revue, Tallulah was sweet, cooperative, gentle, and well liked by the members of the cast. Once again, however, it was because she was clearly un-threatened and totally in charge. Her fellow players, Jimmy among them, were mostly deferential kids in their early twenties.

She exploded only once and that was at the Cape Playhouse in Massachusetts. Jimmy Kirkwood had an impossibly quick cos-tume change, after which he was to reappear onstage, dance a Charleston with a group of young dancers, all of whom fall flat on their faces with exhaustion as Tallulah—the Inexhaustible—comes onstage.

One night, however, Jimmy's quick change did not come off. He appeared onstage disheveled, dancing with his shirt sticking out of his fly. He laughed. The kids in the cast laughed. The au-dience laughed. Tallulah did not laugh.

She played to a giggly audience in the midst of a group of giggly actors. When the curtain came down, she walked over to Jimmy, who was convulsed with laughter and lying in an appropriately supine position. She began to kick him in the side and the gut with the point of her shoe: "You unprofessional sonofabitchprick-bastard," Tallulah screamed. "How dare you break up during one of my numbers!"

Tallulah turned and charged toward her dressing room. She was followed by Rose Reily, a black woman, who was functioning as Tallulah's right hand and theater maid.

The audience, separated from these scenes only by a curtain, remained in their seats. The next voice they heard was Rose's as she yelled, "Don't, Miss Bankhead. Please don't. Stop it. Stop it."

Tallulah had grabbed a knife, lunged toward her wardrobe, and was ripping apart all her costumes.

She liked and trusted Herbert Machiz well enough to begin another venture with him, this one an adaptation of Henry James' *The Europeans*, which was called, in its adaptive form, *Eugenia*. It was the first role she had actually created since Philip Barry's *Foolish Notion* twelve years before. Machiz, who had experienced a sober, humble, professional Tallulah Bankhead struggling against impossible odds in *Streetcar,* now experienced the other side of the coin. It was the limp reed syndrome. Tallulah was at her worst when she suddenly lost faith in a male figure on whom she previously depended. And now she took the inadequacies of *Eugenia* out on Machiz. He describes it as "impossible, a nightmare."

On tour with the play before the scheduled New York opening, she broke her hand by banging it violently against one of the sets. In Philadelphia, she stumbled and broke four ribs. The accidents were beginning to proliferate: a combination of pills, drinking, brittleness, and vanity. Her eyes were getting weaker and weaker, and she refused to wear her glasses for anything but reading. After a short stay at the hospital, she returned and fired a French lead actor whom she had originally approved. She watched a run-through of the play, called Machiz aside, and said peremptorily, "Fire him. I don't understand a word he says." She demanded extensive rewrites, read them hastily, and tore them to shreds in the presence of the author.

Her acting apparently had infinite variety. While one reviewer out of town said she was flirting with a great performance, another said she had been totally unintelligible. Elliott Norton of the Boston *Daily Record* wrote ominously: "Miss Bankhead can no longer keep a poor play alive by good acting. Not in 1957. However, her performance was good enough to keep her own reputation intact and that is important. For she had lost a good deal of lustre and some of her high standing in the last few years." That she was obviously still passionately concerned with her reputation was evidenced by the frequent press conferences she held in which she explained every bruise, every hospital stay, every missed performance. When necessary, she lied.

Eugenia limped to New York. The *New Yorker* had great fun describing her opening-night performance: "she snarls, gurgles, bays and purrs, much the usual way; she manipulates parasols like pool cues and fans like discuses; she launders the stage from wing to wing with the skirts of her spectacular gowns."

What neither the *New Yorker* nor the other journals picked up was a certain gratuity with which she endowed the script. As directed, Tallulah in the character of Eugenia, a ruthless European fortune hunter, is foiled completely in the last scene. At the de-nouement, she was to walk over to her mirror, turn it away, go stage right, ascend a flight of steps, and, in the ascension, slowly regain her confidence and hauteur. In a series of mute gestures, she was to indicate that she wasn't finished yet. As Tallulah played it, however, during the opening-night New York premiere at the Royal Theater, she ascended the steps, reached the top, and ut-tered the line "I shall go around the world in a mackintosh." Machiz and the rest of the cast froze in amazement. They had never heard the line before. She simply made it up.

At yet another performance, opposite a stunned young actor named Tom Ellis, Tallulah segued mid-scene from *Eugenia* into *The Little Foxes*. She stood on a stage, in a theater whose mar-quee read *Eugenia*, played the play for a time and suddenly, with-out any indication to her fellow actors or to the audience, enacted a scene from the Hellman melodrama. Ellis did the best he could to stay with her; the audience seemed to be unaware of the change in gears.

During the run of *Eugenia*, Tallulah was tripling the already heavy dose of Tuinal her doctor had prescribed for her. Machiz asked her one night, while she swallowed nine pills, how many it would take to kill her. "Thirty-five," she replied nonplussed. Dur-ing the same period, for assorted injuries, demanded sleep, and simply to alter her consciousness, she was ingesting a quart of bourbon a day, Benzedrine, Dexamyl, Dexedrine, and morphine.

She missed one performance of the twelve *Eugenias* played in New York. She was found at home sitting in her tub.

27

Crazy October

TED HOOK was in his late teens when Tallulah was doing *The Big Show* by day and streaming into the slumbering American psyche by night as the girl most likely to do what she damn well pleased. Six years later he met her in Las Vegas. She was headlining at the Sands; he was dancing in the chorus. California born and bred, he was redheaded, blue-eyed, trim and adoring, with a freckled but chiseled face, the deep perpendicular lines around his mouth betraying his Scandinavian ancestry. He took her out several times.

In 1958, Ted called Tallulah on a whim. She was in Hollywood in the middle of the pre-Broadway run of *Crazy October*. Ted's call came at a time when she and Rose Reily were battling royally. When the phone rang at the Knickerbocker Hotel, Rose was out, and Tallulah answered it herself.

She screamed with delight on hearing Ted's voice again and commanded him to come to the hotel *immediately*. Drinking, gesticulating, gazing over his shoulder constantly to touch and palpate her immaculate hair, she offered him a job. "Rose is getting impossible," she said. "I need a man to take over my life. I need someone to handle my affairs, to be my escort in public. I'll pay a hundred a week, plus a lovely room in my new town house on East Sixty-second Street. Your laundry, liquor, cleaning, food —*awl* included. But I *insist* that you buy your own goddamned cigarettes."

Tallulah gave Ted twenty-four hours to think over her proposition, the serious particulars of which—money, food, cleaning—she had spit out like Regina Giddens in *The Little Foxes*. Ted didn't need any time. He was living in a small apartment, had no serious emotional commitments, and his career wasn't going anywhere in particular. Ted joined Tallulah's life when the troublesome play was about to limp into San Francisco.

Crazy October was the work of another young man who was fast becoming an important part of Tallulah's life—James Leo Herlihy. It was adapted from his own short story, "The Sleep of Baby Filbertson." Tallulah, in wedgies and rolled-down red socks, was playing Daisy, the proprietress of a West Virginian wayside inn. Joan Blondell, fresh from a much-lauded performance in *The Rope Dancers* on Broadway, played an earthy waitress. And Estelle Winwood was doing the part of a widow who had paid Daisy $1,500 to cremate her husband properly and whom Daisy had instead buried in a parking lot. It was a mordant and not very good black comedy.

Tallulah had dismissed the play, on first reading, as "one of those down-trodden, downbeat, degenerate Southern plays." When Herlihy, its charming, blue-eyed young creator, personally read it to her, she saw the "marvelous comedy in it." Talent and its bearer were often "as one" to Tallulah. While she had good instincts about other people's abilities, she frequently invested too much faith in too nascent talent. She was smelling the goose, but it wasn't quite cooked.

Tallulah had just come off the summer circuit in an eminently forgettable mystery called *House on the Rocks*. *Crazy October* was scheduled to open on Broadway after an extensive and hopefully therapeutic tour. The play was capitalized at $100,000. Tallulah's continuing ability to pull people into the theater in spite of everything—sometimes because of everything—was evidenced by her contract, a star's contract and no mistaking it.

She was getting $1,500 a week against 15 percent of the box office; approval of director, cast, set designer, company manager, and press agent. She had solo star billing over the title of the play; $100 toward expenses on her theater maid; first-rate accommodations in transit; general approval of lighting scheme, plus guaranteed footlights. Her contract was always explicit about the use of footlights. They were considered old-fashioned, and hardly anyone employed them anymore.

One of the first things she did upon arriving at a new theater was personally supervise the lighting scheme under which she was going to be seen. She chose a young actress whose facial structure was similar to hers, set her up on the stage, and scrutinized this Tallulah manquée from every part of the auditorium, shouting up orders to the technician in the lighting booth. Tallulah knew what she was doing. The results of her expertise were always extraordinarily rejuvenating.

There was also a clause in her contract which gave her the right to miss a performance in order to appear on television upon payment to the producer of $6,000. During this period, Tallulah was receiving very lucrative guest-shot appearances, including a $100,000 proposal from *The Ed Sullivan Show*—ten appearances at $10,000 apiece. She tried it once. But she objected to the pace and the speed of it. "I will not be shot out of a cannon," she told Ted.

Joan Blondell agreed to do *Crazy October* because she wanted the experience of playing with the legendary actress. She was shaken and shocked in the beginning by what she was seeing of Tallulah's behavior.

On the morning that the cast was to depart from Grand Central Station to New Haven, where they would have their first and only dress rehearsal, Tallulah showed up at the very last minute, steered through the cavernous, commuter-jammed station in an unaltered mink, followed by Rose, James Herlihy, a friend of James Herlihy's, two yapping Yorkies, and several old-fashioned stand-up trunks. Tallulah was groggy with the effects of heavily drugged sleep. That she had thrown her mink coat over nothing at all was made painfully obvious to the waiting cast of *Crazy October* and to several hundred astounded commuters.

At the dress rehearsal, she arrived drunk, argued violently about the placement of a staircase, threw up, and stalked out. No rehearsal was held. Subsequent rehearsals were cut short as she retired to her dressing room to watch the soap operas on television.

Rose Reily, though still functioning as her theater maid, had ceased playing nursemaid to Tallulah. Rose stood in the wings, at each performance, holding a glass of scotch and a tube of lipstick, each of them on ice. On her exit cues, Tallulah dashed over to Rose, gulped the scotch, and swiped her mouth with the pointed tube. As her *maquillage* thickened, so did her speech.

Tallulah had never drunk so much, so visibly, so regularly, and so unprofessionally. She was breaking all her own rules. Ted was still a reticent novitiate and couldn't say much. Blondell had not got to know her yet. Estelle took Tallulah as she was, and the young men who had come in droves to watch this particular hoot got exactly what they expected.

During the first part of the tour, Tallulah had very little to do with Joan Blondell. They went their separate ways at lunch and after the theater—Tallulah with her claque of young men, Joan frequently by herself. She had ceased to be appalled or shocked by Tallulah's behavior and was really rather fascinated with her, but a natural shyness kept her at a distance.

Tallulah did not like most women or at least pretended not to. If, for instance, a woman entered her life as the wife of a friend and impressed Tallulah in no other way, Tallulah simply ignored her with the exception of the mandatory amenities. For another woman to impress Tallulah was a delicate and precipitous venture. It could be done, however, by paying Tallulah the proper kind of attention.

During the run of *Welcome, Darlings*, Liz Smith, the motion-picture critic and magazine writer, was then a callow and unsophisticated new girl in town. She was taken to a party by a close friend of Tallulah's, Gus Schirmer, Jr. Tallulah grabbed Gus away at the beginning of the evening, disappeared with him into the bedroom where they talked about Tallulah's life, emerged with him several hours later—all this time, totally ignoring Liz. As Schirmer and Liz were about to leave, Tallulah kissed Gus and shook Liz's hand rather perfunctorily. Liz, working under a kind of high wind of compulsion to say something to the fabulous Tallulah Bankhead, drawled in a rather heavy Texas: "Miss Bankhead, I want to tell you that, until I saw you do Blanche in *Streetcar*, I had never understood the character nor what the play was about."

Tallulah, who had been glaring at her through the critique, and had been rather dour and nervous all night, suddenly broke into a wide and gracious smile. She grabbed Liz's hand and tugged her out into the center of the party, screaming for quiet in the room. "Everybody, attention," she said. "Everybody pay attention. Now I want you to listen to what this *divine* child here has to say. I've given her permission to call me by my first name because she is obviously one of the intelligentsia."

Joan Blondell got through to Tallulah in much the same way, paying the proper kind of attention. Joan had noticed that Tallulah seemed to be in a constant state of not only frenzy, but disarray. She was continuously misplacing her cigarettes, her frownies —which were little patches she wore on her forehead to make the skin taut and keep it from wrinkling further—her matches, and her lipstick and shrieking for TEEEEEED to fetch. Joan had an apron made for her with a patchwork of pockets, individually labeled with Tallulah's needs: FROWNIES, LIPSTICK, CIGARETTES. Tallulah was amused and touched by the whole idea of it. From that time on, their whole relationship changed.

As she had given the party to Liz, she now gave the stage to Joan, feeding her lines as one actor can do for another, standing stock still for her onstage, taking special care to make Joan look good. Joan Blondell began to get fantastic notices. Tallulah exulted in them as though they were her own.

It was not simply that Tallulah was touched with the frownie apron, she was intrigued with Joan Blondell, especially with her family life, the comparative normality of its structure. It was Joan's habit to arrive very early at the theater before each evening's performance. She liked the slumbering quality of the backstage area at twilight and enjoyed spending time in a duster, applying her makeup with complete leisure. Her quiet times were shattered, however, by the uncharacteristically early arrivals of Tallulah.

Joan had had a gate put up, not to keep Tallulah out of her dressing room, but to keep her dog, Bridie, in. Tallulah, with her makeup already on, tumbled over it every night, and scraped her derriere every night, and hollered every night, "You make me feel so unwelcome!"

While Joan applied her makeup, Tallulah sat and inundated her with questions: about her ex-husbands, about her children, about her grandchildren, about the fact that she had never wanted or sought personal publicity. Tallulah seemed to find it all vaguely astonishing. She referred to Joan jocularly as Earth Mother. But when the poignancy of her inquest became too apparent, Tallulah reverted to role playing, climbing out as hoydenishly as she had climbed in, rumbling for the benefit of the now more populous backstage area, "You're soft, Joannie, soft! All you think about are your goddamned children and your goddamned grandchildren. Softie!"

Tallulah would occasionally ask her to one of her little gatherings back at her hotel. "She had a special chair," Joan Blondell recalled. "She balanced a tray on her lap with makeup, cream for her face, and these little precut tissues. There was always a very good light facing her, and she constantly applied cream to this beautifully structured face, drank her drink, and talked constantly.

"She would ask me to tell stories to the group about funny things *she* had done. I watched her enjoy me telling them. A kind of warm light would go on in her eyes. But if she caught me watching, the light would go out immediately. It was fantastic. She reminded me of John Barrymore, whom I met under similar circumstances. Both of them—stoned out of their minds, talking. The beauty of a Barrymore. Tallulah had the beauty of a Barrymore, and she was a lovely, lovely person.

"I wanted to say to her 'Stop this foolishness.' But that image. . . ."

They were at the Geary Theater in San Francisco as Christmas approached. Joan, who was planning a little party for the cast, came around to collect money from Tallulah. Tallulah, however, had decided to ignore the holidays completely that year or at least to Scrooge it up for a time.

"I want no part of Christmas," she screamed. "I will not give a penny. Not a thin penny."

She called for Ted and issued facts. "Ted, there will be no fucking Christmas this year. I despise Christmas. And I will not give in this time. There will be no fucking presents. No fucking parties. No fucking good cheer."

"Yes, Miss B," he said.

The next day Ted informed Tallulah that Joan had put up in her dressing room a tiny and marvelous little tree. "How disgusting," Tallulah said, and ripped into Joan's dressing room.

"Hi, Tallulah."

"I've come to see your little tree, and I've seen it."

"What do you think of it, Tallulah?"

Tallulah made one of her gasping, baritone noises to indicate absolute disapproval, turned her back, and walked out.

By December 23 the large Christmas tree had gone up backstage at the Geary, and the Salvation Army was doing its thing in the streets. Tallulah called for Ted.

"Do you realize," she said, staring into a mirror, applying eye liner, "that it is December twenty-third and we haven't done a thing about Christmas?"

"But Miss B, you said—"

"I know what I said, Ted. But I've been a star for forty years, and I'm entitled to change my mind. Now you're to find out the sizes of everybody in the cast and crew. I want to give the boys silk dressing gowns and a bottle of their favorite liquor. I think the women should have cashmere sweaters. Two each."

On Christmas Eve, after the performance of *Crazy October*, Tallulah trundled out from behind the curtain and made a pitch for the Actor's Fund. She showed her legs, did a Charleston, and sang "May the Good Lord Bless and Keep You" tearfully. She arrived at the cast party overloaded with the presents which Ted had rushed out frantically to buy, insisting that they be opened and tried on immediately. When a stagehand's $100 dressing gown turned out to be too large, she screamed at Ted, "I told you *medium* fat, not *fat!*" She threw a gift-wrapped bottle of very expensive perfume at Joan Blondell.

Joan laughed. "TAH-lu-lah Bankhead! For chrissakes! You're the one who wasn't gonna have any Christmas!"

Tallulah, at the party's end, stepped into very good light and wished the cast of *Crazy October* *au revoir*. "Merry Christmas, dahlings," she said. "And I hope it will be my last."

28

Miss B's Boy

Crazy October closed in San Francisco. Tallulah and Ted returned to the town house on East Sixty-second Street and to a particularly lean period in Tallulah's theatrical career. Stories of her behavior in *Eugenia* and *Crazy October* had, of course, circulated. Tallulah was hard to please at best; the pool from which her choices issued was getting more and more shallow.

But she was deriving an almost maternal satisfaction from Ted Hook. She taught him that one did not make one's own bed in a fully staffed house. That one stayed out of cook's kitchen. That brunch was an ugly and a silly word and that "byes," short for "beddie byes," was less clinical and far nicer than "sexual intercourse."

He learned how to shave her Elizabeth Arden Victory Red lipstick to just the right point after keeping it on ice for forty-five minutes and that Elizabeth Arden was one of a multitude of quirky, Southern loyalties that she maintained. When she was doing a television show for Revlon, a splendiferous gift kit was sent by the company to the town house. Tallulah was called to the door for the presentation. A midget in a Call-for-Philip-Morris midget suit, wearing a pillbox hat, chanted: "Mr. Charles Revson presents *you*, Miss Tallulah Bankhead, with this—" She cut him off. "You can tell Mr. Charles Revson to take his makeup and shove it. I'm an Elizabeth Arden girl. I've always been an Elizabeth Arden girl. And I intend to remain an Elizabeth Arden girl."

She taught Ted how to adjust the living-room lights so that her facial structure was splashed at eventide with the most complimentary pink hues; *not* to jump up and light the more than one hundred imported Craven A cigarettes that she smoked daily or to shut off the radio that played all night lest it awaken her; where to get the best caviar for blinis; *never* to give her a key on those rarer and rarer occasions when she ventured out, but to give it to her escort, because she invariably lost it and could not in any case open a door even sober, and, on such occasions, to check her purse for:

handkerchief
lipstick
frownies
her saints' medals
a rabbit's foot
two packs Craven A's
an assortment of Canadian and Japanese coins
various pills.

He learned where to find the baby-boy blue cashmere sweaters that she slept in all the time and where to buy new ones when the old were tattered with cigarette burns; where to purchase the long red silk robes she wore during most of her waking hours; how much Old Grand-Dad she liked in her ginger ale and that, if the company was interesting enough, he could get away with no Old Grand-Dad at all; and, for the sake of his sanity and despite the very real love he had for her, to insist on taking his day off off:

"Ted, dahling."
"Yes, Miss B."
"I'll give you three hundred dollars if you don't go off today."
"I have to go off today. I promised a friend I'd come and see him."

"We can have him over here, Ted. We'll have a party and we'll have champagne."

"Miss B, we've been together for ten days. I need a day off."

When she was awakened at about 3:30 P.M., Ted had already marshaled the appurtenances of her ablutions. Toothpaste was squeezed onto toothbrush. Listerine was premixed with water. Her warmish tub was drawn, with a tart and never-varying cake of Rogers & Gallet imported English soap emplaced handily. Once she was in the tub, Ted was instructed when to fully awaken her with a shower of ice-cold water or cubes. She caterwauled with delight and stepped out of the tub into an awaiting bath towel, drying herself vigorously while Ted hurtled Chanel #5 at her. He was expected to keep his eyes up. "You're not to look at my bottom," she said. "It looks like an *accordion*."

After Tallulah was dried and perfumed, she walked into the library, where the television was tuned to the first of her "soapies." She drank her heavily laced coffee in front of the set totally engrossed, flicking ashes helter-skelter. When and how Tallulah's soap opera obsession began remains undetermined, but from the late fifties on, the passive act of sitting and observing the sinuous loll of *Edge of Night* and *Secret Storm* was her primary afternoon activity. When it was not feasible for her to watch the programs herself, she paid others to do it for her and make a full report. No telephone calls were taken and no visitors seen during the soapies. There were no exceptions, and she became annoyed if a friend, who should have known better, endeavored to have her disturbed. She expected the people who knew her to be thoroughly acquainted with her habits of life.

At four thirty one afternoon, the telephone rang and Ted answered it. It was Harry Truman's secretary. Ted ran into the den excitedly. "Miss B," he said, "Harry Truman is on the telephone."

She signaled him away with a languorous wave of her arm.

Ted came closer. "It's Harry Truman."

"Tell him," she said, "to call between five and six."

"Miss B"—he laughed, obstructing her vision—"I cannot tell Harry Truman to call back because you're watching a soapie."

"You certainly can," she replied. "I practically elected him to the Presidency with my speech in Madison Square Garden. And he should know better than to call at this hour."

Ted returned to the telephone and began to explain his predicament to the secretary. The ex-President jumped in. "Don't tell me she's watching those damned soap operas! I'll call her back after five."

Ted stared at the mouthpiece incredulously and heard three separate clicks: Mr. Truman, Mr. Truman's secretary, and—softly —Tallulah.

Tallulah was, to a large degree, what other people expected of her. And because Ted's expectations were high and fond, she came alive on his behalf. Resting her small, gaudily polished hand on the telephone one afternoon, she asked him to pick any two people in the world with whom he would like to sup. He specified Dorothy Parker and Truman Capote. She handed him the instrument and told him to call.

He did and they came. Ted and Tallulah dressed formally, he in a white dinner jacket, she in a diaphanous Don Loper gown. Capote, fresh from a trip to Mexico, entered lugging a huge, native-made wicker object, the size of a hamper. Tallulah descended the steps. "Truman," she gasped, "wherever did you get that *vulgar* purse?" They dined on Robert's fried chicken. Capote asked Dorothy Parker whether she had been up to the Guggenheim to see some new exhibit. "No, my dear," she answered. "If I go above Seventy-second Street, I get a nosebleed."

Tallulah glanced at Ted, loving his delight in it all.

She camped outrageously on Ted's behalf. She would agree to be seen under fluorescent lights only at their occasional forays to the neighborhood Nedick's, which she insisted was pronounced to rhyme with "medics." She flapped down the street in her mink and wedgies, delighted when she was recognized. To the questions "Are you Tallulah Bankhead?" she answered invariably, "I'm what's *left* of her, dahling."

At Nedick's, she leaned over, touching the arm of the counterman in his cheesecloth hat, insisting, by her attitude, upon intimacy. She got close to his ear, hoping probably that he would get close to hers. Her hearing was quite bad by this time, and she would not even consider Ted's suggestion that she use some kind of hearing aid. She ordered her hot dog in great, explicit detail. "I'd like a hot dog, please. I'd like it done medium. Sliced in half. And, on it, I'd like some mustard *and* a little mayonnaise. I don't suppose you have any béarnaise sauce?"

The plays continued to arrive at the house. One of them, by a new playwright just out of his teens—with the radical and unlikely title of *Oh Dad, Poor Dad, Mamma's Hung You in the Closet and I'm Feelin' So Sad*—was sent with high commendation. Tallulah called in Ted and insisted that they each take a copy, read it, and talk about it together. Tallulah stayed on her floor. Ted repaired to his.

At five in the morning, Ted came into Tallulah's darkling bedroom. She was propped up in one of her sweaters, chalked by this time with the ashen residue of the night's cigarettes. Her glasses rested on her head, and Doloras, a Maltese named after a character in *Kukla, Fran and Ollie*, slept on a separate pillow above Tallulah's head.

"What do you think?" she asked timorously.

"No, you tell me first," Ted insisted. "I don't want to influence your judgment."

She demanded that Ted talk first.

"Well," he said, sitting beside her on the bed. "I think it's trash and vulgar, and I hate it."

Tallulah closed her eyes in relief, held open her arms, and mashed Ted in a desperately tight hug. She started to cry, "Thank Gawd I have you, Ted. I was afraid to say it. I want to be chic. I want to be with it. But that *monologue*. I just can't talk that way. I was raised in the South. I have beautiful manners, when I choose to execute them. I cannot be common."

Ted handed her a tissue. She wiped her eyes and regained her composure. "Besides," she said, "Shelley Winters has the market cornered on whores and tarts."

Whether she was right or not in this particular case—not about Shelley Winters but in her judgment of the play—Tallulah's tastes and sensibilities were rigidly old-fashioned. She knew what lady-like conduct was. She believed in *style* as a constant, something one had in spite of the way one behaved, and that became, in a strange way, somewhat self-fulfilling: the pride that constituted her *quality*. She believed, too, in the theater as self-presentation. It would not be some character saying all those nasty things up on a stage. It would be Tallulah Bankhead. And she turned down play after play, using this complicity of delusion and rigidity as her rationale.

There are sundry stories about Tallulah and *Sweet Bird of Youth*, disagreement about whether she was ever offered the part of the Princess, an aging, drug-addled, washed-up movie star. She did, however, say one night in a state of logorrheic attitudinization, trying on thoughts like gloves, "I will never play an actress or a drunk."

"We got so automatic that I could look at her and know when she wanted her lipstick and when she wanted her frownies. But she almost never wanted to go out," Ted Hook recalled. "She was a terrible recluse. 'Oh, it's just too much trouble, dahling,' she'd say."

Ted functioned like a social director, combatting her growing desuetude with perky and solicitous suggestions, almost in the form of play therapy. One day they called CBS and invited Joe Sirola of *Secret Storm* over to the house for drinks. She coaxed him into revealing the future convolutions of the plot, which is against network policy, swore she wouldn't tell a soul, and rushed to the phone as soon as he had left to call everyone she knew.

Carol Channing and Tallulah celebrated their birthday on the same day. Earl Blackwell threw a party at Arthur's for Carol to which Tallulah was invited. Tallulah attended the party in a sailor-boy outfit, had a wonderful time, and cajoled Morton Da Costa, who was enjoying a huge success as a director, to come home with her.

He sat by the bed as she slipped into her sweater. He helped her into bed. A night of mutual reminiscences turned into disjointed monologue. At dawn, Da Costa made a motion to leave.

He was sitting on one side of the bed, Ted on the other. Da Costa reached over to take her hand just as she was about to pass out. Ted motioned him away mute and frantic, but too late. Her eyes rolled into her head and her hand clamped around his wrist. He had to be pried loose.

It had been for Morton Da Costa an upsetting evening. He had several times cast glances at Ted Hook, who could easily have passed for a younger brother or son: red, kinky, luxuriant hair; blue eyes; an erect almost gibbonoid bearing.

As he got to the head of the steps, Ted approached him. "Mr. Da Costa, she'd kill me if she knew I asked you. But she needs work. She needs a job. Can't you do something?"

Da Costa hemmed and hawed. Tallulah called his office the next day, but the director did not take the call. "It was devastating to me," Da Costa recalled, "I didn't take the call because I just knew it was a matter of survival. I just couldn't get into all that again."

Ted was afraid to leave her. One night, after a few hours out, he returned to the town house and smelled smoke. He rushed into Tallulah's bedroom. Doloras, the Maltese that ordinarily slept above Tallulah's head, was on fire like some flaming halo. Tallulah had apparently just fallen asleep, after flicking her ashes onto the sleeping dog. Ted now rushed into the bathroom for water, yelling, "Tallulah, Doloras is on fire!"

She awakened. "What is it?"

"Tallulah, Doloras is on fire!"

"Well, for chrissakes, put her out," she said and went back to sleep.

Ted fought quixotically against the pills. The day after the Doloras incident, she promised to allow him to regulate her. He had her down from popping several Demerol tablets a day to Darvon, a weaker synthetic, and finally to Anacin. When she relapsed, he resorted to slipping her placebos, which seemed to do the trick for a time. She cried gratefully at his good intentions. But she wanted her opiates back.

She had the first of a new series of groggy accidents, ripping open her hand on a broken lamp. She bled profusely. Several of her caddies spilled out of the lidless house in a mad search for assistance. Sixty-second Street looked like Satyricon besieged. After breaking several ribs, Tallulah was admitted to Flower-Fifth Avenue. She became violent under sedation, awakened several patients with her screams, kicked a nurse in the breast, mistook Ted for Adlai Stevenson. Her caddies were called in to quiet her and hold her down.

When it became obvious that the staff nurses were susceptible to Tallulah's bribes—she offered to introduce one to Marlon Brando —a private nurse was engaged, who remained with her after she left the hospital. On a recuperative visit to British Columbia to visit Dola Cavendish, Tallulah suffered the first of several psychotic episodes, in which she was very Southern, very proud.

She grunted at it, claimed it had bored, betrayed, and short-changed her—and she was right on all three counts—but the *the-ater* remained the only thing in life that came close to slaking her enormous energies and finally the only thing for which she would temporarily stop killing herself.

The manuscript of *Midgie Purvis* arrived. Ted tossed it at Tallulah, commenting, "This is your next play." Tallulah concurred enthusiastically. Mary Chase, the creator of *Harvey* and *Mrs. Mc-Thing*, had filled another universe with pockets of warmth, whimsy, and sagacity. The play went into rehearsal under the direction of Burgess Meredith. It was produced by Robert Whitehead.

She went into a training period unlike anything since *Streetcar*. This time she had moral and medical assistance. The nurse, who had been kept on after Tallulah's last violent hospitalization, laid down strict laws. No booze during showtime. B$_{12}$ shots would replace the opiates and the amphetamines. Tallulah called her "that Germanic bitch," but she obeyed her.

Tallulah began to eat again: ice-cream sodas for breakfast, a strange assortment of small shellfish during the day. She went so far as to lecture a reporter from the Philadelphia *Inquirer* on the evils of drug use. They had been talking, over lunch, about peyote buttons. "This is the worst kind of abuse," she was quoted as saying. "I cannot and will not try to understand people who take Things."

In *Midgie Purvis*, Tallulah played the title role of a mature woman who finds middle age dull and cold. Instead of electing to make herself young again, Midgie pretends to be much older and hires herself out as a baby-sitter. Life as a dotard is far more tolerable.

In this dual role of Midgie at fifty and Midgie pretending to be eighty, Tallulah agreed to do most of the physical things she had claimed she was incapable of doing. She had a three-minute change at one point in the play, and in another she was required to slide down a banister. She groused, but she did it. She had turned down *Mame* and several other marvelous properties because of the physical exertion required.

The most upsetting of Tallulah's experiences during *Midgie* had to do with other people. She had her usual approval of cast and, during the preproduction period, sat in a darkened, empty theater with Burgess Meredith and Robert Whitehead while a legion of sixtyish actresses read for a part. To the general annoyance of the production people present, Tallulah engaged those she recognized in lengthy, nostalgic conversation. Then, suddenly, with no explanation, she rose and walked out of the auditorium into the backstage area. She told Ted later that she simply could not sit and watch her fellow performers go through the cold business of auditioning. "There's no dignity in it," she said. "After forty years, you're still a commodity to those goddamned producers and those goddamned theater party ladies."

The play wasn't right from the beginning, and it could not be made right. There were cast changes, constant and extensive rewriting. The reviews in Philadelphia were generally bad. Mary Chase, Burgess Meredith, and Robert Whitehead attempted to pull it into shape for the opening. Tallulah was learning whole new scenes from one night to the next.

Tallulah's usual claque awaited her on the night of the New York opening. They heard first her unmistakable singing voice from offstage tremulating, "Yes, we have no bah-nah-nahs"; she entered to wild catcalls and general hysteria, in a dazzling white evening ensemble.

There were radical critical differences of opinion regarding *Midgie*, though no one suggested that the play had worked. For many reviewers and spectators, *Midgie Purvis* was one of those lovable, corruscating cripples that burns moments onto memory and gives critics material for expanded Sunday thoughts. Walter Kerr, who was always very sentimental about Tallulah wrote:

> Half the time in "Midgie Purvis" you won't know where the people have come from, and half the time you won't know where they're going, but in some spooky and entirely impenitent way they always get there. For instance, toward the end of the first act there's a downright disorderly scene in which Tallulah Bankhead, dressed to look like a crone of eighty and driven by at least eighty-horse, clambers all over a huge empty house in the company of three obviously insane children while a band of shuddering interlopers trail them with flashlights and a detachment from the local police force trails *them*. This scene just doesn't make any sense at all, and I'd be lying if I said it did. It isn't even any good. But then, suddenly, all the Mack Sennett shenanigans stop dead in their tracks, a pause like the end of the world cuts short everyone's breath, and almost before you have noticed, Miss Bankhead and the children are slowly streaming away in the increasing darkness as though they'd heard a lonely whistle from a weary Pied Piper—and the moment, for no reason whatever, is lovely to look at and helplessly touching.

Kerr referred to the preceding and disastrous decade in Tallulah's career and concluded: "She is serving notice that an actress is back in town."

Howard Taubman, however, assessed blame for what *Midgie* was not. He claimed Tallulah was at fault:

> Instead of a fey, childlike creature, Midgie Purvis has become a vulgar clown. She has been turned into a product of show business. The public personality of Miss Bankhead, as it has manifested itself on radio, television, and the gossip col-

umns, has been catered to. If there was freshness in Midgie to begin with, it has been dissipated by a pursuit of the commonplace.

Though Taubman's tone was harsh, he was basically correct. What happened to *Midgie Purvis*, however, had less to do with "catering" than with making accommodations. It was a weak and structurally flawed play to begin with. But in the rewriting, Mary Chase, Burgess Meredith, and Robert Whitehead had to take cognizance of Tallulah's limitations as an actress.

Whitehead recalled: "She gave herself. She wasn't drinking much. Tallulah was trying to do her job. But her talent was, in many ways, limited to voice tricks. Everything that was delectable had happened so easily for her that she never really learned how to characterize. I think Tallulah really wanted to act in the last ten years of her life, but the groundwork from which that kind of actress is created was never there—although what was there was quite special and quite extraordinary."

29

Carrying the Bag

TALLULAH, BY 1962, was finding it more and more difficult to get and keep a household staff. Madam, of course, did not set the best example. A cook was fired for answering the door naked; a maid for smoking pot while on the job.

"It wasn't the pot that I objected to," Tallulah laughed. "But the very least she could have done was to offer *me* some."

Estelle Winwood scolded her about the situation: "I submit, Tallulah, that it's your own fault. You offer them liquor and then complain that they're alcoholics. You fraternize, and then you object to intimacy. It's a very confusing household you run, Tallulah."

Ted Hook interviewed domestics around the clock for three days. He finally found Emma Anthony, a soft-spoken, soft-stepping black woman, very old, very tiny—who could cook, clean, and keep books. "Does she play bridge, Ted?" Tallulah asked.

"Jesus, Miss B!"

Tallulah, as it turned out, developed an immediate and protective attachment to Emma Anthony. She called the old woman Mama and, as a symbol of respect, spelled dirty words *sotto voce* when Emma was in earshot, though Emma spelled as well as, if not better than, Tallulah: "As I was saying, Ted, the man is a b-a-s-t-a-r-d."

Soon after Emma came into her life, Tallulah lost Ted to Jerome Cargill, Inc., a firm which advises and oversees amateur theatrical productions. Ted was reluctant and anxious about abandoning Tallulah, but she insisted. "There's less fun and more nursemaid in your job every day," she told him. "If I didn't think you had another talent, I wouldn't mind. But you can't waste your life here, Ted. There will always be someone around to look after me. I haven't been a star for forty years for nothing. Ask Cargill for a good salary. Don't undersell yourself."

Ted's decision convinced Tallulah that she had finally to put her town house on the market. Though she had assured her young friend that there would always be qualified people around to look after her, they both knew better. Tallulah was sixty years old. There was the recurring problem of drinking, cigarettes, and fires. Her life had been saved several times only by a combination of alacrity and luck. She had dreaded being alone all of her life; now the problem was less subtle: It was a matter of *assistance*. Tallulah knew that she would be safer in an apartment house, with around-the-clock neighbors and a twenty-four-hour staff.

And then there was the stair problem. The climb from floor to floor was becoming difficult for Tallulah. It meant a completely debilitating struggle for breath, a desperate fatigue which exhausted her for minutes afterward. Tallulah's "smoker's cough" —a term from the halcyon days of "T-Zones," "unpleasant aftertaste," and walking a mile for a Camel—dated back as far as England. She had always had a certain rushy, breathy quality. Age and cigarettes had made it all much worse. Though the diagnosis "emphysema" had not yet been applied, she had all the symptoms, and any fool knew that stair climbing was counterindicated.

She sold her beloved town house at a fat profit to Huntington Hartford and assigned her caddies the job of finding a suitable apartment, preferably on the thirteenth floor. Thirteen was Tallulah's lucky number that year. A five-room condominium was found for her, at 447 East Fifty-seventh Street. The floor and the price were right.

During the move to Fifty-seventh Street and just before his departure, Ted helped Tallulah rummage through her basement to decide what was to be retained and what discarded. They came upon *thousands* of yellowed, unopened letters in dusty cardboard cartons. There were some small checks whose negotiability they pondered, but most of it was fan mail, postmarked as early as 1924.

"Do you think it's too late to answer it?" Tallulah laughed.

The bulk of the packing, however, was finished by an interregnum group of caddies, their friends, and friends of their friends. Dishes were broken, and valuable silver was pilfered.

During the move, Al Morgan, editor of the newly launched *Show* magazine, came into Tallulah's life. He paid Tallulah for the privilege of sitting down to do an in-depth, four-part profile. He sat with her for hours while she rapped about life and death and being an actress. He grew fond of her along the way and, as he started putting things together, realized he could not do the story because he did not have the heart to write about the fading years. Among her favorite subjects: her boys, the caddies. "She told me with great glee," Morgan recalled, "that her boys never left her. The ones that I knew were always very elegant fags who just fawned on her the way fags will on an aging queen."

They were, no doubt, becoming more and more exclusively Tallulah's sole environment. People like Jean Dalrymple and Robert

Whitehead, who genuinely loved Tallulah and cared about her, found it fatiguing and sad to be around too much. Certain others, such as Morton Da Costa, preferred not to get too intimately involved with Tallulah. Ruth Mitchell, who got her start in the theater through Tallulah, was successful and busy. Mildred Dunnock and her banker husband continued to see her, but they could never give what Tallulah required: nothing less than total commitment.

So the caddies took over. They came from the theater, from advertising, television, merchandising, the art world, the idling rich. Tallulah had more respect and love for some than for others. There were court favorites. A pecking order. They were as various as any group of heterosexuals. There were vast differences in their accomplishments. But to be of interest to Tallulah, they had to be, more or less, between twenty and thirty-five, handsome or at least *interesting*-looking; well dressed; charming; risible; able to tell and listen to a good story; unfettered; able to do the work of a servant with the pure devotion of a freedom fighter. When there was a certain concurrence of desire and an ample imbibition of alcohol, she even had sex with some of them.

Onstage, she had played to them, when all else failed, with huge and hysterical success. And now, in life, she made the same choice.

Tallulah's favorite friend in 1962 was a businessman with an ex-wife and two small children. She informed him, at their first meeting, that she didn't like his real Christian name and would prefer to call him Johnny since many of the important men in her life had been so named: Granddaddy, whose exploits and accomplishments she regaled him with; Barrymore, whose early pass at her grew more and more successful as she retold the story over decades; Emery, her husband; and a childhood playmate with whom she had first experimented sexually.

"Johnny" began taking all his evening meals with Tallulah. He convinced her even to venture out of the house for dinner and then a movie, the latest James Bond adventure. They were sitting in a chic restaurant when socialite Hope Hampton walked in. Tallulah hissed at Johnny, "There's Hopie Hampton. My Gawd, she's seen us! Now I want you to be just you and me, Johnny, so you're to tell her that we're going to Connecticut to play bridge. Under no circumstance is she to be allowed to come to the movie with us."

Hope Hampton came over. Tallulah introduced Johnny, invited the reluctant socialite to sit down, warmed to her immediately, and asked her to join them at the movies.

"But, Tallulah," Johnny said, perplexed, "we've got to be in Connecticut in less than an hour."

"What, dahling?" Tallulah said.

"Our bridge game in Connecticut."

"Damn Connecticut," Tallulah expostulated. "That game is never very interesting anyhow, and how often do I get to go to a neighborhood movie with two of my dearest friends in the world?"

Tallulah had a regard for Johnny that she had for few of her other young men. She loved families and family life. It was the saddest and the loveliest of Tallulah's many passions. That Johnny had produced and reared a family was, in Tallulah's eyes, a prodigious accomplishment. And, of course, she insisted upon meeting with his young children. The occasion was Thanksgiving and she invited them and their father to share holiday dessert with her. She received them wearing long centipedal eyelashes, a red Malibu smoking jacket, dragging on a cigarette holder that resembled a pole vault. The children were fascinated.

After dinner, they all went into Tallulah's bedroom. Johnny sat on the foot of the bed. Tallulah motioned the children to come, one on each side, in a flurry of down and throw pillows. She put on her smudged reading glasses and told them the story of Thanksgiving from notes she had scrawled in a hand, which like her voice, was so rapid and impatient it was close to a straight line.

The little boy, heavy with thought, craned his neck to stare at Tallulah through the entire recitation. After she had finished the story, he said to her, "Are you an actress or something?"

Tallulah laughed her very soft, Southern laugh, resisted the joke, and asked him how in the *woooorld* he could tell.

"Well, I think you must be an actress because while you were reading the story, you made me laugh and then you made me cry."

"Bless you," she said, hugging the boy. "And that's the best definition of actress I have ever heard."

They were lying about, drinking eggnog, when the telephone rang. Tallulah picked it up and apparently was asked what she was doing. "You won't believe this," she said. "But I'm in bed with my best friend and his two children."

In and out during these years was a dark, rugged advertising man who, to Tallulah's chagrin, had recently turned actor. Since he had made the decision very late in life and was seldom employed, Tallulah bristled when he designated himself actor and went half-mad when he spoke cozily of "their profession." He lived in for a while, traveled with her, poured drinks, sat around with Tallulah through the languorous afternoons watching quiz shows and soap operas.

He was a proud young man who had a great deal of difficulty resigning himself to the role he played with Tallulah. She deferred to his pride but only on her own terms. They had dinner out once a week together at Sardi's East. On one such occasion, as they were entering the restaurant, she leaned proudly against his arm, and whispered, "Dahling, do you mind at all being out with a much older woman?"

They were greeted effusively and led to Tallulah's favorite corner table. "No, not at all," he replied.

Tallulah then said, quite earnestly, "I'm delighted to hear that. But if it did begin to bother you, I wouldn't mind at all if you called me *Mummy*."

She and the young actor spent most of their time sitting around Tallulah's, guessing along with the quiz shows. They had frequent and ferocious arguments about unimportant things—such as whether or not he should continue to whiten the moons of his well-pared nails with a Cutex pencil. She thought it looked "Forty-second Street" and told him so. "You won't believe this," he countered, "but I read that your favorite man in the world, John F. Kennedy, uses a Cutex stick on his nails."

"You're right I don't believe it. You're making it up."

"He does."

"He doesn't."

"He does, Tallulah."

"You're full of shit."

Such arguments were typical but unserious. Their relationship was irreparably torn, however, when, in front of a group of distinguished guests she asked him to fix her a drink. He grew tight and petulant.

"Tallulah, I'm not going to caddy for you," he said.

He slammed out of the house and subsequently sent Tallulah an angry, explanatory note. Tallulah could brook fury, anger, or rebellion; she understood them well enough. But petulance and heady notes were hybrid and womanish. You carried the bag proudly or you got the hell off the green. She tore up the note and never consented to see him again.

When her various boys entered or left the room, Tallulah customarily extended her tiny hand. The motion was meant less as a gesture of friendliness than as a precaution, a distance-keeping device. Tallulah, toward the end of her years, literally did not want to be touched.

She made her excuses as a rule: "I don't like being mauled; I break easily," or "I've just put on makeup, dahling." And both of them were true. She was always putting on makeup, and she was extremely fragile, given to bruising inexplicably, finding at times the pressure of a high collar unbearable. But there were undoubtedly psychic underpinnings to the "Don't touch me!" phenomenon.

She joked about her diminishing beauty, but she felt it as intensely as she felt anything in her life, not as a harbinger of death, because she wasn't afraid to die, but as a token of waning power, which petrified her. She had felt something close to self-esteem and love through her sudden gift of beauty; now that it was gone, surely she was less worthy and considerably less lovable. She did not want to be touched because she did not feel worth touching.

Tallulah had never been vain in the conventional sense about her beauty. Her statements of bald self-admiration, which shocked people or made them laugh—her statements about the "marvelous structure of her face" or "her perfect teeth" or her skin—were expressions of a kind of gratitude, which is the opposite of vanity. She was as generous about other people's good looks. "You have beautiful teeth," she would say. "Don't thank me. Take care of them. They're a gift."

The world had changed for Tallulah when she became suddenly beautiful. She experienced the externality of her attractiveness as no child born with beauty can experience it . . . as a concise, sudden, beneficent gift of power because of which the world had yielded its riches to her. Not to her essence but to something that had happened to her. In any case, that was, if not good enough, at least better than her prior state of unloveliness.

As she began to watch her attractiveness wane—and she could watch and scrutinize her face in the mirror for hours at a time—there was a commensurate change in the way she dealt with money and personal possessions. It was as if she had a second engine ready to take over when the first failed.

That is not quite accurate because for some time there had been a neurotic linkup between her sexuality and her personal wealth. During the run of *Eugenia* in 1959, she made love to a bisexual actor in his twenties. He had for some time been her companion-caddy, and as just good friends, they had often shared Tallulah's bed.

One night Tallulah was feeling more than friendly toward him as they lay together in bed. She slashed her mouth thickly with a coat of Victory Red, rolled upon the actor. In the aggressor's position, she began to fantasize aloud. He became, in her mind, a jewel thief who had stolen into her bedroom as she slept.

"How did you get in here?" she asked the pinioned young actor. "How dare you? What are you doing? You came to take my jewels, but you are ravishing my beauty."

It was a remarkably satisfying experience for both of them, somewhere between Krafft-Ebing and *opéra bouffe*. And the young man gathered from her oblique references afterward that she had been robbed by a jewel thief, in her London years, who entered her bedroom forcibly. He was unable to determine if there had actually been a sexual attack or whether Tallulah merely used the experience as a highly charged stimulant simile.

By the early 1960's she no longer felt attractive enough to offer

her beauty and began to play the coquette with material possessions. She drew up a will. She left it around her Fifty-seventh Street
apartment and made constant changes in her legatees. Her paintings were most frequently traded off. They included two Eisen-
decks, a seascape called "The Harbor of Dieppe" by Max Bond, a
Grandma Moses, a Corot, a portrait of Tallulah by Ambrose Mc-
Evoy, a little Renoir, various other works of art, mostly Impression-
ist. She never disported her Augustus John portrait; she treasured
that more with the passing years and always assumed it would be
left to a museum.

During the course of the *Show* interview, Tallulah took Al Morgan around her place, showing him all her paintings and naming
the people to whom they were currently bequeathed. Morgan recalled, "If you displeased Tallulah, she notified you that you'd just
lost your painting, but there was always the possibility that you
could get it back." Tallulah eventually became so attached to Morgan that she informed him she was leaving him the Corot. Morgan
gradually faded out of Tallulah's life—as many did. He was not left
anything at all. The early will became a patchwork quilt, an ear-
marked dean's list of Tallulah's current favorites.

The beauty-personal possessions-money calculus was extremely
involved. The possessions she used as surrogate sexuality. Her attitudes toward money, on the other hand, reflected her feelings
about her diminished personal beauty.

Al Morgan, for instance, agreed to pay Tallulah for the *Show*
interview, which is not a customary procedure in profile journal-
ism, because he was of the impression that she was flat broke. And
he was not alone in that surmise. None of her close friends knew
how much Tallulah had, and most of them believed she was penniless. They believed it because she told them so time and time and
time again.

She poor-mouthed. Asked why she had not attended the funeral of a lifelong friend, she sobbed that she did not have enough
money for the plane ticket. In fact, Tallulah had a great deal of
money. Since the Cronin case, it had been managed fastidiously
by Ezra Shine, a certified public accountant. She had a healthy
folder of blue chip stocks: hundreds of thousands of dollars of

Eastman Kodak and Christiana, purchased before the famous split.

She knew exactly what she had. Shine visited her regularly. They went over her assets and her liabilities, and she would say to him, "Well, Ezra, am I rich or poor?" He was able to tell her at one point that she could retire, never work another day in her life, and expect a guaranteed income of at least $35,000 a year. "That's not enough," she would say. Indeed, it was not a great deal considering Tallulah's habits of life, but it was enough to put the lie to her fears of insolvency or her pitiable bouts of poor-mouthing. She cried poor because she felt depleted—and she would cry poorer and poorer.

30

The Death of a Clown

SHE WENT ON THE ROAD with Estelle Winwood in 1962. The play was called *Here Today*, and they traveled for fourteen weeks. She then settled into a period of desuetude. Robert Williams, who was back with her temporarily, watched as she sat in her darkened hotel suite and plucked out the gray hairs which were mixing more and more abundantly with the auburn.

"Don't do that, Tallulah," he begged. "Each one means something."

"I'm getting old, Robert."

For months at a time, she refused even to be seen on the street. Her home was her life, such as it was. She sat with her legs under her on a long blue couch and hardly moved at all. A Kleenex, or a drink, or a pencil was fetched for her. She complained about taxes, talked about moving out of the country to avoid them, went out to vote for Mayor Lindsay though there was a great deal about him that she resented, especially the comparisons made with John F. Kennedy, whom she adored. Her political talk was still party-centered, and fusion tickets she considered apostasy.

She continued to read enormously, but the books had to be lightweight so she could rest them on her chest while she was supine. The occult interested her, though she remained skeptical, and she fooled around occasionally with a crystal ball. Once she did a quick reading for a friend. "I see a puppet manipulated by three people," she reported. The friend went out for a pack of cigarettes late that night and was mugged by three assailants.

Odd medical facts and theories fascinated her. She knew things like the Scandinavian suicide rate, spit it out with vigor but could not discuss and had no desire to probe the complexities of the Scandinavian psyche. She claimed that one could actually go blind from contact with syphilitic tissue. When one of her caddies disputed the theory, she touched her genitals and then her eye and said, "There, I'm not blind, so I don't have syphilis."

She continued to disapprove of the way Eugenia was leading her life. Her older sister was in Tangier at the time seeing a great deal of a tall, rather rugged-looking Gary Cooper type. Tallulah insisted that the man was a bounder and a fortune hunter.

Though they could come together for short periods of time and amuse each other enormously, the sisters never really got along. The last of the debacles had occurred in 1958, the year Eugenia first went off to Tangier. Eugenia, at the time, left sixteen-year-old Billy in the care of Louisa Carpenter, the Bankhead sisters' mutual friend.

When, in the course of her residency in Tangier, Eugenia petitioned Tallulah for some money to open a filling station there, the actress hit the ceiling. She had a letter drafted by her lawyer. It was sent to Sister. The money, in the first place, was denied. In the second, Tallulah maintained that she was not "obligated, morally or otherwise," to give Eugenia any assistance. Tallulah reiterated that she was "shocked" by Eugenia's decision to return to Tangier.

Tallulah's lawyer phrased his final paragraph more emphatically. He apprised Eugenia that Tallulah no longer regarded her as a sister.

As breathing became more and more arduous for Tallulah, she tried again and again to stop smoking. She had her friends blow their smoke in her face or, better yet, inhale themselves and then blow the smoke resuscitatively into Tallulah's mouth. The latter method comprised the compleat filter—other people's lungs. Robert Williams, who had never smoked in his life, performed that service for a time. He was up to two packs a day before he decided it couldn't go on.

Tallulah had another one of her accidents as a result of falling asleep with a lit cigarette and burned her hand so badly that amputation was considered.

These periods of insularity and inactivity had at one time led to melancholia. Now there were psychotic episodes. She thought there were people in her living room who were there to kill her. She jammed her dresser against her bedroom door and screamed for help.

"Tallulah, there's no one here," a frightened caddy assured her.

"Don't lie to me. I crept out on the window ledge and saw them," Tallulah bellowed.

Tallulah was perfectly herself by the morning with no memory of the events of the night before. She attacked a maid once. It is difficult, if not impossible, to separate the psychic wheat from the chemically induced chaff. Tallulah swallowed opiates, alcohol, amphetamines, barbiturates, cocaine—enough to cause psychotic behavior in even a healthy person.

There was talk of commitment or at least consultation with a psychiatrist. Tallulah never knew about the first possibility and of course would not consider the second. "No doctor on earth can understand me," she objected. She considered psychoanalysis worthless, psychoanalysts quacks, and submission to same a sign of weakness.

Her salvation was, as always, work.

In the mind of anyone over thirty, Tallulah Bankhead was still legend and, therefore, box office. She was not without offers, even though their quality naturally changed. She was asked to appear opposite Bette Davis in a film called *What Ever Happened to Baby Jane?* the first of a spate of motion pictures in which glamorous personalities of the recent past emerged from forced retirement wrinkles and all. Tallulah was never loose enough or secure enough professionally to pioneer or set that kind of style.

She talked constantly about making a "Laurette Taylor comeback"—a great, prestigious, brilliantly reviewed, commercially successful coup. And then maybe she would consider that quick but triumphant fade to retirement. Her expression, to the caddies, was: "Mama needs a hit!"

She had several of her boys over one night when she brought up the Laurette Taylor theme. She was drunk and reaching out for the usual reassurance. But one of the young men, a writer who knew that Tallulah needed a jolt, refused to comfort her.

"Nothing is going to happen for you," he said excitedly, "because you apparently don't want it enough. You don't care, or you would *do* something. Laurette Taylor loved the theater. You don't love it, or you'd be part of it. They're not even telling Tallulah stories anymore. They've forgotten you exist."

Tallulah, almost apoplectic, ordered him out of her house. Then, as he was about to leave, she burst into tears and threw her arms around him.

In the late fall of 1963 she received a telephone call from Tennessee Williams, who was in Puerto Vallarta watching the filming of his *Night of the Iguana*. Did she finally want to play Flora Goforth in a revised version of *The Milk Train Doesn't Stop Here Anymore?* Though the character had been written with Tallulah in mind, the play had been produced three times with another actress doing the role. Tallulah accepted enthusiastically.

Tallulah had always boasted that all of Tennessee's plays were written for her. Williams admits, however, only to four occasions when his creative processes were inhabited in some way by Tallulah's presence. Whether Williams wrote *for* her as an actress or *of* her as a person has never been made clear, but the plays involved were *Battle of Angels, Streetcar Named Desire, Sweet Bird of Youth,* and *Milk Train Doesn't Stop Here Anymore.*

This last had premiered at Italy's Spoleto Drama Festival in 1962 with Hermione Baddeley in the Goforth part. Though Tallulah knew about the play and reportedly wanted very much to do it, Williams was so pleased with Miss Baddeley's performance in Spoleto that he permitted her to go with it to Broadway in late 1962. *Milk Train* received bad notices then, and its run was further handicapped by a newspaper strike, which began soon after the opening. "It was produced too soon," Tennessee Williams explained. "It had not gestated in my mind."

The play focuses on the dying of a Georgia-born, ex-Follies girl, named Flora Goforth. She is living in a sun-drenched villa on the Italian Riviera, dictating her Proustian memoirs to a secretary named Blackie. Flora is angry, drug-addled, and out of grace. Into her life comes a young, very beautiful gigolo who has survived by making himself companionable to rich, moribund females. The international set, which both he and Flora inhabit, have nicknamed him the Angel of Death. He teaches Flora peace and acceptance.

Williams described his play thus: "Essentially the death of Miss Flora Goforth is the death of a clown. There is hardly a bit of nobility, nor even of dignity, in her fiercely resistant approach to life's most awful adventure which is, of course, dying.

"But, if the play achieves, even partially, its artistic intention, you will find it possible to pity this female clown even while her absurd pretensions and her panicky last effort to hide from her final destruction makes you laugh at her."

This gestated, full-term version of the "death of a clown" went into rehearsal soon after the telephone call from Tennessee Williams to Tallulah. The David Merrick Foundation was producing, Tony Richardson, directing. Richardson had seemed one of the most attractive parts of the package presented to Tallulah. The youthful Englishman was enjoying a monumental success at the time. His *Tom Jones*, in films, won fantastic plaudits and enjoyed great commercial success. For Merrick on Broadway he had recently directed *Luther* and *Arturo Ui*. In November, 1963, when the play went into rehearsal, he was the hottest director in films and the theater.

Tallulah, as usual, changed gears to prepare to perform. She modified all her habits considerably and, for beauty and vigor, even tried eating regularly. In the past, her health regimens had always worked. Over a period of days and to the astonishment of everyone around her she had been able to get into glowing, vital physical and mental health. No such miracle occurred now. The pain of the burn, a gaping thing between her two smoking fingers which she was instructed not to bandage, sapped her strength and limited her dexterity. She tired with the slightest exertion. And, for the first time in her life, she feared that her great trap of a mind would not retain lines.

There was a prerehearsal gathering at Tallulah's apartment. Richardson appeared with the cast: Tab Hunter, Ruth Ford, and Marian Seldes. Hunter, who had been an important teen-age idol in Hollywood for years, compensated for his understandable insecurity about this, his first Broadway appearance, by talking at great length about the problems involved in having his horses shipped from one part of the country to another. Ruth Ford was an old friend. Richardson seemed intelligent, if a little intense.

Tallulah gravitated immediately to Marian Seldes, the tall, raw-boned daughter of critic Gilbert Seldes and an enormously gifted actress. Tallulah sensed Marian's sense of tradition, of deference. She liked her good manners, and she just instinctively trusted her. She confided to Marian her fears about not being able to remember her lines, and twice before rehearsal, the younger actress visited Tallulah's apartment to work with her on those lines.

Rehearsals began on November 19. The hassling started soon thereafter. Tab and Tallulah stood center stage one afternoon as he wound up a long, long speech written to end: "The man held out the money to me. And I . . . And I", to which Tallulah was to say, "You took it. You took it, didn't you?" He neglected to say the second "And I." Tallulah said gently, "Dahling, you have another line." Tab jumped up in the air and screamed, "What the *fuck* difference does it make?" Tallulah looked out into the darkened theater at David Merrick, Tennessee Williams, and Tony Richardson and simply shrugged stoically. She said to her caddy that night, "If I were ever going to be the temperamental Tallulah Bankhead, it would have been right there."

She and Richardson had incompatibility problems. He spoke a cryptic, intellectual, modern actors' language. He would not defer to her past. He cared only about her performance that day. There was a cold contemporaneity about him very different from the gallant, traditional, sympathetic "woman's director" to which she was accustomed, the kind who treated his distaff stars as if they were continuously premenstrual. Some of them may have been inept, but they had elegant theater manners and a sense of tradition. In any case, the brilliant, working-class Briton was unable to create the environment in which Tallulah functioned best.

The most niggling but emblematic difference between them had to do with bows. Tallulah, at one point, reminded her director that they have not gone over their curtain calls. He looked at her a bit askance. She explained patiently that she took her calls in the traditional way and proceeded to show him how: after the play, the curtain rises swiftly, catching her *mise en scène*, as though she had just finished the play and settled into the set. She is caught in the act of being, either fluttering a handkerchief, fixing a vase of flowers, or chatting with a fellow actor. With aplomb, startled but gracious, she acknowledges the exultant audience, gathers up the rest of the cast, and steps downstage.

"That went out fifty years ago," Richardson laughed. Tallulah was adamant. The call stayed in.

Early in the proceedings, Richardson gave up. He and Tallulah had argued about everything, and rather than turn the stage into an arena, he simply let her have her way. Then she felt abandoned and undirected, and in the middle of rehearsing a particular scene, she threw up her hands, walked toward Richardson, and complained, "I can do this scene any way, Tony. Upside down. Inside out. Doing a cartwheel. But will you tell me how you would like me to play it!"

His response was a very fluty: "You're the actress, Tallulah."

Given even optimum conditions, it is unlikely that Tallulah could have managed to give any kind of performance for any extended period of time. She was weak and feeble, and she could hardly remember her lines. She walked through rehearsals and out-of-town tryouts, saving a performance that she never gave.

She came through just once. It was in a final dress rehearsal. Tony Richardson decided to take one last shot at directing Tallulah. There is, in the play, a scene in which the dying Flora talks glowingly about what she had with one of her ex-husbands, the only man she ever really loved. In a burst of inspired, vulgar eloquence, Richardson told his star what that man must have meant to Flora, what they had together as a man and a woman.

Tallulah read those lines as she had never read them before. She stunned and electrified everyone present. Marian Seldes commented: "I remember thinking that it was going to be all right, as great as *Little Foxes*. The reading was terrible and it was beautiful, and I felt that I was there at the *end* of something, looking at something I was not supposed to see."

Tallulah finished the speech. Richardson told her it had been brilliant. And she said, in no way vindictively but as a matter of simple fact, that she would never do it that way again. And she did not.

This particular *Milk Train* was staged Kabuki style, with two actor stage managers supplying props to the actors and telling jokes to the audience. Separations between interior and exterior settings were defined in semi-abstraction by lighting, and the entire production, according to Williams, was supposed to be suffused with "the mountain-sea-sky" feeling of "Italy's 'Divina Costiera'" in summer. Williams' conception was rendered real by set designer Rouben Ter-Artunian. Music was by Ned Rorem.

Out of town, Tallulah rattled around wanly on that Orientalized stage, delivering those lines which she managed to remember as rapid, peakless explosions of breath. People walked out of the theater disgusted with her unintelligibility. Richardson flew to London to cast a production of *The Sea Gull*; Tallulah castigated him for leaving a sinking ship, in spite of the fact that his departure had been understood from the beginning and that he intended to return before the New York opening. There was talk even of closing out of New York, and at the last minute plans were made to bring it in. One of the actors purchased a tiny box of soap flakes, for hotel use, about the size of a cigarette pack. When asked why he purchased such a small box of powder, he held it up and said, "That's about as long as I expect the play to run."

Christmas came to Baltimore, where *Milk Train* played a week before the New York opening. It snowed big, thick flakes, and Tallulah invited Marian Seldes and her eight-year-old daughter Katharine, who was with her mother for the holiday, to her suite at the Lord Baltimore. She had two gifts for the child: a red dress and a white cashmere sweater.

She asked Katharine, that December, 1963, whether she believed in Santa Claus. The child answered that she did not. Tallulah said that she had believed very firmly in Santa Claus as a child, that she was hurt and disappointed when she discovered that there was no Santa Claus, and that she had not been hurt in such a way again until the recent death of President Kennedy.

The Milk Train Doesn't Stop Here Anymore closed in New York after five performances. Enid Bagnold attended the last matinee and wrote to Marian Seldes, "Why couldn't we hear Tallulah? What was that?" Many of Tallulah's friends stayed away because they had heard that she was forgetting lines. Tallulah arranged for seats for an actor friend, Tom Ellis, who was bringing actress Lovelady Powell. Miss Powell, who'd been eager to meet Tallulah Bankhead, told Tom that she just couldn't go backstage to meet her after that performance.

Tom told Tallulah that Miss Powell was ill. Tallulah said, "I don't blame her. I wouldn't want to meet me right now either."

31

Fanatic

SHE GREW OLDER still around her immutably garish Victory Red lips. Breathing became more and more of a fight against reluctant tissue. The doctors now gave it a name—emphysema. With a cigarette in her hand, she telephoned Glenn Anders, who had retired to a modest apartment in Guadalajara, Mexico. She was thinking of moving to a more salubrious climate. Was the Burton-Taylor villa in Puerto Vallarta for sale? Could he get a price without mentioning the bidder? Would it please him to retire with her, just the two of them, living out their last days together?

Glenn, who had answered the call from New York on his hall telephone, was gathering a crowd of curious Mexicans. Thinking quickly, he told her that two American women had died just that last week in the area from emphysema. Certainly this was not the place to come with the disease, nor was Puerto Vallarta. They discussed their pensions. At Tallulah's bidding, Glenn reluctantly whispered a figure into the phone.

"That's what I'll get every week when my annuity starts, Glennie."

"I get that for a *month*, Tallulah."

"Promise to call me twice a week, but not before five o'clock. Do you know that Estelle is eighty-five?"

"Well, Tallulah, I'm seventy-eight. We're all getting up there."

Had Glenn not improvised the death of two emphysema victims, Tallulah would probably not have thrown in the towel for sun, sea, and Glenn Anders. Laurette Taylor finish or not, Tallulah's desire to be *seen* was stronger now than ever. She knew that, after the *Milk Train* experience she would never again step on a Broadway stage, but she adjusted her rigid standards and began taking more or less what was offered to her in the other media.

She was in British Columbia visiting Dola Cavendish in 1964 when she received, through Joyce Selznick, the script of a chilling horror story called *Fanatic*, which was to be filmed in England. Tallulah's part in the picture would be that of an old, unattractive religious fanatic who loses her mind after the death of an only son. When the dead boy's erstwhile fiancée comes to visit her in her huge Gothic house, she traps the girl and endeavors to murder her.

Since *Baby Jane*, a big commercial success which was filmed finally with Bette Davis and Joan Crawford, there had been a rash of similar pictures in which other glamorous ladies, including Olivia De Havilland and Barbara Stanwyck, had agreed to look their worst amid murder and mayhem. A precedent had been established for Tallulah, who had not been prepared at that earlier date to be so heinously deglamorized. Now, with some final coaxing from Dola, Tallulah agreed to do what was unquestionably a character role.

She left for England accompanied by Laura Mitchell, Dola's niece, a widow in her late forties who was said vaguely to resemble Tallulah. The flight over was uneventful. Tallulah slept most of the way, awakening about half an hour before the scheduled early-morning landing to fix her face and hair.

There were no placards this time, of course. Tallulah didn't expect that there would be. But she had hoped to be met by her director, Silvio Narizzano, or at least by her producer. They had sent, instead, a liveried Rolls. Only Kenneth Carten bothered to come to meet the plane. And as Tallulah and Laura emerged from customs inspection, he ran ebulliently toward them, calling Tallulah's name. He had not seen Tallulah for several years and threw his arms erroneously around Laura.

With typical sentimentality, Tallulah had asked to stay at the elegant, old Ritz in Piccadilly, where she had first come in 1923. She and Laura were walking up the stately steps of the hotel. Tallulah, jet-lagged but happy, was telling Laura about the first time she had encountered the snobbish Ritz bell captain, when a pass-erby recognized Tallulah and called out her name. She turned abruptly, her heel somehow caught, and she flopped. When Laura bent to help her up, Tallulah grimaced and whispered, "I suppose they'll say I was drunk." At that very moment, a picture was snapped. It ran prominently, captioned with various degrees of tendentious coyness, in newspapers and magazines throughout the world.

With *Fanatic*, Tallulah instituted a new, almost inflexible work pattern. She conserved all her energies—such as they were—for the job. She slept whenever she could for as long as possible. She held only one press conference, though several were scheduled. And she saw very few people. Among those were Elizabeth Lock, her companion of old who was now eighty and living quietly in the north of England, and Dorothy Dickson, former star of the English stage on whose bed Tallulah had sat in 1923 and talked about her role in *The Dancers*. She put off Lord Dudley, who asked to visit, and Judy Garland, who wanted to party.

Tallulah changed her habits, but she was still Tallulah. About a week before shooting was to start, an insurance investigator came to see her. Columbia, which was producing *Fanatic*, had re-quested the customary insurance policy on Tallulah's health, which would indemnify them against possible loss in the event she could not work. When the agent asked her about her health history, she waxed prolix on every ailment from childhood croupe to her em-physema, exaggerating the severity of each illness as though she were comparing fever charts with Eugenia. "I've had triple pneu-monia *twice*," she boasted to the astonished gentleman, who thanked her for her candor and advised the company against in-suring Columbia.

A Columbia executive came to see Tallulah after this episode and told her that they would have to replace her since the risk of continuing a picture with an uninsured star was much too high. She pleaded with him to reconsider, assured him that her most serious ailments were way in the past, and suggested that, to ver-ify that, he read her autobiography. They worked out some kind of deal. Tallulah's $50,000 salary was held as a guarantee against loss. She was not replaced.

It became a matter of honor now for Tallulah to remain healthy. She had a doctor come in several times a week to administer a high-potency vitamin cocktail; she avoided drafts and drank very little.

After three days of rehearsing—a week before the actual filming was to begin—Tallulah awakened at 6 A.M. coughing wickedly. She felt that her face and jaw were in places where neither had ever been before. She called terrified to Laura, who came running into her bedroom. Tallulah's head had ballooned enormously. A doctor was called; he confessed his perplexity and gave her a shot of penicillin. He told her that work, for at least a couple of days, was simply out of the question. Several hours later Tallulah covered her head with a scarf and reported to the set. She told her director that she had a head cold. With subsequent injections, the swelling went down gradually. The cause of this particular episode, like so many of Tallulah's eruptive, violent, and seemingly unique ailments, was never determined.

Tallulah had her best time, on the set of *Fanatic*, picking and betting on horses. She missed gambling in America and complained bitterly that there were no honorable bookies left in New York City. In England, she bought every racing sheet available, studied them assiduously, and conferred with a certain wardrobe man about the horses and their jockeys before placing her daily two-pound wager. She won about 80 percent of the time, and the crew was astonished. They liked Tallulah, as the so-called little people always did. She talked to them, greeted them, asked about their homes and their families, and tipped all of them, especially the cameramen, generously.

Tallulah's relationship with her director, Narizzano, has been described as a "love-hate" amalgam. She truly enjoyed him as a man. The little bit of socializing she did in England involved him, his wife, a deck of cards, and a poker table. He had intelligence, talent, and, most important, he could make Tallulah laugh. But though they joked about it, she bitterly resented what he, as a director, compelled her to do.

There were no compromises with the filmic aging process. The bone structure of her face, in which she took such great pride, was compromised with a mound of putty. Her face was furrowed like new-plowed farmland. Her hair grayed so that it wasn't even interesting and twisted up into a severe, New England knot. And then he zoomed his cameras in for a series of merciless close-ups.

To Stephanie Powers, the ingenue whom she did not want in the first place, she was civil but cool. Tallulah fought hard against what she knew was an unworthy and cheap sensibility, to resent the young and the beautiful, but she did not usually succeed. In a scene in which Tallulah was called upon to slap the girl in the face, she warned Stephanie Powers that the blow would be vigorously realistic. Apparently, it was that and more so. A minor press debacle resulted. Tallulah explained that nobody could really fake a slap, and besides, she said, "It tones up the complexion."

In the middle of the ten-week shooting schedule, Tallulah discovered to her chagrin that the name of the picture was going to be changed, for the American market, to *Die! Die! My Darling!* She strenuously objected. At this point in her career, the "dahling" phenomenon had become an abomination to Tallulah, a symbol of all the gimmicks which had made her a legend but at the same time encrusted and limited her. The word had been extirpated from the scripts of her last Broadway shows. Now that it reappeared, and so sneakily, in the title of what she hoped would be a major motion picture, she felt exploited and double-crossed.

Tallulah consulted her contract to find that *Fanatic* had been designated as a *working* title subject to change and that, therefore, she had no legal recourse. Had a younger Tallulah been informed of such a devious and dastardly alteration *in medias res* she probably would have refused to finish the movie. This Tallulah, however, was wiser and weaker.

Back in the States, the movie was screened for Tallulah and a group of her closest friends. She sat and watched mostly in silence. When Narizzano's most unkind cut—a microscopic close-up of a leathery, evil, ugly old Tallulah—appeared on the screen, she allayed everyone's tensions, including her own, by standing and shouting, "I want to apologize to all of you for my appearance on the screen, looking older than *God's wet nurse.*"

If the movie had somehow caught on, Tallulah might have forgiven Silvio Narizzano and herself for anything. But it was a boring, graceless movie with no redeeming Gothic values. The reviews were horrific in general except for one which appeared in *Life,* written by Dora Jane Hamblin, on April 9, 1965.

"I imagine," she wrote, "that the whole enterprise may have been partly designed to make Tallulah look ridiculous. If so, the idea backfired. Her superb acting is the saving grace of the film, and she may well be launched—at 60 or 65—on a new career."

In the warmest part of the review, she said that save for "that lethal basso profundo, 'half British, half pickaninny,'" she would have been unable even to recognize the star. When she did, however, recognize her she wanted to get up from her seat and shout, "Hey, everybody, Tallulah's back!"

Tallulah clipped the review.

32

Jesse

BUT SHE WAS NOT launched on a new, vital career. When the picture was over, she sank into her old rut. Emma bathed her in the morning. Television amused her in the afternoon. A quart of Old Grand-Dad and an assortment of pills worked their manipulative, slaking services. And the caddies reassured her by night.

Her total dependence on her young men was more evident than ever:

"I get all mixed up when George or somebody isn't here to tell me what to do. . . .

"I've been screaming at Philip, my best friend all day; I wouldn't blame him if he killed me.

"My watch is set ahead for me so that I don't miss the beginning of mysteries.

"I fell last night. Johnny was out. I have Daddy's knees."

She took them less for granted. She tried to control her demonic temper. In various conversations with one of her caddies, she seemed continuously to be grappling with her natural testiness and impatience, two layers side by side: "Why am I wasting my time with you?" and "Thank God you're still there."

Dola Cavendish was always there. She had moved to Victoria, British Columbia, in 1955. Though the family castle there was turned into a hospital, she lived on a nearby mountaintop in a house that could have been designed with Tallulah in mind. Fireplaces abounded. The bedrooms were huge and lavish. Mattresses were made of down. And the bar was impeccably stocked.

In 1959, Tallulah began to make rather lengthy visits to see Dola, whose uncritical and abiding love she had begun to appreciate and reciprocate. They both had mellowed with the years, and their arguments were less frequent and less highly charged.

Tallulah chose to spend Christmas of 1964 at Dola's. On the way into Canada, a customs' man had recognized Tallulah and asked her to come to the head of the line. When he began perfunctorily to check through her luggage, she said, "Oh, you don't have to bother with that, baby. Nothing in them but liquor and dope." Tallulah stayed on that year through New Year and then to her birthday, January 31, 1965. Dola had a small party for her at which Tallulah reversed tradition and gave all the guests presents.

During her visits, Tallulah and Dola took long walks in the rugged, magnificent Victorian terrain. Though her staff was large, Dola insisted on taking personal care of Tallulah. She kept her bedroom fire going all night and sometimes sat by Tallulah's bed-side for hours just watching her sleep.

Dola had cirrhosis of the liver for years and, during this last visit, was not looking well. Tallulah and a caddy were sitting in a darkened cocktail lounge in the Canadian airport when she broke down and cried, "I have a feeling that I'll never see Dola again." She did not. Dola had a stroke in March, 1966, and died.

Though most of her considerable fortune had been eaten away by dependents and by her own illnesses, Dola left Tallulah several pieces of exquisite jewelry. There was a problem, however, about bringing them in from Canada to the United States—the duties were exorbitant. Edie Van Cleve, whose advice in such matters Tallulah usually took, suggested that she sell the jewels in Canada. But Tallulah was unable to do it. "Dola wouldn't have wanted me to," she said.

Tallulah's own jewelry was interred in a bank vault somewhere in New York City. It was worth approximately $50,000, and she called the gems collectively "my tragedy fund." She considered them a last recourse in the event of a very rainy day. Her favorite piece was a diamond and sapphire ring which John Hay Whitney had given to her in the thirties. She loved to tell the story of how Jock had sent a tray of precious jewels up to her in her suite at the Elysee, the diamond and sapphire ring among them, with the in-struction CHOOSE!

Tallulah hardly ever went to the vault. On those few occasions when she did go out socially, she wore either her pearls, which were real, or the imitation paste that had been made for her when it was feared that she might either lose or give the stuff away. Her real jewels were saved for extraordinary events. Such an occasion was Truman Capote's black-and-white ball in 1966, to which the author invited 540 of his closest friends, Tallulah among them.

The little that continued to happen in Tallulah's life took on tre-mendous import. She prepared for the masked ball for weeks. Since her wardrobe was scant and she was dead set against spend-ing a great deal of money on a gown she could wear only once, Tallulah decided to finagle. Her machination made Regina Gid-dens look like an amateur. Finally, she was taken to the ball by a couturier, who made her a dress in return for the opportunity to attend the Capote party.

Dripping mink, diamonds, her face half-covered with a fringed, feline white mask, and looking very beautiful, Tallulah had a wonderful time, though, because of her illness, she could not dance at all.

She made a rule before she left for the party that she wasn't going to go up to anyone unless they approached her. Just about everybody did, including Lillian Hellman, to whom she had not spoken since *The Little Foxes* trouble of decades past. Tallulah's "Don't touch me" caveat was rescinded for the night, and she and Lillian hugged affectionately. Tallulah blamed the whole thing on *Time* magazine. "We never had a cross word," she said to the playwright. "You just stopped coming backstage."

Tallulah invited several people back to the house that night. Among them was Jesse Levy, a charming, urbane, self-proclaimed "retired playboy—not too old to play." Tallulah and Jesse had met several times through the years. He traveled if not with, at least near, the jet set and was a friend of both Eugenia Bankhead and Louisa Carpenter.

Tallulah was enchanted with Jesse's looks, which have been described as a "felicitous cross between Claude Rains and Nelson Rockefeller." He has dark gray eyes, almond in shape, heavily lidded with what Tallulah called "Mongolian folds." His hair is steel gray. His voice is slow and quirky in emphasizing words in a W. C. Fields fashion, and he seems sometimes to be peering at the words he has just spoken.

Jesse Levy was forty-five years old when he went home with Tallulah after the Capote party. He held two degrees in business administration though he never took a regular job. He served in the Navy during World War II and in Korea, discharged with the rank of lieutenant commander—inactive.

He was the last remaining guest at Tallulah's post-Capote party. When he made a motion finally to leave, Tallulah pointed to her jewelry which she had lain helter-skelter throughout the apartment. "You can't leave me alone, Jesse," she begged. "The jewelry is worth *thousands*, and I'm terrified to be here with it alone." She asked if he would stay the night in the guest bedroom until she could arrange to have the gems taken back to the vault in the morning.

By the time Jesse and Tallulah had straggled out of their bedrooms, gathered themselves together, and acknowledged the existence of the jewelry, the bank's limited civilian hours had come and were long gone. Several days passed. The jewelry and Jesse Levy remained. He became her new drinking companion, confidant, and—temporarily—Brink's guard.

They formalized the deal when Jesse said to Tallulah, "If I stay on any longer, *you're* gonna have to put me on salary."

Tallulah smiled. "I was hoping you'd say that. How much do you want?"

"Just take the figure you had in mind and add an *o* to it."

So Jesse stayed with Tallulah. He and Emma shared the work of her, Jesse answering the telephone, taking care of some of the one hundred or so pieces of correspondence she received weekly, shopping, cooking between cooks, and, most important, listening to Tallulah. Though he was theoretically free to go at night, he seldom did. After the *Huntley-Brinkley Report* and a dinner which she very seldom touched, she would ask him what his plans were for the evening, to which he would reply, "Well, I'm not spoken for," and they would sit and drink until three, or four, or five the next morning.

She signed a picture for him: TO JESSE/WHO SAVED MY LIFE/ BLESS YOU, TALLULAH. She bought him some beautiful clothes, which he carried well. She lit Chanakah candles with him on the holiday and demanded to know everything he had on the Maccabees. On the few occasions when he did go away, she called him continually. An accomplished pianist, he played Chopin for her on her Baldwin grand piano. They had fights, of course, and they were violent fights; but Tallulah fought with everyone.

She became increasingly dependent on Jesse, and many of the other people in her life were shut out entirely. Some of Tallulah's friends resented and distrusted him; others agreed with her that she was damn lucky to get him.

Unlike Ted Hook, Jesse never tried to reform Tallulah. He never scolded her about her habits and seemed to accept in its entirety Tallulah's self-presentation. He believed she worked just for the money, was blessedly free of ambition, and had never had any to speak of.

They wanted her to romp about as the Dragon Lady on the phenomenally successful, seminally camp *Batman* television series. She turned down the initial offer, but as she saw other prestigious stars appear with the dynamic duo, she consented to do it—"for the children." She was paid $20,000 to play a sort of butch black widow in a two-program episode.

Cal Schumann, the voice behind the weather puppet of a popular Baltimore news program and devoted friend to Tallulah, telephoned her right after she had closed the deal. He recalls the conversation as follows:

"I'm going to California," she said in a small and frail-deep voice. "I've stooped *not* to conquer. I'm going to do *Batman*."

Cal answered, "Why not!"

"What, my dahling?"

"Why not?" he repeated. "Why not do *Batman?* Everybody else is!"

"Exactly," Tallulah replied, pleased with Cal's grasp of the subject. "I leave the sixteenth of February—February sixteenth."

"Your birthday is soon, Tallulah!"

"I don't want anybody to know about it. An order—"

"Yes, Tallulah."

"*Not* to send me anything to drink. *Not* to send me roses. (They die in eight hours in this town.) My beloved Dola always sent me white flowers which that lady who *stole* always took home. Send me flowers five days *after* Christmas or five days *after* New Year. I haven't got a flower in sight right now, for instance. On Christmas or on my birthday or on New Year this place looks like a gangster's funeral. In two days everything is dead. But it will be better if you wait five days after my birthday. Send me the long-stemmed American Beauty roses. When you order them, say they're to be delivered between noon and one o'clock. But I don't want the little biddy roses. Obey me, dahling! *I must do some-*

thing good. I must do something good. What time is it, dahling? My watch is always fast so I won't miss the beginning of mysteries."

"It's seven forty, Tallulah."

"What, dahling?"

"It's seven forty."

"It's *not* seven forty. *It's twenty minutes of eight.* I have nothing to look at until eight thirty. Good-bye, my dahling."

"I love you, Tallulah."

"And I love you. Good-bye."

She and Jesse flew to California. They were put up in a two-bedroom suite at the Beverly-Hillcrest. For ten days, Tallulah rose in time to be at the Desilu Studios at six in the morning. She made jokes there about the tight black pants suit that she was required to wear for the part ("There goes one ball," she said to Batman, as she was being fitted into it) and yelled a good deal. Jesse was finally put on salary by the production organization to act as a sort of emissary between them and the tempestuous Tallulah. When she heard about that, she was pleased on Jesse's behalf but astonished and not a little hurt. "I'm the easiest person in the *world* to get along with," she bellowed.

She and Jesse dined out just twice: once with *Batman* producer Bill Dozier and his wife, Ann Rutherford, once with dear friend George Cukor. Cukor planned a small dinner party in Tallulah's honor to which he also invited Katharine Houghton, the niece of Katharine Hepburn. Hepburn thought it would be a good experience for Kathy to meet Tallulah, and Tallulah came through magnificently. She was sweet and attentive throughout dinner, but took amused exception to the girl's demure Eastern college appearance. She handed her a tube of Victory Red and commanded, "Put on some of this and stop trying to look like that Boston spinster aunt of yours." Hepburn showed up after dinner and sat on the floor.

Katharine Hepburn recalled that evening: "Tallulah never disappointed anyone. She always lived up to people's expectations of her—even at the very end when she was ravaged."

Tallulah and Jesse got on the first plane back to New York the night of the last day of shooting. A fog was lifting as they climbed into one of the motorized little carts that the airport provides to take VIP's from the terminal to the awaiting plane. Tallulah was asked if she objected to sharing her cart with a third person. "Who is it?" she asked wearily.

She was told Cary Grant.

"I should say not. I gave him his first job."

Grant approached the vehicle stealthily, hiding behind his Foster Grants, hoping apparently that Tallulah would not see him and that he could sleep on the flight to New York.

"Cary, dahling."

"Ta-loooo-la."

Cary Grant was not annoyed by Tallulah on the flight East. She was too bone weary even to sip a cup of coffee. In New York, Robert Williams, who drove for Tallulah occasionally now, met the plane at about four in the morning. He saw Tallulah disembark, leaning heavily on Jesse's arm. Her feet had swollen en route, and she was in great pain. Robert picked her up in his arms and carried her to the limousine.

33

Last Will and Testament

IN NOVEMBER, 1967, the day before she was scheduled to leave for the West Coast, to appear with the Smothers brothers on their weekly variety show, Tallulah decided to change her will. Three attorneys and a secretary were summoned to Fifty-seventh Street.

Tallulah dealt this time not with the allocation of paintings to caddies, but with the more serious matter of heirs: the people who would share all the profits of her rather large estate after specific bequests were made.

The result of the most crucial business transacted that afternoon—witnessed by her elevator man—was simple. Jesse Levy, after a year of devoted service and good companionship was *in;* Eugenia, after sixty-five years of infuriating Tallulah was, more or less, *out.*

The Tangier debacle of 1958, at which time Tallulah claimed she was disowning Eugenia, was the least of it. The sisters had spoken to and seen each other many times since then, though nothing had been resolved. Tallulah had built up a blistering catalogue of grievances against Eugenia over the years. There were long periods during which she simply refused to see her witty, multimarrying, globe-trotting older sister. In any case, Eugenia's bequest was altered considerably by the terms of Tallulah's new will.

On November 24, 1967, Jesse Levy of 447 East Fifty-seventh Street was bequeathed one-fourth of Tallulah's estate, plus $10,000, plus the Baldwin grand piano.

The two children of Donald Seawell, her friend and lawyer, and Seawell's wife, actress Eugenia Rawls, were together bequeathed one-half of the estate. Tallulah had acted opposite Eugenia Rawls in *The Little Foxes,* thrown rice at her wedding, and been godmother to their boy, Brockman, and their girl, Brook. She had watched them grow up and had recently attended Brook's wedding. They were handsome, affectionate, impeccably mannered young people who never forgot Tallulah's birthday, visited on Christmas, and were unflagging in their devotion to Tallulah.

The last quarter was to go to Eugenia Bankhead's grandchildren, the children of Billy Bankhead: Mary Eugenia, four, and Tallulah Brockman Bankhead, one. At the time that she drew up the will, Billy's children were virtual strangers to Tallulah. She was not happy at all when she heard that Billy's second daughter was to be her namesake, and bellowed, upon hearing of the second Tallulah, "That bitch better have blue eyes!"

Billy, their father, was left only $5,000. She never forgot or forgave the fact that he had not acknowledged a gold cigarette case which she had sent to him while he was attending the School of Agriculture at Cornell.

Though Eugenia was not among her heirs, the bequest to her grandchildren certainly indicated that Tallulah had not ceased to regard her as a sister, however disappointing or wayward she might be.

Tallulah saw to it, too, in the will, that Eugenia, in the event that she survived her, would never be without necessities. She left her a bequest of $5,000, plus provisions for an annuity of $250 a month to be purchased by the estate. The annuity, however, was specifically ordered to be "without cash value or refund provisions." Moderation in all things was mandated by the terms of the will. It was a dole of sorts really—Tallulah's final bequest to Eugenia. She would never take a feckless trip to Tangier or set a man up in business with Tallulah's money!

Eugenia was also bequeathed Tallulah's annuity of $650 a month to be paid to her for the remaining years between the time of Tallulah's death and the year in which she would have been seventy.

Old friends, like George Cukor and Mildred Dunnock, who were set rather well financially but who had admired some little thing of Tallulah's over the years, were bequeathed that object.

Servants and secretaries all were remembered, though a year or so of diminished attention, even if it followed years of faithful service, altered a bequest considerably. Ted Hook was left a painting and only $1,000. Robert Williams, who was with her more than twenty years but from whom she had not heard in several months, was left $500.

Her last will and testament was as typical of Tallulah as anything had been in her life. It was impulsive but not spontaneous; sentimental but unforgiving. It rewarded fidelity even to those she did not especially love and especially rewarded those she had loved last.

On the West Coast, set to appear with the rapscallion Smothers Brothers, Tallulah once again refused to take calls or to see people. One of the very rare exceptions was a San Diego man, whom she had met once before twenty-six years ago. His name was Fred Hall, and at their first meeting he was a frightened boy in a soldier suit about to be shipped overseas; she was touring military installations. Tallulah had embraced Hall, pulled back and spit ritually dry in his face. For good luck. "You'll come back unharmed," she told him. When he did, he naturally attributed his survival to her.

Since that time, he had written at least seven long and personal letters to Tallulah *every* week. He was now in his late forties, owned some property in California, and played the piano in a local bar on weekends.

After she had consented to see him, he sat timorously quiet in her suite while she regaled him with the wit and wisdom of Tallulah Bankhead. She was sweet and gracious always about such things. Jesse Levy walked him to the door at the end, placed his arm around Hall's shoulder, and remembers saying apologetically, "Fred, you ought to know that she very rarely, *if ever*, reads your letters."

Hall shrugged and smiled. "That's all right. She doesn't have to read them, but I have to write them."

During this five-day sojourn, Tallulah taped about twenty minutes of show. She played Mata Hari in an opening sketch; she sang a hoarse "My Funny Valentine" to one of the brothers, though she could never remember which; she narrated a group of satirical tidbits about gun control; and, with particular zeal, she introduced a group of black singers called the Temptations. With her old-timey fervor, Tallulah considered that segment a bravura example of interracial harmony. It was just a white Southern lady introducing some black gentlemen who sang; but in Tallulah's day, of course, people had flambéed crosses on lawns for less. When her introduction was cut eventually from the show, she was certain that Governor Wallace, whom she abhorred, had somehow intervened.

Tallulah was confused and frightened by the new crosscurrents in race relations. Lena Horne, for instance, had that year published *Lena*, her autobiography written with Richard Schickel. In it, she attacked various white Southern celebrities whom she had met through the years for racial attitudes that she found offensive. Miriam Hopkins drew some very heavy fire, and Tallulah, too, was criticized, though Miss Horne was forced to admit that, in spite of everything, she couldn't help liking her. She wrote: "I had the feeling she was a lady and that she was a genuine, dyed-in-the-wool Southerner who really thought she was protective of Negroes—misguided, I thought, but essentially kind. When she talked about how cute the little pickaninnies were and discussed the non-Negro-ness of my features she was being honestly herself."

That was the first racial rap Tallulah Bankhead had ever taken. Her crude Rooseveltian egalitarianism just wasn't good enough anymore. The Negroes with whom she had come in contact had always seen through Tallulah's self-presentation. They understood her guilt and even forgave the occasional lapse. The new black was less tolerant.

Nor was Tallulah pleased with the new black. She watched the peace strikes, the sit-downs, and the emergence of the new-style militant on the television news, and she was repelled and frightened by much of what she saw. She told friends repeatedly in these last years: "I used to think that if I were ever in real trouble I would run to Harlem for friends and shelter; now I'd be afraid to go up there alone."

Her half-fantasy Harlem—a kind of *Porgy and Bess* setting, peopled with dignified Uncles and gentle, maternal Mamas—was no more, indeed had never been.

"That bitch," Tallulah boomed when she heard what Lena Horne had written about her. "I never used the word 'pickaninny' in my life. She's a liar."

Back in New York, Tallulah eagerly awaited the *Smothers Brothers* broadcast. She was pleased to observe that the show was promoted extensively on the network, but displeased because her participation in it was cut severely. Neither her introduction to the Temptations nor her own musical number was used. She blamed it on a combination of political cowardice, bad judgment, and Mama Cass Elliot, who was a guest on the same show and, more or less, monopolized the final program. "If it hadn't been for that idiot fat woman," Tallulah complained, "I could have gotten my song on!"

One of Tallulah's loyalest caddies telephoned after the show to tell Tallulah that it was the best television appearance yet but that he was appalled at the drastic cuts. He had drafted an indignant letter to CBS and wanted her to hear it. Tallulah's attention suddenly riveted. She called to Jesse for her listening gear—a cigarette and her drink—and told him to pick up the extension.

"I hope that you haven't mentioned that you're a friend," she said to the caller. "Are you sending it on your professional stationery? Not that they'll answer it!"

The letter began with a historical parallel: a reference to the fact that Agnes Moorehead, who had been a guest on a prior show with the Smothers Brothers, had been given only three minutes of time. He went right into his: "dismay, better still *disgust,* at the limited use of Tallulah Bankhead."

Tallulah's silence was audible. The caddy continued, "Tallulah Bankhead may be old hat to sophisticated producers on the Coast, but she's a legend to us in the hinterlands."

"I wouldn't say 'old hat,' dahling. It's a bad line."

"We want to see her and not for a brief five minutes. There are stars in Hollywood, but Tallulah Bankhead is an entirely different—"

"Just scratch that out, and say 'Not only a star in Hollywood—' You know, 'Someone who's a legend in her own time, a great tragedienne as well as a great comedienne—' And go on with that."

"Yes, Tallulah."

"Well, the Smothers Brothers are darling boys. But it's a long time before I go back there . . . *until I'm asked.*"

She made her last appearances anywhere with television personality Merv Griffin. She had tried the *Tonight* show with Johnny Carson, but she felt "used" by Carson, as she never did by Griffin.

Even with Griffin, however, whom she trusted and loved, her several appearances were ordeals to prepare and agony to perform. For weeks she decided what to say and how to dress. She called various people connected with the Griffin show at all hours of the day and night and kept them on the phone for hours, with her personal problems and her free associations. On the day of the show, the Griffin office extended courtesies to her which they extended to no one else in the business. Makeup technician Barbara Armstrong was sent to Tallulah's house in the early afternoon. One of Griffin's production assistants was dispatched, with a car, to pick her up and escort her to the studio in time for the taping.

"Her attitude toward a guest shot was all out of proportion to what it really meant," one of Merv Griffin's associates remembered. "It was as if it were a special with her starring in it.

"She was always sitting in a chair when I arrived at the apartment, with a cigarette going, coughing, her hair being done and the makeup, screaming at Jesse. I'd sit down and I'd look up and suddenly I'd be staring up her dress. Invariably. It was no accident. That's how she had it set up. One day she showed me her breast operation. 'Do you like them, darling?' she asked me.

"Then it would be a kind of ceremony. I'd be her 'date' for the show. Take her arm, escort her to the car, help her fend off any autograph seekers we'd meet along the way. She was frantic about that. 'Don't let them near me!' she'd say. She knew what she looked like."

The cameramen, at the studio, were told to stay back and to leave her legs out of the picture. Backstage, tense and shaking, she invariably had trouble getting her breath. The walk from the backstage area to the chair next to Merv, only several feet, took full minutes.

While she was held up backstage, Griffin would say:

ONE OF THE MOST FASCINATING PERSONALITIES IN THE ENTERTAINMENT WORLD IS HERE WITH US TODAY . . . THERE'S SO MUCH TO SAY ABOUT HER THAT I DON'T WANT TO LOSE ANY TIME. I JUST WANT TO BRING HER RIGHT OUT HERE. SHE IS ABSOLUTELY THE ONE AND ONLY . . . MISS TALLULAH BANKHEAD.

As soon as Tallulah got to the desk at which he sat, Griffin would grab her by the hand. She sat down, reached for a glass of water which wasn't water, and they talked about the subjects which were prepared before hand: politics, bridge, soap operas, Tallulah's desire to buy a farm in the country, and why she didn't get out much anymore.

After one of her appearances, Merv Griffin asked Tallulah why she bothered to do the show at all. "It's one way of proving to people that I'm not dead," she replied.

That Tallulah should have made her last professional appearance on one of television's personality exploitation programs was suitable and right. *The Big Show* was an epochal event in the Carson-Griffin-Cavett-Frost phenomenon. It was there, in a new way and for the first time, that actors, singers, dancers, politicians, and writers did something other than act, or sing, or dance, or wield power, or write. They consented publicly "to be," to exhibit a projectile of reality the modern term for which is "image."

And of the many "images" which have since fascinated the public, Tallulah's was archetypally modern. She informed people, through her own projectile, that she was an open, wayward, free, cosmopolitan, liberated, sensuous human being. In thus systematically invading her own privacy, she was the first of the modern personalities, the sort Walter Kerr described in a memoriam to Tallulah. He wrote:

> She was nowhere near a great actress, though once in a while a surprisingly good one. And now all the truths had to be set down, given back, added up—even if they added up to an image of on-the-whole failure, of fabulous waste.
>
> I don't think we expected to see her give a good performance. I think we expected to meet her someday. Really meet her. In person. I think she was too real to us to be good in most parts. She lacked camouflage. There was no chameleon in her.

34

The Eastern Shore

TALLULAH WAS on her long sofa, in her silk wrapper, leaning over to light a cigarette when her living-room ceiling fell in on her. Great patches of plaster had come loose, suddenly and inexplicably. She was safe but stunned, her hair whitened by the freshly fallen blizzard of plaster. While the necessary repairs were being done on the apartment, Tallulah and Jesse drove to Rock Hall, Maryland, to visit Eugenia.

Though she continued her global peregrinations in search of something better, Eugenia Bankhead's home base for many years had been Rock Hall. There, on the rich and rural Eastern Shore, she owned two charming, cozily appointed houses nestled close together on a lakefront, her own and a cottage for guests.

The air there is clear and tasty. The area abounds in wild birdlife, and at certain times of the year, the skies darken and roar intermittently from the overhead flights of ducks and geese. It is great hunting country.

Though Eugenia never cultivated a taste for such sport, she consented on several occasions to accompany Louisa Carpenter, who owns a sizable portion of Rock Hall, on her venatic adventures. Eugenia refers to the months when hunting the wild birds is permitted as "the mud, blood, and feathers season."

Tallulah arrived, with Jesse, on July 6, 1968. They had waited for the holiday traffic to abate. Though Eugenia had made heady preparations for Tallulah's arrival and intended, in general, to show her famous sister off to her friends on the Eastern Shore, it was painfully obvious that Tallulah would not be up to much of anything.

It was almost as if their childhood positions had been reversed. Tallulah was the sickly one now. She weighed less than 100 pounds, she threw up frequently, and she ate virtually nothing at all. At sixty-seven, Eugenia was round, in the way of the Bankhead women, and peppery. She took great pride in her still-youthful body and her well-shaped legs. Though her eyesight was very poor, and she had literally to press her nose against a page to read it, the disfigurement was no longer apparent.

Tallulah and Jesse settled into their little cottage, and she took up her city habits: bath, booze, television, and bridge. She interrupted her rigid afternoon viewing schedule once when Cindy, Billy Bankhead's wife, brought the children over to visit. Fortunately, little Tallulah, whom everyone called Tally, did have blue eyes. She was two years old and precocious, and Tallulah took to her immediately.

She did not, however, extend the same courtesy to the child's grandmother. When Eugenia visited in the middle of one of Tallulah's soapies, Tallulah indicated a chair and said, "Just sit down and be quiet, Sister."

Eugenia obeyed, peering at the ongoing program, making a genuine effort, in the beginning, to understand what it was that could so enthrall her younger sister. Watching the endless recitation of interrelated tragedies, Eugenia could not finally resist a crack. "It's like a flea circus, Sister," she laughed.

Tallulah yelled, "If you don't understand it, then don't watch." That was the last time Eugenia interrupted Tallulah's afternoon soap operas.

At night they played bridge in Tallulah's cottage. Tallulah was bright in the beginning, but she drank and took pills all through the game until she could hardly remain in a sitting position.

The two sisters were sometimes able to talk but only in their reminiscences of childhood could they avert the inevitable tensions and arguments which were about everything and nothing, from who was left Daddy's gold walking stick to whether or not

Eugenia really had tuberculosis when she spent all that time in Ortisei.

Their dual presence in a room surcharged the area with static. In spite of Eugenia's near blindness and Tallulah's half deafness, they were both always completely tuned into and scrutinizing the other. A friend of Eugenia's compared it to "an old Bette Davis-Miriam Hopkins movie."

Tallulah said several times that Daddy had loved Eugenia more, and Eugenia replied, "Well, somebody had to!"

Tallulah was sick and frightened and failing fast. She told Eugenia, "I'm through, and I know it, and I don't care. Every night when I go to sleep, I pray to God that I won't wake up in the morning."

"Which God do you pray to, baby," Eugenia replied, "the one you don't believe in anymore?"

If Tallulah had come to Maryland to seek some kind of *détente*, she didn't find it, though she stayed two months beyond the intended several weeks. Then, with Jesse, she returned to New York.

That December, during a bad epidemic, Tallulah contracted the Asian flu. She did not respond to a traditional medical regimen, and after a period of days, Jesse called Dr. Lumus Bell, who had been treating Tallulah's emphysema. Wary of possible respiratory complications, Dr. Bell suggested immediate hospitalization. To Jesse's utter astonishment, Tallulah offered no resistance to the idea. She dressed, took her checkbook, her pills, a rabbit's foot which had been Will Bankhead's good-luck piece, her dressing gown, and waited for the ambulance.

It was evening when they got to St. Luke's Hospital. Jesse checked her in and returned to Fifty-seventh Street. Tallulah proceeded to make life hell for the hospital staff by screaming about the linens, the hospital smock, and pulling the intravenous needle out of her arm. The last was the most serious, since Tallulah had not eaten anything for several days before she arrived at the hospital. A sedative was ordered so that she could be forcibly nourished.

It was several days before anyone was informed of Tallulah's illness. She did finally ask for her sister, and Eugenia flew up the next morning. By the time she arrived in New York Tallulah had sunk into a coma and was placed in the intensive care unit of the hospital, where a roaring machine breathed on her behalf. Pneumonia had set in. During her time in the machine, Tallulah tried to talk, but her only discernible words were "codeine-bourbon." On December 12, 1968, Dr. Bell called Jesse to say, "We've lost Tallulah."

Arrangements were made by Louisa Carpenter. The body was taken to Maryland for burial. A simple casket was chosen at Frank Campbell's and lined, at Robert Williams' suggestion, in Tallulah's favorite baby-boy blue. She was dressed in one of her favorite silk wrappers, cigarette burns and all. Before the lid was closed, Louisa Carpenter slipped in the rabbit's foot that had belonged to Will. There was a simple Episcopal prayer book service. She was interred in Rock Hall on a quiet lakeside by some children's graves.

Then thirty of the closest friends went back to Louisa's house and told Tallulah stories.

Index

Valiant Lady, 308
Van Cleve, Edith, 195–97, 228, 231, 354
Vanity Fair, 54, 76, 77
Van Wyck, Robert, 24
Variety, 178, 190, 261, 266
Vaughan, Sarah, 280
Victoria Bouquet, 81
Viertel, Berthold, 140
Viertel, Salka, 140
Vincent, Alan, 143, 145
Von Sternberg, Joseph, 134

Wales, Prince of, 95, 106
Wallace, George, 362
Wallace, Henry, 201
"Waltz, The," 293, 307
Wanger, Walter, 132, 134, 136
War Brides, 45
Warner, Jack, 266
Warner Brothers, 262–64
Washer, Ben, 196–97
Watts, Richard, Jr., 136, 180
Webb, Clifton, 116
Welcome, Darlings, 308–11, 315
Well of Loneliness, The, 127
Welles, Orson, 178, 179, 181, 184, 215, 247
West, Mae, 240, 306
Westminster, Duchess of, 115
Westport, Conn., 171, 249
Wetempka, Ala., 20
What Ever Happened to Baby Jane?, 341, 348
When Men Betray, 53
White, Edward Ennis, 165, 166
Whitehead, Robert, 326, 329, 331–32
Whitney, John Hay "Jock," 157, 167, 170, 171, 172, 219, 228, 354
Whitney, Payne, 157
Wilder, Isabel, 215
Wilder, Thornton, 212, 214, 215–16
William Morris Agency, 274

Williams, Hope, 149, 269
Williams, Robert, 222, 264, 273, 301, 338, 340, 359, 361, 370
Williams, Tennessee, 263, 264, 301–4, 341–44
Willkie, Wendell, 202
Willson, Meredith, 270, 272, 274, 289
Wilson, Frank, 271
Wilson, Jack, 256
Wilson, John C., 133, 247, 248
Wilson, Tony, 121–22, 125
Wilson, Woodrow, 15, 65
Winchell, Walter, 276
Windows, 220 ff., 248, 263–64, 276, 290, 292, 296, 300
Winters, Shelley, 323
Winwood, Estelle, 54, 71, 75–78, 158, 212, 222–24, 228, 229, 230, 263, 296, 303, 313, 315, 330, 338, 347
Woman's Home Companion, 207
Wong, Anna May, 171
Woodruff, Gussie, 37
Woollcott, Alexander, 67
World War I, 15
World War II, 206, 225, 246
WPA Federal Theatre Project, 194–97, 198
Wright, Frank Lloyd, 241, 243
Wylie, Elinor Hoyt, 65
Wyndham, Lady, 86
Wyndham Theater, 82, 86–87
York, Duke and Duchess of, 84
Young, Robert, 252
Yurka, Blanche, 194
Yvonne of Braithwaite, 163

Zanuck, Daryl, 240
Ziegfeld, Florenz, 83
Ziegfeld Follies, The, 307
Zolotow, Maurice, 187, 188, 230, 239
Zukor, Adolph, 134, 136–37